The Tutorverse
MAKING THE UNIVERSE BRIGHTER, ONE STUDENT AT A TIME

Upper Level ISEE®
1500+ Practice Questions

Upper Level ISEE®: 1500+ Practice Questions

February 2023

Published in the United States of America by:

The Tutorverse, LLC

222 Broadway, 19th Floor

New York, NY 10038

Web: www.thetutorverse.com

Email: hello@thetutorverse.com

For information about buying this title in bulk or to place a special order, please contact us at hello@thetutorverse.com.

ISBN-13: 978-1515297352
ISBN-10: 1515297357

ISEE® is a registered trademark of the Educational Records Bureau, which was not involved in the production of, and does not endorse, sponsor, or certify this product.

Neither the author or publisher claim any responsibility for the accuracy and appropriateness of the content in this book, nor do they claim any responsibility over the outcome of students who use these materials.

The views and opinions expressed in this book do not necessarily reflect the official policy, position, or point of view of the author or publisher. Such views and opinions do not constitute an endorsement to perform, attempt to perform, or otherwise emulate any procedures, experiments, etc. described in any of the passages, excerpts, adaptations, cited materials, or similar information. Such information is included only to facilitate the development of questions, answer choices, and answer explanations for purposes of preparing for the ISEE®.

Table of Contents

Upper Level ISEE®
1500+ Practice Questions

Welcome

Dear Students, Parents, and Educators,

We believe that the key to scoring well on the Upper Level ISEE is practice – a lot of practice. While test taking tips and tricks can be helpful, we believe a solid foundation of core learning and subject-matter proficiency to be the bedrock on which high-performance relies.

That's why this workbook contains over 1,500 practice questions – more questions than 10 actual exams! We've painstakingly identified core concepts and crafted questions of varying difficulty to help prepare students for the exam. Questions in this workbook build on fundamentals and grow progressively more challenging. Our questions help to build confidence, test mastery, and introduce new concepts, skills, and knowledge.

Online and computer-based testing is more prevalent than ever. Because of this, and due to the overwhelming demand for even more ISEE content, we've launched our ISEE Digital platform on www.thetutorverse.com. As of this book's publication, students, parents, and educators can access over thousands of additional practice questions from their internet-connected devices. We have big plans for this platform, and can't wait for you to check it out!

This workbook will help students to identify skills and concepts requiring further development. This workbook will also provide ample practice for many of the subject-areas on the Upper Level ISEE. Whether you use this workbook for independent study or with a professional tutor or teacher, we believe that the practice you will receive will benefit you both on the Upper Level ISEE and beyond.

Best wishes, good luck, and welcome to The Tutorverse!

Regards,

The Team at The Tutorverse

The Tutorverse
www.thetutorverse.com

How to Use This Book

Overview

The purpose of this workbook is to provide students, parents, and educators with practice materials relevant to the Upper Level ISEE. Though this workbook includes information with respect to the test's structure and content—and includes tips, suggestions, and strategies—the primary goal of this workbook is to provide copious practice and to introduce new words, concepts, and skills as necessary.

Organization

This workbook is organized into six main sections. Each section is designed to accomplish different objectives. These sections and objectives are as follows:

🐢 Diagnostic Practice Test (Form A)
This section is designed to help students identify topics requiring the most practice. The diagnostic test mirrors the actual length of a real Upper Level ISEE test, including questions that would not be graded on the real test. This is done in order to ensure that students begin to get accustomed to the actual length of the test. The diagnostic test should be used as a gauge to estimate the amount of additional practice needed on each topic, not as an estimate of how the student will actually score on the test.

🐢 Verbal Reasoning
Verbal Reasoning is the first of four practice sections in this workbook. This section provides practice for synonym and sentence completion questions found on the first two sections of the Upper Level ISEE. Both the synonym and sentence completion questions are further divided into sub-sections, which can help students focus more accurately.

🐢 Reading Comprehension
This section is the second of four practice sections in this workbook and includes many passages and questions that assess many of the skills tested on the Upper Level ISEE. The Reading Comprehension section is further divided into four types of passages: narrative, persuasive, descriptive, and expository.

🐢 Quantitative Reasoning & Mathematics Achievement
This is the third of four practice sections. There are many topics in this section which are organized as indicated in the table of contents.

🐢 The Essay
The final practice section of this workbook, The Essay provides information about the writing prompts on the actual exam and includes several practice prompts.

🐢 Final Practice Test (Form B)
The final practice test helps to familiarize students with the format, organization, and time allotments on the Upper Level ISEE. Like the diagnostic test, the length of the test mirrors that of the real test, including questions that would not otherwise be graded on the real test. This test should be taken once students have completed the diagnostic and spent sufficient time answering the appropriate questions in the practice sections.

At the beginning of each of the above listed sections are detailed instructions. Students should carefully review these instructions, as they contain important information about the actual exam and how best to practice.

Strategy

Every student has different strengths and abilities. We don't think there is any one strategy that will help every student ace the exam. Instead, we believe there are core principles to keep in mind when preparing for the Upper Level ISEE. These principles are interrelated and cyclical in nature.

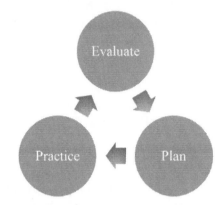

☞ Evaluate

A critical step in developing a solid study plan is to have a clear idea of how to spend your time. What subjects are more difficult for you? Which types of questions do you frequently answer incorrectly? Why? These and many other questions should be answered before developing any study plan. The diagnostic test is just one way to help you evaluate your abilities.

☞ Plan

Once you've taken stock of your strengths and abilities, focus on actions. How much time do you have before the test? How many areas do you need to work on during that time? Which areas do you need to work on? How many questions (and of which type) do you need to do each day, or each week? The answers to these and other questions will help you determine your study and practice plan.

☞ Practice

Once you settle on a plan, try to stick with it as much as you can. To study successfully requires discipline, commitment, and focus. Try turning off your phone, TV, tablet, or other distractions. Not only will you learn more effectively when you're focused, but you may find that you finish your work more quickly, as well.

☞ Reevaluate

Because learning and studying is an ongoing process, it is important to take stock of your improvements along the way. This will help you see how you are progressing and allow you to make adjustments to your plan. The practice test at the end of this workbook is designed to help you gauge your progress.

Help

Preparing for a standardized test such as the Upper Level ISEE can be a difficult and trying time. In addition to challenging material, preparing for a standardized test can often feel like an extra responsibility. For these reasons, it's important to recognize when students need extra help.

Because the Upper Level ISEE is administered to students in various grade levels, some students may find material in this workbook to be difficult or entirely new. This is normal and to be expected, as certain material included in this workbook may not yet have been taught to some students. For example, 8th graders may not yet have learned some of the concepts taught to 10th graders.

Though students will only be scored against other students in their grade (9th graders vs. other 9th graders; 10th graders vs. other 10th graders, etc.), mastering advanced materials can often provide a competitive advantage in achieving higher scores. This workbook includes such materials.

We encourage you to reach out to trusted educators to help you prepare for the Upper Level ISEE. Strong tutors, teachers, mentors, and consultants can help you with many aspects of your preparation – from evaluating and reevaluating your needs to creating an effective plan to helping you make the most of your practice.

Diagnostic Practice Test (Form A)

Overview

The first step in an effective study plan is to know your strengths and areas for improvement.

This diagnostic test assesses your mastery of certain skills and concepts that you may see on the actual exam. The main difference between the diagnostic test and the actual test is that the diagnostic test is scored differently from how the actual exam is scored. On the actual exam, certain questions will not count towards your actual score, and your score will be determined how you did compared with other students in your grade. On this diagnostic test, however, we will score every question in order to gauge your mastery over skills and concepts.

This diagnostic test should *not* be used as a gauge of how you will score on the test.

Format

The format of the diagnostic test is similar to that of the actual test. The number of questions included in each section mirror those of the actual test, *even though the actual test includes questions that will not be scored*. This is done by design, in order to help familiarize you with the actual length of the test.

The diagnostic includes the following sections:

Diagnostic Test Section	Questions	Time Limit
Verbal Reasoning	40	20 minutes
Quantitative Reasoning	37	35 minutes
Break #1	N/A	5 minutes
Reading Comprehension	36	35 minutes
Mathematics Achievement	47	40 minutes
Break #2	N/A	5 minutes
Essay Prompt	1	30 minutes
Total	**161**	**170 minutes**

Answering

Use the answer sheet provided on the next several pages to record your answers. You may wish to tear these pages out of the workbook.

Diagnostic Practice Test
(Form A)

Diagnostic Test Answer Sheet

Section 1: Verbal Reasoning

1. Ⓐ Ⓑ Ⓒ Ⓓ	8. Ⓐ Ⓑ Ⓒ Ⓓ	15. Ⓐ Ⓑ Ⓒ Ⓓ	22. Ⓐ Ⓑ Ⓒ Ⓓ	29. Ⓐ Ⓑ Ⓒ Ⓓ	36. Ⓐ Ⓑ Ⓒ Ⓓ
2. Ⓐ Ⓑ Ⓒ Ⓓ	9. Ⓐ Ⓑ Ⓒ Ⓓ	16. Ⓐ Ⓑ Ⓒ Ⓓ	23. Ⓐ Ⓑ Ⓒ Ⓓ	30. Ⓐ Ⓑ Ⓒ Ⓓ	37. Ⓐ Ⓑ Ⓒ Ⓓ
3. Ⓐ Ⓑ Ⓒ Ⓓ	10. Ⓐ Ⓑ Ⓒ Ⓓ	17. Ⓐ Ⓑ Ⓒ Ⓓ	24. Ⓐ Ⓑ Ⓒ Ⓓ	31. Ⓐ Ⓑ Ⓒ Ⓓ	38. Ⓐ Ⓑ Ⓒ Ⓓ
4. Ⓐ Ⓑ Ⓒ Ⓓ	11. Ⓐ Ⓑ Ⓒ Ⓓ	18. Ⓐ Ⓑ Ⓒ Ⓓ	25. Ⓐ Ⓑ Ⓒ Ⓓ	32. Ⓐ Ⓑ Ⓒ Ⓓ	39. Ⓐ Ⓑ Ⓒ Ⓓ
5. Ⓐ Ⓑ Ⓒ Ⓓ	12. Ⓐ Ⓑ Ⓒ Ⓓ	19. Ⓐ Ⓑ Ⓒ Ⓓ	26. Ⓐ Ⓑ Ⓒ Ⓓ	33. Ⓐ Ⓑ Ⓒ Ⓓ	40. Ⓐ Ⓑ Ⓒ Ⓓ
6. Ⓐ Ⓑ Ⓒ Ⓓ	13. Ⓐ Ⓑ Ⓒ Ⓓ	20. Ⓐ Ⓑ Ⓒ Ⓓ	27. Ⓐ Ⓑ Ⓒ Ⓓ	34. Ⓐ Ⓑ Ⓒ Ⓓ	
7. Ⓐ Ⓑ Ⓒ Ⓓ	14. Ⓐ Ⓑ Ⓒ Ⓓ	21. Ⓐ Ⓑ Ⓒ Ⓓ	28. Ⓐ Ⓑ Ⓒ Ⓓ	35. Ⓐ Ⓑ Ⓒ Ⓓ	

Section 2: Quantitative Reasoning

1. Ⓐ Ⓑ Ⓒ Ⓓ	8. Ⓐ Ⓑ Ⓒ Ⓓ	15. Ⓐ Ⓑ Ⓒ Ⓓ	22. Ⓐ Ⓑ Ⓒ Ⓓ	29. Ⓐ Ⓑ Ⓒ Ⓓ	36. Ⓐ Ⓑ Ⓒ Ⓓ
2. Ⓐ Ⓑ Ⓒ Ⓓ	9. Ⓐ Ⓑ Ⓒ Ⓓ	16. Ⓐ Ⓑ Ⓒ Ⓓ	23. Ⓐ Ⓑ Ⓒ Ⓓ	30. Ⓐ Ⓑ Ⓒ Ⓓ	37. Ⓐ Ⓑ Ⓒ Ⓓ
3. Ⓐ Ⓑ Ⓒ Ⓓ	10. Ⓐ Ⓑ Ⓒ Ⓓ	17. Ⓐ Ⓑ Ⓒ Ⓓ	24. Ⓐ Ⓑ Ⓒ Ⓓ	31. Ⓐ Ⓑ Ⓒ Ⓓ	
4. Ⓐ Ⓑ Ⓒ Ⓓ	11. Ⓐ Ⓑ Ⓒ Ⓓ	18. Ⓐ Ⓑ Ⓒ Ⓓ	25. Ⓐ Ⓑ Ⓒ Ⓓ	32. Ⓐ Ⓑ Ⓒ Ⓓ	
5. Ⓐ Ⓑ Ⓒ Ⓓ	12. Ⓐ Ⓑ Ⓒ Ⓓ	19. Ⓐ Ⓑ Ⓒ Ⓓ	26. Ⓐ Ⓑ Ⓒ Ⓓ	33. Ⓐ Ⓑ Ⓒ Ⓓ	
6. Ⓐ Ⓑ Ⓒ Ⓓ	13. Ⓐ Ⓑ Ⓒ Ⓓ	20. Ⓐ Ⓑ Ⓒ Ⓓ	27. Ⓐ Ⓑ Ⓒ Ⓓ	34. Ⓐ Ⓑ Ⓒ Ⓓ	
7. Ⓐ Ⓑ Ⓒ Ⓓ	14. Ⓐ Ⓑ Ⓒ Ⓓ	21. Ⓐ Ⓑ Ⓒ Ⓓ	28. Ⓐ Ⓑ Ⓒ Ⓓ	35. Ⓐ Ⓑ Ⓒ Ⓓ	

Section 3: Reading Comprehension

1. Ⓐ Ⓑ Ⓒ Ⓓ	7. Ⓐ Ⓑ Ⓒ Ⓓ	13. Ⓐ Ⓑ Ⓒ Ⓓ	19. Ⓐ Ⓑ Ⓒ Ⓓ	25. Ⓐ Ⓑ Ⓒ Ⓓ	31. Ⓐ Ⓑ Ⓒ Ⓓ
2. Ⓐ Ⓑ Ⓒ Ⓓ	8. Ⓐ Ⓑ Ⓒ Ⓓ	14. Ⓐ Ⓑ Ⓒ Ⓓ	20. Ⓐ Ⓑ Ⓒ Ⓓ	26. Ⓐ Ⓑ Ⓒ Ⓓ	32. Ⓐ Ⓑ Ⓒ Ⓓ
3. Ⓐ Ⓑ Ⓒ Ⓓ	9. Ⓐ Ⓑ Ⓒ Ⓓ	15. Ⓐ Ⓑ Ⓒ Ⓓ	21. Ⓐ Ⓑ Ⓒ Ⓓ	27. Ⓐ Ⓑ Ⓒ Ⓓ	33. Ⓐ Ⓑ Ⓒ Ⓓ
4. Ⓐ Ⓑ Ⓒ Ⓓ	10. Ⓐ Ⓑ Ⓒ Ⓓ	16. Ⓐ Ⓑ Ⓒ Ⓓ	22. Ⓐ Ⓑ Ⓒ Ⓓ	28. Ⓐ Ⓑ Ⓒ Ⓓ	34. Ⓐ Ⓑ Ⓒ Ⓓ
5. Ⓐ Ⓑ Ⓒ Ⓓ	11. Ⓐ Ⓑ Ⓒ Ⓓ	17. Ⓐ Ⓑ Ⓒ Ⓓ	23. Ⓐ Ⓑ Ⓒ Ⓓ	29. Ⓐ Ⓑ Ⓒ Ⓓ	35. Ⓐ Ⓑ Ⓒ Ⓓ
6. Ⓐ Ⓑ Ⓒ Ⓓ	12. Ⓐ Ⓑ Ⓒ Ⓓ	18. Ⓐ Ⓑ Ⓒ Ⓓ	24. Ⓐ Ⓑ Ⓒ Ⓓ	30. Ⓐ Ⓑ Ⓒ Ⓓ	36. Ⓐ Ⓑ Ⓒ Ⓓ

Section 4: Mathematics Achievement

1. Ⓐ Ⓑ Ⓒ Ⓓ	9. Ⓐ Ⓑ Ⓒ Ⓓ	17. Ⓐ Ⓑ Ⓒ Ⓓ	25. Ⓐ Ⓑ Ⓒ Ⓓ	33. Ⓐ Ⓑ Ⓒ Ⓓ	41. Ⓐ Ⓑ Ⓒ Ⓓ
2. Ⓐ Ⓑ Ⓒ Ⓓ	10. Ⓐ Ⓑ Ⓒ Ⓓ	18. Ⓐ Ⓑ Ⓒ Ⓓ	26. Ⓐ Ⓑ Ⓒ Ⓓ	34. Ⓐ Ⓑ Ⓒ Ⓓ	42. Ⓐ Ⓑ Ⓒ Ⓓ
3. Ⓐ Ⓑ Ⓒ Ⓓ	11. Ⓐ Ⓑ Ⓒ Ⓓ	19. Ⓐ Ⓑ Ⓒ Ⓓ	27. Ⓐ Ⓑ Ⓒ Ⓓ	35. Ⓐ Ⓑ Ⓒ Ⓓ	43. Ⓐ Ⓑ Ⓒ Ⓓ
4. Ⓐ Ⓑ Ⓒ Ⓓ	12. Ⓐ Ⓑ Ⓒ Ⓓ	20. Ⓐ Ⓑ Ⓒ Ⓓ	28. Ⓐ Ⓑ Ⓒ Ⓓ	36. Ⓐ Ⓑ Ⓒ Ⓓ	44. Ⓐ Ⓑ Ⓒ Ⓓ
5. Ⓐ Ⓑ Ⓒ Ⓓ	13. Ⓐ Ⓑ Ⓒ Ⓓ	21. Ⓐ Ⓑ Ⓒ Ⓓ	29. Ⓐ Ⓑ Ⓒ Ⓓ	37. Ⓐ Ⓑ Ⓒ Ⓓ	45. Ⓐ Ⓑ Ⓒ Ⓓ
6. Ⓐ Ⓑ Ⓒ Ⓓ	14. Ⓐ Ⓑ Ⓒ Ⓓ	22. Ⓐ Ⓑ Ⓒ Ⓓ	30. Ⓐ Ⓑ Ⓒ Ⓓ	38. Ⓐ Ⓑ Ⓒ Ⓓ	46. Ⓐ Ⓑ Ⓒ Ⓓ
7. Ⓐ Ⓑ Ⓒ Ⓓ	15. Ⓐ Ⓑ Ⓒ Ⓓ	23. Ⓐ Ⓑ Ⓒ Ⓓ	31. Ⓐ Ⓑ Ⓒ Ⓓ	39. Ⓐ Ⓑ Ⓒ Ⓓ	47. Ⓐ Ⓑ Ⓒ Ⓓ
8. Ⓐ Ⓑ Ⓒ Ⓓ	16. Ⓐ Ⓑ Ⓒ Ⓓ	24. Ⓐ Ⓑ Ⓒ Ⓓ	32. Ⓐ Ⓑ Ⓒ Ⓓ	40. Ⓐ Ⓑ Ⓒ Ⓓ	

Section 5: Essay

_____

_____

_____

_____

_____

_____

_____

_____

_____

_____

_____

_____

_____

_____

_____

_____

_____

_____

_____

_____

_____

_____

_____

_____

Section One: Verbal Reasoning (Part One – Synonyms)

Questions: 40

Time Limit: 20 minutes

Directions: Select the word that is most nearly the same in meaning as the word in capital letters. You have 20 minutes to complete part one and part two.

1. PRECISE:

   (A) approximate
   (B) exact
   (C) mistaken
   (D) nearby

2. RANDOM:

   (A) calculated
   (B) deliberate
   (C) rehearsed
   (D) spontaneous

3. HAMPER:

   (A) carry
   (B) delay
   (C) expedite
   (D) scurry

4. ABOLISH:

   (A) eliminate
   (B) establish
   (C) prevent
   (D) promote

5. HAUGHTY:

   (A) arrogant
   (B) base
   (C) flighty
   (D) sufficient

6. CHASTISE:

   (A) drink
   (B) prevent
   (C) punish
   (D) purify

7. SPARSE:

   (A) analytical
   (B) dense
   (C) extra
   (D) meager

8. RELINQUISH:

   (A) abandon
   (B) anguish
   (C) conquer
   (D) savor

9. REBUFF:

   (A) accept
   (B) pacify
   (C) polish
   (D) spurn

10. AUGMENT:

   (A) argue
   (B) amplify
   (C) minimize
   (D) reduce

11. WANTON:

    (A) dumpling
    (B) keen
    (C) necessary
    (D) unprovoked

12. VENERABLE:

    (A) esteemed
    (B) insignificant
    (C) invincible
    (D) susceptible

13. IMPUDENT:

    (A) careful
    (B) disrespectful
    (C) gracious
    (D) reckless

14. POMPOUS:

    (A) ceremonial
    (B) minor
    (C) vain
    (D) valuable

15. USURP:

    (A) bequeath
    (B) confer
    (C) seize
    (D) surrender

16. TIRADE:

    (A) denunciation
    (B) riot
    (C) tyrant
    (D) vacation

17. ONEROUS:

    (A) arboreal
    (B) ardent
    (C) arduous
    (D) argent

18. SLOVENLY:

    (A) fatherly
    (B) heavenly
    (C) lovingly
    (D) messy

19. ERUDITION:

    (A) eruption
    (B) illiteracy
    (C) knowledge
    (D) strangeness

Section One: Verbal Reasoning (Part Two – Sentence Completion)

Directions: Select the word or pair of words that best completes the meaning of the sentence.

20. The flash of lightning was gone in an instant, its ------- blaze disappearing as quickly as it had appeared.

    (A) ephemeral
    (B) indelible
    (C) perpetual
    (D) unwavering

21. Edward rarely studied and never thought too much about a decision, instead relying upon his ------- to help him succeed.

    (A) emotions
    (B) humor
    (C) intuition
    (D) knowledge

22. The young musician was widely regarded as a(n) ------- because he was able to play pieces that adults found nearly impossible.

    (A) angel
    (B) loon
    (C) outsider
    (D) prodigy

23. Removing ------- words helped to simplify and clarify the main idea of the book.

    (A) appealing
    (B) concise
    (C) silvery
    (D) superfluous

24. The touching and deeply moving nature documentary ------- within him a previously unknown love of plants and animals.

    (A) curbed
    (B) doused
    (C) dulled
    (D) kindled

25. The designer specialized in ------- clothing; she was an expert at creating customized, made-to-order garments.

    (A) beautiful
    (B) bespoke
    (C) plain
    (D) trendy

26. Some governments have ------- intelligence organizations which operate in secret and without public oversight.

    (A) bureaucratic
    (B) clandestine
    (C) efficient
    (D) overt

27. Many countries consider treason to be a particularly ------- crime to be punished severely.

    (A) anodyne
    (B) heinous
    (C) justifiable
    (D) pardonable

28. The rote memorization and hours of practice left an ------- mark on Sally; even decades later, she still remembered how to read sheet music.

    (A) impermanent
    (B) indelible
    (C) opaque
    (D) unknown

29. Gripped by strong feelings of -------, the government banned all immigration.

    (A) equality
    (B) fraternity
    (C) sorority
    (D) xenophobia

30. The roommates' friendship hung by a(n) ------- thread; despite their formal agreement, Sally had not taken out the garbage, and Ruth had not cleaned the bathroom.

    (A) broken
    (B) industrious
    (C) substantial
    (D) tenuous

31. It is the ------- of the mouse that has enabled it to avoid detection, and to continue to thrive in the modern world.

    (A) assertiveness
    (B) blitheness
    (C) bravery
    (D) furtiveness

32. Lack of sleep has been shown to severely ------- judgement and ------- decision-making abilities, resulting in below average performance.

    (A) damage . . . facilitate
    (B) enhance . . . ease
    (C) impair . . . hinder
    (D) improve . . . debilitate

33. Instead of ------- opposition, the new and oppressive laws actually ------- a stronger and more unified dissent to the corrupt government.

    (A) cultivating . . . pacified
    (B) encouraging . . . triggered
    (C) stifling . . . provoked
    (D) suppressing . . . prevented

34. The lecturer had a tendency to -------; this quality made it even more difficult for the audience to maintain an interest in the already ------- topic.

    (A) blame . . . tiresome
    (B) joke . . . riveting
    (C) prattle . . . enthralling
    (D) ramble . . . mundane

35. Cracking open the oyster, the diver peered at the most ------- pearl he had ever seen; the light reflecting off of the pearl was so ------- that he needed to shield his eyes.

    (A) burnished . . . potent
    (B) illustrious . . . intoxicating
    (C) leaden . . . lackluster
    (D) luminous . . . brilliant

36. The ------- gangster was at once feared and loved by the public; he had a ------- personality that belied a taste for physical violence.

   (A) infamous . . . threatening
   (B) nefarious . . . menacing
   (C) notorious . . . charismatic
   (D) reputable . . . charming

37. The professional boxer was ------- even outside the ring; his ------- disposition resulted in many fights that landed him in trouble with the law.

   (A) amiable . . . diplomatic
   (B) bellicose . . . serene
   (C) genial . . . quarrelsome
   (D) pugnacious . . . truculent

38. The delicious smells wafting from the kitchen only served to ------- his appetite; his growing hunger ------- him from his bed.

   (A) hone . . . perched
   (B) quell . . . lulled
   (C) taper . . . ousted
   (D) whet . . . roused

39. The thief's success at ------- candies was due in part to his -------; the store clerks never suspected that a thief could be so calm and collected.

   (A) hawking . . . confidence
   (B) peddling . . . apprehension
   (C) pilfering . . . nonchalance
   (D) sneaking . . . trepidation

40. The man had grown ------- in his old age; he had lost interest in many of the passions he had once pursued as a young man and led a ------- and uneventful life.

   (A) active . . . charming
   (B) dull . . . fascinating
   (C) lively . . . tedious
   (D) stodgy . . . sedentary

Section Two: Quantitative Reasoning (Part One – Word Problems)

Questions: 37   **Time Limit:** 35 minutes

Directions – Choose the best of the four possible answers. You have 35 minutes to complete part one and part two.

1. The sum of all the integers from 100 to 1,000, inclusive, is x. Which expression represents the sum of all integers from 104 to 1,000, inclusive?

   (A) $x - 103$
   (B) $x - 404$
   (C) $x - 406$
   (D) $x - 896$

2. What is the value of 0.513 in scientific notation?

   (A) 5.13×10^{-3}
   (B) 5.13×10^{-1}
   (C) 51.3×10^{-1}
   (D) 513×10^{-1}

3. Ingrid and Hubert are jogging through a park, each at a constant speed. When Ingrid started jogging, Hubert had already jogged 200 meters. If Ingrid was jogging faster than Hubert, which one additional piece of information would be needed to determine how long it took Ingrid to catch up to Hubert?

   (A) Ingrid was jogging at a speed of 6 kilometers per hour.
   (B) Hubert was jogging at a speed of 3 kilometers per hour.
   (C) Their combined speed was 10 kilometers per hour.
   (D) The difference of their speeds was 1 kilometer per hour.

4. A cube is shown.

Which figure is a possible net for the cube?

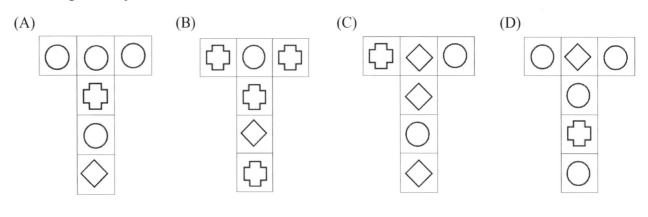

(A)   (B)   (C)   (D)

5. If $n*m = 3m + \dfrac{n}{m}$, what is the value of n if

$n*2 = 7$?

(A) 1
(B) 2
(C) 4
(D) 6

6. What is the greatest common factor of $5a^2b^4$, a^3b, and $8a^4b^3$?

(A) a^2b
(B) a^2b^4
(C) $5ab^4$
(D) $5a^2b^4$

7. If $(x - 11)^2 = x^2 + n + 121$, what is the value of n?

(A) 22
(B) $22x$
(C) -22
(D) $-22x$

8. The sum of three consecutive odd integers is 69. Which equation could be used to find the integers?

(A) $3x + 6 = 69$
(B) $x^3 + 6 = 69$
(C) $x + (x + 1) + (x + 3) = 69$
(D) $3x + 3 = 69$

9. $f(x) = x^4$
$g(x) = x^3$

Which of the following statements must be true?

(A) $f(x)$ must be odd
(B) $g(f(x))$ must be odd
(C) $g(x)$ must be positive
(D) $f(g(x))$ must be positive

10. Square MNOP is similar to Square QRST.

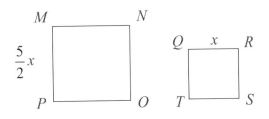

If side MN is 10 inches, what is the length of ST?

(A) 4
(B) 6
(C) $4x$
(D) $6x$

11. A bucket contains 10 yellow pencils, 4 white pencils, 6 green pencils, and 10 black pencils. Damon picks out a pencil and does not place it back into the bucket, then picks out another pencil. If the first pencil Damon picked out was yellow, what is the probability that the second pencil he picked out was black?

(A) $\dfrac{1}{3}$

(B) $\dfrac{10}{29}$

(C) $\dfrac{1}{3} \times \dfrac{1}{3}$

(D) $\dfrac{10}{29} \times \dfrac{1}{3}$

12. James has 8 more dimes than nickels. The total value of all his coins is $1.55. How many nickels does he have?

(A) 5
(B) 6
(C) 7
(D) 8

13. Joan earned scores of 69, 77, and 88 on her first three tests. Her final test will count as two tests towards her final mean. What grade must she get on her last test to raise her average to an 80?

(A) 86
(B) 84
(C) 83
(D) 82

14. What is the value of $\sqrt{6} \times \sqrt{3}$?

(A) $9\sqrt{2}$
(B) 9
(C) $3\sqrt{2}$
(D) $2\sqrt{3}$

15. Which of the following represents 4^9 in terms of 64?

(A) 64^3
(B) 64^4
(C) 64^{12}
(D) 64^{18}

16. Corinne is donating old toys to charity. She wants to donate 3 out of her 4 old teddy bears. How many different combinations of 3 bears can she make to donate?

(A) 4
(B) 8
(C) 12
(D) 16

17. A political party keeps track of how many votes they receive in each state. They received 45,000 votes in all, 9,000 of which came from New York. A circle graph was made from the data. What was the central angle of the portion of the graph representing New York?

(A) 20°
(B) 36°
(C) 72°
(D) 90°

18. What is the sum of the four interior angles of any quadrilateral?

(A) 180°
(B) 270°
(C) 360°
(D) 540°

19. What is the value of the expression $\dfrac{(5^2 + 5^1)}{(3^3 + 3^1)}$?

(A) 1
(B) 2.5
(C) 3.3333
(D) 4.4444

20. If $\dfrac{a}{b} = c$, then which expression is equal to b?

(A) a
(B) $\dfrac{a}{c}$
(C) $\dfrac{c}{a}$
(D) ac

21. The first three terms of a geometric sequence of numbers are shown.

$$\frac{1}{4}, \frac{1}{2}, 1$$

What is the 7th term of this sequence?

(A) 7
(B) 16
(C) 32
(D) 64

Section Two: Quantitative Reasoning (Part Two – Quantitative Comparisons)

Directions – Compare the amount in Column A to the amount in Column B using the information provided in each question. All questions in this part have the following answer choices:

(A) The amount in column A is greater.
(B) The amount in column B is greater.
(C) The two amounts are equal.
(D) The relationship cannot be determined from the information provided.

A girl playing a game spins a spinner with 4 equally-sized sections numbered 1-4 and rolls a 6-sided die.

Column A	Column B
22. The probability she will spin an odd number on the spinner and roll an even number on the die	$\frac{1}{2}$

B

$\frac{1}{24}$

$d, e, f, p, q,$ and r are all positive integers

Column A	Column B
23. $\dfrac{d^3 e^{-5} f}{3pq^{-2}r^{-8}}$	$\dfrac{2d^3 fq^2 r^8}{6e^5 p}$

D

A pair of pants was on sale for 20% off the original price. The sale price after the discount was $48.

Column A	Column B
24. The original price before the discount	$58

A

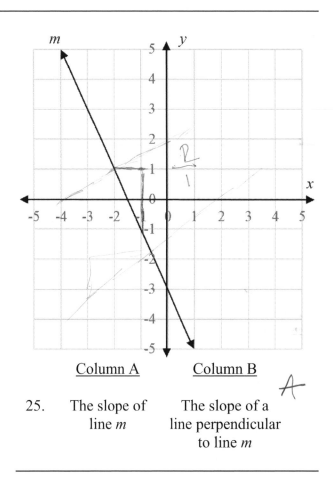

Column A	Column B
25. The slope of line m	The slope of a line perpendicular to line m

A

A rectangle has a perimeter of 36 inches. The length and width are both integers.

Column A	Column B
26. The smallest possible area of the rectangle	36 square inches

C

36
[36 in]

	Column A	Column B
27.	$(x + 5)(x + 3)$	$x^2 + 8x + 16$

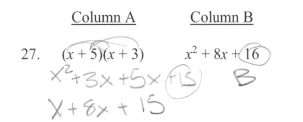

An abandoned city lot has a 5-foot-wide sidewalk around it, as shown by the shaded area.

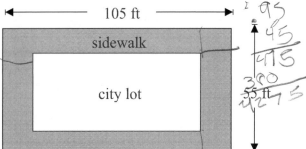

← 105 ft →

sidewalk

city lot

55 ft

Note: Figure not drawn to scale.

	Column A	Column B
28.	The area of the lot without the sidewalk	5,000 ft^2

Missy's science test had a typo in it, so the teacher decided to give all 24 students in the class an extra 2 points on their test grades.

	Column A	Column B
29.	The change in the median grade	The change in the range of the grades

	Column A	Column B
30.	64^2	2^{36}

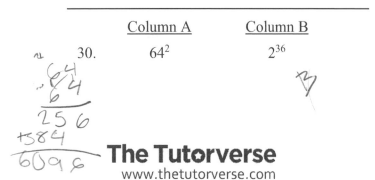

A school held a fundraiser. Every family that attended was asked to donate at one of the pre-chosen levels: $20, $50, $100, $200, $500. The school then graphed the results of the fundraiser.

FUNDRAISER

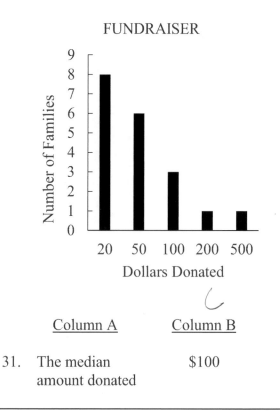

Number of Families

Dollars Donated

	Column A	Column B
31.	The median amount donated	$100

Cube M has a volume of $64x^3$, where x is greater than 0.

	Column A	Column B
32.	The volume of a cube with a side length 2 times the side length of Cube M.	The volume of a cube with a side length of $8x$.

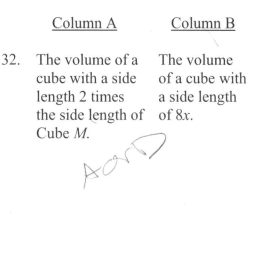

$$(x - y)^2 = 60$$
$$x^2 + y^2 = 30$$

skipped

Column A	Column B
33. The value of $2xy$	30

A coin is flipped three times.

Column A	Column B
34. If the first two flips both result in heads, the probability of the third flip resulting in heads	If the first two flips both result in heads, the probability of the third flip resulting in tails

skipped

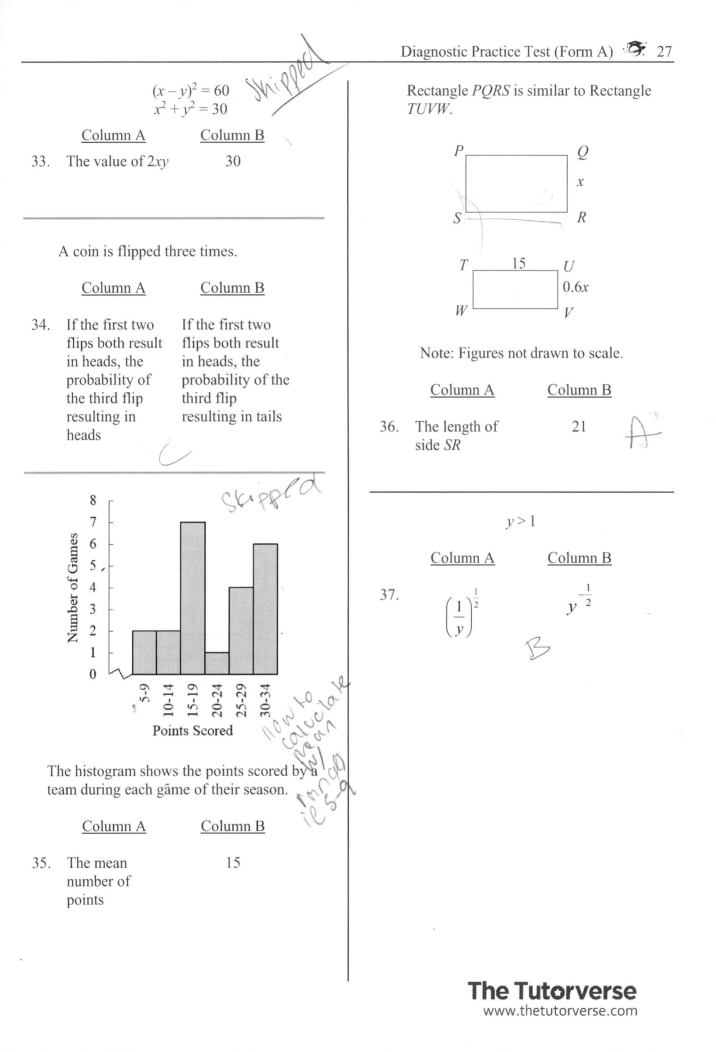

The histogram shows the points scored by a team during each game of their season.

how to calculate mean w/ range ie 5-9

Column A	Column B
35. The mean number of points	15

Rectangle _PQRS_ is similar to Rectangle _TUVW_.

Note: Figures not drawn to scale.

Column A	Column B
36. The length of side _SR_	21

_A_

$$y > 1$$

Column A	Column B
37. $\left(\dfrac{1}{y}\right)^{\frac{1}{2}}$	$y^{-\frac{1}{2}}$

_B_

Section Three: Reading Comprehension

Questions: 36   **Time Limit:** 35 minutes

Directions – Answer the questions following each passage based on what is either stated or implied in the passage. You have 35 minutes to complete 36 questions.

Questions 1-6

1   Easter Island is a small island in the
2 southeastern Pacific. One of the island's
3 greatest claims to fame are the moai,
4 monolithic stone sculptures of human
5 figures. On Easter Island, many of the
6 surviving moai were buried to their
7 shoulders. As a result, the sculptures
8 became mistakenly known as the "Easter
9 Island heads." Many mysteries surround the
10 moai, not least of which is the method by
11 which the sculptures were transported
12 around the island.
13   Many of the moai scattered around the
14 island were quarried from the same rock
15 quarry on the island. This meant that the
16 rock was somehow moved from the quarry
17 to the moai's final destination. The average
18 moai weighed approximately 14 tons, with
19 several being significantly larger, in excess
20 of 80 tons. Created between the 13th and
21 16th centuries – a time before mechanized
22 construction equipment – moving the large,
23 heavy sculptures was a feat of engineering
24 and human ingenuity. Yet historians are
25 unsure precisely how the native islanders
26 were able to accomplish such a feat.
27   Oral histories describe how powerful
28 rulers wielded supernatural or divine powers
29 and caused the statues to come to life and
30 walk themselves around the island. Though
31 many considered such stories to be
32 outlandish, they had difficulty determining
33 any alternative.
34   One early theory was that the islanders
35 transported quarried rock across the island

36 by means of a conveyer belt-type system.
37 The idea was that trees were cut down and
38 used as rollers across which the stones could
39 be moved. But by the time Europeans
40 arrived on Easter Island in the 18th century,
41 the island was completely treeless. This
42 added fuel to the mystery of the moai, which
43 persists even today.
44   More recently, some archaeologists and
45 historians attempted to "walk" moai replicas
46 across the island. They did so by tying
47 ropes around the head and the base of the
48 replica, rocking the replica from side to side.
49 The team was able to shuffle the replica
50 forward, which they considered proof that
51 such a methodology was likely employed by
52 the island's old inhabitants.
53   However, not everyone was convinced.
54 Some historians and archaeologists
55 questioned the basic premise behind the
56 "walking" experiment. They argued that the
57 replica used in the "walk" was not
58 representative of actual moai weight, and
59 that the replica did not behave as a real moai
60 would have. Thus, they argued, no
61 definitive conclusions could be drawn from
62 the "walking" experiment.
63   We are no closer to discovering the truth
64 behind how the Easter Island natives moved
65 the moai than we were decades ago. For all
66 we know, perhaps the moai really did get up
67 and walk themselves from the quarry to their
68 current locations.

1. Which best expresses the main idea of the passage?

   (A) Easter Island natives wielded divine powers.
   (B) Moving large statues is impossible without trees.
   (C) Some historical phenomena are not well understood.
   (D) Most historical phenomena are understood through oral traditions.

2. According to the first paragraph (lines 1-12), many people mistakenly think that the sculptures on Easter Island are merely heads because

   (A) the heads are already so large.
   (B) they only see a portion of each statue.
   (C) moai on other islands also consist only of heads.
   (D) they know that the sculptures broke in transit, leaving only the heads.

3. According to lines 27-33, it can be inferred that the method for transporting moai was

   (A) not documented in historical records.
   (B) unknown even to the native islanders.
   (C) discovered by early European visitors, but later lost.
   (D) certainly the result of divine or supernatural powers.

4. In line 61, "definitive" most nearly means

   (A) authoritative.
   (B) basic.
   (C) impressive.
   (D) uncertain.

5. The author's tone in the final sentence of the passage (lines 65-68) can best be described as

   (A) certain.
   (B) cryptic.
   (C) decisive.
   (D) tolerant.

6. The author of the passage does all of the following EXCEPT

   (A) describe several theories.
   (B) highlight a historical mystery.
   (C) present two sides to an argument.
   (D) explain an island's geological history.

Questions 7-12

1   My friend's parents had purchased the
2 abandoned summer camp several years ago,
3 just before they retired. Since then, they had
4 spent a lot of time and money renovating the
5 facilities.
6   The camp's seven structures – formerly
7 a mess hall, administrative office, and cabins
8 – were arranged in a semi-circle near a small
9 lake. The lake and buildings were
10 surrounded by a native forest of the sort that
11 can be found in other small upstate New
12 York towns; everywhere were oaks, maples,
13 aspens, and birches.
14   My friend's parents, ever enterprising
15 and entrepreneurial – even in retirement! –
16 had decided to capitalize on the natural
17 resources that came with the camp. After
18 converting the old mess hall into their
19 vacation home, they turned their attention to
20 the woods. In the summer and early fall,
21 they hired workers to comb the woods for
22 mushrooms and usually ended the season
23 with a large harvest of chanterelles, hen-of-
24 the-woods, and morels. Though they had
25 several years' success harvesting
26 mushrooms, this was only the second year
27 that they had decided to focus on their maple
28 trees.
29   As I looked around the property on a
30 cold, spring morning, I could see around the
31 lake and through the woods bright blue
32 plastic bags tied around the trunks of various
33 trees. I guessed correctly that these trees
34 were in fact sugar maples, and that the
35 plastic bags were collecting the sap needed
36 to make maple syrup.
37   Walking toward one of the maples with
38 my friend, I passed by a skeleton of a
39 building. All that remained of the former
40 cabin were framed walls supporting a roof;
41 the sides of the structure were completely

42 open to the elements, and allowed me to
43 clearly see an evaporator sitting in the
44 middle of the shack. The old cabin had been
45 repurposed into a sugar shack – the place
46 where sap was boiled down into syrup.
47   The evaporator oozed character. That a
48 glorified stove could be so beautiful actually
49 took my breath away. I walked toward the
50 evaporator through one of the "walls" to
51 take a better look.
52   It was about the size of a dining room
53 table. At one end, low to the ground,
54 intricately carved cast iron doors guarded
55 the furnace in its underbelly. Above the
56 furnace, about waist height, were two large
57 vats where sap would undergo its
58 metamorphosis. At the opposite end of the
59 cast iron doors was a chimney that rose up
60 to the roof, allowing steam and smoke to
61 vent. Perhaps the most beautiful aspect of
62 the evaporator was its copper plating,
63 covering everything from the furnace to the
64 vats to the chimney in a soft, warm glow.
65 The copper was polished to a high shine,
66 reflecting its otherwise spartan surroundings
67 in a warm, bronze radiance.
68   The evaporator was covered in little
69 dings, scratches, and dents from years of
70 syrup making. Rather than making it look
71 dingy and dilapidated, these scars instead
72 gave it a dignified and weathered patina.
73 My friend confirmed that the evaporator
74 was, indeed, an antique.
75   I took another look around the sugar
76 shack and through its "walls" into the
77 surrounding forest. The chance to work in
78 such an idyllic setting, with good friends and
79 beautiful tools, filled me with a strange but
80 comforting sense of nostalgia.
81   I was ready to get to work.

7. The primary purpose of the passage is to

    (A) describe a place.
    (B) describe an event.
    (C) describe a person.
    (D) describe a process.

8. According to lines 14-17, it can be inferred that the current owners of the camp

    (A) enjoy swimming in the lake.
    (B) like to go camping in the mountains and forests.
    (C) previously owned several businesses.
    (D) renovate and sell abandoned properties.

9. "Chanterelles, hen-of-the-woods, and morels" (lines 23-24) are most likely

    (A) names of trees.
    (B) types of mushrooms.
    (C) brands of maple syrup.
    (D) names of the old buildings.

10. In line 54, "intricately" most nearly means

    (A) elaborately.
    (B) plainly.
    (C) simply.
    (D) superficially.

11. In lines 57-58, the phrase "undergo its metamorphosis" refers to

    (A) the renovation of the evaporator.
    (B) the renovation of the sugar shack.
    (C) the process of turning sap into syrup.
    (D) a caterpillar transforming into a butterfly.

12. In describing the evaporator, the author's tone can be best described as

    (A) admiring.
    (B) defensive.
    (C) mysterious.
    (D) lackadaisical.

The Tutorverse
www.thetutorverse.com

Questions 13-18

This passage is an excerpt from a speech delivered by John F. Kennedy at the White House.

1　　I want to tell you how welcome you are
2　to the White House. I think this is the most
3　extraordinary collection of talent, of human
4　knowledge, that has ever been gathered
5　together at the White House, with the
6　possible exception of when Thomas
7　Jefferson dined alone.
8　　Someone once said that Thomas
9　Jefferson was a gentleman of 32 who could
10　calculate an eclipse, survey an estate, tie an
11　artery, plan an edifice, try a cause, break a
12　horse, and dance the minuet. Whatever he
13　may have lacked, if he could have had his
14　former colleague, Mr. Franklin, here we all
15　would have been impressed.
16　　In any case, I am delighted to welcome
17　you here. We are delighted to have the
18　Norwegian Ambassador and the Swedish
19　Minister to represent their governments, and
20　we are delighted to have the Nobel prize
21　winners of the Western Hemisphere here at
22　this dinner.
23　　I know that the Nobel prize does not
24　have any geographic or national
25　implications. Mr. Nobel in his will, in fact,
26　made it very clear when he said that he
27　hoped that in the giving of the prize that no
28　attention would be paid to nationality. He
29　declared it to be "my express desire that in
30　awarding the prize, no consideration
31　whatsoever be paid to the nationality of the
32　candidates; that is to say, the most deserving
33　be awarded the prize, whether he or she be
34　Scandinavian or not."

35　　In any case, there is no nationality in the
36　Nobel prize, just as there is no nationality in
37　the acquisition of knowledge. I know that
38　every man here who has won the Nobel
39　prize, not only does he build on the past,
40　which goes back hundreds and thousands of
41　years, on the efforts of other men and
42　women, but he also builds on the efforts of
43　those in other countries; and therefore, quite
44　rightly, the Nobel prize has no national
45　significance.
46　　But I think we can take some satisfaction
47　that this hemisphere has been able to
48　develop an atmosphere which has permitted
49　the happy pursuit of knowledge, and of
50　peace; and that over 40 percent of the Nobel
51　prizes in the last 30 years have gone to men
52　and women in this hemisphere.
53　　And of particular pleasure today is the
54　fact that 13 Nobel prizes for peace have
55　gone to those who live in this hemisphere. I
56　think the pursuit of knowledge, the pursuit
57　of peace, are very basic drives and pressures
58　in this life of ours – and this dinner is an
59　attempt, in a sense, to recognize those great
60　efforts, to encourage young Americans and
61　young people in this hemisphere to develop
62　the same drive and deep desire for
63　knowledge and peace.
64　　So I want you to know that you are most
65　welcome here. I regard this as the most
66　distinguished and significant dinner that we
67　have had in the White House since I have
68　been here, and I think in many, many years.

13. The passage is primarily concerned with

    (A) preparing for a fancy dinner.
    (B) honoring distinguished guests.
    (C) interpreting the will of Mr. Nobel.
    (D) explaining the importance of the Nobel prize.

14. The mood of lines 1-15 can best be described as

    (A) contentious.
    (B) hospitable.
    (C) remorseful.
    (D) solemn.

15. The author quotes Mr. Nobel's will (lines 28-34) in order to

    (A) compare Mr. Nobel with Mr. Jefferson.
    (B) explain that Mr. Nobel was Scandinavian.
    (C) wholly reject nationalism and patriotism.
    (D) emphasize that the prize prioritizes merit.

16. In lines 35-45, the author suggests that knowledge is advanced by all humanity because

    (A) all ideas build off of other ideas.
    (B) all ideas are novel and wholly original.
    (C) Nobel prize recipients are given unlimited access to historical records.
    (D) the acquisition of knowledge is only important to people of certain nationalities.

17. According to lines 46-52, it can be inferred that the author attributes the number of Nobel prize winners in his hemisphere in part to

    (A) freedoms and liberties.
    (B) studiousness and discipline.
    (C) government support and subsidies.
    (D) the availability of libraries and universities.

18. In line 62, "drive" most nearly means

    (A) happiness.
    (B) motivation.
    (C) optimism.
    (D) satisfaction.

Questions 19-24

1   The definition of the workplace has
2   changed throughout human history. In times
3   past, work was conducted alone or in small
4   groups – in fields, in the woods, or in small
5   shops and factories. As societies became
6   more advanced and people began relying
7   more and more on each other to carry out
8   their responsibilities, people began to work
9   in what we today call offices – buildings
10 dedicated to the centralized administration
11 of a business. Such offices were important
12 to the development of a knowledge and
13 service-based economy. However, new
14 technology and forms of communication
15 have begun to render the office obsolete.
16 More and more people both desire to and are
17 enabled to work remotely. We are entering
18 a new age of work – an age where, for the
19 first time, people working together towards
20 a common goal need not actually ever meet.
21   The idea of a centralized workplace
22 where people could come together and
23 exchange ideas was crucial to the
24 development of certain industries. Indeed,
25 certain professions continue to thrive on an
26 office culture where coworkers can meet
27 face to face. Meeting people in-person has a
28 great many advantages, not least of which is
29 the ability for people to read and assess body
30 language, which has been shown to greatly
31 affect communication. Not only do offices
32 facilitate in-person communication, but they
33 also help to establish a cohesive culture for
34 workers. Like any other community, office
35 workers bond over shared experiences. This
36 in turn helps to create new social circles and
37 friendships, and can even lead to new ideas
38 and improved efficiencies.
39   Technology has inadvertently begun to
40 supplant the office, offering cheaper, faster,
41 and more convenient ways to accomplish the

42 same goals. Many people do not live near
43 their office. For many workers, commuting
44 to an office represents untold hours of
45 unproductive time, in addition to added
46 expense and stress. The people that do live
47 near their offices tend to live in cities, where
48 the cost of real-estate and office space can
49 be very high. Technology offers a solution
50 to the problem of high rents and long
51 commutes: telecommuting.
52   The widespread use of technology to
53 facilitate communication has already begun
54 to change the way people do business and
55 work together. Just as the advent of the
56 telephone changed the way people lived and
57 worked, so too does the advent of the
58 internet. People can conduct face-to-face
59 meetings with others on the other side of the
60 planet as easily as they can speak to one
61 another on the phone. People can share
62 documents and collaborate with one another
63 as if they were sitting next to each other.
64 People can discover and share new ideas
65 with one another with the click of the mouse
66 and a stroke of the keyboard. Faster,
67 cheaper, and sometimes more effective,
68 technology is quickly making the idea of
69 working remotely attractive to industries and
70 businesses that may not require a permanent,
71 centralized location from which to run a
72 business.
73   Technology is no panacea. Businesses
74 and groups must weigh carefully the
75 advantages and disadvantages of a
76 disaggregated workplace powered by
77 technology alone. A business with no
78 central office is more suitable for some
79 industries than others. After all, shaking
80 hands with someone is still very different
81 from waving at them through a computer
82 screen.

19. The main purpose of the passage is to

(A) explain different styles of communication.
(B) advocate for technology-based workplace solutions. *- less strong*
(C) staunchly oppose the continued use of traditional office spaces. *-strong*
(D) describe how technological advances change all aspects of human behavior.

20. In line 40, "supplant" most nearly means

(A) conceal.
(B) establish.
(C) ingrain.
(D) replace.

21. According to lines 52-72, the author suggests that all of the following can be accomplished more cheaply and quickly through the use of technology EXCEPT for

(A) exchanging new ideas.
(B) building a unified culture.
(C) communicating with other people.
(D) working together to review a project.

22. The author of the passage appears to care most deeply about

(A) discontinuing the use of offices.
(B) fully transitioning to virtual offices.
(C) saving people time and businesses money.
(D) the evolution of the workplace through history.

23. In the final paragraph (lines 73-82), the phrase "technology is no panacea" refers to the

(A) notion that technology is critical to communication.
(B) misguided belief that technology can solve all problems.
(C) fact that technology can be applied to any and all industries.
(D) idea that virtual meetings are as effective as in-person meetings.

24. The author of the passage does all of the following EXCEPT

(A) present an argument supporting an opinion.
(B) compare and contrast different points of view.
(C) describe how technology can be applied to different industries.
(D) explain the advantages and disadvantages of working in an office.

Questions 25-30

1   For three hundred years, from the
2 fourteenth through the seventeenth
3 centuries, the European Renaissance swept
4 across the continent. During this time,
5 Europe witnessed an unprecedented
6 explosion of new ideas, innovative art, bold
7 invention, and booming prosperity. Like
8 many significant historical events, there is
9 no one reason for this blossoming that took
10 place. Rather, a confluence of events –
11 some social, some political – paved the way
12 for one the most important periods in human
13 history.
14   During the Renaissance, Italy was not
15 the unified country that it is today. Instead,
16 what we today know as Italy was a
17 collection of city-states and small republics.
18 One of the unique features of these small
19 states was their innovative form of social
20 and political order. While much of Europe
21 continued to exist under a model of
22 feudalism, which derived political and social
23 order from land ownership, Italy had, by the
24 twelfth century, achieved stability through
25 commerce and trade. Because the economy
26 was paramount, these new Italian republics
27 favored secular governance, and preferred to
28 keep monarchical and religious authority
29 outside of the realm of politics. This new
30 republicanism highly valued individual
31 liberties.

32   Because of these values, significant
33 freedom was afforded to scholars and artists.
34 As a result, great advances in science, math,
35 engineering, art, and philosophy occurred
36 during this time. As the economic
37 importance of the various republics
38 increased, more money became available to
39 fund the burgeoning class of artists and
40 scholars. Meanwhile, booming trade led to
41 the production of new goods, and the city-
42 states and republics soon became central to
43 global commerce. The republics of Florence
44 and Venice, for example, were major trading
45 centers, drawing traders from as far away as
46 the Middle East. Fresh thinking and new
47 ideas traveled with the various traders who
48 passed through Florentine and Venetian
49 gates.
50   As Italian merchants increased their
51 fortunes, they also grew their political power
52 and social influence. In many cases, they
53 utilized their newfound power and position
54 to advance the arts. Particularly in Florence,
55 families such as the Medicis were extremely
56 wealthy, politically well connected, and
57 socially influential. They patronized artists
58 and thinkers such as Leonardo da Vinci,
59 Michelangelo Buonarroti, and Sandro
60 Botticelli, helping them to realize many of
61 their dreams and visions.

25. The passage is primarily concerned with

    (A) comparing feudalism with republicanism.
    (B) underscoring the importance of patrons to artists.
    (C) highlighting the relationship between money and art.
    (D) explaining the factors that contributed to an important era in human history.

26. The author uses the phrase "swept across the continent" (lines 3-4) in order to

    (A) invoke a solemn tone.
    (B) anthropomorphize the Renaissance.
    (C) show the widespread impact of the Renaissance.
    (D) explain how the Renaissance cleansed Europe of heretical thinking.

27. In line 26, "paramount" most nearly means

    (A) central.
    (B) fantastic.
    (C) lofty.
    (D) unimportant.

28. In lines 32-49, the author does all of the following EXCEPT

    (A) blame religious decline on economic growth.
    (B) describe the impact of commerce on the global flow of new ideas.
    (C) explain how growing wealth benefited both thinkers and artists.
    (D) provide specific examples in which republics became central to global trade.

29. According to the final paragraph, lines 50-61, many works created by artists such as Michelangelo and da Vinci were the result of

    (A) a feudalistic society.
    (B) unique genius and ability.
    (C) religious fervor and divine inspiration.
    (D) the patronage of rich, powerful merchants.

30. The author implies that the European Renaissance may not have taken place without which of the following?

    (A) Widespread social, political, and economic changes.
    (B) A respect for and adherence to old ideas and philosophies.
    (C) The ongoing popularity and widespread support of feudalism.
    (D) The continuation of monarchical and religious authority within politics.

The Tutorverse
www.thetutorverse.com

Questions 31-36

1   Also known as twisters or cyclones, a
2 tornado is a rapidly rotating column of air
3 that is concurrently in contact with the earth
4 and a cloud. Tornadoes are typically found
5 in areas where the atmospheric pressure is
6 lower than that of surrounding areas.
7   Most tornadoes are short lived, traveling
8 for several miles before disappearing.
9 However, even these weaker formations
10 have wind speeds that can reach up to 110
11 miles per hour. On the other hand, more
12 violent and powerful tornadoes can have
13 wind speeds exceeding 300 miles per hour
14 and can travel for many miles before
15 dissipating.
16   There are three primary scales that rate
17 the strength of tornadoes. These scales are
18 the Fujita scale, the Enhanced Fujita Scale,
19 and the TORRO scale. Under the Fujita and
20 Enhanced Fujita scales, respectively, the
21 weakest tornadoes, F0 or EF0 tornadoes, can
22 cause damage to trees but not to substantial
23 structures. The strongest tornadoes, F5 or
24 EF5, can completely destroy smaller
25 buildings and cause substantial damage to
26 large skyscrapers. While the Fujita scales
27 rely on damage potential in order to classify
28 tornadoes, the TORRO scale uses wind
29 speed. Under the TORRO scale, T0
30 tornadoes are extremely weak, having wind
31 speeds between 39 and 54 miles per hour.

32 The TORRO scale increases based upon a
33 mathematical formula; the maximum rating
34 for a tornado under this scale is T11, which
35 applies to tornadoes with wind speeds
36 exceeding 300 miles per hour.
37   Most tornadoes, regardless of size or
38 strength rating, take on a funnel-like
39 appearance, though the shapes of these
40 funnels can vary widely. "Stovepipe"
41 tornadoes possess a cylindrical profile,
42 whereas "wedge" tornadoes are low to the
43 ground and wide; "rope" tornadoes are
44 narrow and twisting. Similarly, the color of
45 tornadoes can vary widely. This variation is
46 due to the location of the sun relative to the
47 observer and to the tornado, as well as to the
48 time of day when the tornado is formed.
49   Because of unique geological features on
50 the North American continent, tornadoes are
51 most frequently observed in the United
52 States. In particular, the central part of the
53 country, aptly named "Tornado Alley,"
54 often sees fronts of warm, tropical air
55 colliding with cool, arctic air – ideal
56 conditions for tornado formation. Because
57 Tornado Alley is large and relatively flat,
58 with no major landmasses to block the
59 meeting of the air flows, these conditions
60 can occur quite frequently. In the last decade
61 alone, the United States averaged over 1,000
62 tornadoes per year.

31. The passage is primarily concerned with

   (A) criticizing certain tornado-strength measurement scales.
   (B) providing the reader with a general overview of tornadoes.
   (C) explaining why tornadoes are more frequent in North America.
   (D) describing in detail the shapes, sizes, and colors of different tornadoes.

32. In line 3, "concurrently" most nearly means

   (A) inconveniently.
   (B) mistakenly.
   (C) separately.
   (D) simultaneously.

33. According to lines 7-15, it can be inferred that tornadoes are unpredictable because

   (A) they reliably travel short distances.
   (B) they seldom endure for less than a minute.
   (C) their appearance, strength, and longevity can vary so widely.
   (D) they are always so powerful that they devastate land and buildings.

34. Which best describes the organization of lines 37-48?

   (A) a compilation of physical tornado attributes
   (B) an analysis detailing the causes of different tornado shapes
   (C) a first-hand account of encountering different types of tornadoes
   (D) a description of the process by which tornadoes achieve different colors

35. Which does the author mention in the last paragraph (lines 49-62) as a reason that tornadoes occur more frequently in North America?

   (A) grassy prairies
   (B) changes in global wind and climate patterns
   (C) high mountains and wide-ranging temperatures
   (D) unobstructed meeting of cold and warm air masses

36. The author includes the term "Tornado Alley" (line 53) in order to

   (A) make a comparison with Hurricane Hub in the Atlantic.
   (B) suggest a nickname for the central part of the United States.
   (C) make light of the frequency of tornadoes occurring in North America.
   (D) reinforce the notion that tornadoes occur frequently in this area of the United States.

Section Four: Mathematics Achievement

Questions: 47   Time Limit: 40 minutes

Directions – Select the best answer from the four answer choices. You have 40 minutes to complete 47 questions.

1. The first five terms of a geometric sequence of numbers are shown.

   ×2 ×2 geometric
   4, 8, 16, 32, 64

   Which expression represents the nth term of this sequence?

   (A) 2^{n-1}
   (B) $2^{n-1}+4$
   (C) $4(2)^{n-1}$
   (D) $4(2)^n$

2. There are 1,760 yards in a mile. Cody can run at a speed of 6 miles per hour. Which expression has a value equal to Cody's speed, in yards per second?

   (A) $\dfrac{6 \times 1,760}{60 \times 60}$

   (B) $\dfrac{60 \times 1,760}{6 \times 60}$

   (C) $\dfrac{6 \times 60}{60 \times 1,760}$

   (D) $\dfrac{60 \times 60}{70 \times 1,760}$

3. Which of the following represents 6^2 in expanded form?

   (A) 6×2
   (B) 6×6
   (C) $6 + 6$
   (D) $2 \times 2 \times 2 \times 2 \times 2 \times 2$

4. Which expression is equivalent to the expression $x^4 - 81$?

   (A) $(x-3)^4$
   (B) $(x-9)(x+9)$
   (C) $(x^2-27)(x^2+3)$
   (D) $(x-3)(x+3)(x^2+9)$

5. The box-and-whisker plot shows the number of gallons of gas every car in a town used in a month.

   35 40 45 50 55 60 65 70 75 80

   What is the median of the data?

   (A) 40
   (B) 57
   (C) 62
   (D) 67

6. Which of the following is the graph of the solution to $2|x+4| - 6 < 8$?

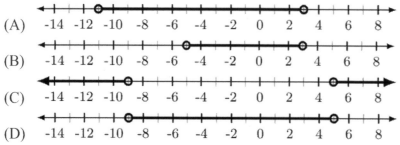

   (A) -14 -12 -10 -8 -6 -4 -2   0   2   4   6   8
   (B) -14 -12 -10 -8 -6 -4 -2   0   2   4   6   8
   (C) -14 -12 -10 -8 -6 -4 -2   0   2   4   6   8
   (D) -14 -12 -10 -8 -6 -4 -2   0   2   4   6   8

7. What type of number results from i^4?

   (A) a complex number
   (B) an irrational number
   (C) a negative integer
   (D) a whole number

8. What is the value of the numerical expression $6.02 \times 10^6 + 4.29 \times 10^4$ in scientific notation?

   (A) 6.02429×10^6
   (B) 6.0629×10^6
   (C) 10.32×10^{10}
   (D) 1.032×10^6

9. What is the value of $\sqrt{54} - \sqrt{24}$?

   (A) $\sqrt{6}$
   (B) $\sqrt{30}$
   (C) $5\sqrt{6}$
   (D) $6\sqrt{5}$

10. If c and d are prime numbers, what is the least common multiple of $2c^5d$, $3c^4d$, and $5d^3$?

   (A) cd^3
   (B) c^5d^3
   (C) $30cd^3$
   (D) $30c^5d^3$

11. What is the solution set for $0 = x^2 + 400$?

   (A) 20
   (B) $20i$
   (C) ± 20
   (D) $\pm 20i$

12. Which is the most reasonable unit to use when measuring the volume of water in a lake?

   (A) grams
   (B) kiloliters
   (C) miles
   (D) square feet

13. What is the value of $\sqrt{p^8 q r^3}$?

   (A) $p^7 r^2 \sqrt{pqr}$
   (B) $p^7 r \sqrt{pqr}$
   (C) $p^4 r^2 \sqrt{qr}$
   (D) $p^4 r \sqrt{qr}$

14. The histogram shows the perimeters of all the parks in a certain town.

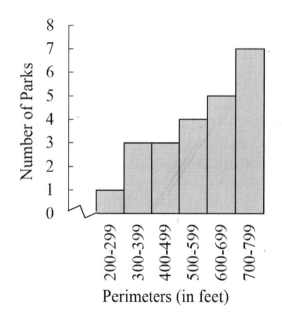

Which of the following could be the median perimeter?

   (A) 429
   (B) 513
   (C) 602
   (D) 789

15. The graph shows the number of kids who signed up for baseball tryouts for various teams. One of the bars is missing.

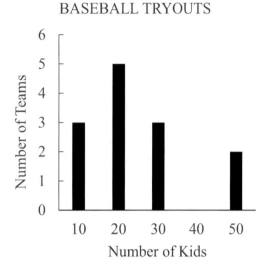

BASEBALL TRYOUTS

If the median is 20, which of the following could be the number of teams that had 40 kids apply?

(A) 2
(B) 3
(C) 4
(D) 5

16. A movie studio is releasing their new animated family film in one week. They want to know what percent of school-age children will be seeing the film on opening weekend. Which sample will give them the most reliable information?

(A) 500 parents waiting for their kids outside a school at 3pm
(B) 1,000 hospital patients
(C) 2,000 passengers boarding a month-long cruise
(D) the entire cast and crew of the film

17. The shaded figure shown has an area of 36 cm^2.

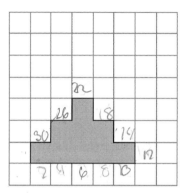

What is the length of each grid square, in cm?

(A) 1
(B) 2
(C) 3
(D) 4

18. A large square has had a smaller square cut from its top left corner, as shown.

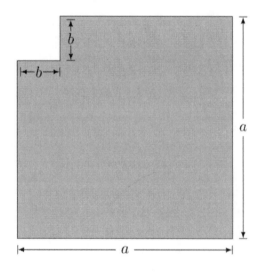

Which expression represents the perimeter of the shaded region?

(A) $4a$
(B) $a^2 - b^2$
(C) $2a - 2b$
(D) $4a + 2b$

19. The table shows the favorite color of all the students in an 8th grade class. The data for orange is missing.

FAVORITE COLOR

COLOR	Number of Students
Red	5
Orange	
Yellow	9
Green	12
Blue	8

A circle graph is made from the data. If the central angle of the portion of the graph representing green is 120°, how many students chose orange?

(A) 0
(B) 1
(C) 2
(D) 3

20. For what value of x is the equation
$$\frac{(x-1)(x+2)}{x^2 - 9} = 0 \text{ true?}$$

(A) $x = 3$ only
(B) $x = 1$ and $x = -2$
(C) $x = 3$ and $x = -3$
(D) $x = 1, x = -2, x = 3,$ and $x = -3$

21. The formula for the volume of a cone is
$V = \frac{1}{3}Bh$ where B is the area of the base
and h is the length of the height. A cone has a volume of 50π in^3, and a base area of 25π in^2. What is the height?

(A) $\frac{2}{3}$ in.
(B) 2 in.
(C) 6 in.
(D) 2π in.

22. Bob has five new books on his desk. He wants to pack three to take to camp. How many combinations of 3 books are possible?

(A) 5
(B) 10
(C) 15
(D) 20

23. Which expression is equivalent to the expression $2m^2n + 3mn^2 - (4mn^2 - 5m^2n)$?

(A) $-3m^2n + mn^2$
(B) $-3m^2n - mn^2$
(C) $7m^2n + mn^2$
(D) $7m^2n - mn^2$

24. The graph of line z is shown.

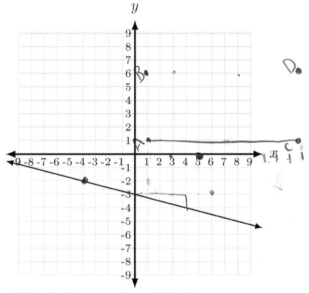

What is the equation of the line perpendicular to line z at $(-4, -2)$?

(A) $y = 4x + 14$
(B) $y = 4x - 14$
(C) $y = \frac{1}{4}x + 14$
(D) $y = \frac{1}{4}x - 14$

25. Rectangle *ABCD* has vertices at (1,1), (1,6), (13,1), and (13,6). What is the length, in coordinate units, of diagonal $\overline{AC}$?

(A) 12
(B) 13
(C) 17
(D) 18

26. A line that passes through points (3,*y*) and (5,0) has a slope of –3. What is the value of *y*?

(A) 6
(B) 7
(C) 8
(D) 9

27. The grid shows two vertices of a right triangle.

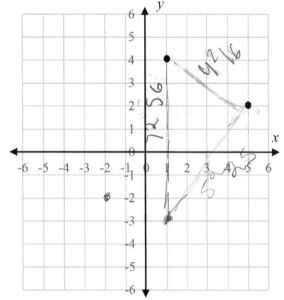

Which could be the coordinates of the third vertex of the right triangle?

(A) (0,3)
(B) (3,0)
(C) (1,–3)
(D) (–2,–2)

28. Triangle *DEF* is shown. The length of $\overline{DE}$ is 2 in. The measure of angle *F* is 35°.

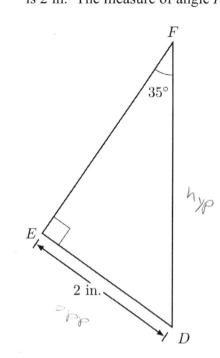

The value of which expression is equal to the length of side $\overline{DF}$?

(A) $\dfrac{2}{\sin 35°}$

(B) $\dfrac{\sin 35°}{2}$

(C) $\dfrac{2}{\tan 35°}$

(D) $\dfrac{\tan 35°}{2}$

29. What is the value of $\sqrt{360} + \sqrt{75} - \sqrt{12}$?

(A) $10\sqrt{6} + 3\sqrt{3}$
(B) $6\sqrt{10} + 3\sqrt{3}$
(C) $10\sqrt{6} + 3$
(D) $6\sqrt{10} + 3$

30. The probability of picking a blue marble out of a bowl is $\frac{1}{2}$. The probability of picking out two blue marbles without replacement is $\frac{1}{6}$. What is the probability of picking the second blue marble?

(A) $\frac{1}{2}$

(B) $\frac{1}{3}$

(C) $\frac{1}{4}$

(D) $\frac{1}{12}$

31. The stem-and-leaf plot below shows the number of fish in various ponds throughout the state.

Stem	Leaf
121	1 4 8 9
125	1 3 4 9 9
213	3 6 7 7 7
257	1 5 7

What is the median of the data?

(A) 7
(B) 1,259
(C) 1,366
(D) 2,137

32. If $i = \sqrt{-1}$, what is the value of i^4?

(A) 1
(B) −1
(C) $\sqrt{-1}$
(D) $-\sqrt{-1}$

33. Two concentric circles are shown.

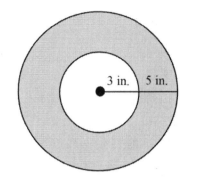

The radius of the inner circle is 3 in. The distance from the edge of the inner circle to the edge of the outer circle is 5 in. What is the area of the shaded region in square inches? $(A = \pi r^2)$

(A) 4π
(B) 10π
(C) 16π
(D) 55π

34. What is the result of the expression

$$3\begin{bmatrix} 4 & -2 \\ 9 & c \end{bmatrix}?$$

(A) $\begin{bmatrix} 34 & -32 \\ 39 & 3c \end{bmatrix}$

(B) $\begin{bmatrix} 7 & 1 \\ 12 & c+3 \end{bmatrix}$

(C) $\begin{bmatrix} 12 & -6 \\ 27 & 3c \end{bmatrix}$

(D) $\begin{bmatrix} 12 & -6 \\ 36 & c^3 \end{bmatrix}$

35. In rhombus WXYZ, angle X has a measure of 102°. What is the measure of its adjacent angle, angle Y?

(A) 45°
(B) 78°
(C) 82°
(D) 88°

36. If the mean of $4x$, $5x$, and $6x$ is 90, what is the value of x?

    (A) 6
    (B) 15
    (C) 18
    (D) 22.5

37. Kevin rolls a six-sided number cube. What is the probability that the first number he rolls is a 1 and the second number he rolls is a 2?

    (A) $\dfrac{1}{36}$

    (B) $\dfrac{1}{12}$

    (C) $\dfrac{1}{6}$

    (D) $\dfrac{1}{3}$

38. Inez and Juan were walking down the street. Inez walked 500 meters in 15 minutes. If Juan's speed is 1 kilometer per hour slower than Inez's, how long will it take him to walk 3 kilometers?

    (A) 30 minutes
    (B) 1 hour
    (C) 2 hours
    (D) 3 hours

39. Bruce and Betty recycled a total of 1,000 bottles. Bruce recycled 100 more bottles than Betty. What percent of the 1,000 bottles did Bruce recycle?

    (A) 60%
    (B) 55%
    (C) 54.5%
    (D) 45%

40. A high-speed train can travel 500 km in 2 hours. If it left its station at noon and traveled nonstop, how many kilometers had it traveled by midnight?

    (A) 1,000
    (B) 3,000
    (C) 6,000
    (D) 12,000

41. A copy center charges $1.75 for the first color copy, and then an additional $0.95 for each copy thereafter. Which expression represents the total cost, in dollars, of making c copies?

    (A) $2.7c$
    (B) $1.75 + 95c$
    (C) $1.75 + .95c$
    (D) $1.75 + .95(c - 1)$

42. The shaded figure shown has a perimeter of 32 cm.

    What is the area of the shaded region, in cm^2?

    (A) 9
    (B) 18
    (C) 36
    (D) 64

43. The average of four consecutive odd integers is 12. Which is the smallest of the integers?

    (A) 3
    (B) 5
    (C) 9
    (D) 11

44. The box-and-whisker plot shows the number of burgers sold by a restaurant each day during the month of July.

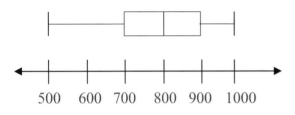

    500   600   700   800   900   1000

    Which value represents the third quartile?

    (A) 600
    (B) 700
    (C) 800
    (D) 900

45. Yesterday, Jeff read 100 pages in his book. Today, he read 150 pages. What was the percent increase in the number of pages he read?

    (A) 1.5%
    (B) 50%
    (C) 100%
    (D) 150%

46. A right triangle is shown.

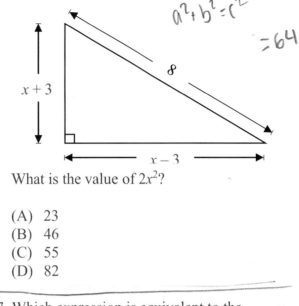

    What is the value of $2x^2$?

    (A) 23
    (B) 46
    (C) 55
    (D) 82

47. Which expression is equivalent to the expression $(x^2 + 9)(x - 3)(x + 3)$?

    (A) $x^3 + 9x^2 - 9x - 81$
    (B) $x^3 - 81$
    (C) $x^4 + 81$
    (D) $x^4 - 81$

Section Five: Essay Prompt

Time Limit: 30 minutes

Directions – You have 30 minutes to plan and write an essay on the topic printed below. Do not write on another topic. How well you write is more important than how much you write. You may only write in the appropriate section of the answer sheet. Write neatly so that someone else can read your handwriting. You may take notes in the section below. Write only in blue or black pen.

TOPIC:

If you could go anywhere in the world for one day, where would you go and why?

NOTES:

Scoring the Diagnostic Practice Test (Form A)

Using your answer sheet and referring to the answer key at the back of the book, calculate the percentage of questions you answered correctly in each section by taking the number of questions you answered correctly in that section and dividing it by the number of questions in that section. Multiply this number by 100 to determine your percentage score. The higher the percentage, the stronger your performance in that section. The lower the percentage, the more time you should spend practicing that section.

Note that the actual test will not evaluate your score based on percentage correct or incorrect. Instead, it will evaluate your performance relative to all other students in your grade who took the test.

Record your results here:

Section	Questions Correct	Total Questions	Percent Questions Correct
Verbal Reasoning	_____	40	_____ %
Quantitative Reasoning	_____	37	_____ %
Reading Comprehension	_____	36	_____ %
Mathematics Achievement	_____	47	_____ %

Carefully consider the results from your diagnostic test when coming up with your study plan. Remember, the Upper Level ISEE is given to students from grades 8 through 12. Unless you've finished high school, chances are that there is material on this test that you have not yet been taught. If this is the case, and you would like to improve your score beyond what is expected of your grade, consider outside help – such as a tutor or teacher – who can help you learn more about the topics that are new to you.

Answer Key

The answer key to this diagnostic test can be found at the back of the book in the Answer Key section. The keys are organized by section, and each question has an answer associated with it. Visit www.thetutorverse.com for detailed answer explanations.

Note that there are no answers provided to the essay sections. Instead, consider having a tutor, teacher, or other educator review your writing and give you constructive feedback.

Get a Scaled Score Report @ thetutorverse.com/digital

Looking for an estimated Scaled Score Report? First, save your printed bubble sheet!

Then, navigate to thetutorverse.com/digital. Scroll to the "Get a Score Report" feature and follow the on-screen instructions. You'll be prompted to create or log in to your account on thetutorverse.com.

More Practice Tests Available Online

Need to take more practice tests? Want to work through more practice sections? Check out our computer-based practice on thetutorverse.com/digital. Take a fully-timed, automated practice test. Or, work through thousands of additional practice questions. Get this workbook for FREE using the code at the front of this workbook.

Verbal Reasoning

On the Actual Test

In the Verbal Reasoning section of the Upper Level ISEE, you will encounter two types of questions:

- 🐦 Synonyms – This section assesses your ability to recognize words and reason through different relationships and subtle differences among words.
- 🐦 Sentence Completion – Sentence completion questions consist of a sentence with one or two words missing from the sentence. Your task is to select the missing word or words that most appropriately complete the sentence.

Both Synonyms and Sentence Completion questions are designed to test your vocabulary and reasoning skills.

There will be 40 questions on the actual Verbal Reasoning section, which you will have 20 minutes to complete. In the Verbal Reasoning section, there will be five questions that will not be scored. These questions are included for trial and research purposes only. You will not know which questions are trial questions.

In This Practice Book

The practice questions in this workbook *are not* structured like an actual ISEE exam. Instead, these sections contain many exams' worth of materials to help you practice. The questions within each of the following sections grow progressively more difficult, as they do on the actual exam. For example, question 50 will be more difficult than question 5.

Verbal Reasoning practice consists of the following sections:

- 🐦 Synonyms
    - 🐦 Connotation
    - 🐦 Root Words
    - 🐦 Vocabulary
    - 🐦 Association
- 🐦 Sentence Completion
    - 🐦 One missing word
    - 🐦 Two missing words

There are additional instructions and recommendations at the beginning of each of the Synonyms and Sentence Completion pages which you should review before starting.

Remember: there are detailed answer explanations available online at www.thetutorverse.com. Be sure to obtain permission before going online.

The Tutorverse
www.thetutorverse.com

Synonyms

Overview

Each synonym question consists of a word written in capital letters followed by four answer choice words written in lower-case letters. Your task is to select one of the four listed answer choices that is most nearly the same in meaning as the word in capital letters. Not every question word will necessarily have an answer choice with the exact same meaning!

How to Use This Section

The questions on the test aren't structured this way, but we've broken down the synonym section further because it has helped many students master this section:

- *Connotation* – These words generally have a positive or negative meaning. If you do not know the exact meaning of the listed words, you should be able to identify which answer choice has a similarly positive or negative meaning as the question word.
- *Root Words* – These words are generally derived from Greek or Latin root words. Researching and learning the underlying root words will help familiarize you with several words all at once!
- *Vocabulary* – Though these words can derive from Greek or Latin root words and may carry certain connotations or associations, we've grouped these words together as students generally rely on memorization and context to understand the word's meaning.
- *Association* – These words tend to appear with other words and are similar to connotation words. Knowing words that frequently appear together can be helpful in determining the meaning of a word you don't know at face value.

Some words may belong to more than one of the above listed sub-sections. For instance, a word that students generally recognize as having a positive or negative connotation may also have a recognizable root word. This is just owing to the history and etymology of those words!

We recommend that you practice at least 15-20 questions per week in preparing for the exam.

You may find many of the words in this section to be challenging. Don't be surprised if you need to look up many of the words that you encounter in this section! The purpose of this section is to introduce you to new words. We encourage you to make a list of words that give you trouble, whether they appear in questions or answer choices. Write down the definition of each word as well as a sentence using the word. You might also want to consider writing down positive or negative associations, any root words that can help you remember the word, or any words that are commonly encountered with that word.

Tutorverse Tips!

Answer choices in this section are always listed in alphabetical order. As you read the question words in capital letters, think of a word that you might use instead of the question word.

Sometimes, words can have more than one meaning. Don't let this confuse you! Look at the answer choices to make an educated guess as to which meaning is being used in the question. Then, use your reasoning skills to select the word that most nearly means the same as the word in capital letters.

Directions – Choose the word that is most nearly the same in meaning as the word in capital letters.

Sample Question:

BOON:

(A) benefit
(B) trouble
(C) vibration
(D) virtue

Sample Answer:

(A) B C D

Connotation

1. CAUTIOUS

   (A) bothered
   (B) unexpected
   (C) righteous
   (D) wary

2. OBVIOUS:

   (A) blatant
   (B) glamorous
   (C) unknown
   (D) unclear

3. DISCREDIT:

   (A) accept
   (B) accrete
   (C) accredit
   (D) malign

4. GLEE:

   (A) decree
   (B) delight
   (C) fee
   (D) failure

5. SUSPECT:

   (A) dubious
   (B) entrust
   (C) established
   (D) respect

6. FIASCO:

   (A) abasement
   (B) disaster
   (C) mediocrity
   (D) triumph

7. DEVIOUS:

   (A) curious
   (B) dishonest
   (C) forthcoming
   (D) truthful

8. TRAVESTY:

   (A) distortion
   (B) facsimile
   (C) replica
   (D) trouble

9. NAIVE:

   (A) apprehensive
   (B) credulous
   (C) indigenous
   (D) innate

10. AMICABLE:

   (A) carefree
   (B) detestable
   (C) friendly
   (D) insolent

11. OUTLANDISH:

   (A) familiar
   (B) ordinary
   (C) plain
   (D) unorthodox

12. MEEK:

   (A) controlling
   (B) insistent
   (C) sleek
   (D) submissive

13. ABUNDANT:

   (A) instant
   (B) profuse
   (C) rare
   (D) restricted

14. RENOVATION:

   (A) destruction
   (B) forgiveness
   (C) improvement
   (D) understanding

15. HINDER:

   (A) enable
   (B) enhance
   (C) finalize
   (D) prevent

16. CONTEMPT:

(A) admiration
(B) disrespect
(C) fondness
(D) regard

17. PROSPERITY:

(A) abundance
(B) entropy
(C) proposal
(D) scarcity

18. PROCRASTINATE:

(A) advance
(B) delay
(C) inspire
(D) promote

19. SQUANDER:

(A) invest
(B) traipse
(C) waste
(D) wonder

20. GULLIBLE:

(A) guilty
(B) innocent
(C) seasoned
(D) suspicious

21. EXEMPLARY:

(A) admirable
(B) excusable
(C) habitable
(D) innumerable

22. HARASS:

(A) entertain
(B) pester
(C) placate
(D) support

23. FRANTIC:

(A) misunderstood
(B) serene
(C) tame
(D) wild

24. AFFLUENCE:

(A) affliction
(B) greed
(C) shortage
(D) wealth

25. LIVID:

(A) distressed
(B) entranced
(C) gleeful
(D) impartial

26. ADMONISH:

(A) adapt
(B) admit
(C) rebuke
(D) reinforce

27. ADVERSE:

(A) auspicious
(B) beneficial
(C) blessed
(D) deleterious

28. TERSE:

(A) baffled
(B) cordial
(C) curt
(D) verbose

29. RECONCILIATION:

(A) agreement
(B) approval
(C) conversion
(D) discord

30. DEVOUT:

(A) pious
(B) stout
(C) superficial
(D) worldly

31. PRUDENT:

(A) diminutive
(B) foolhardy
(C) sensible
(D) unimaginative

32. FUTILE:

(A) fruitful
(B) meaningful
(C) profound
(D) vain

33. TRITE:

(A) banal
(B) original
(C) short
(D) exclusive

34. PROVINCIAL:

(A) foreign
(B) patriotic
(C) simple
(D) victorious

35. DISPARAGE:

(A) adore
(B) appraise
(C) despair
(D) vilify

36. PALATIAL:

(A) beautiful
(B) flat
(C) glacial
(D) grand

37. DERISION:

(A) contempt
(B) desires
(C) erosion
(D) volition

38. INFAMY:

(A) disrepute
(B) popularity
(C) remembrance
(D) reminiscence

39. OMINOUS:

(A) decadent
(B) promising
(C) symphonic
(D) threatening

40. INSATIABLE:

(A) desirable
(B) greedy
(C) improper
(D) angry

41. INGENUITY:

(A) imagination
(B) madness
(C) perpetuity
(D) reliability

42. QUARRELSOME:

(A) adaptive
(B) argumentative
(C) burdensome
(D) fulsome

43. QUANDARY:

(A) explanation
(B) problem
(C) reason
(D) setting

44. PREPOSTEROUS:

(A) absurd
(B) analogous
(C) lucid
(D) reasonable

45. EXASPERATE:

(A) aerate
(B) breathe
(C) desire
(D) frustrate

46. APPALL:

(A) apprehend
(B) fortify
(C) obey
(D) shock

47. ONEROUS:

(A) exhausting
(B) heinous
(C) singular
(D) trivial

48. DESECRATE:

(A) enshrine
(B) ooze
(C) specify
(D) violate

49. SURREPTITIOUS:

(A) clear
(B) open
(C) repetitive
(D) stealthy

50. TRAVAIL:

(A) avail
(B) countervail
(C) struggle
(D) success

51. ROIL:

(A) agitate
(B) burn
(C) recoil
(D) work

52. BEDLAM:

(A) chaos
(B) frustration
(C) insanity
(D) peace

53. SLOVENLY:

(A) effective
(B) heavenly
(C) lovingly
(D) sloppy

54. HEEDLESS:

(A) effortless
(B) impetuous
(C) measured
(D) steady

55. TREPIDATION:

(A) concern
(B) courage
(C) consolation
(D) leisure

56. CONSTERNATION:

(A) comfort
(B) composure
(C) dismay
(D) transition

57. LISTLESS:

(A) enthused
(B) giddy
(C) languid
(D) thoughtless

58. PALLID:

(A) bright
(B) colorful
(C) dark
(D) pale

59. PRECOCIOUS:

(A) mature
(B) oblivious
(C) precious
(D) slow

60. SERENDIPITOUS:

(A) deliberate
(B) foolish
(C) fortuitous
(D) witless

61. INFERNAL:

(A) annoying
(B) enjoyable
(C) understandable
(D) welcome

Root Words

Directions – Choose the word that is most nearly the same in meaning as the word in capital letters.

1. HYPOTHESIS:

(A) affirmation
(B) fact
(C) forecast
(D) guess

2. APPRENTICE:

(A) artisan
(B) instructor
(C) master
(D) novice

3. ADHERE:

(A) advertise
(B) defy
(C) obey
(D) object

4. ADEPT:

(A) infirm
(B) new
(C) proficient
(D) unable

5. CREDIBLE:

(A) appetizing
(B) opinionated
(C) plausible
(D) tasty

6. LAVISH:

(A) frugal
(B) meager
(C) opulent
(D) wish

7. ADVOCATE:

(A) champion
(B) libeler
(C) mentor
(D) solicitor

8. SUBTLE:

(A) apparent
(B) complex
(C) sublime
(D) understated

9. ACCLAIM:

(A) claim
(B) demand
(C) laud
(D) reclaim

10. CONGREGATION:

(A) corporation
(B) dissipate
(C) gathering
(D) line

11. AMIABLE:

(A) accurate
(B) eloquent
(C) indecisive
(D) pleasant

12. BENIGN:

(A) approaching
(B) imminent
(C) kind
(D) livid

13. CONFORMIST:

(A) follower
(B) iconoclast
(C) leader
(D) radical

14. MALICIOUS:

(A) cruel
(B) delicious
(C) loving
(D) savory

15. INNOVATE:

(A) recreate
(B) rescind
(C) resplendent
(D) respond

16. BENEFICENCE:

(A) avarice
(B) generosity
(C) jealousy
(D) stinginess

17. FALLIBLE:

(A) flawless
(B) impeccable
(C) imperfect
(D) unspoiled

18. VOLATILE:

(A) apathetic
(B) futile
(C) unstable
(D) voluntary

19. PONDEROUS:

(A) buoyant
(B) cumbersome
(C) nimble
(D) thoughtful

20. ORATOR:

(A) entertainer
(B) listener
(C) dentist
(D) speaker

21. BELLIGERENT:

(A) abiding
(B) compliant
(C) hostile
(D) varicose

22. SUPERFLUOUS:

(A) enviable
(B) excessive
(C) fluid
(D) peerless

23. SERVILE:

(A) docile
(B) masculine
(C) repulsive
(D) revile

24. INCESSANT:

(A) eternal
(B) finite
(C) interrupted
(D) yielding

25. EMPATHY:

(A) apathy
(B) compassion
(C) indifference
(D) telepathy

26. PERTURB:

(A) bother
(B) excite
(C) pacify
(D) reassure

27. INTEGRITY:

(A) compromise
(B) hysteria
(C) sympathy
(D) unity

28. INCANDESCENT:

(A) luminous
(B) lusterless
(C) matte
(D) translucent

29. RECAPITULATE:

(A) defeat
(B) prevail
(C) summarize
(D) surrender

30. EXACERBATE:

(A) curtail
(B) exact
(C) intensify
(D) mollify

31. PHILANTHROPIST:

(A) accountant
(B) donor
(C) lawyer
(D) soldier

32. SINUOUS:

(A) direct
(B) illustrious
(C) luscious
(D) winding

33. PERVADE:

(A) dilute
(B) evade
(C) mediate
(D) saturate

34. IMMUTABLE:

(A) changeable
(B) enduring
(C) passing
(D) transitory

35. DISPARITY:

(A) equality
(B) disparage
(C) imbalance
(D) symmetry

36. SOLACE:

(A) calm
(B) goad
(C) incite
(D) rouse

37. PROTRACTED:

(A) indefinite
(B) limited
(C) minimal
(D) predictable

38. LUCID:

(A) abjure
(B) ambiguous
(C) ambivalent
(D) articulate

39. INNOCUOUS:

(A) depressing
(B) harmless
(C) poisonous
(D) risky

40. DEXTEROUS:

(A) clumsy
(B) deterrent
(C) preventive
(D) skillful

41. ASSIDUOUS:

(A) attentive
(B) careless
(C) insidious
(D) topical

42. PORTEND:

(A) entrench
(B) extend
(C) pretend
(D) prophesize

43. VITRIOLIC:

(A) alcoholic
(B) gloomy
(C) spiteful
(D) upbeat

44. SALUBRIOUS:

(A) detrimental
(B) healthy
(C) loquacious
(D) sacred

45. COMPLACENT:

(A) comprehensive
(B) disgruntled
(C) incomplete
(D) satisfied

46. DEMAGOGUE:

(A) judge
(B) populist
(C) priest
(D) synagogue

47. SACCHARINE:

(A) asinine
(B) sacrifice
(C) supine
(D) sweet

48. ANACHRONISTIC:

(A) antiquated
(B) modern
(C) opportune
(D) unfortunate

49. TENACIOUS:

  (A) amorous
  (B) inquisitive
  (C) perilous
  (D) resolute

50. DESULTORY:

  (A) ambitious
  (B) discerning
  (C) intermittent
  (D) resilient

51. PRODIGAL:

  (A) careful
  (B) enormous
  (C) judicious
  (D) lavish

52. ESPOUSE:

  (A) contradict
  (B) disagree
  (C) endorse
  (D) marry

53. PARSIMONY:

  (A) charity
  (B) congruence
  (C) dissonance
  (D) miserliness

54. RISIBLE:

  (A) fantastic
  (B) funny
  (C) logical
  (D) rational

55. ASPERSION:

  (A) dispersion
  (B) praise
  (C) revulsion
  (D) slander

56. JOCULAR:

  (A) boring
  (B) dangerous
  (C) humorous
  (D) serious

57. TORPOR:

  (A) exception
  (B) excitement
  (C) normalcy
  (D) weariness

58. ELUCIDATE:

  (A) clarify
  (B) darken
  (C) impede
  (D) muddle

59. ACUITY:

  (A) authenticity
  (B) ignorance
  (C) intelligence
  (D) sincerity

60. DOLOROUS:

  (A) engaged
  (B) exultant
  (C) indolent
  (D) miserable

61. IMPLACABLE:

  (A) impersonal
  (B) merciless
  (C) supple
  (D) unbearable

Vocabulary

Directions – Choose the word that is most nearly the same in meaning as the word in capital letters.

1. SPONTANEITY:

  (A) deliberation
  (B) intent
  (C) purpose
  (D) randomness

2. COMPROMISE:

  (A) advertise
  (B) believe
  (C) concede
  (D) pledge

3. DECEPTIVE:

  (A) accessible
  (B) amenable
  (C) furious
  (D) misleading

4. CONSUME:

(A) complete
(B) devour
(C) presume
(D) resume

5. POSSIBLE:

(A) feasible
(B) intricate
(C) strenuous
(D) unreasonable

6. LETHARGIC:

(A) deadly
(B) energetic
(C) lazy
(D) vigorous

7. PASSION:

(A) ennui
(B) fashion
(C) style
(D) zeal

8. BLUNDER:

(A) calculate
(B) flounder
(C) mistake
(D) standardize

9. INCOMPATIBLE:

(A) appropriate
(B) fitted
(C) mobile
(D) opposite

10. GREED: ✓

(A) avarice
(B) aversion
(C) aviary
(D) aviation

11. RAMPAGE:

(A) adage
(B) campaign
(C) devalue
(D) riot

12. DIVERGENT:

(A) comparable
(B) contradictory
(C) resurgent
(D) verdant

13. CARELESS:

(A) negligent
(B) precise
(C) thorough
(D) thoughtful

14. CONVERGENCE:

(A) edge
(B) intersection
(C) resurgence
(D) separation

15. ANECDOTE:

(A) ancillary
(B) cure
(C) dotage
(D) story

16. HOLISTIC:

(A) complete
(B) partial
(C) projected
(D) prophesied

17. TRANSIENT:

(A) fleeting
(B) ineffaceable
(C) lasting
(D) permanent

18. DILIGENT:

(A) harmful
(B) industrious
(C) insurgent
(D) lacking

19. DEFERENCE:

(A) defense
(B) interruption
(C) obedience
(D) position

20. DIGRESSION:

(A) concentration
(B) detour
(C) emphasis
(D) focus

21. GUILE:

(A) confusion
(B) honesty
(C) persuasion
(D) trickery

22. CAVALIER:

(A) healthier
(B) nonchalant
(C) superior
(D) valiant

23. RESOLUTE:

(A) doable
(B) tenacious
(C) wavering
(D) weak

24. PERIPHERAL:

(A) central
(B) essential
(C) fringe
(D) relevant

25. EPITHET:

(A) description
(B) personality
(C) slur
(D) temperament

26. ABSOLUTION:

(A) accusation
(B) conviction
(C) outcome
(D) pardon

27. DISSIPATE:

(A) condense
(B) demolish
(C) reappear
(D) vanish

28. RAUCOUS:

(A) distinct
(B) noisy
(C) quiet
(D) vague

29. INCORRIGIBLE:

(A) dynamic
(B) erratic
(C) flexible
(D) hopeless

30. PRISTINE:

(A) expansive
(B) feral
(C) pure
(D) sullied

31. CAMARADERIE:

(A) convention
(B) reverie
(C) trust
(D) wariness

32. POTABLE:

(A) adulterated
(B) clean
(C) filthy
(D) foul

33. ASCETIC:

(A) acidic
(B) certain
(C) humble
(D) mysterious

34. BASTION:

(A) adoption
(B) faction
(C) home
(D) stronghold

35. EXPEDIENT:

(A) peculiar
(B) pernicious
(C) persistent
(D) practical

36. SHIRK:

(A) avoid
(B) quirk
(C) expect
(D) vex = ?

37. GRAPPLE:

(A) apprehend
(B) struggle
(C) understand
(D) verify

38. RAPACIOUS:

(A) covetous
(B) delicious
(C) distinctiveness
(D) indifferent

39. PROSAIC:

(A) expert
(B) mosaic
(C) mundane
(D) poetic

40. EXTRICATE:

(A) ingrain
(B) inter
(C) observe
(D) remove

41. TREMULOUS:

(A) assertive
(B) ferocious
(C) nervous
(D) tremendous

42. PIQUE:

(A) apex
(B) appease
(C) glimpse
(D) intrigue

43. REDOLENT:

(A) bitter
(B) blinding
(C) evocative
(D) supplemental

44. INDOLENCE:

(A) audacity
(B) idleness
(C) insolence
(D) sadness

45. DISSONANCE:

(A) assonance
(B) conflict
(C) harmony
(D) recurrence

46. EUPHONIOUS:

(A) brash
(B) chaotic
(C) loud
(D) melodious

47. HACKNEYED:

(A) common
(B) creative
(C) imagined
(D) unique

48. RANCOROUS:

(A) content
(B) grateful
(C) putrid
(D) resentful

49. CENSURE:

(A) bond
(B) criticism
(C) forfeiture ⊃?
(D) guarantee

50. PRESCIENCE:

(A) history
(B) intuition
(C) sorcery
(D) skill

51. SAGACITY:

(A) absurdity
(B) inanity
(C) quackery
(D) wisdom

52. EVINCE:

(A) depress
(B) evict
(C) express
(D) suppress

53. UMBRAGE:

(A) craze
(B) protection
(C) resentment
(D) tribute

54. CAPRICE:

(A) accountability
(B) instability
(C) threshold
(D) worth

55. ASSUAGE:

(A) persuade
(B) pressure
(C) relieve
(D) upset

56. INTERCEDE:

(A) intervene
(B) relinquish
(C) remediate
(D) secede

57. OBSOLESCENT:

(A) graceful
(B) radiant
(C) useless
(D) youthful

58. CAPACIOUS:

(A) ample
(B) eager
(C) fickle
(D) impulsive

59. GARRULOUS:

(A) taciturn
(B) talkative
(C) temperamental
(D) typical

60. FASTIDIOUS:

(A) exacting
(B) intellectual
(C) negligent
(D) ravenous

61. OBSTREPEROUS:

(A) discreet
(B) private
(C) restrained
(D) rowdy

Association

Directions – Choose the word that is most nearly the same in meaning as the word in capital letters.

1. NOVEL:

   (A) slum
   (B) spade
   (C) traditional
   (D) unfamiliar

2. LIBERATE:

   (A) abdicate
   (B) release
   (C) spite
   (D) subjugate

3. FLUENT:

   (A) affluent
   (B) conventional
   (C) remarkable
   (D) versed

4. ARROGANT:

   (A) elegant
   (B) intrusive
   (C) meek
   (D) proud

5. CORRUPTION:

   (A) abstraction
   (B) dishonesty
   (C) infection
   (D) resolution

6. INTREPID:

   (A) animated
   (B) fearless
   (C) tepid
   (D) wonderful

7. INCONSEQUENTIAL:

   (A) orderly
   (B) paltry
   (C) random
   (D) significant

8. LONGEVITY:

   (A) brevity
   (B) endurance
   (C) seniority
   (D) weakness

9. CONDITIONAL:

   (A) dependent
   (B) improved
   (C) refined
   (D) suggestive

10. ATROCIOUS:

    (A) anxious
    (B) horrible
    (C) passable
    (D) vicarious

11. INEVITABLE:

    (A) destined
    (B) detested
    (C) eventful
    (D) viable

12. ESTEEM:

    (A) approximation
    (B) reverence
    (C) surplus
    (D) vapor

13. ENIGMA:

    (A) dogma
    (B) riddle
    (C) solution
    (D) stigma

14. TENTATIVE:

    (A) contemplative
    (B) experienced
    (C) known
    (D) temporary

15. DENOUNCE:

    (A) announce
    (B) condemn
    (C) err
    (D) report

16. STRUT:

    (A) construct
    (B) parade
    (C) stir
    (D) structure

17. SCRUTINIZE:

    (A) forge
    (B) identify
    (C) inspect
    (D) organize

18. RECLUSIVE:

    (A) alternate
    (B) hidden
    (C) preventative
    (D) resting

19. EPIPHANY:

   (A) cacophony
   (B) dream
   (C) idea
   (D) regret

20. EMULATE:

   (A) detain
   (B) mirror
   (C) regulate
   (D) scar

21. CADENCE:

   (A) echo
   (B) resonance
   (C) reverberation
   (D) rhythm

22. EXASPERATION:

   (A) annoyance
   (B) aspiration
   (C) beauty
   (D) breath

23. SEDATE:

   (A) astute
   (B) composed
   (C) populate
   (D) rapid

24. ENDEAR:

   (A) disavow
   (B) dissuade
   (C) employ
   (D) recommend

25. DISCORD:

   (A) pandemonium
   (B) record
   (C) tranquility
   (D) uniformity

26. MOTLEY:

   (A) consistent
   (B) diverse
   (C) identical
   (D) uniform

27. ERRATIC:

   (A) committed
   (B) secure
   (C) static
   (D) turbulent

28. ECSTASY:

   (A) fantasy
   (B) happiness
   (C) melancholy
   (D) simplicity

29. IMMATERIAL:

   (A) ethereal
   (B) irrelevant
   (C) substantial
   (D) weighty

30. JOSTLE:

   (A) encroach
   (B) jeopardize
   (C) joke
   (D) push

31. DWINDLE:

   (A) coil
   (B) disappear
   (C) engage
   (D) kindle

32. PROLIFIC:

   (A) abundant
   (B) bland
   (C) resourceful
   (D) vital

33. FORTHRIGHT:

   (A) duplicitous
   (B) fraudulent
   (C) honest
   (D) opaque

34. SUBSTANTIATE:

   (A) enlarge
   (B) prove
   (C) subsist
   (D) trick

35. REVERE:

   (A) honor
   (B) provoke
   (C) understand
   (D) vision

36. PARAMOUNT:

   (A) finicky
   (B) important
   (C) petty
   (D) trifling

37. CODDLE:

   (A) addle
   (B) deny
   (C) indulge
   (D) rebuff

38. IMMACULATE:

   (A) aflame
   (B) graduate
   (C) impassioned
   (D) perfect

39. ASYLUM:

   (A) bottle
   (B) family
   (C) prophesy
   (D) refuge

40. SEETHE:

    (A) beam
    (B) smolder
    (C) squirm
    (D) teethe

41. FLIPPANT:

    (A) deferential
    (B) disrespectful
    (C) elusive
    (D) polite

42. LOBBYIST:

    (A) advocate
    (B) collector
    (C) doorman
    (D) receptionist

43. DISSENT:

    (A) consent
    (B) insult
    (C) oppose
    (D) promote

44. PROVOCATIVE:

    (A) irritating
    (B) miserly
    (C) pronounced
    (D) vocal

45. COERCE:

    (A) associate
    (B) buttress
    (C) complement
    (D) force

46. CONTRITE:

    (A) banal
    (B) pointless
    (C) repentant
    (D) unoriginal

47. DRONE:

    (A) admire
    (B) buzz
    (C) copy
    (D) whisper

48. DOGMATIC:

    (A) automatic
    (B) carnivorous
    (C) rigid
    (D) tolerant

49. EXTENUATING:

    (A) expected
    (B) extensive
    (C) mitigating
    (D) tenuous

50. DISCERN:

    (A) contest
    (B) detect
    (C) hold
    (D) worry

51. HERETIC:

    (A) applicant
    (B) defendant
    (C) dissenter
    (D) hearsay

52. ATROPHY:

    (A) award
    (B) decay
    (C) grow
    (D) improve

53. TANGENT:

    (A) conformity
    (B) departure
    (C) following
    (D) path

54. MAGNANIMOUS:

    (A) generous
    (B) helpful
    (C) magnetic
    (D) stingy

55. FLORID:

    (A) flushed
    (B) fragrant
    (C) joyful
    (D) pretty

56. ABSCOND:

    (A) escape
    (B) greet
    (C) pilfer
    (D) rupture

57. FERVENT:

    (A) adopt
    (B) encourage
    (C) passionate
    (D) preclude

58. MENDACITY:

    (A) capacity
    (B) lies
    (C) repairs
    (D) towns

59. CONSTITUENT:

    (A) component
    (B) document
    (C) folio
    (D) parcel

60. OSTENTATIOUS:

    (A) friendly
    (B) gaudy
    (C) hazardous
    (D) ostensible

Sentence Completion

Overview

Sentence completion questions assess your ability to understand the meaning of words and how they are used in sentences. Each question consists of a sentence with one or two missing words. Your task is to choose the word or words that best complete the sentence based on the context and logic of the sentence and the meaning of the word or words.

How to Use This Section

The Sentence Completion section consists of single and double blank questions. There are approximately two single blank questions for every double blank question. Try to preserve this ratio as you practice. For example, if you do 5 double blank questions, try to do 10 single blank questions.

We recommend that you practice at least 5-10 questions per week in preparing for exam.

You may find many of the words in this section to be challenging. Don't be surprised if you need to look up many of the words that you encounter in this section! The purpose of this section is to introduce you to new words. We encourage you to make a list of words that give you trouble, whether they appear in sentence questions or answer choices. Write down the definition of each word as well as a sentence using the word. You might also want to consider writing down positive or negative associations, any root words that can help you remember the word, or any words that are commonly encountered with that word.

Remember: there are detailed answer explanations available online at www.thetutorverse.com. Be sure to obtain permission before going online.

Tutorverse Tips!

Context clues are very important. Read the sentence in its entirety in order to understand the overall meaning.

Then, focus on key words and clues that might help you determine the correct answer. For example, words such as "though" and "despite" can signal that the correct answer choice might be one that implies the opposite of what is given in the sentence. Similarly, words such as "because" and "since" can signal that the correct answer choice might be one that implies the same meaning of what is given in the sentence. Pay special attention to the meaning or connotation of adjectives, as the description of subjects they modify will give you a clue as to the right answer choice.

Once you've decided on an answer choice, reread the sentence by including your answer choice words in the sentence to make sure the sentence makes sense with the overall meaning.

Remember that on the Upper Level ISEE, there is no penalty for guessing. If you don't know the answer to a question, take your best guess.

Single Blank

Directions – Choose the word that best completes the sentence.

> Sample Question:
>
> Joe forgot to bring his books to school and was ------- for class.
>
> (A) absent
> (B) ready
> (C) unprepared
> (D) waiting
>
> Sample Answer:
>
> A B **C** D

1. Due to its ------- properties, the diamond on Tabetha's finger nearly blinded the crowd as she waved to her adoring fans.

   (A) dull
   (B) permanent
   (C) scintillating
   (D) unassuming

2. The executive cared only for more and more profits and did not care about his employees; his ------- knew no bounds.

   (A) avarice
   (B) generosity
   (C) guidance
   (D) passion

3. Although Karl was usually even-tempered and slow to anger, the high-pressured sales tactics left him in a(n) ------- mood.

   (A) bellicose
   (B) enlightened
   (C) optimal
   (D) satisfied

4. The dog was -------; he would not abide by his master's commands and could not be trained.

   (A) guilty
   (B) loyal
   (C) obedient
   (D) recalcitrant

5. The professor gave the student a failing grade because of the illogical and ------- arguments written in the paper; the examples provided by the student were riddled with errors.

   (A) fallacious
   (B) judicious
   (C) reasonable
   (D) valid

6. Because average global temperatures have increased over time, the scientist's claims about global warming were certainly -------.

   (A) incomplete
   (B) paranoid
   (C) plausible
   (D) uneventful

7. The younger brother copied the way his older brother dressed and talked; this pleased their parents, who felt that the older brother was a role model worthy of -------.

   (A) defending
   (B) emulating
   (C) ignoring
   (D) instigating

8. The playwright's ------- jokes were hurtful and slanderous; as such, she made many enemies over the course of her career.

   (A) definitive
   (B) lighthearted
   (C) malicious
   (D) playful

9. The poker player's face was -------; his opponents had no way of telling whether he held a good hand or a bad hand.

   (A) inscrutable
   (B) revealing
   (C) transparent
   (D) understandable

10. The group of friends walked toward their favorite movie theater only to find that it had closed for the night; it was ------- to find that the theater, normally open past midnight, would be closed so early on a weekend.

    (A) aberrant
    (B) normal
    (C) uninteresting
    (D) unsurprising

11. After being discharged from military service, the soldier learned that she had become much more -------, always thinking about things realistically and logically.

    (A) manic
    (B) optimistic
    (C) pragmatic
    (D) predictable

12. The artist was known for her ------- sense of style; she paired colors and shapes together in unusual, clashing combinations that other artists typically avoided.

    (A) conservative
    (B) conventional
    (C) eccentric
    (D) fraudulent

13. Ronald stared at the test question, certain that there were two correct answers; he grew frustrated because the question seemed so ------- that it invited the possibility of multiple answers.

    (A) ambiguous
    (B) apparent
    (C) clear
    (D) lengthy

14. The criminal was further punished for attempting to ------- the facts pertaining to the crime; he had attempted to tamper with the evidence and had lied about his whereabouts.

    (A) clarify
    (B) dissuade
    (C) obfuscate
    (D) understand

15. The overbearing mother accused her son of being -------; he never applied himself in school, and she felt that he led a life of leisure.

    (A) brazen
    (B) indolent
    (C) questionable
    (D) transitory

16. Many of the wandering salesman's customers thought him ------- ; the customers found that the salesman did not always fully disclose the shortcomings of his product and so did not recommend him to their friends.

    (A) genuine
    (B) honest
    (C) perfidious
    (D) pretentious

17. The baby girl displayed a strong ------- for her security blanket; she would take it out with her wherever she would go and would cry whenever she was without it.

    (A) affinity
    (B) exclusion
    (C) gratuity
    (D) repulsion

18. After investigating the claims made in the paper, the review board found that the arguments were baseless, unsubstantiated, and utterly -------.

    (A) innocent
    (B) subversive
    (C) unusual
    (D) vacuous

19. It was not uncommon for the school's guidance counselor to see students ------- between different potential career paths.

    (A) gravitate
    (B) question
    (C) socialize
    (D) vacillate

20. During the trial, the prosecution attempted to ------- the character of the defendant, mounting an argument that the defendant was untrustworthy and unreliable.

    (A) impugn
    (B) laud
    (C) nullify
    (D) validate

21. John had difficulty understanding the theoretical nature of advanced calculus; the concepts were too ------- to understand without concrete examples.

    (A) absolute
    (B) abstract
    (C) easy
    (D) simple

22. A(n) ------- malady plagued the victim; despite their best efforts, the doctors could not determine the cause of the gradual but irrevocable weakening of the patient's immune system.

    (A) insidious
    (B) looming
    (C) obvious
    (D) virulent

23. Stephen was in awe of his mother's -------; she always seemed to know where he was, what he was doing, and what he was thinking.

    (A) apathy
    (B) empathy
    (C) happiness
    (D) omniscience

24. Though the party was scheduled to end before midnight, the revelry continued well into the wee hours of the morning, and showed no signs of -------.

(A) abating
(B) continuing
(C) enclosing
(D) escaping

25. The way John washed his hands was ------- in its frequency and intensity; he washed them after every handshake, and only used the best soaps.

(A) complementary
(B) fanatical
(C) irreverent
(D) understated

26. The townsfolk were unaccustomed to the traveler's strange mannerisms and ways of speech; some were even offended by his behavior, which they found to be rather -------.

(A) adherent
(B) harmless
(C) rash
(D) uncouth

27. The dinner conversation became heated as half of the guests argued with the other half about ------- political issues.

(A) boring
(B) contentious
(C) spiteful
(D) vapid

28. The concierge greeted them with a(n) ------- smile; the guests could tell that he cared genuinely for their happiness.

(A) apathetic
(B) dour
(C) effusive
(D) forced

29. The young, newly elected politician firmly believed he could change decades of corruption and nepotism; his more experienced colleagues laughed at his optimism and called him -------.

(A) indulgent
(B) naïve
(C) particular
(D) seasoned

30. Though only a few people in the world shared her interest in ancient Mayan basket weaving practices, Linda did not mind pursuing such a(n) ------- course of study, as she felt truly passionate about the topic.

(A) arcane
(B) lackluster
(C) ordinary
(D) widespread

31. George was difficult to travel with due to his ------- personality; he was continually changing his mind about which tourist attraction he wanted to visit next.

(A) appealing
(B) harmonious
(C) mercurial
(D) unswerving

32. Some environmentalists believe that our society's ------- view of environmental issues will lead to significant environmental problems in the future; they believe that our short-term worldview is mistaken.

(A) accepting
(B) enthusiastic
(C) myopic
(D) nonchalant

33. Large boulders sit ------- atop thin stone formations in Arches National Park; some boulders seem as if they could topple over from the slightest breeze.

    (A) irregularly
    (B) precariously
    (C) securely
    (D) steadfastly

34. Relatively speaking, there are only a few, scattered islands that dot the world's oceans; these ------- landmasses play an important role in migratory bird behaviors.

    (A) continuous
    (B) enormous
    (C) sporadic
    (D) ubiquitous

35. Though captive animals may appear -------, many are in fact wild at heart and can be dangerous if provoked.

    (A) docent
    (B) docile
    (C) permissive
    (D) tempestuous

36. Accepting that he had done something wrong, the little boy was ready to ------- to his mother's punishment.

    (A) accentuate
    (B) acquiesce
    (C) avoid
    (D) resist

37. Despite receiving a harsh sentence, the criminal did not display even a ------- of remorse.

    (A) memento
    (B) progeny
    (C) riddle
    (D) vestige

38. The art critic found the works displayed in the new gallery to be -------; she found them uninteresting and lackluster and went on to write a scathing review of the artist.

    (A) baffling
    (B) engaging
    (C) insipid
    (D) wonderful

39. The homeowners were convinced by the logical, ------- argument put forth by the real-estate agent; as a result, they followed the agent's advice, and sold their property.

    (A) cogent
    (B) intentional
    (C) malevolent
    (D) muted

40. In the fashion world, designers realize that certain styles are ------- whereas others are classic and timeless.

    (A) blatant
    (B) customary
    (C) ephemeral
    (D) grandiose

41. Abigail did not realize that her comments were insulting; she did not understand that what she said was ------- and disrespectful.

    (A) derogatory
    (B) honest
    (C) oblivious
    (D) traditional

42. Despite insurmountable odds and almost certain defeat, the general vowed to fight to the last man and would not negotiate terms; he would not -------.

    (A) capitulate
    (B) defy
    (C) hasten
    (D) wager

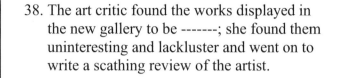

43. Joyce stared ------- at the flying pig; in disbelief and shock, she stood with her mouth open, unable to believe her eyes.

   (A) incredulously
   (B) obliviously
   (C) unrelentingly
   (D) wistfully

44. In the chef's experience, few people are ------- about cilantro; people either seem to love it or hate it.

   (A) ambivalent
   (B) compulsory
   (C) excited
   (D) foolhardy

45. The early European colonizers of the western hemisphere first had to overcome a long and ------- journey, for the trip was fraught with hardships.

   (A) ardent
   (B) arduous
   (C) blissful
   (D) bountiful

46. That the new engineer asked for a raise after only being with the company for a few months was -------; his coworkers knew that it was a bold and risky move.

   (A) audacious
   (B) exciting
   (C) imaginative
   (D) irrational

47. The ------- fumes emanating from the mouth of the volcano prevented any plant or animal life from thriving nearby.

   (A) aromatic
   (B) lustrous
   (C) noxious
   (D) pungent

48. The doctor's ------- smile put Rachel at ease; Rachel could sense that the doctor only had her best interest at heart.

   (A) benevolent
   (B) cavernous
   (C) frosty
   (D) misanthropic

49. The students found that reading the centuries-old original text was nearly impossible, as their understanding was severely limited by the old, ------- words used by the author.

   (A) arid
   (B) esoteric
   (C) fashionable
   (D) loquacious

50. Harry's dreams were -------; she could recall bits and pieces, but as soon as she focused on a particular detail, the memory would slip away.

   (A) evanescent
   (B) paramount
   (C) pleasant
   (D) unimportant

51. The idea of eating meat, though customary in many cultures and to many people, was ------- to the vegetarian, who was wholly repulsed by the notion.

   (A) abhorrent
   (B) affable
   (C) misjudged
   (D) tolerable

52. The advent of the internet has rendered newspapers and other print media virtually -------.

   (A) artificial
   (B) indecipherable
   (C) indispensable
   (D) obsolete

53. The teacher said, in words that allowed for no -------, that there would be no tolerance for cheating on the exam.

    (A) collaboration
    (B) confrontation
    (C) equivocation
    (D) vacancy

54. The principal would not grant the tardy student a(n) ------- from detention; she was tired of the student's excuses, many of which had proven in the past to be fabricated.

    (A) exemption
    (B) freedom
    (C) nomination
    (D) parlance

55. The wispy curls of steam rising from the hot cup of tea were -------, fading in and out of existence as they floated like ghosts in the air.

    (A) abrasive
    (B) ethereal
    (C) marginal
    (D) reserved

56. The contract was nullified by the judge because the plaintiff had signed the contract under -------; the judge learned that the plaintiff was coerced into signing the contract.

    (A) contention
    (B) duress
    (C) fiat
    (D) prognosis

57. In order to sell more copies, the publishers of the newspaper were deliberately inciting social unrest by publishing ------- remarks about the politician.

    (A) incendiary
    (B) irrelevant
    (C) logical
    (D) unbiased

58. Floating down the Mississippi River without a care in the world, Huckleberry Finn must have – at least momentarily – enjoyed the ------- experience.

    (A) arboreal
    (B) bracing
    (C) fervent
    (D) idyllic

59. The legal document asked all signatories to ------- the owners against all liability; the owners wanted to make sure they were protected in case of any accidents.

    (A) indemnify
    (B) modify
    (C) objectify
    (D) teach

60. The racehorse moved with great -------; the speed with which it overcame its competitors and maintained its position was incredible.

    (A) absolve
    (B) agency
    (C) alacrity
    (D) ambivalence

61. In an attempt to ------- the minority protesters, the majority government made several nominal concessions.

    (A) inflame
    (B) interrogate
    (C) mollify
    (D) rouse

62. Despite the threat of jail time, the ------- protestor refused to stop his impassioned evangelizing.

    (A) dastardly
    (B) demure
    (C) jovial
    (D) zealous

63. The fortune teller was certain that the alignment of the planets was a(n) ------- event; he told his client that they should expect great fortune in the coming days.

(A) auspicious
(B) ominous
(C) pessimistic
(D) rapacious

64. The activist was ------- in her beliefs; no amount of convincing or rhetoric could convince her otherwise.

(A) adamant
(B) condescending
(C) malleable
(D) yielding

65. The monk had found a spiritual ------- in his studies; he felt like he had finally achieved balance.

(A) aesthetic
(B) conundrum
(C) equilibrium
(D) forbearance

66. At the ------- of two rivers can be found a whirlpool; this is due to the meeting of two different currents.

(A) confluence
(B) conspiracy
(C) delta
(D) divergence

67. As they approached the principal's office, the two students could feel a(n) ------- fear in their chests; while extremely subtle at first, the fear grew and grew as they neared the door.

(A) amorous
(B) decent
(C) incipient
(D) redolent

68. The Olympian demonstrated a(n) ------- spirit; despite numerous setbacks and injuries, she persevered and took home the gold medal.

(A) apparent
(B) indomitable
(C) miniscule
(D) tortuous

69. The activist was a staunch, ------- opponent of the proposed legislation; he shared his many opinions with anyone who would listen.

(A) capricious
(B) charitable
(C) defensible
(D) vociferous

70. The lawsuit poisoned the partners' relationship, which devolved from cooperative prosperity to -------.

(A) acrimony
(B) nobility
(C) novelty
(D) propensity

71. Upon being cross-examined by the prosecuting attorney, the defendant often -------; he shifted uncomfortably in his seat and refused to answer any of the questions directly.

(A) arbitrated
(B) imagined
(C) mitigated
(D) prevaricated

72. After waiting months for the payments to be -------, Phillip realized that he had to find an alternative means to pay for his education.

(A) detained
(B) diminished
(C) disbursed
(D) dispersed

The Tutorverse
www.thetutorverse.com

73. There was no respite from the ------- of insects at night in the jungle; even with earplugs, the explorer did not sleep well for all the unbearable noise.

(A) cacophony
(B) cloud
(C) swarm
(D) symphony

74. The hillside was dotted with ------- flowers, which helped to break up the uniform sameness of the grass.

(A) curious
(B) desultory
(C) plain
(D) prearranged

75. Lobbyists are often blamed for entrenching industries in the status quo; if we are to progress as a society, we must not allow them to ------- creativity, innovation, and invention.

(A) cultivate
(B) foster
(C) nurture
(D) stymie

76. In certain authoritarian regimes, the judicial review process is a -------, a show with no substance, put on for appearances only.

(A) concert
(B) farce
(C) lie
(D) program

77. The graduate student expected her astrophysics classes to be easy to understand, but instead she realized that she had underestimated just how ------- the topic could be.

(A) abstruse
(B) entertaining
(C) intangible
(D) literal

Double Blank

Directions – Choose the pair of words that best completes the sentence.

Sample Question:

The interior decorator suggested a ------- wall color so as not to ------- any prospective buyers.

(A) bold . . . attract
(B) drab . . . tempt
(C) neutral . . . offend
(D) tawdry . . . upset

Sample Answer:

A B C D

1. Her attempt to ------- herself with the well-heeled backfired, causing her would-be friends to ------- her flattering overtures.

(A) ingratiate . . . detest
(B) justify . . . admire
(C) market . . . embrace
(D) promote . . . accept

2. The judge valued ------- arguments as he had a(n) ------- of time.

(A) pithy . . . plethora
(B) rational . . . abundance
(C) succinct . . . paucity
(D) verbose . . . scarcity

3. Though many people believe football players to be ------- and -------, I have often found that a good many are instead quiet and reserved, trying their best to stay out of the spotlight.

(A) boisterous . . . gregarious
(B) discreet . . . unreserved
(C) docile . . . unassuming
(D) energetic . . . timid

4. Because the billiards player had a(n) ------- for showing off his skills, his defeat at the hands of a novice filled him with a sense of -------.

(A) antipathy . . . humiliation
(B) fondness . . . honor
(C) liking . . . esteem
(D) penchant . . . ignominy

5. Built both as architectural monuments and as ------- places for people to -------, churches in the Middle Ages were spacious structures where townspeople often assembled.

(A) capacious . . . congregate
(B) diminutive . . . diffuse
(C) petite . . . gather
(D) voluminous . . . disperse

6. The monks ------- themselves in remote monasteries in order to concentrate on their studies; by ------- themselves away from outside distractions, they believe they can better focus on spiritual matters.

(A) cloister . . . sequestering
(B) divulge . . . shielding
(C) humble . . . enclosing
(D) protect . . . disclosing

7. Possessing both ------- and strength of will, the explorer ------- his last ounce of stamina and stepped onto the top of the mountain.

    (A) agility . . . misplaced
    (B) fortitude . . . summoned
    (C) frailties . . . depleted
    (D) stamina . . . dismissed

8. Other than the color, there was no ------- difference between the red bell pepper and the green bell pepper; as the recipe did not specify which type of pepper to use, the confused shopper found himself in a -------.

    (A) appreciable . . . quandary
    (B) insignificant . . . predicament
    (C) negligible . . . dilemma
    (D) trivial . . . fix

9. Despite a(n) ------- of damning evidence, the lawyer's ------- led to the absolution of his client.

    (A) abundance . . . ineptitude
    (B) copiousness . . . sophistry
    (C) mountain . . . hysterics
    (D) quantum . . . aptitude

10. The dog displayed a strong ------- for its tennis ball; it would only play with the tennis ball and would ------- all other toys.

    (A) affinity . . . eschew
    (B) aversion . . . refuse
    (C) disdain . . . engage
    (D) preference . . . prefer

11. Normally a paragon of peace and -------, the yoga instructor grew ------- when the cell phone continued to ring in class; he shouted a stream of obscenities that shocked the class.

    (A) anxiety . . . composed
    (B) panic . . . incensed
    (C) prudence . . . listless
    (D) tranquility . . . irate

12. Though many consumers today are ------- and consider the impact of their shopping habits on the environment, many more utilize such simple ------- as single-use plastic bags and water bottles to the detriment of the environment.

    (A) conscientious . . . indulgences
    (B) dishonorable . . . conveniences
    (C) fastidious . . . securities
    (D) scrupulous . . . bureaucracies

13. Many considered Zachary and Bill to be an unlikely pair; while Zachary was ------- and disinclined to speak or to share his feelings, Bill often spoke too much, sharing unnecessary and ------- details about his life with anyone who would listen.

    (A) excitable . . . redundant
    (B) reserved . . . valuable
    (C) reticent. . . superfluous
    (D) silent . . . beneficial

14. Edouard Manet had a ------- impact on the art world; his works helped to permanently propel the art world away from the declining, ------- school of Realism and towards the more progressive school of Impressionism.

    (A) fleeting . . . inert
    (B) lasting . . . stagnant
    (C) persisting . . . avant-garde
    (D) transitory . . . vivacious

15. Many health experts had previously believed that large doses of vitamin supplements had no ------- health effects; in a shocking reversal, these same experts now warn that large doses of vitamins can in fact be ------- to the body.

    (A) advantageous . . . injurious
    (B) beneficial . . . neutral
    (C) damaging . . . impartial
    (D) punitive . . . detrimental

16. Galileo Galilei's -------, that the planets orbit the sun, was ------- to heresy; his proposition that the Earth was not the center of the solar system challenged commonly held beliefs.

(A) belief . . . contradictory
(B) denial . . . synonymous
(C) hypothesis . . . tantamount
(D) refutation . . . identical

17. The city approved funding to renovate the ------- building as part of an effort to ------- the neighborhood's appeal.

(A) austere . . . condemn
(B) decrepit . . . absolve
(C) derelict . . . revitalize
(D) pristine . . . rejuvenate

18. To ------- the tragic civil war battle that had taken place in the town's main square, City Hall approved a plan to build a(n) ------- memorial by the entrance to the square.

(A) commemorate . . . somber
(B) ignore . . . dismal
(C) lament . . . colorful
(D) observe . . . exuberant

19. For early American explorers, nature was a(n) ------- friend; it seemed that nature could just as easily bless explorers with good luck and ------- fortune as plague them with famine and disease.

(A) fickle . . . exorbitant
(B) steadfast . . . trifling
(C) unpredictable . . . . vacuous
(D) unwavering . . . inordinate

20. Each time he told the lie, Adam added a few more ------- details; eventually, the lie grew so complex that he could not ------- between the lie and the truth.

(A) contrived . . . waver
(B) fabricated . . . discern
(C) genuine . . . distinguish
(D) simplistic . . . . decide

21. Scaling the side of a mountain without safety gear ------- considerable risk and requires ------- skills.

(A) debunks . . . . superior
(B) demands . . . negligible
(C) entails . . . commensurate
(D) involves . . . minimal

22. Utilizing the internet to ------- classroom learning is ------- and helps students learn when performed in a coordinated manner.

(A) facilitate . . . demoralizing
(B) supplant . . . efficacious
(C) supplement . . . effective
(D) undermine . . . promising

23. Gregory was a(n) ------- and amiable man; he had none of his brother's animosity and -------.

(A) affable . . . fervor
(B) affluent . . . wealth
(C) blithe . . . enmity
(D) incorruptible . . . scruples

24. Smith's latest book is widely considered to be ------- and -------, as the plot advances fantastically out of control and characters react in a way that is larger than life.

(A) hyperbolic . . . sedate
(B) melodramatic . . . exaggerated
(C) realistic . . . measured
(D) conservative . . . embellished

25. The ------- way in which John complimented Jane was a signal to her that John had ulterior motives; she felt that his overtures were nothing more than a -------.

(A) disingenuous . . . compliment
(B) glib . . . ruse
(C) insincere . . . truth
(D) sincere . . . fabrication

26. The ------- party was at its apex as the friends cheerfully engaged with one another; rather than -------, the conversation showed no sign of stopping.

    (A) convivial . . . subsiding
    (B) genial . . . intensifying
    (C) inauspicious . . . dwindling
    (D) portentous . . . escalating

27. Even miles away from town, travelers could hear the tolling of the famous bells ------- through the canyon; the acoustic properties of the canyon's walls ------- the sound.

    (A) contracted . . . augmented
    (B) echo . . . muffled
    (C) reverberate . . . amplified
    (D) ricochet . . . dampened

28. The celebrity unwittingly endorsed a defective product, landing her in a legal -------; however, despite the difficulties wrought by the scandal, she was made rich by the ------- deal.

    (A) dream . . . luxurious
    (B) hiatus . . . brusque
    (C) morass . . . futile
    (D) quagmire . . . . lucrative

29. Some frogs, being ------- creatures, are most active at night; as night progresses, more and more frogs join the growing ------- of croaking.

    (A) belligerent . . . harmony
    (B) carnivorous . . . ballad
    (C) diurnal . . . cacophony
    (D) nocturnal . . . crescendo

30. Growing up in the upper ------- of society, the girl was only ever used to a(n) ------- of wealth and privilege.

    (A) analog . . . atmosphere
    (B) echelon . . . milieu
    (C) parallel . . . routine
    (D) ranks . . . command

31. So talented that her show sold out in seconds, the musician was famous for her rare ability to produce ------- tones from a challenging instrument; sound flowed ------- from her horn, enrapturing her audience.

    (A) callous . . .melodiously
    (B) dulcet . . . mellifluously
    (C) pleasant . . . languidly
    (D) thundering . . . dreamily

32. Standing at the end of the jetty, ------- by the beauty and mystery of the waves, Susan watched as the ------- waves rolled towards her.

    (A) drawn . . . deliberate
    (B) enraptured . . . undulating
    (C) enthralled . . . tippling
    (D) gravitated . . . rippling

33. In -------, the little girl realized that she should have heeded her mother's advice and not worn her long dress on the field trip; this realization did little to comfort her as she continued to ------- the long rip that had sundered the dress.

    (A) circumspect . . . bemoan
    (B) hindsight . . . venerate
    (C) prospect . . . contemplate
    (D) retrospect . . . lament

34. Some argue that ------- landlords are contributing to the decline of culture in the city; ------- rents have driven out stores, restaurants, and even long-standing tenants.

    (A) avaricious . . . plummeting
    (B) frugal . . . spiraling
    (C) rapacious . . . escalating
    (D) spendthrift . . . mounting

35. As café culture becomes more -------, more and more cafés have been opening around the city to meet the demand; a logical ------- to this pattern, however, is that coffee beans will become more expensive as more cafés clamor over supplies.

    (A) appalling . . . consequence
    (B) causal . . . conjecture
    (C) prevalent . . . expedient
    (D) ubiquitous . . . corollary

36. Ever since he was thirteen years old, Neil was ------- by the idea of being an astronaut; the powerful ------- to be up among the stars was finally satisfied twenty years later.

    (A) afflicted . . . draw
    (B) captivated . . . yearning
    (C) inspired . . . option
    (D) jaded . . . longing

37. Though on the surface the play seemed to merely be about a nun going through a dilemma, a deeper reading of the play suggests that it was actually quite -------; the playwright, desiring to teach his audience a lesson, cleverly concealed a(n) ------- message on morality.

    (A) didactic . . . covert
    (B) ostensible . . . candid
    (C) perceptive . . . agreeable
    (D) superficial . . . surreptitious

38. The professor was impressed by how ------- the students in his new class seemed; already he had seen several students grasp complex concepts and furiously pursue ------- solutions to age-old problems.

    (A) astute . . . elusive
    (B) erratic . . . enthusiastic
    (C) infatuated . . . maneuverable
    (D) shrewd . . . specious

Reading Comprehension
Overview

In the Reading Comprehension section, students are asked to read passages and answer questions that pertain to those passages. The reading passages cover a variety of subject areas including the sciences, arts, history, and modern life. Questions are one to two sentences in length and ask students to respond to questions related to a number of different topics.

On the Actual Test

In the Reading Comprehension section of the Upper Level ISEE, you will encounter six reading passages, each between 300-600 words long. There will be 36 questions on the actual Reading Comprehension section, which you have 35 minutes to complete. The questions you will see relate to:

- ✏ *Main Idea* – What is the general message, premise, or idea in a section or passage? What is the author trying to tell the reader?
- ✏ *Supporting Ideas* – What are specific ideas supporting the important messages, premises, or ideas? How does the author expand on his or her main idea?
- ✏ *Inference* – What are some conclusions that can be drawn from the passage? What should a reader be able to infer based on the passage?
- ✏ *Vocabulary* – What do certain words or phrases mean?
- ✏ *Logic & Organization* – How is the passage structured? What type of writing does the author use?
- ✏ *Mood, Tone, Style, & Figurative Language* – What feeling is the author trying to convey? How does the author use figurative language such as metaphors and similes to establish a mood or set a tone?

Of the 36 questions, six questions in the Reading Comprehension section will not be scored. These questions are included for trial and research purposes only. You will not know which questions are trial questions.

In This Practice Book

Similar to the actual Upper Level ISEE exam, we have included side-by-side passages and questions and have numbered each line of each passage. As with the actual exam, our passages are all between 300-600 words in length and our questions are presented based on the order in which the subject-matter appears in the passage. This is unlike questions in other sections of the exam, which are ordered by difficulty.

The questions on the test aren't structured this way, but we've grouped similar passages together into the following genres because doing so has helped many students master this section:

- ✏ Narrative Passages – often used to tell a story, such as a memory or a fantasy
- ✏ Persuasive Passages – often used to persuade or convince the reader of an opinion or idea
- ✏ Descriptive Passages – often used to describe something, such as a person, place, thing, or event
- ✏ Expository Passages – often used to explain something, such as a process, or to present facts

The Tutorverse

How to Use This Section

We recommend that you practice at least 4-5 passages per week in preparing for exam. A good way to practice might be to do 1 passage from each genre each week.

You may find many words and concepts in this section to be challenging. Don't be surprised if you need to look up many of the words that you encounter in this section! We encourage you to make a list of words that give you trouble, whether they appear in passages, questions, or answer choices. Write down the definition of each word as well as a sentence using the word. You might also want to consider writing down positive or negative associations, any root words that can help you remember the word, or any words that are commonly encountered with that word. Reach out to a trusted educator for help learning new or confusing words or concepts.

Tutorverse Tips!

Remember that on the Upper Level ISEE, there is no penalty for guessing. If you don't know the answer to a question, take your best guess.

Identifying Main Ideas & Genres

Think about what the main idea might be as you read the passage. Remember, some passages may appear to fall into multiple genres. For example, a very descriptive passage may also be narrated by the author or a character in the passage. In those instances, think about which two genres might best fit to help you eliminate incorrect answer choices. Here are some clues:

- 🐟 Narrative Passages – may include dialogue, characters, or the word "I"
- 🐟 Persuasive Passages – may include opinions supported by reasons or facts; may ask the reader to do something or agree with something
- 🐟 Descriptive Passages – may be very descriptive, using many adjectives to appeal to the senses
- 🐟 Expository Passages – may be very logical and sequential; may describe how to do something or explain a concept or idea

Identifying Question Types

- 🐟 Reading Comprehension questions *are not* listed in order of difficulty. They are ordered based on the order of ideas in the passage. For example, questions related to Line 1 of a passage will be listed before questions related to Line 60.
- 🐟 Main idea questions tend to be listed first. They often ask about the passage's "primary purpose" or about "what the passage is primarily concerned with."
- 🐟 Supporting idea questions typically ask you to find something explicitly stated in the passage. Inference items typically ask you to think about ideas and interpret the passage in order to make a conclusion about something you've read. These questions tend not to ask for explicit support.
- 🐟 Vocabulary questions usually ask what a specific word or phrase "most nearly means."

Narrative Passages

Directions: Answer the questions following each passage on the basis of what is stated or implied in that passage.

Narrative – Passage 1

1   We had packed our bags and equipment
2   the night before: a waterproof tent, complete
3   with stakes and a wind shield; a tarp to lay
4   on the ground, to prevent moisture from
5   seeping in from the ground; another tarp, to
6   drape over the top of the tent, to prevent rain
7   from coming in; and of course, our down-
8   filled sleeping bags and pillows from home.
9   This was a big step for me. The only
10   camping I had ever done before this was in
11   our backyard. That time, I was so scared to
12   sleep outside by myself that I didn't even
13   make it through the night; I was constantly
14   running back and forth to the bathroom and
15   to the kitchen, just to satisfy my craving for
16   light, warmth, and company. Eventually, I
17   ended up sleeping in my bedroom that night.
18   This time, though, I was determined not
19   to have a repeat of that backyard camping
20   fiasco. I wanted to show my parents and
21   myself that I was a serious camper. To
22   make sure of this, in addition to the
23   necessary propane lamps and candles, I also
24   packed with me the biggest, brightest
25   flashlight that we had, as well as extra
26   batteries for my cell phone. In addition, I
27   brought my laptop and my tablet. I needed
28   to make sure that I had all of the trappings
29   that I knew I would miss, and that might
30   make me miss home. I even asked my
31   parents if I could bring a generator, but they
32   just looked at me strangely.
33   After a three hour drive, my parents and
34   I pulled up to an empty patch of dirt in the
35   woods. All I could see were trees and a

36   circular clearing where we were to set up
37   camp.
38   My parents were camping experts. They
39   showed me how to pitch the tent, how to
40   gather firewood and build a fire, and how to
41   cook over an open flame. But all of that
42   took only a few hours. By the end, I was
43   bored. I took my phone out from my pocket
44   and stared at a warning that read: "No
45   Service". The phone was basically useless,
46   but I still thumbed around for some games to
47   play.
48   My parents were deep in conversation
49   with one another, and I had nothing to do. I
50   knew there was a lake nearby, but I was too
51   scared to go alone and my parents showed
52   no signs of wanting to explore. I didn't
53   want to venture too far into the woods,
54   either, as I had read about bears and
55   mountain lions living in this area. Instead, I
56   went to the car to get my laptop.
57   On my way back from the car, my
58   parents looked up from their conversation
59   and asked me if I wanted to listen to stories
60   by the fire. The familiar weight and feel of
61   my laptop reminded me of how excited I
62   was to watch the new movie I had
63   downloaded the other day. I said I would
64   pass, and headed toward the tent to watch
65   my movie.
66   As I passed them, I once again saw my
67   parents give me one of their strange looks,
68   the meaning of which I couldn't quite
69   understand.

Narrative – Passage 1 Question Set

Main idea

1. The primary purpose of the passage is to

   (A) describe camping guidelines.
   (B) explain why the author was excited to go camping.
   (C) show how a child has nothing in common with his parents.
   (D) explain the differences between the author's definition of camping and his parents'.

tone/mood

2. The mood of the second paragraph can best be described as one of

   (A) pride and resolve.
   (B) humor and boredom.
   (C) remorse and fondness.
   (D) regret and embarrassment.

3. Which does the author of the passage mention as a reason that the first backyard camping experience (lines 9-17) was a fiasco?

   (A) The author's loneliness.
   (B) The author's lack of equipment.
   (C) The author's batteries and lights stopped working.
   (D) The author's parents did not allow him to sleep outside at night.

authors

4. The sentence "I even asked my parents if I could bring a generator, but they just looked at me strangely" (lines 30-32) is included in order to *why how does it move text forward*

   (A) enumerate the importance of a generator to camping.
   (B) show how the author's parents lack technological savvy.
   (C) illustrate a specific example to emphasize a larger disparity.
   (D) list some of the comforts that the author misses while camping.

5. In line 46, "thumbed" most nearly means

   (A) browsed.
   (B) jerked.
   (C) pointed.
   (D) wiggled.

Inference

6. In the final sentence (lines 66-69), which conclusion can best be drawn from the way the parents look at the author?

   (A) The author enjoys the comforts of home.
   (B) The parents are unable to empathize with the author.
   (C) The parents understand why the author prefers to watch movies while camping.
   (D) The author is tired from a long day and wants to relax in the tent with a movie.

Narrative – Passage 2

This passage is adapted from Franklin D. Roosevelt's first fireside chat address.

1   I want to talk for a few minutes with the
2 people of the United States about banking –
3 with the comparatively few who understand
4 the mechanics of banking but more
5 particularly with the overwhelming majority
6 who use banks for the making of deposits
7 and the drawing of checks. I want to tell you
8 what has been done in the last few days,
9 why it was done, and what the next steps are
10 going to be. I recognize that the many
11 proclamations from state capitols and from
12 Washington, the legislation, the Treasury
13 regulations, etc., couched for the most part
14 in banking and legal terms should be
15 explained for the benefit of the average
16 citizen. I owe this in particular because of
17 the fortitude and good temper with which
18 everybody has accepted the inconvenience
19 and hardships of the banking holiday. I
20 know that when you understand what we in
21 Washington have been about I shall continue
22 to have your cooperation as fully as I have
23 had your sympathy and help during the past
24 week.
25   First of all let me state the simple fact
26 that when you deposit money in a bank the
27 bank does not put the money into a safe
28 deposit vault. It invests your money in many
29 different forms of credit-bonds, commercial
30 paper, mortgages and many other kinds of
31 loans. In other words, the bank puts your
32 money to work to keep the wheels of

33 industry and of agriculture turning around.
34 A comparatively small part of the money
35 you put into the bank is kept in currency --
36 an amount which in normal times is wholly
37 sufficient to cover the cash needs of the
38 average citizen. In other words the total
39 amount of all the currency in the country is
40 only a small fraction of the total deposits in
41 all of the banks.
42   What, then, happened during the last few
43 days of February and the first few days of
44 March? Because of undermined confidence
45 on the part of the public, there was a general
46 rush by a large portion of our population to
47 turn bank deposits into currency or gold – a
48 rush so great that the soundest banks could
49 not get enough currency to meet the
50 demand. The reason for this was that on the
51 spur of the moment it was, of course,
52 impossible to sell perfectly sound assets of a
53 bank and convert them into cash except at
54 panic prices far below their real value.
55   By the afternoon of March 3rd scarcely a
56 bank in the country was open to do business.
57 Proclamations temporarily closing them in
58 whole or in part had been issued by the
59 governors in almost all the states.
60   It was then that I issued the proclamation
61 providing for the nation-wide bank holiday,
62 and this was the first step in the
63 government's reconstruction of our financial
64 and economic fabric.

Narrative – Passage 2 Question Set

1. The passage is primarily concerned with

   (A) assigning blame for the banking crisis.
   (B) teaching the public about technical banking.
   (C) explaining why gold is preferable to cash currency.
   (D) explaining the rationale for the bank holiday, and the events that led up to it.

2. Which conclusion can best be drawn from lines 7-16?

   (A) The general public was confused.
   (B) The average person understands banking and legal terms.
   (C) The general public was unsympathetic during the bank holiday.
   (D) Many Americans understand the difference between currency and gold.

3. According to lines 25-41, banks keep a relatively small amount of money in the form of currency because

   (A) they invest it in industry and agriculture.
   (B) there is not enough room in safe deposit vaults.
   (C) they are required to convert all currency into gold.
   (D) they are not required to satisfy customer withdrawal requests.

4. In line 64, "fabric" most nearly means

   (A) clothing.
   (B) forgery.
   (C) framework.
   (D) manufacture.

5. The author's tone in this passage is best described as

   (A) angry and practical.
   (B) wistful and yearning.
   (C) hysterical and pragmatic.
   (D) realistic and matter-of-fact.

6. According to the author of the passage, all of the following were reasons that the government closed banks EXCEPT

   (A) there was an excess of currency available to the public.
   (B) the loss of public confidence resulted in a rush to withdraw currency.
   (C) it was not possible to properly or fairly convert investments into currency.
   (D) there was not enough money in the banks to satisfy currency withdrawal requests.

Narrative – Passage 3

1　　An otherworldly blue shone all around
2　me, like a giant pale sapphire. Even with
3　my sunglasses on, the light was bright and
4　blinding. I stopped for a moment, to take
5　stock of my situation. Somewhere in the
6　back of my mind, the pulsing of a coming
7　headache registered dimly. I ignored it,
8　however, and looked up: beyond the jagged
9　crack, some thirty or forty feet above me,
10　shone the unmistakable blue of the sky,
11　dotted with white. And yet the blue
12　surrounding me looked different from that of
13　the sky. It was less solid; shifting and
14　dynamic, changing with the light, this blue
15　was the blue of pure ice.
16　　Thankfully, I had not fallen into this
17　crevasse. I had simply walked into the crack
18　in the side of this glacier, along with a few
19　other hikers. We were exploring Franz Josef
20　Glacier in New Zealand, one of the most
21　unique glaciers in the world. Its lowest
22　point a mere thousand feet above sea level,
23　the glacier itself was surrounded by a
24　temperate rainforest. The temperature was
25　significantly warmer than I had expected,
26　especially since I was walking on, and
27　surrounded by, a fortress of ice.
28　　The walls of the crevasse were slippery
29　and smooth. The ice wasn't melting so
30　much as it was perspiring, covering itself in
31　a fine sheen of water. The bottom of the
32　crevasse was so narrow that I half-shuffled
33　and half-slid through the crack, sidling
34　sideways with my breath sucked in. It hit me
35　that I hadn't taken a full breath since the
36　beginning of the walk.
37　　I stopped, looking at the pure and
38　flawless ice just inches in front of me, and
39　stared into the soul of the glacier. With no
40　air bubbles or blemishes to obstruct my
41　view, I stared hundreds of years into the
42　past, at snowfall that had accumulated and
43　compacted and become ice: snow from
44　when man first walked on the moon, and
45　maybe even from when the world's earliest
46　explorers first sailed around the world.
47　　The beauty was astounding, and I
48　stopped to savor it, to burn it into my
49　memory, to will it into permanence in my
50　mind.

Narrative – Passage 3 Question Set

1. Which best expresses the main idea of the passage?

   (A) The author is describing a vivid memory.
   (B) Glaciers are dangerous and can cause headaches.
   (C) The author is providing data and information about glaciers.
   (D) The author is comparing the Franz Josef Glacier with other glaciers.

2. The second paragraph (lines 16-27) suggests that walking a glacier is typically

   (A) colder.
   (B) more tiring.
   (C) less dangerous.
   (D) more enjoyable.

3. In lines 37-46, which is a reason that the author is able to look hundreds of years into the past when looking at the ice?

   (A) The author is exhausted and is experiencing hallucinations of the past.
   (B) The author believes the ice behaves like a fortuneteller's crystal ball.
   (C) The ice is flecked with tiny imperfections, each of which represents a past event.
   (D) The snow takes hundreds of years to accumulate into ice this deep and pure, so it is as if he is looking directly into the past.

4. The mood of the final paragraph (lines 47-50) can best be described as

   (A) contemptuous.
   (B) detached.
   (C) grave.
   (D) reverent.

5. In line 48, "burn" most nearly means

   (A) etch.
   (B) ignite.
   (C) pare.
   (D) shave.

6. The author of the passage does all of the following EXCEPT

   (A) describe the beauty of the glacier.
   (B) give advice about how best to climb a glacier.
   (C) explain the impact of the glacier on his body and mind.
   (D) compare the Franz Josef Glacier with other glaciers around the world.

Narrative – Passage 4

1　　When I was much younger, all I wanted
2　was to visit Greece. I remember passing by
3　the travel agency with my mother and seeing
4　a picture hanging in the window of crystal
5　clear, blue-green water. When I saw it, I
6　froze, and pictured myself with persons
7　unknown on the rugged coastline of the
8　Aegean Sea.
9　　The sun shone down on us in a single,
10　unbroken ray, filling us with its warmth and
11　its life. There was no one around for miles –
12　at least, no one that we could see. We were
13　utterly alone on the gravelly beach, with the
14　whole world to ourselves. Not one of us
15　spoke for hours, for there was nothing to
16　say: we were completely and utterly content.
17　　I rolled onto my stomach and realized
18　that I was alone. Did I fall asleep? I
19　couldn't be sure, but I realized that I didn't
20　even care. All I knew was that I found

21　myself alone, staring at the tiny pebbles and
22　grains of sand along the shoreline.
23　　My mother's voice pulled me back to
24　reality. The azure waters faded from my
25　mind's eye, leaving only the illusory smell
26　of salt water lingering in my nose. I was
27　suddenly back in front of the travel agency,
28　staring at the picture of the jagged cliffs and
29　the glass-like water. I felt, for a moment,
30　completely befuddled. The experience was
31　so visceral that I was shocked at being back
32　in the suburbs. And yet the whole episode
33　had clearly just been a dream.
34　　It's no wonder that now, some twenty
35　years later, I find myself vacationing on a
36　very similar beach, with very similar rocks,
37　and feeling a very similar warmth
38　enveloping me from above. Isn't it strange
39　how the events of the past can influence the
40　events of the present, and of the future?

Narrative – Passage 4 Question Set

1. The primary purpose of the passage is to

   (A) complain about boredom.
   (B) convince the reader to travel to Greece.
   (C) express a feeling of nostalgia and wonderment.
   (D) convey a dissatisfaction with the state of Greek beaches.

2. The author's tone when describing the dream of being on the beach (lines 9-22) is best described as

   (A) bemused.
   (B) ethereal.
   (C) euphoric.
   (D) muted.

3. According to the passage, the author of the passage was awoken from her daydream (lines 23-33) by

   (A) her mother's voice.
   (B) shock and confusion.
   (C) the splashing of water.
   (D) the brightness of sunlight.

4. In line 31, "visceral" most nearly means

   (A) disappointing.
   (B) exciting.
   (C) realistic.
   (D) vicarious.

5. It can be inferred from lines 34-40 that

   (A) the best vacations are beach vacations.
   (B) rocky beaches are very similar to sandy beaches.
   (C) the author's present-day beach vacation is in Greece.
   (D) the past has little to do with the present or with the future.

6. The author of the passage does all of the following EXCEPT

   (A) give instructions.
   (B) describe a present-day vacation.
   (C) use imagery to describe a vivid daydream.
   (D) explain how events of the past influenced events of the present.

Narrative – Passage 5

This passage is adapted from John F. Kennedy's inaugural address.

1   Let every nation know, whether it
2   wishes us well or ill, that we shall pay any
3   price, bear any burden, meet any hardship,
4   support any friend, oppose any foe to assure
5   the survival and the success of liberty.
6   This much we pledge – and more.
7   To those old allies whose cultural and
8   spiritual origins we share, we pledge the
9   loyalty of faithful friends. United there is
10   little we cannot do in a host of co-operative
11   ventures. Divided there is little we can do –
12   for we dare not meet a powerful challenge at
13   odds and split asunder.
14   To those new states whom we welcome
15   to the ranks of the free, we pledge our word
16   that one form of colonial control shall not
17   have passed away merely to be replaced by a
18   far more iron tyranny. We shall not always
19   expect to find them supporting our view. But
20   we shall always hope to find them strongly
21   supporting their own freedom – and to
22   remember that, in the past, those who
23   foolishly sought power by riding the back of
24   the tiger ended up inside.
25   To those people in the huts and villages
26   of half the globe struggling to break the
27   bonds of mass misery: we pledge our best
28   efforts to help them help themselves, for
29   whatever period is required – not because
30   the Communists may be doing it, not
31   because we seek their votes, but because it is
32   right. If a free society cannot help the many
33   who are poor, it cannot save the few who are
34   rich.
35   To our sister republics south of our
36   border, we offer a special pledge – to
37   convert our good words into good deeds – in
38   a new alliance for progress – to assist free
39   men and free governments in casting off the
40   chains of poverty. But this peaceful
41   revolution of hope cannot become the prey
42   of hostile powers. Let all our neighbors
43   know that we shall join with them to oppose
44   aggression or subversion anywhere in the
45   Americas. And let every other power know
46   that this hemisphere intends to remain the
47   master of its own house.
48   To that world assembly of sovereign
49   states: the United Nations – our last best
50   hope in an age where the instruments of war
51   have far outpaced the instruments of peace,
52   we renew our pledge of support – to prevent
53   it from becoming merely a forum for
54   invective – to strengthen its shield of the
55   new and the weak – and to enlarge the area
56   in which its writ may run.
57   Finally, to those nations who would
58   make themselves our adversaries, we offer
59   not a pledge but a request: that both sides
60   begin anew the quest for peace, before the
61   dark powers of destruction unleashed by
62   science engulf all humanity in planned or
63   accidental self-destruction.

Narrative – Passage 5 Question Set

1. The passage is primarily concerned with

   (A) pacifying enemies.
   (B) admonishing allies.
   (C) threatening enemies.
   (D) summarizing national policies.

2. In lines 35-47, the author pledges an alliance with southern republics in order to

   (A) improve trade relations and commercial profit.
   (B) advance the common interest of technological innovation.
   (C) remind them that the United States alone will control the hemisphere.
   (D) signal that the hemisphere is united in opposing aggression and subversion.

3. The metaphor in lines 19-24 ("But...inside") most likely implies that

   (A) tigers are wild animals who sometimes prey on humans.
   (B) powerful friends can be capricious and double-dealing.
   (C) what happens in the past is unlikely to happen again.
   (D) one should train tigers before attempting to ride them.

4. In line 54, "invective" most nearly means

   (A) collaboration.
   (B) condemnation.
   (C) cooperation.
   (D) engagement.

5. The purpose of the last paragraph is to

   (A) deny requests for peace.
   (B) open a dialogue for diplomacy.
   (C) unleash dark powers of destruction.
   (D) explain how science will engulf humanity.

6. The mood of the passage can best be described as

   (A) candid yet steadfast.
   (B) confident yet nervous.
   (C) adoring yet disdainful.
   (D) understated yet comforting.

Narrative – Passage 6

1　　The knapsack, a relic from a time when
2　efficiency and practicality were valued over
3　aesthetics and form, was one of my favorite
4　things. Its leather exterior had grown soft
5　from the thousands of times that it had been
6　smoothed, opened, and closed over the
7　years. Despite its age, the bag didn't smell
8　or look dirty. Instead, it gave off a rich,
9　earthy scent, which reminded me of a walk
10　through the woods. Just looking at the old
11　knapsack made me smile, as it made me
12　think about all of the different adventures
13　my father, and my grandfather before him,
14　must have had with it.
15　　The knapsack was a special family
16　heirloom, and when my father gave it to me
17　on my fourteenth birthday, he told me
18　something that, at the time, I found
19　unusual. This was that I should be very
20　careful with the knapsack, and make sure
21　that it survives daily wear and tear. This
22　practice of taking good care of things was
23　unfamiliar to me, as I grew up in a world of
24　convenience and plenty – a world in which
25　everything is replaceable. For instance, each
26　year I bought a new backpack for school,
27　and it occurred to me that, after the school

28　year ended, I wasn't really sure where the
29　old ones went. Whenever I shopped for
30　groceries or went to the convenience store, I
31　received plastic or paper bags with my
32　purchase. I didn't really give these things
33　much thought until my father gave me his
34　father's leather knapsack.
35　　For some reason, using and caring about
36　this bag began to change the way I behaved.
37　I started using the bag everywhere. I took it
38　with me to school and carried my books in
39　it. I brought the bag with me to stores and
40　carried my groceries in it. More recently,
41　I've been bringing the bag with me on my
42　travels. I've found that using the bag has
43　changed the way I think about all the things
44　that we use only once and then throw away,
45　such as paper bags or plastic bottles. I've
46　begun to wonder why we don't have things
47　that are built to last anymore. As a result,
48　I've now made a conscious decision to stop
49　being so wasteful in my day-to-day
50　routines. I've decided to invest in a few
51　items that will keep my belongings in good
52　condition, such as polish for my
53　grandfather's bag.

Narrative – Passage 6 Question Set

1. Which best expresses the main idea of the passage?

   (A) One should always listen to one's elders.
   (B) Leather bags, if properly taken care of, become more beautiful in time.
   (C) An old object from the past has changed the author's point of view and behavior.
   (D) Though knapsacks are superior to backpacks, both are inferior to paper and plastic bags.

2. The sentences in lines 4-10 are included to

   (A) make the reader jealous.
   (B) criticize those who are unchanging and stubborn.
   (C) describe the ways in which the knapsack is special.
   (D) explain why the author's thinking changed over time.

3. In line 16, "heirloom" most nearly means

   (A) bag.
   (B) container.
   (C) furniture.
   (D) treasure.

4. Why did the father's instructions to care for the knapsack surprise the author?

   (A) The author's father rarely spoke about his father.
   (B) The author had always needed to take good care of things.
   (C) The author's mother had always taken good care of everything.
   (D) The author had never needed to take good care of anything before.

5. According to the final paragraph, the reason the author's behavior began to change (lines 35-45) was because

   (A) the knapsack was heavy and cumbersome.
   (B) the author's grandfather instructed him to change.
   (C) the author realized that disposable products are designed to be reusable.
   (D) in using the knapsack to carry books and groceries, the author realized that disposable bags were an unnecessary convenience.

6. The author of the passage appears to care most deeply about

   (A) polishing the leather knapsack.
   (B) prioritizing convenience over all else.
   (C) no longer living as a creature of habit.
   (D) banning all plastic bags and water bottles.

Narrative – Passage 7

This narrative is adapted from Lyndon B. Johnson's State of the Union address.

1   We are in the midst of the greatest
2 upward surge of economic well-being in the
3 history of any nation.
4   Our flourishing progress has been
5 marked by price stability that is unequalled
6 in the world. Our balance of payments
7 deficit has declined and the soundness of our
8 dollar is unquestioned. I pledge to keep it
9 that way and I urge business and labor to
10 cooperate to that end.
11   We worked for two centuries to climb
12 this peak of prosperity. But we are only at
13 the beginning of the road to the Great
14 Society. Ahead now is a summit where
15 freedom from the wants of the body can help
16 fulfill the needs of the spirit.
17   We built this Nation to serve its people.
18   We want to grow and build and create,
19 but we want progress to be the servant and
20 not the master of man.
21   We do not intend to live in the midst of
22 abundance, isolated from neighbors and
23 nature, confined by blighted cities and bleak
24 suburbs, stunted by a poverty of learning
25 and an emptiness of leisure.
26   The Great Society asks not how much,
27 but how good; not only how to create wealth
28 but how to use it; not only how fast we are
29 going, but where we are headed.
30   It proposes as the first test for a nation:
31 the quality of its people.
32   This kind of society will not flower
33 spontaneously from swelling riches and
34 surging power.

35   It will not be the gift of government or
36 the creation of presidents.
37   It will require of every American, for
38 many generations, both faith in the
39 destination and the fortitude to make the
40 journey.
41   And like freedom itself, it will always be
42 challenge and not fulfillment.
43   And tonight we accept that challenge.
44   I propose that we begin a program in
45 education to ensure every American child
46 the fullest development of his mind and
47 skills.
48   I propose that we begin a massive attack
49 on crippling and killing diseases.
50   I propose that we launch a national effort
51 to make the American city a better and a
52 more stimulating place to live. I propose
53 that we increase the beauty of America and
54 end the poisoning of our rivers and the air
55 that we breathe.
56   I propose that we carry out a new
57 program to develop regions of our country
58 that are now suffering from distress and
59 depression.
60   I propose that we make new efforts to
61 control and prevent crime and delinquency.
62   I propose that we eliminate every
63 remaining obstacle to the right and the
64 opportunity to vote.
65   I propose that we honor and support the
66 achievements of thought and the creations of
67 art.
68   I propose that we make an all-out
69 campaign against waste and inefficiency.

Narrative – Passage 7 Question Set

1. Which best expresses the main idea of the passage?

    (A) America should adopt an isolationist policy.
    (B) The dream of a perfect America is unreasonable.
    (C) America has achieved the status of a Great Society.
    (D) America has accomplished much, but still has much to accomplish.

2. The author of the passage suggests that America is "in the midst of the greatest upward surge of economic well-being" (lines 1-3) because

    (A) every American has a home.
    (B) the dollar is sound and prices are stable.
    (C) prices of goods and services fluctuate wildly.
    (D) America has already climbed to the peak of prosperity.

3. Lines 18-20 imply that people have done all of the following EXCEPT

    (A) abandoned creative and progressive pursuits.
    (B) prioritized, at times, creation and progress over humanity.
    (C) succumbed to ignoble motivations to pursue creation and progress.
    (D) lost sight of the underlying purpose behind creation and progress.

4. In line 23, "blighted" most nearly means

    (A) neglected.
    (B) pleasant.
    (C) prodigious.
    (D) radiant.

5. Which best describes the organization of lines 44-69?

    (A) The author lists and describes goals.
    (B) The author outlines a chronological process.
    (C) The author presents an account of past accomplishments.
    (D) The author describes an opinion and supports it with facts.

6. The author of the passage appears to care most deeply about

    (A) describing America's prosperity.
    (B) admonishing Americans for being lazy.
    (C) outlining a future course for America.
    (D) how much progress America has already made.

Narrative – Passage 8

1   Whenever I fly on an airplane, I try to
2 get a window seat. I think most people try
3 to reserve an aisle seat, but for the life of
4 me, I can't understand why. Let's say you
5 need to go to the bathroom. True, if you're
6 sitting in the aisle, you can come and go
7 whenever you please, but when has sitting in
8 the window seat prevented anyone from
9 getting up to go to the bathroom? Sure, it
10 might briefly inconvenience the person
11 sitting by the aisle, but who cares? It's not
12 very likely that you'll ever see that person
13 again.
14   For me, the reason I like to sit by the
15 window is because I like to look out and
16 enjoy the view, especially when we're flying
17 in a cloudless sky.
18   My favorite things to look out for are
19 rivers. And there are, surprisingly, a lot of
20 rivers out there.
21   Why do I like to look at rivers? Well, I
22 like to imagine myself a couple of hundred
23 years ago when there were no airplanes or
24 cars or anything like that. Back during that
25 time, people needed to get from place to
26 place, just like they do now. But back then,

27 people weren't in such a rush to get around.
28 And one of the best ways to travel happened
29 to be by boat.
30   Big or little, steam powered or human
31 powered, I love the idea of boat travel. It's
32 just so romantic, to drift lazily downstream
33 or chug along upstream. What a scenic way
34 to travel, too, taking in the sights and smells
35 along sinuous shorelines, feeling the wind,
36 and smelling the fresh air! Now that I think
37 about it, maybe looking at the rivers below
38 helps me forget that I'm squeezed like a
39 sardine into my seat and hurtling through the
40 sky at 35,000 feet while breathing in stale,
41 recycled air.
42   Nowadays, when you look out of your
43 airplane window at a river, or drive by one
44 on the highway, the rivers are, for the most
45 part, empty. While there are a few
46 waterways that remain commercially active,
47 it seems that rivers now are mostly used for
48 recreation – or not at all. It's kind of sad to
49 see these grand, age-old parts of our world
50 go unused. How I wish we could all just
51 slow down and travel by boat again.

Narrative – Passage 8 Question Set

1. The primary purpose of the passage is to

    (A) provide information about rivers.
    (B) explain the author's preference for boat travel.
    (C) describe the author's preference for window seats.
    (D) convince readers that inconveniencing your neighbor is a small price to pay for a window seat.

2. The author of the passage implies that people's desire to move around quickly resulted in all of the following EXCEPT

    (A) the proliferation of boat travel.
    (B) a decreased use of waterways for transportation.
    (C) speedier but less enjoyable forms of transportation.
    (D) a preference for the destination over the experience of the journey itself.

3. In line 35, "sinuous" most nearly means

    (A) depraved.
    (B) polluted.
    (C) unyielding.
    (D) winding.

4. In the last paragraph (lines 42-51), the author's tone when discussing the current state of rivers and travel can best be described as

    (A) contemplative.
    (B) disdainful.
    (C) threatened.
    (D) uncertain.

5. According to the author of the passage, boat travel is more enjoyable than air travel because

    (A) boat travel is less romantic.
    (B) boat travel is more efficient.
    (C) air travel is inherently unsafe.
    (D) boat travel is less claustrophobic.

6. By always taking a window seat, the author of the passage

    (A) avoids motion sickness and feeling cramped.
    (B) is able to forget about present discomforts.
    (C) can freely and conveniently use the bathroom.
    (D) is able to converse with fellow travelers regarding the state of air travel.

Narrative – Passage 9

1   Brad spun around in a circle, lost,
2 confused, and overwhelmed. He was
3 supposed to have met his friend at the train
4 station, but was having a difficult time
5 finding her. She should have arrived twenty
6 minutes ago, and he was getting nervous.
7   Brad didn't realize that this train station,
8 Shinjuku Station in the heart of Tokyo, was
9 the busiest in the entire world. An
10 astounding 3.5 million people passed
11 through its halls each day, and each of the
12 station's multiple levels was a labyrinth unto
13 itself. The station had over 200 exits!
14 Suddenly, Brad realized that his friend was
15 right when she said that meeting here was
16 going to be a bad idea. And now, as a result
17 of his hubris – he thought that because he
18 had lived in New York for a decade and
19 navigated many different public
20 transportation systems – they were separated.
21   Because he hadn't specified a more exact
22 location in advance, he now stood by one of
23 the many information booths, hoping to
24 catch a glimpse of his friend. Brad kicked
25 himself for not signing up for international

26 phone service, as he realized that he had no
27 way of contacting her. He kicked himself
28 even harder for not knowing Japanese and
29 for being so naive. He should have known
30 better.
31   Completely bewildered, Brad found it
32 difficult to focus. The signs overhead were
33 too many to count, and written only in
34 Japanese. The surging crowds were
35 disorienting. Shoulder to shoulder,
36 businessmen in suits walked purposefully,
37 this way and that, while clusters of
38 eclectically dressed schoolchildren loitered
39 off to the sides, chattering happily. Lining
40 the passageway were stores, mobbed by
41 shoppers. Flashing advertisements and the
42 cacophonous din of the station only served to
43 add to his confusion.
44   Shinjuku Station made Times Square in
45 New York City look like a quiet day at the
46 park. Not knowing what to do – should he
47 stay put, or should he search actively for his
48 friend? – Brad felt helpless. He looked
49 around once again, hoping to see his friend's
50 familiar face.

Narrative – Passage 9 Question Set

1. The passage is primarily concerned with

   (A) explaining why Shinjuku Station is so large and so busy.
   (B) illustrating the importance of learning a foreign language.
   (C) comparing Brad's experiences in New York with those in Tokyo.
   (D) describing Brad's predicament in the world's busiest train station.

2. It can be inferred from lines 16-20 that Brad

   (A) was born in New York.
   (B) is a seasoned traveler.
   (C) does not enjoy traveling.
   (D) travels only if he can use public transportation.

3. The mood of lines 31-43 can best be described as one of

   (A) growing worry.
   (B) vivacious energy.
   (C) unabashed apathy.
   (D) emphatic empathy.

4. In line 42 "cacophonous" most nearly means

   (A) cadaverous.
   (B) noisy.
   (C) quiet.
   (D) ringing.

5. The sentence "Shinjuku Station made Times Square in New York City look like a quiet day at the park" (lines 44-46) is included in order to

   (A) emphasize the busyness of Shinjuku Station.
   (B) describe how Times Square is similar to a park.
   (C) provide an example of a typical day in the park.
   (D) highlight Shinjuku Station's relative tranquility.

6. According to passage, all of the following were reasons why Brad could not find his friend EXCEPT

   (A) Brad cannot speak or read Japanese.
   (B) Brad is unable to use a phone to contact his friend.
   (C) Brad did not specify a specific location to meet with his friend.
   (D) Brad was busy musing about overhead signs and flashing advertisements.

Persuasive Passages

Directions: Answer the questions following each passage on the basis of what is stated or implied in that passage.

Persuasive – Passage 1

1　　I love the idea of having a vegetable
2　garden in the backyard, don't you? At a
3　time when most Americans are spending
4　more and more on groceries and produce,
5　having a vegetable garden is a great way to
6　save money on one's monthly food bill. In
7　addition, at a time when consumers are
8　increasingly concerned about the health
9　ramifications of consuming food grown with
10　pesticides, a vegetable garden can allow you
11　to know for certain that your food is 100%
12　organically produced. Not only are
13　vegetable gardens a great way to save
14　money and eat more healthily, but they are
15　also a great way to spend more time outside
16　and reap the health benefits of physical
17　activity. On top of the physical and
18　monetary benefits of having a vegetable
19　garden, many gardeners report a feeling of
20　satisfaction and contentedness associated
21　with caring for a garden.
22　　Vegetable gardens, in fact, have had a
23　huge impact on the course of human
24　history. In times past, people gardened as a
25　matter of necessity. In more recent history,
26　however, farms adopted more automated
27　and scientific agricultural cultivation
28　techniques, and were able to increase yields
29　and minimize the effects of droughts and
30　pest problems. Combined with improved
31　storage methods and more efficient
32　transportation, food became cheaper and
33　more accessible. As a result, fewer and
34　fewer people needed to sustain their own
35　vegetable gardens at home.

36　　One exception to this general trend has
37　been during times of global crises, such as
38　World War I and World War II. As these
39　conflicts surged around the globe, involved
40　countries encouraged their citizens to
41　cultivate "victory gardens," or private and
42　communal vegetable gardens. In 1917,
43　Charles Pack founded the US National War
44　Gardens Commission, which, by the end of
45　World War I, helped to promote and
46　organize over five million gardens in the
47　United States. These gardens were planted
48　on both public and private land and helped
49　to ease the burden on the public food
50　supply. The people involved were very
51　resourceful, planting wherever there was
52　arable land: on backyards and in parks, as
53　well as on rooftops, in railroad yards, and
54　even in vacant city lots. During World War
55　II, First Lady Eleanor Roosevelt planted a
56　victory garden on the White House grounds,
57　and more recently, First Lady Michelle
58　Obama planted a kitchen garden, also on
59　White House grounds, to promote awareness
60　of the need for healthy, fresh food options.
61　　Like many other people who live in a big
62　city and who don't often get the chance, I
63　often have an urge to work outside with my
64　hands. Looking back at victory gardens, I
65　can't help but feel envious of war-time
66　ingenuity and need-based creativity. It's too
67　bad that vegetable gardens today are more a
68　thing of the past. I think that many people
69　would enjoy and benefit from cultivating a
70　vegetable garden.

Persuasive – Passage 1 Question Set

1. Which best expresses the main idea of the passage?

    (A) There are many different places where one can plant vegetable gardens.
    (B) People should stop buying produce from supermarkets and grow their own instead.
    (C) Vegetables are healthier than other types of food and should be produced by individuals, not farms.
    (D) In addition to having many virtues and benefits, vegetable gardens have played a large role in world history.

2. Which best describes the organization of lines 1-21?

    (A) Historical gardening methods are explained.
    (B) A detailed process for growing vegetables is outlined.
    (C) The various benefits of caring for a vegetable garden are listed.
    (D) A balanced argument is presented, discussing both the benefits and drawbacks of vegetable gardens.

3. According to lines 36-60, strain on the American public food supply during World War I was somewhat alleviated as a result of

    (A) the organization of victory gardens.
    (B) Eleanor Roosevelt's White House garden.
    (C) the lack of resourcefulness on the part of the public.
    (D) Charles Pack's personal contribution of fruits and vegetables to the war effort.

4. The author of the passage uses the term "victory garden" (line 41) in order to _why does_ _Infrence author_ _include_

    (A) emphasize a contribution to the success of a war effort.
    (B) explain how vegetable gardens help athletes attain victory.
    (C) bestow a nickname upon vegetable gardens around the world.
    (D) confuse the reader by adding another term to describe vegetable gardens.

5. In line 52, "arable" most nearly means _Vocab_

    (A) available.
    (B) dry.
    (C) fertile.
    (D) flat.

6. It can be inferred from the last paragraph of _Infrence_ the passage that the author of the passage

    (A) dislikes working outdoors.
    (B) works with her hands frequently.
    (C) wants to start her own vegetable garden.
    (D) is frequently engaged in creative pursuits.

Persuasive – Passage 2

1   Though not all restaurants take
2 reservations, those that do are often plagued
3 by diners who make reservations, but then
4 fail to show up for their meal. This
5 ultimately results in a loss for the restaurant,
6 since the no-show causes a table to sit
7 empty, when it could otherwise have
8 accommodated diners who were ready and
9 willing to pay. Indeed, no-shows pose a real
10 problem to a restaurant's financial success,
11 and they are a contributing factor to the
12 closing of many restaurants.
13   To help manage the problem, many
14 restaurants that do accept reservations
15 employ disincentives. Some restaurants
16 require a customer to provide his or her
17 credit card information in order to make and
18 hold a reservation, and then charge the credit
19 card a fee in the event the diner does not
20 honor the reservation.
21   Rather than charging reservation holders
22 a fee for a no-show, other restaurants have
23 attempted to commoditize reservations,
24 putting some or all of their reservations up
25 for sale or auction. This practice is highly
26 contentious, with strong proponents and
27 opponents. The reservation is a service, the

28 former argue, and like many other services,
29 businesses should be able to receive
30 compensation for their service. Proponents
31 also argue that people who pay for their
32 reservations will be more likely to keep
33 them, thereby preventing the problems
34 posed by no-shows. The opponents to this
35 practice argue that it is contrary to the idea
36 of hospitality itself, and that it gives an
37 unfair advantage to the wealthy. They argue
38 that other ways, such as requiring a credit
39 card number to hold reservations, are
40 equally effective at managing no-shows.
41   Perhaps there is a happy middle ground
42 – one that is already employed by some
43 restaurants. Some restaurants that offer
44 fixed-priced meals and dining experiences
45 sell tickets for a specific date and time.
46 These tickets are priced at the cost of the
47 meal, which is known in advance.
48 Effectively, diners buying tickets are pre-
49 paying for their meal, and thus they are
50 highly incentivized to show up at the
51 appointed ticket time. In this way customers
52 are not charged more than the cost of their
53 meal and restaurants will not lose money in
54 the event of a no-show.

Persuasive – Passage 2 Question Set

1. The primary purpose of the passage is to

   (A) discuss the history of dining reservations.
   (B) advocate for a particular remedy to the problem of no-shows.
   (C) provide specific examples where no-shows have hurt restaurants.
   (D) impartially compare and contrast different solutions to a problem.

2. In line 2, the author most likely uses the word "plagued" in order to

   (A) support his opinion about no-shows.
   (B) minimize the impact of no-shows on restaurants.
   (C) emphasize the frequency and magnitude of no-shows.
   (D) contrast no-show diners with diners who show up for their meals.

3. In line 26, "contentious" most nearly means

   (A) bland.
   (B) controversial.
   (C) satisfied.
   (D) tame.

4. In the final paragraph, lines 41-54, the author gives which of the following as a reason why pre-paying for meals might be a "happy middle ground"?

   (A) No-shows will be completely eradicated.
   (B) Restaurants will see fewer customers making reservations.
   (C) Customers will be happy to pay for their meals months in advance.
   (D) Diners are motivated to honor their reservation without being charged extra fees.

5. The author of the passage mentions all of the following as a possible solution to the problem of no-shows EXCEPT

   (A) selling reservations.
   (B) allowing tables to sit empty.
   (C) requiring diners to pre-pay for a meal.
   (D) requiring a credit card in order to hold a reservation.

6. The author of the passage appears to care most deeply about the fact that

   (A) hospitality is a dying art.
   (B) fees and penalties are unfair to diners.
   (C) disincentives are more powerful and influential than incentives.
   (D) eliminating no-shows should be fair to both diners and restaurants.

Persuasive – Passage 3

1 Trees are an invaluable part of our
2 ecosystem. They provide a host of benefits
3 that we are only beginning to understand.
4 Have you ever walked, hiked, or
5 exercised in the blazing summer sun? Well,
6 if you exercised in the shade, you'd feel
7 between 10 and 15 degrees cooler. That's
8 because trees absorb sunlight and solar
9 radiation, and use them as energy to grow.
10 Thus, trees are essential in helping to
11 regulate temperatures, both for the planet, as
12 well as for animals like us who are trying to
13 find respite from the heat. According to the
14 USDA Forest Service, trees that are properly
15 placed around buildings can reduce air
16 conditioning needs by 30%, and save
17 between 20-50% in energy used for climate
18 control.
19 Another way that trees benefit our
20 environment, besides the absorption of solar
21 energy, is the absorption of carbon.
22 Specifically, trees absorb carbon dioxide
23 from the atmosphere and use it as an
24 ingredient in their cellular processes. This is
25 helpful to the environment, because carbon
26 dioxide, a powerful greenhouse gas, can trap
27 solar radiation in our atmosphere, thereby
28 causing the average temperature on Earth to
29 rise. Estimates suggest that a single tree can
30 capture between 18 and 50 pounds of carbon
31 dioxide per year! And trees do more than
32 just provide us with a beautiful, inexpensive
33 way to absorb carbon. In the process of
34 converting carbon dioxide into energy, trees
35 release oxygen into the atmosphere. Thus,
36 together with other plants and
37 photosynthetic organisms, trees provide us
38 with the very air that we breathe!
39 In addition to removing excess carbon
40 from the atmosphere, adding oxygen to the
41 air, and keeping things shady and cool, trees

42 also help fight soil erosion. Deep roots
43 absorb and store water, thereby holding soil
44 together and helping to prevent landslides or
45 the washing away of soil in the rain.
46 Furthermore, trees help to block wind,
47 which prevents the wind from whipping up
48 dust and removing fertile topsoil. And every
49 Autumn in temperate climate zones, colorful
50 fallen leaves decompose into minerals and
51 nutrients that enrich the soil.
52 Trees are also important to our physical
53 health. Many trees bear fruit that are fit for
54 human consumption, and even those that do
55 not are important to insects and animals that
56 are critical to the success of our crops. Not
57 only do trees produce things that are good to
58 eat, but they have contributed in our fight
59 against illnesses and cancers as well. For
60 example, an asthma drug has been derived
61 from a certain tree in the Amazon rain
62 forest, and an anti-cancer drug has been
63 derived from a tree found in the Pacific
64 Northwest.
65 The value people receive from trees
66 comes not only in the form of foods,
67 medicines, shade, and oxygen. Many people
68 derive spiritual or other personal value from
69 trees. Trees, being majestic in size and
70 diverse in shape and color, are aesthetically
71 pleasing. People have also planted trees as
72 monuments to life-changing events – living
73 monuments that grow with the people they
74 commemorate. The personal, spiritual, and
75 aesthetic value of trees is not only
76 intangible, but can also help increase the
77 economic value of a home or property.
78 So the next time you want to cut down a
79 tree, think twice. If the tree needs to be cut
80 down, consider planting a new one – or
81 better yet, plant a new tree anyway!

Persuasive – Passage 3 Question Set

1. Which best expresses the main idea of the passage?

   (A) Trees absorb carbon and sunlight.
   (B) Trees are useful for their beauty and spiritual value.
   (C) Trees are a vital part of our ecosystem and provide many benefits to people.
   (D) Though trees are important and beneficial, other plants are just as important and helpful.

2. In line 13, "respite" most nearly means

   (A) hatred.
   (B) resolve.
   (C) shelter.
   (D) spirit.

3. In lines 4-18, the author cites facts and statistics about temperature differences in order to

   (A) shock the reader.
   (B) build credibility for his argument.
   (C) explain why trees should never be cut down.
   (D) emphasize the importance of the USDA Forest Service.

4. The author of the passage does all of the following in lines 19-38 EXCEPT

   (A) document general biological processes.
   (B) explain the impact of rising temperatures.
   (C) provide details and specific examples to support an opinion.
   (D) explain how trees contribute to the overall health of the atmosphere.

5. According to lines 39-51, trees help fight soil erosion

   (A) by converting fallen leaves into new soil.
   (B) through the washing away of soil in the rain.
   (C) by blocking wind that can turn topsoil into dust.
   (D) by absorbing sunlight that can dry and weaken the soil.

6. The author would most likely support which of the following statements?

   (A) It is unnecessary to harvest timber sustainably.
   (B) There are no further medical benefits to be derived from trees.
   (C) The passage describes an exhaustive list of all benefits provided by trees.
   (D) Trees likely provide many more benefits to people than are described in the passage.

The Tutorverse
www.thetutorverse.com

Persuasive – Passage 4

1 Of all the different forms of land-based
2 aerobic exercise, race-walking is
3 undoubtedly the most efficient. Because of
4 its positive impact on the circulatory,
5 respiratory, and muscular systems, many
6 people choose to engage in regular race-
7 walking. In addition, race-walkers tend to
8 suffer fewer injuries than their running or
9 cycling peers. These benefits cause many
10 within the fitness world to extol race-
11 walking's virtues.
12 Many experts consider one's resting
13 heart rate to be an indicator of
14 cardiovascular health, and believe that the
15 lower one's resting heart rate, the healthier
16 the cardiovascular system. One study
17 showed that those who regularly engaged in
18 race-walking have resting heart rates as low
19 as the heart rates of those who regularly
20 engaged in cycling or running. Still other
21 studies have shown that those who race-
22 walk have lung capacities as efficient as
23 those of their cycling or running
24 counterparts. This was measured based on
25 the amount of oxygen and carbon dioxide
26 exchanged in each breath.
27 At the right intensity and pace, race-
28 walking also strengthens and defines many
29 muscles throughout the body. As in running
30 and cycling, race-walking engages the
31 calves, quads, hamstrings, and glutes. Like
32 running, proper race-walking posture
33 engages the abdominal muscles, helping to
34 improve core strength and definition.
35 Compared with other forms of exercise,
36 race-walking is relatively low impact,
37 resulting in fewer injuries and longer-lasting
38 participation. Unlike running or cycling,
39 where one's joints can suffer from repeated
40 pounding and strain, proper race-walking
41 form dictates that one's heel always be in
42 contact with the ground. This has the effect
43 of limiting one's stride and preventing undue
44 strain on the knees and other joints.
45 Common ailments that afflict runners and
46 cyclists, such as tendonitis, shin splints, and
47 sprains, can be avoided by observing proper
48 race-walking form and technique. Over the
49 long term, race-walking may even help to
50 stave off arthritis and joint degradation. As
51 a result, people who race-walk are less prone
52 to exercise related injuries and are more
53 likely to continue exercising as they grow
54 older. Many experts cite ongoing and
55 regular exercise as integral to maintaining
56 one's overall health.

Persuasive – Passage 4 Question Set

1. The primary purpose of the passage is to

   (A) describe race-walking technique and form.
   (B) malign other forms of land-based aerobic exercise.
   (C) deter readers from engaging in running or cycling.
   (D) educate the reader about the many benefits of race-walking.

2. In line 10, "extol" most nearly means

   (A) detract.
   (B) promote.
   (C) retract.
   (D) suppress.

3. Which conclusion can best be drawn from the study summarized in the second paragraph (lines 12-26)?

   (A) High resting heart rates are a sign of good physical fitness.
   (B) Race-walking is better for the lungs than cycling and running.
   (C) Cardiovascular health is the best indicator of physical fitness.
   (D) Race-walking is likely as good for the cardiovascular system as running and cycling.

4. The author of the passage suggests that in order to engage the abdominal muscles in a fashion similar to running and cycling (lines 27-34), one must

   (A) walk as quickly as possible.
   (B) prioritize intensity over form.
   (C) ensure proper posture and pacing.
   (D) actively utilize all muscles in the leg.

5. The author's tone when discussing different exercise related injuries (lines 38-48) is best described as

   (A) apologetic.
   (B) blithe.
   (C) critical.
   (D) professional.

6. Which best describes the organization of the last paragraph (lines 35-56)?

   (A) The author supports her opinion with facts.
   (B) The author compares the relative danger of different types of injuries.
   (C) The author explains different types of exercise related injuries in detail.
   (D) The author describes the chronological relationship between injury, exercise, and health.

Persuasive – Passage 5

1   The designation of national parks and
2 protected wilderness areas is one of the
3 greatest accomplishments of governments
4 around the world. Governments and their
5 constituents recognize the importance of
6 setting aside land for recreational enjoyment
7 and preservation. Often running contrary to
8 the interests of industry and commerce, the
9 legislation and mandates that protect some
10 of the world's most beautiful and often
11 fragile ecosystems are proof that profit and
12 monetary gain need not require the
13 wholesale destruction and exploitation of
14 natural resources. In fact, the preservation
15 and maintenance of unique environments
16 can lead to their own economic benefits.
17   Yellowstone National Park in the United
18 States was established in 1872 as the
19 world's first national park. Ferdinand
20 Hayden, explorer and conservationist, is
21 widely credited with helping to convince the
22 United States Congress to withdraw the
23 region from public auction, stating that
24 instead the country should "set aside the
25 area as a pleasure ground for the benefit and
26 enjoyment of the people." He warned that
27 otherwise, people would "make merchandise
28 of these beautiful specimens," citing the
29 commercialization of Niagara Falls as an
30 example. Hayden went on to say that
31 "vandals who are now waiting to enter into
32 this wonder-land, will in a single season
33 despoil, beyond recovery, these remarkable
34 curiosities, which have required all the
35 cunning skill of nature thousands of years to
36 prepare."

37   Though many countries already afforded
38 certain areas national protection and reserve
39 status, the widespread classification of
40 national parks in other countries did not
41 flourish until after the creation of
42 Yellowstone. Royal National Park was
43 established in Australia in 1879; Rocky
44 Mountain National Park was established in
45 Canada in 1885. The first national parks in
46 Europe were established in Sweden in 1909,
47 followed by the Albert National Park in the
48 Congo in 1925.
49   At the time, many contemporaries of
50 conservationists and preservationists
51 bemoaned the loss of economic opportunity.
52 But while, in the short-term, industry lost
53 the ability to capitalize on natural resources
54 such as timber and various minerals, it
55 gained a long-term opportunity in the form
56 of profitable and sustainable eco-tourism.
57 Today, domestic and international tourists
58 flock to national parks around the world,
59 increasing tourism and encouraging
60 sustainable development and investment.
61 Countries such as Costa Rica have seen,
62 over the past two decades, a pronounced
63 increase in their tourism rates.
64   Surviving two world wars and countless
65 other threats, national parks are a treasure
66 for all humanity, worthy of preservation for
67 future generations. Natural wonders are so
68 easily destroyed, yet take so long to develop.
69 It would be a shame to see works of nature
70 destroyed forever for the sake of short-term
71 profit.

Persuasive – Passage 5 Question Set

1. The passage is primarily concerned with

    (A) explaining the cultural importance of
         Yellowstone National Park.
    (B) convincing the reader to travel to
         national parks in Costa Rica.
    (C) comparing national parks in the United
         States to national parks elsewhere.
    (D) convincing the reader of the economic
         and environmental benefits of national
         parks.

2. The author of the passage quotes Ferdinand
    Hayden in the second paragraph (lines 17-
    36) in order to

    (A) provide a brief history of Yellowstone
         National Park.
    (B) illustrate the principles behind
         environmental conservation.
    (C) highlight the specific circumstances
         leading to the commercialization of
         Niagara Falls.
    (D) ridicule those who would seek to
         exploit natural wonders for monetary
         gain.

3. The author suggests that the proliferation of
    national parks has facilitated economic
    growth (lines 49-63) because

    (A) national parks are an inexpensive
         vacation.
    (B) the national parks have been privatized
         and are controlled by corporations.
    (C) people have been spending increasing
         amounts of money on environmental
         tourism.
    (D) the national parks have restricted
         access to timber and other natural
         resources.

4. In line 51, "bemoaned" most nearly means

    (A) capered.
    (B) devastated.
    (C) inspired.
    (D) lamented.

5. Which conclusion can best be drawn from
    the fact that Costa Rica has seen an increase
    in tourism rates due to its national parks
    (lines 61-63)?

    (A) Tourism in Costa Rica will detract
         from tourism in other places.
    (B) Countries will lose economic
         opportunity by designating national
         parks.
    (C) Other countries that invest in national
         parks can also attract tourists.
    (D) Costa Rica would have made more
         money by selling timber and other
         natural resources.

6. In order to show that environmental
    preservation and monetary gain are not
    mutually exclusive, the author

    (A) makes unsubstantiated claims and
         judgments.
    (B) advocates for short-term solutions over
         long-term thinking.
    (C) describes in detail the many different
         national parks throughout the world.
    (D) provides a specific example where
         environmental protection has led to
         monetary gain.

Persuasive – Passage 6

1   Crop diversity is important to the
2   security and stability of our food supply.
3   We should not allow the convenience and
4   affordability of "monoculture" – the
5   cultivating of a single crop only – to blind us
6   to the costly and dangerous consequences of
7   relying too greatly upon any one single plant
8   for food. In fact, there are many historical
9   disasters that have shown us that
10 monoculture is not only risky but potentially
11 disastrous. One of the most well-known
12 disasters due to monoculture was the Irish
13 Potato Famine of the mid-nineteenth
14 century.
15   During the seventeenth and eighteenth
16 centuries, Irish Catholics were prevented
17 from owning land, voting, holding office,
18 getting an education, gaining any kind of
19 professional employment, and living near
20 large towns or cities. These stringent laws,
21 enacted by the ruling British powers, helped
22 mire the Irish in poverty for several
23 generations. The Irish had no power over
24 their circumstances; they were forced to
25 work for British absentee landlords, paying
26 rents by working the fields and subsisting on
27 what little crop they had time to cultivate on
28 their own. By the mid-nineteenth century, a
29 census conducted by the British government
30 found that poverty was rampant in Ireland:
31 one-third of all Irish worked parcels of land
32 so small that they could not support their
33 families after paying rent to their landlords.
34 At the time, two-thirds of the eight million
35 Irish were dependent on agriculture for
36 survival, even though they were not given
37 enough land to do so. Given the paucity of
38 land, the only crop that could be grown in
39 sufficient quantities was the Irish Lumper
40 potato.
41   Lumper potatoes were not only used as
42 food for the people, but were used also as
43 feed for livestock. And yet the crop had
44 already begun to fail in the years leading up

45 to the Great Famine due to frost and pre-
46 existing diseases such as dry rot and curl.
47   A few months after its arrival in Europe,
48 the blight spread to Ireland. In 1845, one-
49 third to one-half of all potato crops had
50 succumbed to the disease. A year later, in
51 1846, the disease had destroyed three-
52 quarters of the crop. For the next several
53 years, potato crop yields shrank to a mere
54 fraction of what they had been. Famine and
55 starvation set in, resulting in the deaths of
56 hundreds of thousands of people. Many
57 hundreds of thousands more left the country.
58   American society today has not been
59 forced into monoculture for social and
60 political reasons, as the Irish were. Instead,
61 Americans willingly accept monoculture as
62 a matter of economic convenience and
63 preference. In order to facilitate the mass
64 production of food, we have come to accept
65 the risk inherent in the cultivation of a single
66 plant crop. This is because the mass
67 production of our crops allows for lower
68 prices. In general, Americans appear willing
69 to trade taste, variety, and food security for
70 lower prices.
71   In 1844, Irish newspapers reported on
72 troubling diseases that, for two years, had
73 attacked potato crops in America. Then in
74 1845, the Gardeners' Chronicle and
75 Horticultural Gazette reported on a strange
76 new potato blight. Though the British
77 government found the reports troubling, they
78 ultimately disregarded them, choosing to
79 believe instead that the reports were
80 exaggerated and written by alarmists.
81 Today, Americans face a similar issue here.
82 Our wheat crop – both a domestic and global
83 staple of the entire food chain – is threatened
84 by a disease called stem rust.
85   Will we let history repeat itself? Or will
86 we be proactive in combating this, as well as
87 all future threats, caused by the myopic
88 practice of monoculture?

Persuasive – Passage 6 Question Set

1. The passage is primarily concerned with

    (A) describing the Irish Lumper potato.
    (B) comparing and contrasting different potato diseases.
    (C) providing a historical account of the Great Famine.
    (D) warning the reader about the dangers of monoculture.

2. According to lines 15-40, all of the following were reasons why the Irish came to depend so heavily on the Lumper potato EXCEPT

    (A) the Irish preferred the taste of the Lumper potato.
    (B) other food farmed by the Irish was sold to pay rent to the British.
    (C) the Lumper potato was the only crop that could be grown sufficiently on a small plot of land.
    (D) the Irish were excluded from professional employment and had no choice but to farm for their food.

3. In line 37, "paucity" most nearly means

    (A) abundance.
    (B) arability.
    (C) fertility.
    (D) scarcity.

4. Which does the author of the passage mention as a reason that the potato blight had such a devastating impact on the Irish?

    (A) Too many potatoes were being used to feed livestock.
    (B) Poor sanitation and hygiene helped to spread the disease.
    (C) The British had inadvertently brought the blight over from America.
    (D) The potato disease targeted the crop that the Irish had come to rely on almost exclusively.

5. In lines 58-84, the author compares monoculture in modern-day America to nineteenth century Ireland in order to

    (A) describe how wheat is different from potatoes.
    (B) convince the reader to accept convenient and inexpensive monoculture.
    (C) illustrate that monoculture could once again pose a grave threat to American welfare.
    (D) highlight that there are no similarities between monoculture today and two hundred years ago.

6. In the final paragraph, lines 85-88, the author uses questions in order to

    (A) contradict opposing points of view.
    (B) understate the risks associated with monoculture.
    (C) call into question the effectiveness of monoculture.
    (D) challenge the reader to oppose a shortsighted practice.

Persuasive – Passage 7

1   Conventional wisdom suggests that
2   consumers consider many different
3   dimensions of a good or service when
4   making a purchase. Such dimensions
5   include, but are not limited to, a
6   commodity's function, quality, appearance,
7   and price. However, not all consumers are
8   the same, and different consumers place
9   different emphases on different factors. For
10 example, some consumers may be more
11 sensitive to price, while others may be more
12 sensitive to quality. There is, for most
13 people, a trade-off between the many
14 different dimensions associated with a
15 purchase. Some goods and services of
16 inferior quality are offered at lower prices
17 than similar goods and services of higher
18 quality. In the end, however, consumers
19 ultimately act with their wallets, paying
20 higher prices for goods and services they
21 believe are worth the premium, and lower
22 prices (or not at all) for those they believe
23 are not.
24   One subset of consumers values low
25 prices above all else. These consumers
26 often frequent multi-national retailers and
27 wholesalers that provide goods and services
28 at prices lower than their competitors. The
29 success of large-scale retailers and
30 wholesalers has coincided with a decrease in
31 the number of small-scale businesses. In
32 many towns, small businesses are unable to
33 compete with large-scale operations offering
34 similar goods and services. Because large
35 businesses are able to buy their supplies and
36 inventory in bulk, they are able to pay a
37 lower cost per unit of the good. Small
38 businesses aren't able to buy their supplies
39 and inventory in such large quantities, and
40 are therefore unable to pass these savings
41 onto consumers. Large businesses rely on
42 volume to generate profit, whereas small
43 businesses rely less on volume and more on
44 price. Thus, small businesses often have to
45 charge more than large businesses for the
46 very same goods, and in time, consumers
47 seeking the lowest possible price will take
48 their business to the conglomerates, thereby
49 pushing small businesses out of business.
50   Some say that small businesses need to
51 get creative in order to survive – that they
52 should not even try to compete with large
53 businesses based on price. Instead, they
54 should think about the different dimensions
55 associated with the good or service they are
56 selling and try to differentiate themselves in
57 some way from the large businesses. For
58 example, smaller businesses might get to
59 learn the names and shopping patterns of
60 their customers, making the shopping
61 experience more enjoyable than at a
62 competing larger business. Another
63 example might be to carry exclusive goods
64 or services that are not sold by their larger
65 competitors.
66   Many people who lament the decline in
67 the number of small businesses often point
68 their finger at the major corporations for
69 pricing small businesses out of the market.
70 Instead, they should think about how their
71 own shopping habits and preferences have
72 contributed to the prevalence of large-scale
73 businesses and the decline of small-scale
74 businesses. In our quest to find the best
75 deal, perhaps we have as a society placed
76 too much emphasis on low prices and not
77 given enough attention to the less tangible
78 qualities of shopping – things like
79 experience, friendliness, and community.
80 The question is: are these qualities worth the
81 price?

Persuasive – Passage 7 Question Set

1. The passage is primarily concerned with

    (A) questioning the practices of large
         businesses.
    (B) explaining different consumer
         preferences and values.
    (C) passing judgment on those consumers
         who value low prices.
    (D) educating consumers about how their
         preferences influence shopping
         experiences.

2. Because suppliers give price discounts for
    buying in large quantities, which of the
    following is true according to the second
    paragraph (lines 24-49)?

    (A) Large businesses never pass price
         discounts onto consumers.
    (B) Small businesses have as much ability
         to purchase in bulk as do large
         businesses.
    (C) Large businesses are at a price
         disadvantage since their supplies are
         more expensive.
    (D) Small businesses that are unable to buy
         in bulk cannot pass price discounts to
         consumers.

3. In line 42, "volume" most nearly means

    (A) applaud.
    (B) decibels.
    (C) quantity.
    (D) sound.

4. According to lines 57-65, we can infer that

    (A) the most important factor for
         consumers is price.
    (B) offering lower prices is the only way
         that large businesses are able to
         compete with small businesses.
    (C) there are no successful small
         businesses because large businesses
         have already crushed their competition.
    (D) there are successful small businesses
         because they appeal to consumers who
         have preferences other than low prices.

5. The author does which of the following in
    lines 57-65?

    (A) Compares the profitability of small
         businesses to large ones.
    (B) Argues that all businesses need to
         make shopping more enjoyable.
    (C) Gives examples of different strategies
         small businesses can use to be
         competitive.
    (D) Hypothesizes that privacy concerns
         will prevent small businesses from
         becoming competitive.

6. The purpose of the final paragraph (lines 66-
    81) is to

    (A) request that consumers boycott large
         businesses.
    (B) suggest that the reader rethink his own
         shopping preferences.
    (C) complain about the consumer's
         inability to make a difference.
    (D) ridicule consumers who blame big
         companies for putting small companies
         out of business.

Persuasive – Passage 8

1   Like many other people who grew up in
2 suburban America during the past century,
3 my childhood home had a grass lawn in both
4 the front and back yards. Many of my
5 fondest and most cherished memories
6 involve those lawns: picnicking with family
7 on the soft grass, under an oak tree; playing
8 tag with friends until dusk, arms and legs
9 stained green; knocking up clumps of grass
10 as I learned how to kick a soccer ball or
11 swing a golf club; the pungent, herbal smell
12 of freshly cut grass.
13   Given all of these pleasant memories,
14 and knowing how important grass lawns are
15 in American culture, I was dismayed to learn
16 that grass lawns have a particularly
17 deleterious impact on the environment.
18   Think about everything it takes to
19 cultivate and maintain a luscious green
20 lawn: seeds, fertilizers, herbicides,
21 pesticides, water, lawn mowers, waste
22 removal, and time. According to some
23 estimates, approximately 25 million acres of
24 land in the United States are devoted to
25 grass lawns, and an incredible 50-70% of all
26 residential water consumption is intended to
27 keep our lawns green. Recently, the
28 Environmental Protection Agency (EPA)
29 has estimated that as many as 70 million
30 pounds of pesticides are used each year to
31 keep our lawns insect-free. And in order to
32 keep grass at an aesthetically pleasing
33 height, the average American spends 40
34 hours a year mowing the lawn. According
35 to the EPA, gas mowers represent
36 approximately 5% of air pollution in the
37 United States.

38   In my mind, the real question is: why
39 does a lawn have to be a certain way, and if
40 it does, is this ideal worth all the time and
41 resources that we spend trying to achieve it?
42 Rather than fighting nature with herbicides,
43 maybe we should tolerate other types of
44 plant life on our lawns, such as clover,
45 dandelion, and other plants typically deemed
46 to be weeds. Rather than draining whole
47 rivers dry to irrigate our lawns in naturally
48 arid or drought-prone areas, maybe we
49 should think about other ways to landscape
50 our properties in places where grass doesn't
51 thrive naturally. Rather than mindlessly
52 doing what we have always done for our
53 lawns, maybe we should think about less
54 harmful, less expensive ways to care for our
55 lawns – ways that don't harm other parts of
56 our ecosystem or use quite as many of our
57 finite resources.
58   I love the look and feel and smell of
59 grass lawns as much as the next person, and
60 I certainly do not advocate that we should
61 ban or outlaw grass lawns. I understand that
62 over time, we as a nation have accepted the
63 idea that a home must have a yard, and that
64 a yard must have a perfectly manicured
65 grass lawn. And while this may be right for
66 some people, it might not be right for
67 everyone. I just think we should spend
68 some time thinking about the consequences
69 of our actions rather than just doing what
70 everyone else is doing. We might have
71 more time to enjoy nature if we spent less
72 time trying to fight it.

Persuasive – Passage 8 Question Set

1. The primary purpose of the passage is to

    (A) relate pleasant memories involving grass lawns.
    (B) describe alternative landscaping philosophies.
    (C) take a dogmatic stance against the environmental impact of grass lawns.
    (D) persuade the reader to think more deeply about the hidden costs of grass lawns.

2. The mood of the first paragraph (lines 1-12) can best be described as

    (A) apathetic.
    (B) critical.
    (C) nostalgic.
    (D) regretful.

3. In line 17, "deleterious" most nearly means

    (A) beneficial.
    (B) effective.
    (C) harmful.
    (D) important.

4. In lines 18-37, the author of the passage mentions all of the following as reasons why maintaining lawns is wasteful EXCEPT

    (A) that maintenance wastes water.
    (B) that lawns are aesthetically pleasing.
    (C) that lawn mowers contribute to air pollution.
    (D) that time caring for lawns could be better spent doing something else.

5. The author of the passage does all of the following in lines 38-57 EXCEPT

    (A) provide alternatives to grass lawns.
    (B) challenge norms and conventional thinking.
    (C) encourage independent thought and decision making.
    (D) convince the reader to continue spending time maintaining lawns.

6. In the final paragraph, lines 58-72, the author of the passage implies that

    (A) it is important to observe and keep all traditions.
    (B) grass lawns should be declared illegal by the government.
    (C) society would be better off if fewer people cultivated grass lawns.
    (D) it is our duty to fight with nature and to control it in every way possible.

Descriptive Passages

Directions: Answer the questions following each passage on the basis of what is stated or implied in that passage.

Descriptive – Passage 1

1   The engine growled as I pushed the gas
2   pedal down further, my foot almost flat
3   against the floor of my roadster. The wind
4   roared even more loudly, drowning out
5   whatever music was pouring out of the
6   speakers. Through the windshield, I
7   watched as the asphalt disappeared under the
8   hood of my car, devoured by my speed.
9   To my left was nothing but parched red
10 dirt and brittle bushes. To my right was
11 more of the same nothingness. But before
12 me – ah, before me was something worth
13 seeing!
14   The horizon had been as flat as
15 everything else around me. I had been
16 surrounded by flatness so absolute that I
17 thought I could see the curvature of the earth
18 itself. As far as I could tell, there was
19 nothing around me but the same shrubs and
20 the same dirt that I had seen for the last
21 several hours. Eventually though, I saw
22 something just above the horizon. At first,
23 the single object appeared no larger than a

24 car, somewhere off in the distance. As I
25 hurtled across the desert at over eighty miles
26 per hour, however, I found myself looking at
27 a number of objects of different shapes and
28 sizes.
29   Beckoning me were magnificent pillars
30 of stratified rock and stone. Proud and
31 imposing, the mesas stood like sentinels,
32 guarding the path to some forgotten
33 kingdom. Having withstood millennia of
34 wind and rain, the mesas seemed to hold up
35 the sky itself with their indomitable strength.
36 After hundreds of miles of nothingness, the
37 sublime vision before me was
38 overwhelming, filling me with a deep
39 yearning and excitement.
40   The mesas grew steadily as I sped
41 toward them. In no time at all, I found
42 myself surrounded by the colossi, so tall and
43 so wide that they blotted out the sun.
44   With a whoop, I realized I had finally
45 made it to the land of giants.

Descriptive – Passage 1 Question Set

[handwritten: analizing author]

1. Which best expresses the main idea of the passage? *[handwritten: shrek?]*

   (A) The author recalls meeting ogres.
   (B) The author explains why he is driving through the desert.
   (C) The author compares his desert drive with his experiences in the city.
   (D) The author recounts a first-hand experience of driving through the desert.

2. In the first paragraph (lines 1-13), the author uses words such as "growled", "roared" and "devoured" in order to *[handwritten: authors resoning]*

   (A) describe his vitality.
   (B) liken his car to an animal.
   (C) exaggerate the importance of his roadster.
   (D) describe the primal and visceral experience of speed.

3. According to lines 14-18, the author claims to have seen the curvature of the earth because *[handwritten: fact]*

   (A) of his unobstructed and expansive view.
   (B) he was travelling at such a great speed.
   (C) the heat of the desert created a mirage.
   (D) changes in elevation created the illusion of roundness.

4. The author includes the sentences "Eventually . . . sizes" (lines 21-28) in order to

   (A) build tension and excitement.
   (B) express a feeling of contentedness.
   (C) clarify what the objects in the distance were.
   (D) explain how the objects in the distance were probably just more cars.

5. In line 37, "sublime" most nearly means *[handwritten: vocab]*

   (A) magnanimous.
   (B) magnificent.
   (C) sour.
   (D) subtle.

6. Based on the final sentence (lines 44-45), we can infer that the author's trip was *[handwritten: Infrence]*

   (A) unintentional; he had gotten lost.
   (B) deliberate; he wanted to see the mesas.
   (C) impulsive; he drove without a destination in mind
   (D) preordained; he had agreed to meet a friend in the desert.

Descriptive – Passage 2

1 The row of buttons was an artifact of the
2 past, but Anne still enjoyed pressing them
3 and watching them light up. Nowadays,
4 many elevator manufacturers were making
5 digital displays that prompted riders to input
6 a combination of numbers to determine their
7 floor destination. Maybe it was more
8 efficient, but she didn't care. Anne liked the
9 feeling of pressing an analog button.
10 The button, cool to the touch and
11 dimpled at its center where the light bulb
12 shone, was the center of the action. These
13 buttons were made of stainless steel. When
14 pressed, the buttons would yield a few
15 millimeters and then stop, though it
16 sometimes felt to Anne as if they should
17 yield a few millimeters more. There was
18 something satisfying about pressing the
19 button and feeling it push back – something
20 tactile that she didn't experience when using
21 her smartphone or other digital touchscreen
22 displays.
23 Next to the buttons were little plaques
24 honoring each button's place upon the board:
25 upon each plaque was inscribed a number
26 that indicated a particular floor of the
27 building. Beneath each of the numerals were
28 intricately patterned dots – Braille, used by
29 the seeing impaired. While Anne herself had
30 no problems seeing, she still liked to run her
31 fingertips over the Braille, silently
32 wondering how the small dots translated into
33 numbers.
34 One of the things Anne enjoyed most,
35 however, had nothing to do with the look
36 and feel of the buttons, nor with their
37 accompanying plaques. To her, the best
38 thing was watching someone join her in the
39 elevator, only to press a button that would
40 simply refuse to light up. She'd watch as the
41 person would press the button again and
42 again, each time hoping in vain that the
43 button might glow. For some riders, it only
44 took a few presses before they would realize
45 that the bulb was broken, and the light
46 wasn't coming on. Others would never stop
47 pressing the button until the elevator reached
48 their floor. Only then, with embarrassment,
49 would they realize that the first press had
50 done the trick all along.

Descriptive – Passage 2 Question Set

1. The passage is primarily concerned with

   (A) detailing the reasons why Anne likes riding elevators.
   (B) understanding why Anne prefers analog to digital displays.
   (C) weighing the advantages and disadvantages of digital elevator displays.
   (D) rationalizing the actions of passengers who repeatedly press broken buttons.

2. The author does all of the following in the second paragraph (lines 10-22) EXCEPT

   (A) explain how the buttons feel.
   (B) explain how the buttons look.
   (C) explain why Anne likes pressing the buttons.
   (D) explain that Anne does not enjoy using her smartphone.

3. In line 20, "tactile" most nearly means

   (A) flexible.
   (B) imaginary.
   (C) physical.
   (D) polite.

4. By using the words "plaques," "honoring," and "inscribed" in lines 23-25, the author

   (A) emphasizes the importance of the buttons to Anne.
   (B) suggests that the buttons are similar to a scoreboard.
   (C) admits that Anne has written numbers on each of the buttons.
   (D) leaves the layout of the buttons to the reader's imagination.

5. According to lines 29-33, Anne enjoys touching the Braille lettering because

   (A) she is bored.
   (B) she is able to translate the Braille.
   (C) she sympathizes with her friend, who is seeing impaired.
   (D) she likes to marvel at the notion that people can interpret the arrangement of bumps.

6. It can be inferred from the final paragraph (lines 34-50) that a normal working button is supposed to

   (A) ring when pressed.
   (B) light up when pressed.
   (C) vibrate when pressed.
   (D) do nothing when pressed.

Descriptive – Passage 3

1   Almost 300 feet long and over 100 feet
2 wide, the Main Concourse of Grand Central
3 Station in New York City is both
4 architecturally and aesthetically impressive.
5 Serving as a major transportation hub, a
6 marketplace, a meeting place, a dining
7 venue, and even a gym, Grand Central is a
8 wonder of design and engineering – a
9 perfect meeting of form and function.
10 Steeped in history, the station is home to
11 some of America's most famous heirlooms;
12 the four-faced clock standing at the heart of
13 the Main Concourse; the vaulted ceilings of
14 the whispering gallery; the original
15 mechanical flap-board destination sign. In
16 the rush to get from one part of the station to
17 another, it's possible to miss one of the most
18 beautiful features of the station: the ceiling
19 of the Main Concourse.
20   The ceiling soars over a hundred feet
21 above the heads of thousands upon
22 thousands of travelers. The ceiling itself is a
23 major tourist attraction. Painted in a
24 turquoise blue-green, the ceiling depicts
25 constellations visible from October through
26 March, which are rendered in gold paint and
27 leaf. The constellations are comprised of
28 almost 2,500 stars. Two golden arches

29 stretch from east to west, and represent the
30 earth's orbit around the sun as well as the
31 earth's equator. Even the Milky Way is
32 visible as a cloud of tiny stars, from the
33 southwest to northeast corners of the ceiling.
34   Though great care was taken during the
35 planning and creation of the ceiling, a
36 mistake was nonetheless made in the
37 rendering of the constellations. Though the
38 correct constellations are depicted, the
39 orientation and placement of several patterns
40 are inconsistent with what we see in the
41 actual night sky. All of the stars on the
42 ceiling are rendered as they would appear
43 from Earth, except for Taurus and
44 Gemini. These constellations are reversed
45 and are depicted as they would be seen
46 looking down at Earth from above. Though
47 Gemini should be near Orion's elevated
48 arm, the ceiling of the concourse displays
49 Taurus in this position. The most likely
50 explanation is that a transcription error
51 occurred when transposing an astronomical
52 sketch onto the ceiling. Despite the
53 inconsistency in its design, the ceiling is
54 nonetheless a beautiful and impressive work
55 of art.

Descriptive – Passage 3 Question Set

1. The passage is primarily concerned with

    (A) describing a ceiling.
    (B) the science of astronomy.
    (C) the history of Grand Central Station.
    (D) the many and varied design features of a train station.

2. The phrase "meeting of form and function" (line 9) is included in order to

    (A) echo the words of a great poet.
    (B) emphasize that Grand Central is both practical and beautiful.
    (C) explain why appearances are less important than functionality.
    (D) support the idea that Grand Central is primarily useful as a train station.

3. In line 10, "steeped in" most nearly means

    (A) filled with.
    (B) lacking in.
    (C) missing from.
    (D) overwhelmed by.

4. According to the last paragraph (lines 34-55), which of the following likely caused some of the constellations to be reversed?

    (A) human error
    (B) water damage
    (C) deliberate design
    (D) a rare astronomical occurrence

5. The author implies that the ceiling of the Main Concourse is beautiful because of all of the following EXCEPT

    (A) the color of the ceiling.
    (B) the size and scale of the ceiling.
    (C) the original flap-board destination sign.
    (D) the depiction of stars and constellations.

6. According to the passage, it can be inferred that the author

    (A) thinks the ceiling is gaudy.
    (B) likes to stop and admire the ceiling.
    (C) thinks the mistake in the ceiling should be fixed.
    (D) is irritated by commuters running around the concourse.

Descriptive – Passage 4

1   The beach town had been decimated in
2 the wake of the once-in-a-lifetime
3 hurricane. The historic boardwalk
4 esplanade, home to classic rides, games of
5 chance, and snack stands had been washed
6 out to sea. The hurricane left in its wake a
7 trail of debris and devastation, washing
8 away not only the physical presence of the
9 boardwalk, but also its intangible presence –
10 all of its memories of happiness on warm
11 summer nights. When the hurricane hit, an
12 entire era was suddenly gone, never to be
13 replicated.
14   What little remained was strewn across
15 the beach and in the water. It was as if an
16 angry child had ripped apart his room and
17 left the pieces lying about. A hundred yards
18 out to sea rested the remnants of the
19 boardwalk's roller coaster; its apex, twisted
20 and gnarled, grew silently out of the waves.
21   Wooden horses and unicorns from the
22 carousel reared up from the sea floor to gaze
23 dolefully up at the sky above, all while
24 sinking further each day, down into their
25 sandy graves. Waterlogged stuffed animals,
26 bloated and demented, moved with the tides,
27 losing their stitching, and slowly
28 disintegrating into pulp. Along the beach,
29 broken pieces of glass, metal, and plastic lay
30 everywhere – a minefield of shattered
31 dreams and happiness.
32   The reclamation would take years – the
33 rehabilitation even longer. Luckily, the
34 community and its inhabitants were resilient,
35 and they would rebuild their boardwalk even
36 better than before. Still, long after the last
37 of the dredges have combed through the
38 sand, and long after the last metal detector
39 has swept across the beach, swimmers,
40 divers, and beachgoers will undoubtedly
41 continue to find detritus from the
42 disaster. Here and there, there will be a
43 reminder of what has been lost: a crystal ball
44 from a fortune teller's booth; glass from
45 tinted light bulbs; tiny bits and pieces from
46 another time – another life.

Descriptive – Passage 4 Question Set

1. The primary purpose of the passage is to

    (A) warn people not to build near the
         ocean.
    (B) illustrate the benefits of perseverance.
    (C) highlight the importance of following
         evacuation orders.
    (D) describe the impact of a natural disaster
         on a community.

2. The author includes the sentence "It was as
    if . . . lying about" (lines 15-17) in order to

    (A) compare the condition of the beach to a
         familiar image.
    (B) advise the reader that children are often
         prone to violent mood swings.
    (C) downplay the power of the hurricane
         by likening it to that of a child.
    (D) convince the reader that beaches and
         bedrooms have certain similarities.

3. In line 30, the author uses the word
    "minefield" to describe the beach after the
    hurricane in order to

    (A) plead with beachgoers to avoid the
         beach.
    (B) request military assistance in the
         disaster.
    (C) illustrate how dangerous the beach had
         become.
    (D) inform the reader that beaches are, like
         minefields, inherently unsafe.

4. In line 41, "detritus" most nearly means

    (A) assets.
    (B) prizes.
    (C) remnants.
    (D) results.

5. According to the final paragraph (lines 32-
    46), the community's recovery efforts
    included

    (A) help from the government.
    (B) the use of metal detectors.
    (C) assistance from other countries.
    (D) humanitarian relief from charity
         organizations.

6. The author implies that, despite
    reconstruction efforts, things will never be
    the same because

    (A) the specter of disaster will always
         loom.
    (B) the townspeople abandoned the
         community after the disaster.
    (C) many of the objects destroyed were
         irreplaceable and priceless.
    (D) the quality of the new boardwalk will
         be inferior to that of the original one.

Descriptive – Passage 5

1   Just southwest of the historic district and
2 running parallel to the town's famous East-
3 West promenade is a veritable gem. The
4 open-air market, open every Monday,
5 Wednesday, and Friday, attracts hundreds
6 from the nearby region.
7   The market itself is well
8 organized. Stalls and booths are arranged in
9 four long rows that run parallel with the
10 promenade. Every four or five stalls there
11 runs a perpendicular intersecting pathway
12 that allows shoppers to walk to a different
13 row of merchants. Floating above the stands
14 and walkways are red-and-white-striped
15 cloth awnings – candy-striped shields that
16 protect both people and goods from the
17 sun's unrelenting gaze.
18   The well-designed market attracts a wide
19 range of merchants. From farmers to florists,
20 butchers to bakers, artisans to artists, the
21 sellers are as varied as the needs and wants
22 of their customers. Fresh produce –
23 peaches, plums, potatoes, parsnips, parsley,
24 and more – sit prettily in baskets, enticing
25 patrons with their honeyed, earthy
26 scents. The spice merchants display
27 samples of cardamom, chilies, and curry

28 powders, which fill the air with their sharp,
29 fragrant smells. Soap vendors lay out brick
30 after brick of their fine, hand-milled scented
31 bars. Bakers and confectioners display rows
32 of buttery breads, jam-filled pastries, and
33 luscious chocolates; the warm, rich smell of
34 butter jostles with that of the soap and the
35 spices for primacy. However, no one scent
36 overpowers another, and the multitude of
37 smells coalesces and combines into
38 something greater: the smell of spring, of
39 summer, and of autumn, all rolled into one.
40   Taking in this grand scene are hundreds
41 upon hundreds of shoppers – customers
42 looking for fresh produce, for soap, for the
43 best cut of meat, or for an original, evocative
44 work of art. But not all visitors to the
45 market are there to shop. On either side of
46 the market, rising two stories into the air, are
47 restaurants, cafes, bars, and lounges replete
48 with both indoor and outdoor seating. Many
49 casual observers simply enjoy sitting and
50 having a cup of coffee, while watching the
51 shoppers shop and the sellers sell. The
52 market indeed has something for everyone –
53 even for those people who have no intention
54 of buying anything.

Descriptive – Passage 5 Question Set

1. The passage is primarily concerned with

   (A) portraying a vibrant shopping
   destination.
   (B) persuading the reader to visit the
   outdoor market.
   (C) contrasting the outdoor market with
   other outdoor markets.
   (D) weighing the good aspects of the
   outdoor market with the bad.

2. In line 3, "veritable gem" most nearly means

   (A) a rarity.
   (B) a valuable stone.
   (C) a hoard of treasure.
   (D) a hidden object of great value.

3. The author compares the floating awnings to
   protective shields (lines 13-17) in order to

   (A) describe the rigid and unchanging
   nature of the awnings.
   (B) illustrate how protective people are of
   the outdoor market.
   (C) explain how cool and comfortable it
   would be without shade.
   (D) emphasize how unpleasant the intense
   heat and light would be without the
   awnings.

4. In lines 22-25, the author lists various
   produce in order to

   (A) show that produce is the best part of
   the market.
   (B) help the reader empathize with the fate
   of the produce.
   (C) allow the reader to pause and
   appreciate the bounty on display.
   (D) to help the reader remember every one
   of the products available.

5. According to lines 18-39, the reason there
   are so many different smells in the market is
   because

   (A) the smell of soap overpowers all other
   smells.
   (B) autumn is approaching, bringing with it
   the smells of the harvest.
   (C) summer is in the air, bringing with it
   the smell of butter and fruit.
   (D) there are a variety of different
   merchants whose products each exude
   a unique scent.

6. The author of the passage does all of the
   following in the last paragraph (lines 40-54)
   EXCEPT

   (A) allude to an alternative way to enjoy
   the market without selling and buying.
   (B) reinforce the idea that the market is a
   place dedicated to buying and selling
   only.
   (C) expand the visual imagery of the
   market beyond the vendor booths to the
   outlying areas.
   (D) describe how, in addition to a place to
   buy and sell, the market is a place to
   relax and take in the sights.

Descriptive – Passage 6

1   The floor and walls of the lobby were
2   polished to a high shine. Tiled with Cararra
3   marble from Tuscany, the opulence of the
4   lobby reflected the high cost to rent in this
5   luxury, hundred-floor skyscraper. The
6   marble reflected its surroundings like a
7   shimmering body of water; the reflections
8   were discernable in form, but imperfect in
9   detail. The marble, white as milk, was
10   striated with the finest gray markings, a
11   pattern neither too bold nor too subtle – a
12   balance so perfect no artist could recreate it.
13   The lobby was tastefully decorated in a
14   minimalist, almost austere fashion. Absent
15   of furniture, picture, or plants, the lobby
16   contained only two objects: the welcome
17   desk – also carved of marble – and the
18   monolith that flanked it. Carved from
19   obsidian, the ink-black sculpture rose to the
20   full three-story height of the lobby. On
21   either side of this imposing sentinel were
22   elevator banks used to access the upper
23   floors.

24   Standing flush against the rear wall of
25   the lobby, the jagged surface of the volcanic
26   glass appeared seamless and whole, despite
27   the fact that it was comprised of multiple
28   pieces taken from Argentina and later
29   assembled by a cadre of artists here in its
30   new home. Wide at the base, the sculpture
31   grew narrower as it approached the ceiling.
32   Its front face sloped down from the edge at
33   which the ceiling met the rear wall of the
34   lobby, and when viewed from the side, the
35   sculpture formed a perfect right triangle with
36   the wall.
37   Down the front of the sculpture flowed a
38   stream of water, which collected in a pool at
39   its base. By design, the water trickled softly
40   through cracks and wrinkles in the dark
41   glass, which helped to prevent unwanted
42   splashing and loss of water. The net effect
43   was such that the sculpture appeared to be
44   alive, its features dynamic and dancing
45   under the water.

Descriptive – Passage 6 Question Set

1. Which best expresses the main idea of the passage?

   (A) Cararra marble is the best in the world.
   (B) Every lobby should have a sculpture in it.
   (C) Marble is expensive and should be used sparingly.
   (D) The lobby and sculpture are beautiful works of art.

2. In line 9, the author likens the color of the marble to that of milk in order to

   (A) help the reader picture the color of the marble.
   (B) boast of the marble's rarity and precious value.
   (C) decry the marble's ordinariness and commonness.
   (D) inform the reader that different marbles have different colors.

3. In line 14, "austere" most nearly means

   (A) floral.
   (B) gaudy.
   (C) stark.
   (D) timid.

4. It can be inferred from lines 13-36 that the sculpture was assembled from pieces because

   (A) the front slope was too steep.
   (B) each piece needed to be inked separately.
   (C) it was too large to be moved from Argentina in a single piece.
   (D) the government of Argentina would not allow the removal of so much obsidian at once.

5. The artist suggests in the final paragraph (lines 37-45) that the sculpture had cracks and wrinkles in it because

   (A) of a flaw in the design.
   (B) the running water had begun to erode the rock.
   (C) there are plants at the bottom of the sculpture that need watering.
   (D) these features prevent the water from splashing as it flows down the face.

6. The author appears to be most concerned with

   (A) advising of the obsolescence of obsidian.
   (B) understanding how the sculpture was assembled.
   (C) describing the lobby and sculpture in great detail.
   (D) comparing this lobby with lobbies in other buildings.

Descriptive – Passage 7

1   Today is a rare day. Wedged in between
2 the dry, freezing cold of winter and the
3 humid, blistering heat of summer, spring
4 weather in the northeast United States only
5 ever seems to last a couple of weeks.
6 Winter, with its icy, gnarled fingers,
7 reluctantly loosens its grip only sometime in
8 late March. The weather in April always
9 seems to follow the old aphorism, raining
10 more often than not. And if April is going
11 to keep with tradition, why shouldn't May?
12   A paragon of pleasantness, today is a
13 perfect spring day in May. The temperature
14 is just right: it's neither too hot in the sun,
15 nor too cool in the shade. It's neither too
16 dry nor too humid. The perfect air
17 temperature and relative humidity are
18 complemented by clear, blue skies.
19   Lying in my hammock, I'm rocked half-
20 asleep by the mild breeze. As I lay in the
21 partial shade of an oak tree and look into the
22 infinite blue above me, I can't help but smile
23 to myself. At that moment, I am overcome
24 with a profound happiness – a contentedness
25 and satisfaction that melts away all of my
26 worries. My whole body sways gently.
27 Maybe I'm just projecting my good mood
28 onto them, but even the birds seem happy.

29   Taking a break from staring up at the
30 sky, I look for the songbirds that are
31 showering me with their melodies. They
32 prove invisible. Instead, I spot robins with
33 rust-orange breasts hopping around on the
34 lawn, rustling their feathers. Perhaps they
35 hop in search of food; perhaps they hop just
36 to hop, and rustle just to rustle. Here and
37 there a flash of bright red – a cardinal. And
38 there, a glimpse of a deep royal blue – a blue
39 jay. My ears strain, trying to make out what
40 the unidentified songbirds are saying to each
41 other. In the end, I give up – after all,
42 they're just singing to sing, and I love it too
43 much to think any more about its meaning.
44   As my ears absorb the acoustic treat, my
45 eyes feast upon colors so vibrant and so real
46 that the scene almost looks artificial, like an
47 all-too-vivid painting. The magenta
48 fireworks of azalea blossoms vie with the
49 gentle pink petals of the nearby cherry
50 blossoms. Irises blossom here and there,
51 their rich indigo petals surrounding a
52 golden, powdery stamen.
53   When will there be another day like
54 today? Maybe tomorrow. Maybe the day
55 after tomorrow. Just because I don't know
56 the next time I'll be able to enjoy a day like
57 today, I will savor it all the more.

Descriptive – Passage 7 Question Set

1. The primary purpose of the passage is to

    (A) complain about the brevity of spring.
    (B) compare the relative virtues of different flowers.
    (C) identify and categorize different species of birds.
    (D) share observations made on a picturesque spring day.

2. Based on the sentences "The weather . . . shouldn't May" (lines 8-11), we can infer that the author

    (A) expects May to be rainy.
    (B) expects April to be rainy.
    (C) expects April to be hot and humid.
    (D) expects April to be sunny and pleasant.

3. In line 12, "paragon" most nearly means

    (A) ideal.
    (B) limitation.
    (C) minimum.
    (D) requirement.

4. The author mentions all of the following as reasons why the day is so pleasant EXCEPT that

    (A) the sky is clear and blue.
    (B) the breeze is strong and persistent.
    (C) the humidity is perfectly balanced.
    (D) the temperature is neither too hot nor too cool.

5. The author includes the phrase "songbirds that are showering me with their melodies" (lines 30-31) in order to

    (A) show how birds also sing while bathing.
    (B) associate the sound of songbirds with that of showering.
    (C) illustrate how the sounds of the birds are surrounding him.
    (D) express how he enjoys listening to birds, even in the rain.

6. The purpose of the final paragraph (lines 53-57) is to

    (A) question why such perfect days are so infrequent.
    (B) convey the precious nature of a perfect spring day.
    (C) predict the next day that will have comparable weather.
    (D) describe the negative impact bad weather has on the author's mood.

Descriptive – Passage 8

1   My knees were practically up against my
2   chest. Well, not really. They were actually
3   pushed up against the velvet seat in front of
4   me rather painfully.
5   Shifting uncomfortably in my seat, I
6   tried to focus on something else. I hated
7   waiting. I had waited to get these tickets for
8   almost a year. After that, I had waited
9   another year for the date of the show itself.
10   And now, I had to wait for everyone to take
11   his or her seats.
12   30 minutes to go.
13   I couldn't understand why it took so
14   long for people to get to their seats. Isn't
15   that why there are ushers? To help people
16   find their seats quickly? I mean, I had found
17   our seats with no problem at all. Didn't
18   even talk to an usher. The sections of the
19   theater were all labeled: Orchestra, this way;
20   Mezzanine, up the stairs; box seats, around
21   to the sides. Each row was clearly lettered;
22   each seat, clearly numbered. This theater,
23   like every other I've been in – and if I had to
24   guess, like every other theater in the world –
25   was laid out logically and was easy to
26   navigate. So why were all these people
27   making me wait even longer?
28   John looked over at me wearing an
29   impatient smile. He was probably the only
30   other person in the theater as excited for the
31   show as I was, but he hated how antsy I got
32   while waiting. All I could talk about for
33   almost two years was the show, about how
34   great it would be, how it would change my
35   life forever, and how it would inform all of
36   my artistic sensibilities.
37   15 minutes to go.
38   I had to distract myself, or I would never
39   make it. Looking around, I took a minute to
40   appreciate the theater. Clad in Gilded Age
41   finery, the theater was, itself, a work of art.
42   As far as I could tell, the theater was
43   perfectly symmetrical down to the last
44   detail. Balustrades supported the railing up
45   and down the stairs. Columns lined the
46   walls and framed the stage, lending a formal
47   if not imposing air to it. The oval crest
48   above the stage itself was highly intricate,
49   though it was difficult to make out any of
50   the particulars of the relief from my seat.
51   Yes, this theater was certainly a good fit for
52   this play.
53   The orchestra warmed up and
54   interrupted my musings. Finally – mere
55   minutes remained. I looked over at John,
56   who had seemingly forgotten all about me –
57   his eyes were already fixed on the stage.
58   Applause filled the room.
59   The curtains were finally rising.

Descriptive – Passage 8 Question Set

1. The primary purpose of the passage is to

    (A) explain how to navigate a theater.
    (B) describe the layouts of theater seating.
    (C) relate the experience of waiting eagerly for a show.
    (D) describe the intricacies of Gilded Age architecture and décor.

2. In lines 12 and 37, it can be inferred that the author indicates the amount of time remaining until

    (A) the opening.
    (B) the finale.
    (C) the reprise.
    (D) the intermission.

3. According to lines 13-27, why is the author frustrated that many audience members have not yet taken their seats?

    (A) There are too many people.
    (B) There are not enough ushers.
    (C) The seats and rows are not labeled in the usual way.
    (D) He thinks that the labeling and directions in the theater are very clear.

4. The author includes the question "So . . . longer" (lines 26-27) in order to

    (A) seek John's guidance.
    (B) assign blame for the delay.
    (C) demonstrate his impatience and annoyance.
    (D) understand the reason why people were still not in their seats.

5. In line 50, "relief" most nearly means

    (A) assistance.
    (B) design.
    (C) gratitude.
    (D) satisfaction.

6. The organization of the passage can best be described as

    (A) a list of facts.
    (B) a chronological series of events.
    (C) a series of unproven and unsubstantiated opinions.
    (D) an argument advancing the merits of the Gilded Age.

Expository Passages

Directions: Answer the questions following each passage on the basis of what is stated or implied in that passage.

Expository – Passage 1

1   Anesthesia enables doctors and surgeons
2 to perform medical procedures by relaxing
3 muscles, inducing analgesia (numbness),
4 and causing amnesia and/or
5 unconsciousness. By suppressing responses
6 in the nervous system, anesthesia helps most
7 patients to be less anxious before a
8 procedure, suffer little if any discomfort or
9 pain during a procedure, and remember little
10 to nothing about a procedure after the fact.
11 While it is now a staple in modern medicine,
12 anesthesia has developed and changed over
13 the years, and its history is as long as it is
14 varied.
15   In ancient times, the most common
16 anesthetics were local plants that happened
17 to be available in a given region. For
18 example, opium poppy in early
19 Mesopotamia and mandrake fruit in early
20 Egypt may have been used as local
21 analgesics. In South America, Inca shamans
22 chewed coca leaves and used the pulp and
23 juice as a local anesthetic. Ether, one of the
24 most well-known anesthetics, was first
25 synthesized in the sixteenth century from
26 ethanol and sulfuric acid. Its use as an
27 anesthetic was popularized by the fact that it
28 not only caused patients to fall asleep, but

29 also caused them to feel no pain during that
30 sleep. Though it was chemically derived
31 during the sixteenth century, it was not until
32 the nineteenth century that ether was used in
33 surgery. One of the first surgeries using
34 ether as an anesthetic was performed by
35 American physician Crawford Long on a
36 student named James Venable, who had two
37 small tumors removed painlessly and
38 successfully. Ether's popularity quickly
39 spread to other countries, and its use became
40 standard practice when performing complex
41 operations.
42   Today, ether has been largely replaced
43 by specialized anesthetic drugs that give
44 anesthesiologists – doctors who specialize in
45 the administration of anesthetics – the power
46 to cause a reversible loss of consciousness
47 that is more reliable and less risky than that
48 caused by ether. These anesthetics also
49 cause a decreased awareness of painful
50 stimuli and are used for complex and
51 invasive operations that would otherwise be
52 extremely painful. These anesthetics can be
53 delivered intravenously or administered via
54 inhalation. Without anesthetics, modern
55 medicine might not have advanced to its
56 current state.

Expository – Passage 1 Question Set

1. The primary purpose of the passage is to

   (A) briefly offer a history of anesthesia.
   (B) explain the science behind anesthesia.
   (C) defend the use of anesthesia in medical procedures.
   (D) instruct the reader on producing home-made anesthetics.

2. The phrase "as long as it is varied" (lines 13-14) refers to

   (A) the static nature of anesthesia.
   (B) the scientific mysteries behind anesthesia.
   (C) humanity's short experiment with anesthesia.
   (D) how the numerous types of anesthesia developed over a long period of time.

3. It can be inferred that the number of patients under anesthesia who suffer pain during a procedure is

   (A) few.
   (B) many.
   (C) average.
   (D) impossible to determine.

4. In lines 23-41, the author states that ether became a widely used anesthetic because

   (A) it was inexpensive to manufacture.
   (B) it helped to render tumors harmless.
   (C) it caused patients to fall into a painless sleep.
   (D) initial surgeries using ether were unsuccessful.

5. In line 50, "stimuli" most nearly means

   (A) desires.
   (B) memories.
   (C) opportunities.
   (D) sensations.

6. According to the last paragraph, lines 42-56, all of the following are reasons why anesthetics are important to modern medicine EXCEPT

   (A) they are convenient to administer.
   (B) their effects are easily reversible.
   (C) judging dosage is often difficult and discretionary.
   (D) they enable operations that would be impossible to perform otherwise.

Expository – Passage 2

1   Archimedes of Syracuse, a Greek living
2 during 200-300 BC, made significant
3 contributions to both math and science.
4 Even now, thousands of years later, his
5 discoveries are still central to our
6 understanding of the physical world.
7   The son of an astronomer, Archimedes
8 was born in 287 BC and died 75 years later.
9 Though a biography of Archimedes' life was
10 written by his friend, Heracleides, the work
11 was later lost. As a result, much of what we
12 know about Archimedes as a person is the
13 product of stories and hearsay.
14   One such story was written by the
15 Roman author Vitruvius, who lived some
16 time after Archimedes had died. According
17 to Vitruvius, Archimedes was once asked to
18 determine whether a crown made for King
19 Hiero II was made of pure gold, or of a less
20 valuable blend of gold and silver. King
21 Hiero II stipulated that Archimedes must not
22 damage the crown, which prevented the
23 latter from simply melting down the crown.
24 Later, while taking a bath, Archimedes
25 realized that the level of water in his tub
26 changed depending on whether or not he
27 was in the tub. As a result, Archimedes
28 knew that he could determine the volume of
29 the crown by submerging it in water, and
30 then dividing the mass of the crown by the
31 volume of the water displaced to calculate
32 the density of the crown. By comparing the
33 density of the crown to the density of real
34 gold, he surmised, he would be able to
35 determine if the crown contained silver – a
36 material with a density less than that of gold.
37 Upon this realization, Vitruvius writes,
38 Archimedes leaped out of his bath and
39 proceeded to run through the streets,
40 shouting "Eureka!"
41   While the veracity of this particular story
42 is questionable, Archimedes did make
43 another significant discovery in the realm of
44 fluid dynamics. His discovery that buoyant
45 force is equal to the weight of fluid
46 displaced by a body in a liquid, dubbed
47 Archimedes' Principle, is a fundamental law
48 of physics that he first described in his
49 treatise, *On Floating Bodies*. This law is
50 essential to our understanding of fluids.
51   One of Archimedes' most famous
52 inventions is the Archimedes' screw, which
53 consists of a screw inside of a hollow pipe.
54 Athenaeus of Naucratis, a Greek writer,
55 described how the same King Hiero II
56 commissioned Archimedes to design a large
57 ship. According to Naucratis, the ship was
58 so large that it constantly took on water. To
59 prevent it from sinking, Archimedes devised
60 the screw as a means of pumping water out
61 of the ship. By rotating the screw, materials
62 such as liquids can be easily transported
63 from one plane to another. On board the
64 ship, the screw was turned by hand in order
65 to remove bilge water. This screw is still
66 used today in irrigation systems and pumps.
67   Although we cannot know with certainty
68 how Archimedes was able to surmise his
69 various theories or create his incredible
70 inventions, the mystery of Archimedes'
71 genius in no way lessens the import of his
72 discoveries. Whether Archimedes was
73 driven by madness, brilliance, or necessity,
74 the fact remains that Archimedean
75 discoveries are central to our everyday way
76 of life.

Expository – Passage 2 Question Set

1. Which best expresses the main idea of the passage?

   (A) Necessity is the mother of invention.
   (B) Written history is more credible than oral history.
   (C) Archimedes' life was devoted to the pursuit of fame and fortune.
   (D) Archimedes' discoveries have had a lasting impact on the world.

2. In the second paragraph (lines 7-13), the author of the passage states that we know little about Archimedes primarily because

   (A) he did not know how to read or write.
   (B) stories have distorted the truth.
   (C) he is a figurative and fictional figure.
   (D) the only contemporaneous account of his life was lost.

3. In line 13, "hearsay" most nearly means

   (A) assurances.
   (B) questions.
   (C) rumors. *or stories / myths*
   (D) speeches.

4. The author includes the story about Archimedes' discovery of the equation of density (lines 14-40) in order to

   (A) entertain the reader by relating a humorous and contrived anecdote.
   (B) showcase the relationship between scientists and royalty in ancient Greece.
   (C) provide step-by-step instructions for calculating the density of an object.
   (D) show that though Archimedes is primarily a figure of legend, his contributions to science were real.

5. It can be inferred that the word "Eureka" (line 40) conveys which emotion?

   (A) anger
   (B) satisfaction *happiness*
   (C) terror
   (D) weariness

6. The author of the passage does all of the following EXCEPT

   (A) compare Archimedes with other notable thinkers.
   (B) describe some of Archimedes' inventions and theories.
   (C) explain how Archimedes' intellect continues to benefit modern-day society.
   (D) highlight historical uncertainties about Archimedes' life and personal history.

Expository – Passage 3

1   Useful for identifying bacteria, staining
2   is a chemical process through which certain
3   biological materials can be differentiated
4   from others. The underlying mechanism
5   that enables this differentiation relates to the
6   electrostatic charges of different
7   biomolecules, such as proteins and nucleic
8   acids. The type of stain used depends on the
9   experiment being performed, as different
10 biological materials have different charges.
11 Certain dyes used in staining are negatively
12 charged, which will bind to proteins and
13 acids having a positive charge. By contrast,
14 other dyes are positively charged, which will
15 bind to materials having a negative charge
16 only.
17   The first step in staining bacteria is to
18 thoroughly sterilize a glass slide. The glass
19 slide must fit under the microscope or other
20 instrument being used to view the bacteria.
21 Though there are a number of ways to
22 sterilize the slide, such as with heat or
23 chemicals, the most convenient method is to
24 use a pre-sterilized slide.
25   Once the slide is sterilized, the
26 technician must transfer the bacteria onto the
27 glass slide. This transfer is typically

28 performed using a sterile loop, which is a
29 small wand with a tiny circle at its end that
30 can hold water or other liquids. This loop is
31 very similar in appearance and function to
32 the wands used to blow bubbles.
33   Using the loop, the technician transfers a
34 single small drop of the liquid containing the
35 bacteria onto the center of the slide and
36 allows it to air dry. The resulting slurry is
37 called a smear. It is important not to attempt
38 to expedite drying time, as doing so may
39 lead to contamination.
40   Once the water has been removed, the
41 next step is called heat fixation. Heat
42 fixation destroys and denatures proteins,
43 which causes cells to stick to the slide as the
44 proteins break down. The denaturing
45 process also kills the bacteria, which allows
46 for safe handling in the final steps.
47   After covering the smear with the
48 predetermined stain, the technician allows
49 the stain to set. Afterwards, any excess stain
50 must be removed with distilled and sterile
51 water. The best method is to blot the stain
52 dry, taking care not to rub. Finally, the slide
53 is placed under the microscope, in order to
54 proceed with the experiment in question.

Expository – Passage 3 Question Set

1. The passage is primarily concerned with

   (A) providing scientific information about dyes.
   (B) explaining why staining bacteria is important.
   (C) describing the overall process of staining bacteria.
   (D) providing a specific list of equipment needed to stain bacteria.

2. According to the first paragraph (lines 1-16), dyes bind to bacteria and other biological materials because

   (A) dyes are magnetically opposed to biomolecules.
   (B) of different electrostatic charges on biomolecules.
   (C) of differences in thermal radiation between dyes and biomolecules.
   (D) dyes possess a stronger gravitational attraction than biomolecules.

3. Which best describes the organization of lines 4-16?

   (A) The author presents a historical account of electrostatics.
   (B) The author presents an opinion supported by scientific facts.
   (C) The author presents a reverse-chronological telling of a story.
   (D) The author presents an unbiased presentation of scientific facts.

4. In lines 30-32, the author compares a loop used in scientific experiments to a wand used to blow bubbles in order to

   (A) prove that science can be fun.
   (B) distract the reader from the main idea.
   (C) clarify the appearance of a sterile loop.
   (D) remind the reader of childhood activities.

5. In line 38, "expedite" most nearly means

   (A) accelerate.
   (B) delay.
   (C) enhance.
   (D) erudite.

6. In the last paragraph (lines 47-54), the author implies that rubbing the stain dry will likely

   (A) cause the smear to reject the stain.
   (B) revive the bacteria, creating a health hazard.
   (C) lead to contamination or otherwise ruin the smear.
   (D) damage the microscope, causing the experiment to fail.

Expository – Passage 4

1   Goddess of the harvest and of fertility,
2 Demeter is known in Greek mythology to be
3 responsible for the changing of the seasons.
4 Demeter, whose gifts to humanity included
5 the knowledge of agriculture itself, oversees
6 the cycle of life and death – the changing of
7 the seasons. One of the twelve major deities
8 of the Greek pantheon, Demeter was born of
9 Cronus and Rhea and was the mother of
10 Persephone, whom she loved dearly.
11   When Demeter's beautiful daughter was
12 abducted by Hades, ruler of the underworld,
13 the goddess searched far and wide for her
14 beloved Persephone. During this time, she
15 was so overcome with worry and grief that
16 the seasons halted and all living things
17 suffered and began to die. While she
18 searched for her daughter, Demeter travelled
19 to the city of Eleusis in the modern day
20 province of West Attica. She sought after
21 Persephone in the palace of King Celeus,
22 taking on the guise of an old woman seeking
23 shelter. Celeus agreed to the old woman's
24 request, but asked her to earn her keep by
25 nursing his sons Demophon and
26 Triptolemus. As a reward, Demeter planned
27 to immortalize Demophon.
28   Demeter anointed the boy with ambrosia
29 and laid his body in the flames of the hearth
30 so that his mortality would burn away.

31 However, the boy's mother accidentally
32 walked in on the ceremony, which caused
33 the disguised goddess to abandon her
34 efforts. Still, Demeter wished to reward the
35 king for his kindness. Instead of
36 immortality for Demophon, Demeter taught
37 Triptolemus the secrets of agriculture, who
38 in turn propagated the knowledge to all who
39 would listen.
40   Eventually, Demeter was reunited with
41 her daughter. The reunion, however, was
42 not destined to be everlasting. During her
43 time in the underworld, Persephone ate a
44 pomegranate offered to her by Hades. As a
45 result, she was not permitted to leave the
46 underworld permanently. A bargain was
47 struck: during certain months each year,
48 Persephone would be permitted to leave the
49 underworld and be reunited with her mother.
50 During the remaining months, Persephone
51 would be required to remain in the
52 underworld with Hades.
53   In the months when Demeter is reunited
54 with her daughter – the spring and summer
55 months in the Mediterranean – the goddess'
56 happiness causes life to blossom. In the
57 months when Demeter is forced to live apart
58 from her daughter, life withers and dies.
59 Thus, this myth explains the eternal cycle of
60 life and death.

Expository – Passage 4 Question Set

1. The primary purpose of the passage is to

   (A) divulge the secret to immortality.
   (B) explain how people learned to cultivate crops.
   (C) illustrate how people used a story to explain natural occurrences.
   (D) tell the story of how a pomegranate changed the fate of the world.

2. The author of the passage most likely includes the story of Persephone's abduction and Demeter's search for her daughter (lines 11-27) for all of the following reasons EXCEPT

   (A) to describe the city of Eleusis.
   (B) to emphasize Demeter's love of Persephone.
   (C) to allude to the influence Demeter has over the seasons.
   (D) to preface the story of how the world came to understand agriculture.

3. In line 38, "propagated" most nearly means

   (A) cultivated.
   (B) distributed.
   (C) hoarded.
   (D) wavered.

4. Which does the author mention as a reason that Persephone could not permanently leave the underworld (lines 40-52)?

   (A) Persephone prefers the underworld during the cold seasons.
   (B) Persephone had eaten a pomegranate while living in the underworld.
   (C) Hades was overcome with Persephone's beauty and would not let her go.
   (D) Demeter had no power in the underworld and was unable to take Persephone away.

5. According to the final paragraph (lines 53-60), Demeter and Persephone are separated during which seasons in the Mediterranean?

   (A) autumn and winter.
   (B) winter and summer.
   (C) spring and summer.
   (D) spring and autumn.

6. In lines 53-56, the author uses the imagery of a plant blossoming and then withering in order to

   (A) underscore the fragility of life.
   (B) describe the natural cycle of life and death.
   (C) draw a connection between Demeter's happiness and the seasons.
   (D) undermine the notion that the seasons are caused by the earth's rotation around the sun.

Expository – Passage 5

1   Painting is a quick and easy way to add
2 character and depth to a room. To do a good
3 job, painting requires prior planning and
4 proper equipment.
5   First, think about what part of the room
6 you're painting so you can start moving
7 furniture and any fixtures. If you're painting
8 the ceiling, the best thing to do would be to
9 empty the room of furniture entirely. This
10 will give you more room to work and will
11 prevent paint from splattering onto the
12 furniture. If this isn't feasible, you should
13 paint the ceiling in sections by grouping
14 furniture in one part of the room, covering it
15 with a tarp or drop cloth, and working only
16 on the part of the ceiling where nothing is
17 sitting underneath. Once these areas are
18 completed, move the furniture to a painted
19 part of the room, and work on the next
20 portion of the ceiling. Though the same
21 principle applies when you're painting the
22 walls, it's actually less complicated than
23 painting the ceiling. This is because you can
24 just group the furniture together in the center
25 of the room, and cover all of it with a drop
26 cloth.
27   Once you've decided how you're going
28 to manage your furniture and safeguard it
29 from painting-related accidents, think about
30 the tools and supplies you'll need. At a
31 minimum, you'll likely need paint and a
32 brush. If you're painting a large area, you'll
33 also probably need a rolling brush to help
34 paint a greater surface area, as well as a tray
35 in which to hold the paint. If you're painting
36 something out of reach, such as the top of a
37 wall or a ceiling, you may want to consider
38 an extension rod for your rolling brush.
39 Otherwise, you'll need to get a footstool or
40 ladder. The extension rod for your brush
41 could save you a lot of time and energy,
42 though it can be more difficult to maneuver
43 and control. In addition to the paint, brush,
44 and these other related implements, you
45 should also consider buying painter's tape.
46 Many people like to use this tape to line
47 edges and corners, as it facilitates precision
48 painting. One of the great features of this
49 tape is that it doesn't leave residue or pull up
50 paint when removed. Painter's tape is
51 particularly useful wherever two planes
52 meet; for instance, it works well when
53 placed at the edge between two walls, along
54 the edge between the wall and the ceiling, or
55 within the nooks and crannies near
56 doorframes and windows.
57   Now that you're properly prepared, it's
58 time to get to work! Prepare the surfaces by
59 fixing any blemishes and wiping them clean
60 of dust and debris. Once cleaned and
61 blemish-free, mix your paint and pour it, as
62 needed, into the tray. Coat the brush in
63 enough paint such that it doesn't drip or run
64 down the walls. Finally, paint in broad,
65 multi-directional strokes. Once you're
66 finished, let the paint dry, and apply a
67 second coat if needed.

Expository – Passage 5 Question Set

1. The primary purpose of the passage is to

   (A) persuade the reader to paint a room.
   (B) praise the virtues of certain painting implements.
   (C) provide instructions and advice about painting a room.
   (D) describe the reasons why painting a room is beneficial.

2. In lines 35-43, the author implies that using an extension rod will help save time when painting a ceiling because without one,

   (A) the painter's arms will tire quickly.
   (B) it will be difficult to paint with precision and accuracy.
   (C) it is impossible to paint out of reach surfaces.
   (D) the painter will need to constantly move a footstool or ladder around the room.

3. Which does the author mention, in lines 43-56, as a reason why painter's tape is helpful?

   (A) The tape helps prevent splatter.
   (B) The tape helps to prevent paint from dripping.
   (C) The tape helps you paint a larger surface area more quickly.
   (D) The tape won't damage or blemish the paint or surface when removed.

4. In line 55, "nooks and crannies" most nearly means

   (A) bright rooms.
   (B) flat surfaces.
   (C) inaccessible spaces.
   (D) round edges.

5. Which best describes the organization of lines 57-67?

   (A) The author lists a sequential order of events.
   (B) The author gives a random list of suggestions.
   (C) The author lists a series of unrelated actions.
   (D) The author gives a detailed account of a specific experience.

6. The author's tone can best be described as

   (A) exuberant.
   (B) exultant.
   (C) pragmatic.
   (D) prescient.

Expository – Passage 6

1   Like many of his contemporaries, John
2 Glover held several different positions in
3 life. After gaining success as a young
4 entrepreneur, Glover eventually earned a
5 leadership role in the Continental Army, and
6 played a critical role in the Army's victory
7 during the American War of Independence.
8 Today, Glover is memorialized across the
9 country for his contributions to the war
10 effort: a statue erected in his honor stands in
11 Boston, Massachusetts, and a frigate, the
12 *USS Glover*, was named after him.
13   The son of a carpenter, Glover was born
14 and raised in Salem, Massachusetts. As a
15 young man, Glover held a number of
16 different occupations. One of his first jobs
17 was as a shoemaker specializing in soft
18 leather shoes and other luxury footwear.
19 After his time as a shoemaker, Glover
20 became a sailor and rum trader, and he
21 eventually purchased a fishing vessel and
22 became a merchant fisherman. Glover used
23 his economic status to his advantage,
24 participating in the militia and in local
25 politics.
26   In 1760, at just 28 years of age, Glover
27 joined the Whig party, which opposed
28 England's rule over the then-American
29 colonies; by then, he had already served in
30 the militia for a year. Some ten years later,
31 and only five years after the infamous
32 Boston Massacre, Glover was elected
33 lieutenant colonel of the 21st Massachusetts
34 Regiment. As war grew imminent across

35 the colonies, Glover soon became close with
36 George Washington. The latter would go on
37 to charter the former's schooner, *Hannah,* as
38 a privateer, authorized to raid British supply
39 ships. Because of this, many today consider
40 Glover's ship to be the first ship in the
41 American Navy.
42   Glover would go on to play a pivotal
43 role in the American War of Independence.
44 Because of his and his regiment's nautical
45 skills, Washington used Glover to great
46 effect throughout the war. In August 1776,
47 after being defeated by the British on Long
48 Island, Glover's militia helped evacuate
49 Washington's forces to Manhattan, thereby
50 preventing the colonial forces from being
51 trapped on Long Island with the enemy.
52 Four months later, Glover's militia ferried
53 General Washington across the Delaware
54 River, surprising the British in Trenton, New
55 Jersey.
56   Late in 1776, Glover's militia was
57 disbanded due to the expiration of
58 enlistment contracts. Glover returned home
59 to attend to personal and business matters,
60 turning down the title of brigadier general in
61 early 1777. It took a personal appeal from
62 George Washington to convince Glover to
63 rejoin the war. Until the end of the war,
64 Glover guarded the Hudson River against
65 British incursion, and helped to contain
66 troop movement in the region. For his
67 service, Glover was promoted to major
68 general at the end of the war.

Expository – Passage 6 Question Set

1. Which best expresses the main idea of the passage?

   (A) Glover's life was dull, unimportant, and of no consequence.
   (B) Trying many different jobs is the key to power, prestige, and success.
   (C) In the eighteenth century, making a lasting impact on society was easy to accomplish.
   (D) Though Glover started life like many of his peers, he went on to play an important role in American history.

2. Which does the author mention as a reason that Glover "is memorialized across the country" (lines 8-9)?

   (A) Glover was a great explorer.
   (B) Glover was a successful businessman.
   (C) Glover played a key role in the American War of Independence.
   (D) Glover established permanent fashion trends in luxury footwear.

3. The sentence "Because of this, many today consider Glover's ship to be the first ship in the American Navy" (lines 39-41) is included in order to

   (A) document the evolution of American naval warships.
   (B) allude to Glover's previous occupation as a rum trader.
   (C) explain the reason for Glover's friendship with Washington.
   (D) draw a parallel between the *USS Glover* and the importance of Glover's naval contributions.

4. In line 65, "incursion" most nearly means

   (A) attack.
   (B) development.
   (C) investment.
   (D) involvement.

5. Which best describes the organization of the passage?

   (A) A series of instructions and processes.
   (B) An exchange of ideas between two parties.
   (C) An opinion supported by a number of facts.
   (D) A chronological account of historical facts.

6. The author's tone can best be described as

   (A) amused.
   (B) impartial.
   (C) incredulous.
   (D) reverent

Expository – Passage 7

1   For thousands of years, people have
2 been seeking after precious metals and
3 minerals. All valuable for different reasons,
4 these materials are obtained through the
5 process of mining. Over the years, as
6 technology has advanced and demand for
7 minerals has grown, different types of
8 mining have developed. The fundamental
9 objective of all mining, however, is the same
10 as it's been through the ages: to extract
11 mineral from rock.
12   Surface mining is a highly efficient
13 though environmentally damaging form of
14 mining. Surface mining refers to any type
15 of mining in which materials covering a
16 mineral deposit are removed. This differs
17 from underground mining, in which the
18 covering materials, such as rock and soil, are
19 left in place. There are three methods of
20 surface mining: strip mining, contour
21 stripping, and open-pit mining.
22   Strip mining is used on flat land. In strip
23 mining, long strips of dirt and rock are
24 removed in order to expose the mineral
25 deposits beneath. As each strip of covering
26 is removed, it is dumped into the previously
27 excavated area.
28   Contour mining, on the other hand, is
29 used in areas where the terrain is sloping.
30 Dirt and rock are removed from the sides of
31 hills and mountains, which allows for
32 extraction to take place along the hillside or
33 mountainside.
34   In open-pit mining, rocks and dirt are
35 removed from a large, deep pit in the earth.
36 Open-pit mines grow larger and larger until
37 the sought-after mineral is depleted, or until
38 it becomes too expensive to keep digging.
39   Once mineral deposits are depleted,
40 efforts are sometimes made to refill the
41 retired mine with dirt, clay, and vegetation.
42 Oftentimes, however, this type of
43 rehabilitation is not completed. Depending
44 on the mining method employed, forgoing
45 rehabilitation can result in anything from a
46 scarred and treeless mountainside to an open
47 pit in the ground. Though valuable and
48 useful, minerals obtained through surface
49 mining methods can be costly from an
50 environmental point of view.

Expository – Passage 7 Question Set

1. Which best expresses the main idea of the passage?

   (A) There are many different types of surface mining.
   (B) Surface mining is the best way to mine for minerals.
   (C) The depleted mines are unimportant and inconsequential.
   (D) Negative side effects of surface mining are inconsequential.

2. According to lines 12-21, surface mining is damaging to the environment because

   (A) it can rarely cause earthquakes and tremors.
   (B) it results in both ground and air pollution.
   (C) it uses harsh chemicals that are dangerous to plant and animal life.
   (D) it entails the complete removal of covering materials such as soil and vegetation.

3. In line 43, "rehabilitation" most nearly means

   (A) construction.
   (B) destruction.
   (C) innovation.
   (D) restoration.

4. It can be inferred that people continue to employ surface mining because they

   (A) need rocks and soil more than minerals.
   (B) value minerals more than they value the environment.
   (C) can easily obtain more minerals from other sources.
   (D) do not understand the costs associated with surface mining.

5. Which best describes the organization of the passage?

   (A) The author lists arguments and rebuttals.
   (B) The author denounces surface mining techniques.
   (C) The author describes different mining techniques.
   (D) The author presents an opinion and supports it with facts.

6. The author uses the word "scarred" (line 46) in order to

   (A) mollify supporters of surface mining.
   (B) emphasize the harmlessness of surface mining.
   (C) satisfy the surface mining industry and its interests.
   (D) help the reader to visualize the effects of surface mining.

Expository – Passage 8

1   In the United States, Memorial Day is
2 observed on the last Monday of May. Often
3 confused with Veterans Day, Memorial Day
4 is a national holiday commemorating those
5 who have died while serving in the
6 country's military. (Veterans Day, by
7 contrast, honors all of those who have
8 served in the country's armed forces, both
9 living and dead.) For many, Memorial Day
10 is a day of rest, relaxation, and reflection.
11 Though the entire nation observes the
12 holiday, few seem to know about the
13 holiday's origins and history.
14   In May of 1966, the 89th Congress
15 adopted House Concurrent Resolution 587,
16 which established Memorial Day as a
17 national holiday. The date of this resolution
18 was no accident, as the first formal
19 observation of Memorial Day had occurred
20 in Waterloo, New York one century prior.
21 On May 26 of the same year, President
22 Lyndon Johnson signed a proclamation
23 formally recognizing Waterloo as the
24 birthplace of Memorial Day. Both the 89th
25 Congress and Johnson's proclamation refer
26 to an event that took place on May 5, 1866,
27 in which the townspeople hung flags at half-
28 mast and draped trees and shrubs with black
29 to honor fallen American soldiers.
30 Residents, veterans, and social organizations
31 in Waterloo marched to the village
32 cemeteries and decorated soldiers' graves.
33 Together with neighboring communities, the
34 people of Waterloo repeated the ceremony
35 annually, though they changed the date to be
36 May 30 of each year. The day of
37 remembrance was not at the time known as
38 Memorial Day. Instead, it was known as
39 Decoration Day, after the act of decorating
40 soldiers' graves with commemorative items
41 such as flowers and wreaths.
42   Though the federal government
43 officially granted Waterloo the distinction of
44 being the birthplace of Memorial Day, many
45 other communities had their own memorial
46 services that predated the events at
47 Waterloo. As a response to the devastation
48 wrought by the Civil War, many
49 communities around the country organized
50 days of remembrance. In 1864, women in
51 Boalsburg, Pennsylvania decorated the
52 graves of soldiers who fought at the Battle
53 of Gettysburg. A year later, another group
54 of women did the same for soldiers who
55 fought and fell at the Battle of Vicksburg in
56 Mississippi. In April of 1866, women from
57 Columbus, Mississippi memorialized both
58 Union and Confederate soldiers with flowers
59 and wreaths.
60   Some hundred years later, after countless
61 celebrations and memorials, Congress
62 unified the nation's observances. In 1968,
63 Congress passed the Uniform Monday
64 Holiday Act which moved Memorial Day
65 from its traditionally observed dates to a
66 specified Monday. As a result, Memorial
67 Day was no longer observed on May 30 – or
68 whatever date it was celebrated in a
69 particular community – but rather on the last
70 Monday in May. Though the law took
71 effect at the federal level in 1971 for all
72 federal employees, it met resistance at the
73 state level. As a result of some confusion
74 and the resistance to break tradition, it took
75 several years for all states to fully comply
76 with the law. Ultimately, all fifty states
77 enacted Memorial Day on the date specified
78 by Congress.

Expository – Passage 8 Question Set

1. Which best expresses the main idea of the passage?

    (A) Memorial Day should be renamed Decoration Day.
    (B) Congress standardized Memorial Day celebrations to become the holiday we recognize today.
    (C) Memorial Day should not be celebrated on a Monday, as it was traditionally observed on the last day of May.
    (D) Congress should not have standardized Memorial Day, as each community's traditions should have been respected and preserved.

2. The author's tone when describing Decoration Day in Waterloo (lines 24-32) can best be described as

    (A) disappointed.
    (B) gleeful.
    (C) irreverent.
    (D) reverent.

3. In line 29, "fallen" most nearly means

    (A) deceased.
    (B) reclined.
    (C) stumbled.
    (D) tripped.

4. In the final paragraph (lines 60-78), the author mentions that it took several years for states to comply with the Uniform Monday Holiday Act because

    (A) Congress allowed states to comply with the law at their leisure.
    (B) some states were granted temporary exemptions to the law by the Supreme Court.
    (C) each community had different and deeply ingrained traditions regarding Memorial Day.
    (D) there were mass rebellions and uprisings by the people, who were angered by Congress' decision.

5. It can be inferred from the state-level resistance to the Uniform Monday Holiday Act that the Act was

    (A) appropriate.
    (B) feared.
    (C) unpopular.
    (D) valid.

6. The author of the passage does all of the following EXCEPT

    (A) compare Memorial Day with Veterans Day.
    (B) criticize Congress for including Memorial Day in its 1968 Act.
    (C) provide historical examples of various Memorial Day celebrations.
    (D) explain the reason why Memorial Day is no longer celebrated on different days.

Expository – Passage 9

1   Because rugby union and rugby league
2 originated from the same progenitor, rugby
3 football, both sports share similar objectives
4 and rules of play. However, subtle
5 differences in the evolution of each game's
6 rules have led to two distinctly different
7 sports.
8   In both forms of rugby, players use an
9 ovoid ball to score points during eighty
10 minutes of gameplay. There are essentially
11 two ways to score points: tries and goals.
12 Tries are scored when the ball, carried by a
13 player, is touched to the ground on or
14 beyond the opponent's goal line. Goals are
15 scored when the ball is kicked by a player
16 above a crossbar and between two upright
17 posts. There are several types of goals. A
18 drop goal is a goal that is scored during
19 regular play; a penalty goal is a goal that is
20 scored as a result of a penalty decision made
21 by a referee. A conversion is a special type
22 of goal opportunity afforded to a team after
23 scoring a try.
24   The ball itself can be advanced across
25 the field in several ways. First, a player can
26 carry it and run with it down the field. The
27 ball may be passed from player to player
28 only in a backwards or sideways direction;
29 the ball cannot be passed forward. Second,
30 a player can kick the ball forward. Third, a
31 ball dropped in a forwards direction results
32 in a scrum. During a scrum, both teams vie
33 for possession of the ball; the prevailing
34 team takes the ball and advances it across
35 the field.

36   Though the methods by which a team
37 scores points are similar, differences exist
38 with respect to the number of points
39 awarded for each method. In both games, a
40 conversion is worth two points. However,
41 tries in league play are worth four points
42 whereas tries in union play are worth five
43 points. Both drop goals and penalty goals
44 are worth three points each in union play,
45 whereas the former are only worth one point
46 and the latter are worth two points in league
47 play.
48   In addition to the aforementioned
49 scoring differences, certain rules governing
50 the possession of the ball differ between
51 union and league. In both versions of the
52 game, possession can change upon
53 interception of a pass, upon recovery of a
54 dropped ball (so long as the ball is not
55 dropped in the forward direction), as well as
56 upon a penalty, a punt, or a missed goal
57 attempt.
58   A player can only be tackled if he or she
59 is in possession of the ball. The completion
60 of the tackle itself differs depending on the
61 version of the game being played. In league,
62 a tackle is completed when held in an
63 upright tackle or else when the elbow of the
64 arm holding the ball touches the ground.
65 The tackled player must formally play the
66 ball by righting himself on both feet, placing
67 the ball in front of one foot, and rolling the
68 ball backwards to another player. In union,
69 a tackle is completed when the carrier is
70 held to the ground.

Expository – Passage 9 Question Set

1. Which best expresses the main idea of the passage?

   (A) The differences between rugby union and league are unnecessary and should be resolved.
   (B) Rugby union and league should continue to change their rules to become even more distinct.
   (C) Because of the similarities between rugby union and league, the two games are played interchangeably.
   (D) Though there are some similarities between rugby union and league, the two games remain distinctly different.

2. In line 4, "subtle" most nearly means

   (A) confusing.
   (B) disingenuous.
   (C) minor.
   (D) powerful.

3. According to the third paragraph, the ball can be advanced the field in all of the following ways EXCEPT

   (A) by kicking it.
   (B) by carrying it and running with it.
   (C) by passing it in a forward direction.
   (D) by passing it in a backwards direction.

4. If a team in rugby league scores a try and also scores a conversion, then according to lines 36-47, the team will have scored:

   (A) six points.
   (B) five points.
   (C) four points.
   (D) seven points.

5. The organization of the passage is best described as

   (A) a list of rules and explanations.
   (B) a chronological explanation of gameplay.
   (C) several facts and statistics supporting an opinion.
   (D) a rule-by-rule comparison of rugby and American football.

6. According to the last paragraph (lines 58-70), it can be inferred that tackling a player who does not have possession of the ball

   (A) is beneficial for both teams.
   (B) has no consequences for either team.
   (C) will result in a negative consequence for the team of the player who was tackled.
   (D) will result in a negative consequence for the team of the player who performed the tackle.

Expository – Passage 10

1   Japanese tea ceremonies can vary both in
2 formality and in procedure due to
3 differences in the time of year, time of day,
4 and overall philosophy of the participants.
5 Typically, the most formal proceedings
6 occur during the noon tea ceremony, when
7 the weather is cool.
8   Arriving at the teahouse just prior to the
9 scheduled time, guests often store their
10 outerwear and accessories in an
11 antechamber. In this antechamber are
12 compartments for storage, a floor mat called
13 a tatami, and an alcove in which hangs a
14 ceremonial scroll. The writing on the scroll
15 typically relates to the theme of the
16 gathering, the season, or some other related
17 matter. While disrobing and contemplating
18 the meanings and allusions written on the
19 scroll, guests are offered an aperitif –
20 typically hot water or roasted barley tea.
21   Once all of the guests arrive, they wait
22 until the host calls for them. Once called,
23 the guests and host exchange silent bows.
24 The former purify their hands and mouths at
25 a basin filled with water before entering the
26 main tearoom. Removing their shoes,
27 sandals, or other footwear, the party enters
28 the tearoom through a small crawl space,
29 which has symbolic as well as practical
30 purposes. Crawling through a small space is
31 meant to remind the participant of the quiet,
32 simple, and small space inside the teahouse:
33 the teahouse is a calm island amidst a
34 chaotic and turbulent world. Some
35 historians believe that the crawl space also
36 made it impossible for soldiers and warriors
37 to bring full-length swords with them into
38 the teahouse.
39   Once inside the tearoom, guests admire
40 the tea equipment and are seated in order of
41 rank. When the last guest enters the room,
42 he or she closes the door audibly to signal to
43 the host that all guests are present. The host
44 then welcomes each guest.
45   Conversation begins with a customary
46 formality: the first and most honorable guest
47 asks the host philosophical questions
48 regarding the significance of the scrolls and
49 any of the tea implements.
50   Once this formality is observed, a
51 charcoal fire is lit, which heats the water for
52 the tea. While waiting for the water to come
53 to temperature, guests are served
54 refreshments or a meal. After the meal,
55 guests retire outside while the host cleans,
56 takes down the hanging scroll, and replaces
57 it with a flower arrangement. The tearoom's
58 shutters are then opened, and once the tea is
59 ready to be served, the host strikes a bell or
60 gong.
61   The guests purify themselves again upon
62 entering. The host then cleans each
63 implement – such as a tea bowl, scoop, and
64 whisk – in front of each guest, working in a
65 precise order and using pronounced motions.
66 The placement of each implement after
67 cleansing is exact, and is prescribed by
68 tradition.
69   Each time the host presents a guest with
70 tea, both parties exchange bows. The guest
71 raises the tea bowl in respect to the host and
72 drinks from the rear of the bowl,
73 complimenting the host on the quality and
74 taste of the tea. Cleaning the rim of the
75 bowl, the guest passes the tea on to the next
76 participant. This process is repeated until all
77 guests have drunk from the bowl and all
78 guests have had the opportunity to admire
79 the tea bowl. The host then leaves the
80 tearoom to rekindle the charcoal fire, which
81 signals the end of the formal tea ceremony
82 and the beginning of a more casual affair.

Expository – Passage 10 Question Set

1. The primary purpose of the passage is to

   (A) tell a story about a specific tea ceremony.
   (B) compare Japanese tea ceremonies with Chinese tea ceremonies.
   (C) describe the rituals involved in a typical Japanese tea ceremony.
   (D) convince the reader that formalities and procedures in tea ceremonies are necessary.

2. In lines 21-38, which does the author mention as a reason that crawl spaces are used in teahouses?

   (A) The crawl space prevents guests from leaving quickly.
   (B) Unimportant guests are required to crawl rather than walk.
   (C) Uninvited guests cannot leave with the host's valuable swords.
   (D) The act of crawling to an inner-room symbolizes shelter and peace.

3. According to lines 39-49, the last guest to enter the room is most likely

   (A) a poet.
   (B) a servant or bodyguard.
   (C) the lowest in social rank and honor.
   (D) the highest in social rank and honor.

4. In line 49, "implements" most nearly means

   (A) actions.
   (B) tools.
   (C) toys.
   (D) vats.

5. The organization of the final paragraph (lines 69-82) can best be described as

   (A) a description of tea bowls.
   (B) a first-hand account of a famous tea ceremony.
   (C) an explanation of why all guests drink from the same bowl.
   (D) a series of steps leading up to the conclusion of a tea ceremony.

6. The author's tone can best be described as

   (A) academic.
   (B) approving.
   (C) contemptuous.
   (D) partial.

Quantitative Reasoning & Mathematics Achievement

Overview

The Upper Level ISEE contains two separate math sections.

In the Quantitative Reasoning section, you may be asked to estimate, compare and contrast amounts, interpret charts and graphs representing data, calculate probability, and understand the appropriate application of measurements. In this section, there are two types of questions and two parts on the exam: Word Problems and Quantitative Comparisons. This section tests your ability to understand broader, more abstract math questions and does not require elaborate calculations.

In the Mathematics Achievement section, you may be asked to apply mathematical rules, procedures, concepts, and formulas to solve questions. This section tests concrete math skills and may require calculations as well as knowledge of some mathematical terms and vocabulary.

Both of these sections are linked by common skills outlined further below.

- *Numbers and Operations* – You may be evaluated on your understanding of various numerical operators, including matrices, permutations, and combinations. You may also be asked to understand the conceptual nature of numbers, both rational and irrational, and real and imaginary.
- *Algebra* – You may be asked to understand algebraic functions, including the use of symbols in functions. You may also be asked to analyze expressions, equivalent expressions, and inequalities. You may also be asked to interpret graphs and tables as they relate to algebraic functions.
- *Geometry* – You may be asked to understand geometric figures, including the identification of those figures as well as how they interact with a coordinate grid and 3-dimensional space.
- *Measurement* – You may be asked to use mathematical formulas to measure different dimensions and qualities of both 2-dimensional and 3-dimensional shapes, including area, perimeter, and volume.
- *Data Analysis and Probability* – You may be asked to look at a data set, graph, or chart and from it draw conclusions or make inferences. You may also be asked to understand statistical concepts and probabilities.

On the Actual Test

In the Quantitative Reasoning section of the Upper Level ISEE, you will encounter 37 questions, which you will have 35 minutes to complete. There will be between 18-21 Word Problems and 14-17 Quantitative Comparisons.

In the Mathematics Achievement section, you will encounter 47 questions, which you will have 40 minutes to complete.

Most answer choices will be ordered from greatest to least or least to greatest.

As with other sections of this exam, a portion of these questions will be unscored, though you will not know which questions are unscored. Five questions from each section are unscored.

In This Practice Book

Because both Quantitative Reasoning and Mathematics Achievement test the same common skills, they are combined in this workbook by topic.

Each topic begins with an example and a brief introduction. Any topic that may be covered in the Quantitative Comparison portion of the test will include several Quantitative Comparison practice problems in this workbook, which can be found at the end of each topic.

The full list of topics can be found in the table of contents at the beginning of this workbook.

Remember: there are detailed answer explanations available online at www.thetutorverse.com. Be sure to obtain permission before going online.

How to Use This Section

As determined by your study plan, including the results of your diagnostic test, we encourage you to focus on the topics that are most challenging to you. Because there may be material on this test that you have not yet learned in school, we encourage you to seek additional help from trusted educators. Bring the materials to your tutor or teacher if you need additional enrichment in any given topic.

The questions in each section are progressive. This means that they start out easier, but then become more and more difficult as they build on more nuanced concepts related to that topic. Don't get discouraged if you find some questions difficult. Instead, consider asking a trusted educator to help you better understand the material.

Tutorverse Tips!

Remember that on the Upper Level ISEE, there is no penalty for guessing. If you don't know the answer to a question, take your best guess.

You won't be able to use a calculator or scrap paper to perform complex calculations, so if, as you answer a question things start to get more and more complicated, take a step back and think about what the question is asking you to do. If necessary, use the answer choices themselves to help you arrive at the correct answer by plugging them into formulas or expressions.

You do not have to memorize unit conversion tables (for instance, the number of feet in a mile), as any such information will be provided. However, metric unit conversions will not be provided (i.e. the number of milliliters in a liter).

Numbers & Operations

Arithmetic

Example: What is the value of the expression $7 - 2 \times 3 + 1$?

(A) 0
(B) 2
(C) 16
(D) 20

Solution: (B). The order of operations is PEMDAS (Parentheses, Exponents, Multiplication & Division, and Addition & Subtraction). Here, there are no parentheses or exponents, so multiply 2×3 first, which gives you 6. Then $7 - 6 = 1$, then $1 + 1 = 2$.

1. What is the value of the expression $9 + 5 \times (6 + 4)$?

   (A) 43
   (B) 59
   (C) 88
   (D) 140

2. What is the value of the expression $20 - 5 \times 2^2 + 4$?

   (A) −76
   (B) 4
   (C) 64
   (D) 240

3. What is the value of the expression $20 - 5 \times (2^2 + 4)$?

   (A) −20
   (B) 4
   (C) 64
   (D) 120

4. What is the value of the expression $(20 - 5) \times 2^2 + 4$?

   (A) 20
   (B) 64
   (C) 120
   (D) 904

5. What is the value of the expression $(20 - 5 \times 2)^2 + 4$?

   (A) −76
   (B) 64
   (C) 104
   (D) 904

6. What is the value of the expression $2 - 2 \div 2^2 + 2$?

   (A) −0.5
   (B) 0.5
   (C) 2
   (D) 3.5

7. What is the value of the expression $\dfrac{15(14)}{10(21)}$?

   (Note: If a division problem involves factors, try cancelling factors before you multiply!)

   (A) 1
   (B) 2.25
   (C) 10
   (D) 420

8. What is the value of the expression $\dfrac{52(12)}{24(13)}$?

   (A) 1
   (B) 2
   (C) 338
   (D) 1.8889

9. What is the value of the expression
$$\frac{2+4}{2^2+2^3}?$$

(A) 0.5
(B) 0.75
(C) 1
(D) 9.5

10. What is the value of the expression
$$\frac{(6+2)(9-2)}{(6-2)(10+4)}?$$

(A) 0
(B) 0.4
(C) 1
(D) 196

11. What is the value of the expression
$$\frac{10(5+5^2)}{5(5+5^2)}?$$

(A) 1.3333
(B) 2
(C) 75
(D) 300

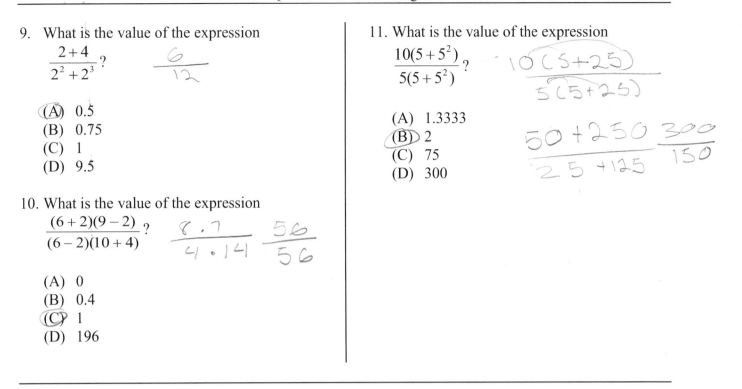

Quantitative Comparison Practice

Answer Choices:

(A) The amount in column A is greater.
(B) The amount in column B is greater.
(C) The two amounts are equal.
(D) The relationship cannot be determined from the information provided.

	Column A	Column B
12.	$1+2-3 \times 4$	0

	Column A	Column B
13.	$20-(5 \times 2)^2+4$	104

	Column A	Column B
14.	$\dfrac{(7+3)(11-5)}{(7-3)(11+5)}$	$\dfrac{15}{16}$

	Column A	Column B
15.	$\dfrac{(2^6-6^2)}{(2^3-3^2)}$	1

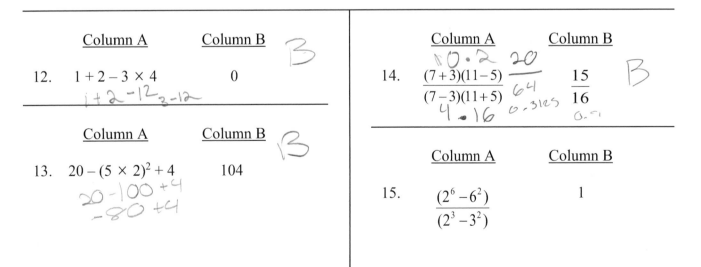

Factors

Example: What is the greatest common factor of $4x^2$ and $6x^3$?

(A) $2x^2$
(B) $2x^5$
(C) $12x^2$
(D) $12x^5$

Solution: (A). To find the greatest common factor (GCF) of any two or more terms, first find the GCF of the coefficients. Here, the GCF of 4 and 6 is 2. Next, take the lowest power of each variable. Here, x^2 is lower than x^3, so the GCF is x^2.

1. How many integers greater than 30 and less than 40 are each the product of two distinct prime factors?

(A) 1
(B) 3
(C) 4
(D) 5

2. What is the greatest common factor of $5y^2$ and $10y$?

(A) $5y$
(B) $5y^2$
(C) $10y$
(D) $20y^2$

3. What is the greatest common factor of $12b^2$ and 18?

(A) 6
(B) $6b$
(C) $12b^2$
(D) $36b^2$

4. What is the greatest common factor of $9a^3$ and $15a^4$?

(A) $3a$
(B) $3a^3$
(C) $9a^4$
(D) $15a^4$

5. What is the greatest common factor of $2x^4$, $4x^3$, and $6x^2$?

(A) $2x^2$
(B) $2x^4$
(C) $12x^2$
(D) $12x^4$

6. What is the greatest common factor of $36m^4$, $18m^8$, and $30m^6$?

(A) $6m^4$
(B) $6m^8$
(C) $12m^4$
(D) $12m^8$

7. What is the greatest common factor of $28p^4$, p^8, and 14?

(A) $28p^8$
(B) $7p$
(C) p^4
(D) 1

8. What is the greatest common factor of $5ab^2$ and a^2b?

(A) ab
(B) ab^2
(C) $5ab$
(D) $5a^2b^2$

9. What is the greatest common factor of $4xy^4$ and $5x^2y^2$?

    (A) $30x^2y^4$
    (B) $4x^2y^2$
    (C) x^2y^2
    (D) xy^2

10. What is the greatest common factor of $40b^2$ and $25a^2b$?

    (A) $5b$
    (B) $5b^2$
    (C) $15b$
    (D) $15b^2$

11. What is the greatest common factor of $81c^5d^8$, $45c^3d^8$, and $63c^4d^2$?

    (A) $27c^5d^8$
    (B) $27c^3d^2$
    (C) $9c^3d^2$
    (D) $9c^4d^3$

12. What is the greatest common factor of $2x^2y^4$, $3y^2z^4$, and $5x^2z^4$?

    (A) $2x^2z^4$
    (B) $2x^2y^2$
    (C) x^2yz
    (D) 1

Quantitative Comparison Practice

Answer Choices:

    (A) The amount in column A is greater.
    (B) The amount in column B is greater.
    (C) The two amounts are equal.
    (D) The relationship cannot be determined from the information provided.

a is a factor of 10 and b is a factor of 15.

	Column A	Column B
13.	The smallest value that ab must be a factor of	30

c, d, x, and y are all distinct positive integers.

x is a factor of c and y is a factor of d.

	Column A	Column B
14.	cx	dy

k is a factor of 6 and m is a factor of 7.

	Column A	Column B
15.	km	42

p is a prime factor of 14 and q is a prime factor of 20.

	Column A	Column B
16.	The largest possible value of pq	35

Multiples

Example: What is the least common multiple of $10x^2$ and $6x^3$?

(A) $2x^2$
(B) $2x^5$
(C) $30x^2$
(D) $30x^3$

Solution: (D). To find the least common multiple (LCM) of any two or more terms, first find the LCM of the coefficients. Here, the LCM of 10 and 6 is 30. Next, take the highest power of each variable. Here, x^3 is greater than x^2, so the LCM is x^3.

1. If y is a prime number, what is the least common multiple of $24y^4$ and $16y^3$?

(A) $8y^7$
(B) $8y^{12}$
(C) $48y^3$
(D) $48y^4$

2. If z is a prime number, what is the least common multiple of $10z^6$, $12z$, and $6z^3$?

(A) $24z$
(B) $24z^6$
(C) $60z$
(D) $60z^6$

3. If a is a prime number, what is the least common multiple of $81a^{12}$ and $9a^6$?

(A) $81a^{12}$
(B) $81a^6$
(C) $9a^{12}$
(D) $9a^6$

4. If x and y are prime numbers, what is the least common multiple of $12x^2y^3$ and $16x^3y$?

(A) $48x^3y^3$
(B) $48x^2y$
(C) $4x^3y^3$
(D) $4x^2y$

5. If a and b are prime numbers, what is the least common multiple of $40a^5$ and $24a^4b^2$?

(A) $120a^5b^2$
(B) $120a^4b$
(C) $80a^5b^2$
(D) $80a^4$

6. If c and d are prime numbers, what is the least common multiple of $6c^2$, $8cd$, and $4d^3$?

(A) $24cd$
(B) $24c^2d^3$
(C) $48cd$
(D) $48c^2d^3$

7. If m and n are prime numbers, what is the least common multiple of $8m^2$, $10m^4n^6$, and $12n^8$?

(A) $120m^4n^8$
(B) $120m^2n^6$
(C) $80m^4n^8$
(D) $80m^2n^6$

8. If p and q are prime numbers, what is the least common multiple of 28, $14pq$, and $7p^7$?

(A) $28p^7$
(B) $28p^7q$
(C) $56pq$
(D) $56p^7q$

The Tutorverse
www.thetutorverse.com

Exponents

Example: Which of the following represents 9^3 in terms of 3?

    (A) 3^3
    (B) 3^6
    (C) 3^9
    (D) 6^3

Solution: (B). 9^3 means $9 \times 9 \times 9$. That equals 729, but that is not what the question is asking, so you do not have to find the actual numerical value. It is asking you to write 729 as a power of 3. Since $3 \times 3 = 9$, every time you see a 9, you can rewrite it as 3×3. $9 \times 9 \times 9$ then becomes $3 \times 3 \times 3 \times 3 \times 3 \times 3$, which is 3^6.

1. What is the value of 3^4?

    (A) 12
    (B) 27
    (C) 64
    (D) 81

2. What is the value of 5^3?

    (A) 15
    (B) 25
    (C) 125
    (D) 243

3. What is the value of 2^5?

    (A) 16
    (B) 25
    (C) 32
    (D) 64

4. Which of the following represents 4^3 in expanded form?

    (A) 4×3
    (B) $4 \times 4 \times 4$
    (C) $4 + 4 + 4$
    (D) $3 \times 3 \times 3 \times 3$

5. Which of the following represents 8^4 in expanded form?

    (A) 8×4
    (B) $8 \times 8 \times 8 \times 8$
    (C) $8 + 8 + 8 + 8$
    (D) $4 \times 4 \times 4 \times 4 \times 4 \times 4 \times 4 \times 4$

6. Which of the following represents 36^2 in terms of 6?

    (A) 4^6
    (B) 6^2
    (C) 6^4
    (D) 6^8

7. Which of the following represents 25^4 in terms of 5?

    (A) 5^4
    (B) 5^6
    (C) 5^8
    (D) 5^{10}

8. Which of the following represents 27^3 in terms of 3?

    (A) 3^6
    (B) 3^9
    (C) 3^{12}
    (D) 3^{27}

9. What is the value of the expression
$$\frac{(5^3)(2^5)}{(5^2)(2^3)}?$$

(A) 2
(B) 10
(C) 20
(D) 10^{10}

10. A Farmer put a chicken in a henhouse. That chicken laid four eggs. When they hatched, each of those chickens laid four eggs. All of the chickens that resulted then laid four eggs of their own. By the time all of the eggs hatched, how many chickens were in the henhouse?

(A) $1 + 4^2$
(B) $1 + 4^3$
(C) $4 + 4^2 + 4^3$
(D) $1 + 4 + 4^2 + 4^3$

11. Which of the following represents 2^6 in terms of 8?

(A) 8^2
(B) 8^3
(C) 8^{12}
(D) 8^{18}

12. Joey gave 2 people each a piece of candy in January. In February, each of those 2 people gave 2 different people a piece of candy, who in turn each gave 2 different people a piece of candy in March. This pattern is repeated until December. Which expression represents the number of people who will have been given a piece of candy by the end of December?

(A) $1 + 2^{11}$
(B) $1 + 2^{12}$
(C) $2 + 2^2 + 2^3 + 2^4 + 2^5 + 2^6 + 2^7 + 2^8 + 2^9 + 2^{10} + 2^{11} + 2^{12}$
(D) $1 + 2 + 2^2 + 2^3 + 2^4 + 2^5 + 2^6 + 2^7 + 2^8 + 2^9 + 2^{10} + 2^{11} + 2^{12}$

Quantitative Comparison Practice

Answer Choices:

(A) The amount in column A is greater.
(B) The amount in column B is greater.
(C) The two amounts are equal.
(D) The relationship cannot be determined from the information provided.

	Column A	Column B
13.	6^6	36^2

	Column A	Column B
14.	$\dfrac{(6^3)(2^3)}{(2^3)(8^2)}$	$\dfrac{27}{8}$

On Day 1, a scientist put 2 fruit flies in a clear box. On Day 2, he observed that the number of fruit flies in the box had doubled. On Day 3, he observed that the number doubled again, and so on.

	Column A	Column B
15.	The number of fruit flies on Day 10	$2 + 2^{10}$

Negative Exponents

Example: Which of the following is equivalent to $\dfrac{w^3 x^2}{6 y^{-2} z^{-1}}$?

(A) $\dfrac{6 y^2 z}{w^3 x^2}$

(B) $6 w^3 x^2 y^2 z$

(C) $\dfrac{w^3 x^2 y^2 z}{6}$

(D) $-y^2 z \dfrac{w^3 x^2}{6}$

Solution: (C). Negative exponents simply mean that the base value should be flipped to the other side of the fraction line (if it's on top, move it to the bottom, and vice versa). Here, w and x both have positive exponents, so they can stay where they are. y and z both have negative exponents, so they get flipped from the bottom to the top, leaving only the 6 in the denominator.

1. What is the value of 7^{-1}?

(A) $-\dfrac{1}{7}$

(B) $\dfrac{1}{7}$

(C) 7

(D) -7

2. What is the value of 6^{-2}?

(A) -36

(B) -3

(C) $-\dfrac{2}{6}$

(D) $\dfrac{1}{36}$

3. What is the value of 3^{-4}?

(A) -81

(B) $-\dfrac{3}{4}$

(C) $\dfrac{1}{81}$

(D) $\dfrac{4}{3}$

4. What is the value of 0^{-1}?

(A) 0

(B) -1

(C) -10

(D) Does not exist

5. What is the value of $\left(\dfrac{1}{2}\right)^{-2}$?

(A) -4

(B) -2

(C) $\dfrac{1}{4}$

(D) 4

6. What is the value of $\left(\dfrac{2}{3}\right)^{-3}$?

(A) $-\dfrac{9}{6}$

(B) $\dfrac{9}{6}$

(C) $-\dfrac{27}{8}$

(D) $\dfrac{27}{8}$

7. What is the value of $\left(\dfrac{5}{4}\right)^{-3}$?

(A) $-\dfrac{125}{64}$

(B) $\dfrac{125}{64}$

(C) $-\dfrac{64}{125}$

(D) $\dfrac{64}{125}$

8. Which is equivalent to $\dfrac{1}{125}$?

(A) -5^3
(B) 5^{-3}
(C) 25^{-2}
(D) 125^{-2}

9. Which is equivalent to $\dfrac{1}{32}$?

(A) -2^5
(B) 2^{-5}
(C) 2^{-6}
(D) 16^{-2}

10. Which is equivalent to $\dfrac{1}{1,000}$?

    I. 10^{-3}
    II. 100^{-2}
    III. $1,000^{-1}$

(A) I and II only
(B) II and III only
(C) I and III only
(D) I, II, and III

11. Which of the following is equivalent to $\dfrac{1}{16}$?

    I. 2^{-4}
    II. 4^{-2}
    III. 16^{-1}

(A) I and II only
(B) II and III only
(C) I and III only
(D) I, II, and III

12. Which of the following is equivalent to x^{-5}?

(A) $-\dfrac{1}{x^5}$

(B) $-x^5$

(C) $\dfrac{x}{5}$

(D) $\dfrac{1}{x^5}$

13. Which of the following is equivalent to m^{-6}?

(A) $-\dfrac{1}{m^6}$

(B) $-m^6$

(C) $\dfrac{1}{m^6}$

(D) $\dfrac{6}{m}$

14. Which of the following is equivalent to $x^2 y^{-3}$?

(A) $\dfrac{1}{x^2 y^3}$

(B) $\dfrac{x^2}{y^3}$

(C) $-\dfrac{x^2}{y^3}$

(D) $-x^2 y^3$

15. Which of the following is equivalent to $12a^{-6}b^2c^{-4}$?

(A) $\dfrac{12b^2}{a^6c^4}$

(B) $-\dfrac{12b^2}{a^6c^4}$

(C) $\dfrac{1}{12a^6b^2c^4}$

(D) $-12a^6b^2c^4$

16. Which of the following is equivalent to $\dfrac{a^{-2}}{c^4}$?

(A) $\dfrac{c^4}{a^{-2}}$

(B) $\dfrac{1}{a^2c^4}$

(C) $\dfrac{1}{a^{-2}c^4}$

(D) $-\dfrac{1}{a^2c^4}$

17. Which of the following is equivalent to $\dfrac{4m^{-6}}{n^5}$?

(A) $\dfrac{4}{m^6n^5}$

(B) $\dfrac{n^5}{4m^{-6}}$

(C) $-\dfrac{4m^6}{n^5}$

(D) $\dfrac{1}{4m^6n^5}$

18. Which of the following is equivalent to $\dfrac{p^4q^{-4}}{r^2s}$?

(A) $\dfrac{r^2s}{p^4q^4}$

(B) $\dfrac{p^4}{q^4r^2s}$

(C) $\dfrac{p^4r^2s}{q^4}$

(D) $-\dfrac{p^4q^4}{r^2s}$

19. Which of the following is equivalent to $\dfrac{w^3x^2}{6y^{-2}z^{-1}}$?

(A) $\dfrac{6y^2z^1}{w^3x^2}$

(B) $6w^3x^2y^2z$

(C) $\dfrac{w^3x^2y^2z^1}{6}$

(D) $-y^2z\dfrac{w^3x^2}{6}$

20. Which of the following is equivalent to $\dfrac{w^{-3}x^{-2}}{y^2z^1}$?

(A) $\dfrac{y^2z^1}{w^3x^2}$

(B) $\dfrac{y^2z^1}{w^{-3}x^{-2}}$

(C) $\dfrac{1}{w^3x^2y^2z}$

(D) $-w^3x^2y^2z$

21. Which of the following is equivalent to $\dfrac{2wx^{-2}}{3y^{-2}z^{-1}}$?

  (A) $\dfrac{6y^2z^1}{wx^2}$

  (B) $\dfrac{2wy^2z^1}{3x^2}$

  (C) $\dfrac{6wy^2z^1}{x^2}$

  (D) $\dfrac{3wy^2z^1}{2x^2}$

22. Which of the following is equivalent to $\dfrac{9d^4e^{-2}f^9}{3uv^9w^{-8}}$?

  (A) $\dfrac{d^4e^2f^9}{3uv^9w^8}$

  (B) $\dfrac{3uv^9w^8}{d^4e^2f^9}$

  (C) $\dfrac{3e^{-2}uv^9}{d^4f^9w^{-8}}$

  (D) $3\dfrac{d^4f^9w^8}{e^2uv^9}$

Quantitative Comparison Practice

Answer Choices:

  (A) The amount in column A is greater.
  (B) The amount in column B is greater.
  (C) The two amounts are equal.
  (D) The relationship cannot be determined from the information provided.

	Column A	Column B
23.	2^{-6}	-64

	Column A	Column B
24.	$\left(\dfrac{3}{2}\right)^{-3}$	$\left(\dfrac{3}{2}\right)^{3}$

	Column A	Column B
25.	y^{-1}	y

a, x, y, and *z* are all positive integers

	Column A	Column B
26.	$\dfrac{a^{-6}b^4c}{12x^2yz^{-8}}$	$\dfrac{b^4cz^8}{12a^6x^2y}$

	Column A	Column B
27.	$\left(\dfrac{2}{5}\right)^{-3}$	$\left(\dfrac{2}{5}\right)^{3}$

	Column A	Column B
28.	$\left(\dfrac{1}{y}\right)^{-2}$	y^{-2}

Fractional Exponents

Example: What is the value of $16^{\frac{1}{2}}$?

    (A) $\frac{1}{32}$

    (B) $\frac{1}{8}$

    (C)   4

    (D)   8

Solution: (C). Fractional exponents tell you to find the root. Whatever the denominator of the exponent's fraction is, that's the root you find. $16^{\frac{1}{2}}$ is the same as $\sqrt{16}$, which is equal to 4. If it had said $16^{\frac{1}{4}}$, you would find $\sqrt[4]{16}$, which is equal to 2.

1. What is the value of $100^{\frac{1}{2}}$?

    (A) $\frac{1}{10}$

    (B)   10

    (C) $\frac{1}{50}$

    (D)   50

2. What is the value of $8^{\frac{1}{3}}$?

    (A) $\frac{3}{8}$

    (B) $\frac{2}{3}$

    (C)   2

    (D)   24

3. What is the value of $125^{\frac{1}{3}}$?

    (A) $\frac{3}{125}$

    (B) $\frac{125}{3}$

    (C)   25

    (D)   5

4. What is the value of $\left(\frac{1}{9}\right)^{\frac{1}{2}}$?

    (A)   3

    (B) $\frac{1}{3}$

    (C)   81

    (D) $\frac{1}{81}$

5. What is the value of $\left(\dfrac{81}{49}\right)^{\frac{1}{2}}$?

  (A) $\dfrac{7}{9}$

  (B) $\dfrac{9}{7}$

  (C) $\dfrac{81}{2,401}$

  (D) $\dfrac{2,401}{81}$

6. What is the value of $\left(\dfrac{27}{64}\right)^{\frac{1}{3}}$?

  (A) $\dfrac{3}{4}$

  (B) $\dfrac{4}{3}$

  (C) $\dfrac{4}{27}$

  (D) $\dfrac{27}{4}$

7. What is the value of $16^{-\frac{1}{2}}$?

  (A)   4

  (B) $\dfrac{1}{4}$

  (C) -4

  (D) $-\dfrac{1}{4}$

8. What is the value of $100^{-\frac{1}{2}}$?

  (A)   10

  (B)   50

  (C) $\dfrac{1}{10}$

  (D) $\dfrac{1}{50}$

9. What is the value of $8^{-\frac{1}{3}}$?

  (A)   2

  (B) $\dfrac{1}{2}$

  (C) $\dfrac{3}{8}$

  (D) $\dfrac{8}{3}$

10. What is the value of $\left(\dfrac{1}{9}\right)^{-\frac{1}{2}}$?

  (A)   3

  (B) $\dfrac{1}{3}$

  (C)   81

  (D) $\dfrac{1}{18}$

11. What is the value of $\left(\dfrac{81}{49}\right)^{-\frac{1}{2}}$?

  (A) $\dfrac{7}{9}$

  (B) $\dfrac{9}{7}$

  (C) $-\dfrac{7}{9}$

  (D) $-\dfrac{9}{7}$

12. What is the value of $\left(\dfrac{27}{64}\right)^{-\frac{1}{3}}$?

  (A) $\dfrac{4}{3}$

  (B) $\dfrac{3}{4}$

  (C) $\dfrac{9}{8}$

  (D) $\dfrac{8}{9}$

Quantitative Comparison Practice

Answer Choices:

- (A) The amount in column A is greater.
- (B) The amount in column B is greater.
- (C) The two amounts are equal.
- (D) The relationship cannot be determined from the information provided.

	Column A	Column B
13.	$-\left(\dfrac{1}{9}\right)^{\frac{1}{2}}$	$-\left(\dfrac{1}{16}\right)^{\frac{1}{2}}$

	Column A	Column B
14.	$\left(\dfrac{1}{8}\right)^{\frac{1}{3}}$	$\left(\dfrac{1}{8}\right)^{-\frac{1}{3}}$

	Column A	Column B
15.	$9^{\frac{1}{2}}$	$\left(\dfrac{1}{9}\right)^{\frac{1}{2}}$

	Column A	Column B
16.	$11^{\frac{1}{2}}$	$\left(\dfrac{1}{11}\right)^{\frac{1}{2}}$

	Column A	Column B
17.	$x^{\frac{1}{2}}$	$\left(\dfrac{1}{x}\right)^{\frac{1}{2}}$

$y > 0$

	Column A	Column B
18.	$y^{\frac{1}{2}}$	$\left(\dfrac{1}{y}\right)^{\frac{1}{2}}$

$z > 1$

	Column A	Column B
19.	$z^{\frac{1}{2}}$	$\left(\dfrac{1}{z}\right)^{\frac{1}{2}}$

	Column A	Column B
20.	$\left(\dfrac{4}{9}\right)^{\frac{1}{2}}$	$\left(\dfrac{9}{4}\right)^{\frac{1}{2}}$

Roots of Numbers

Example: What is the value of $\sqrt{72}$?

    (A) $2\sqrt{6}$
    (B) $6\sqrt{2}$
    (C) $24\sqrt{3}$
    (D)   36

Solution: (B). 72 is not a perfect square like 4, 9, or 25, so its square root will not be an integer. Instead, split the radicand into two factors, one of which must be a perfect square. Here, $72 = 36 \times 2$, so $\sqrt{72} = \sqrt{36} \times \sqrt{2}$. $\sqrt{36} = 6$, so $\sqrt{36} \times \sqrt{2} = 6\sqrt{2}$.

1. What is the approximate value of $\sqrt{4}$?

    (A)   1.414
    (B)   2
    (C)   2.333
    (D)   4

2. What is the value of $\sqrt{121}$?

    (A)   11
    (B)   12.1
    (C)   13
    (D)   60.5

3. What is the value of $\sqrt{225}$?

    (A)   5.5
    (B)   15
    (C)   25
    (D)   35

4. What is the value of $\sqrt{25-9}$?

    (A)   2
    (B)   4
    (C)   6
    (D)   8

5. What is the value of $\sqrt{100-36}$?

    (A)   4
    (B)   8
    (C)   12
    (D)   16

6. What is the value of $\sqrt{144+25}$?

    (A)   13
    (B)   14
    (C)   16
    (D)   17

7. What is the value of $\sqrt{16+9} - (\sqrt{16} + \sqrt{9})$?

    (A)   –2
    (B)   0
    (C)   4
    (D)   6

8. Which expression represents a rational number?

    (A) $\sqrt{64+36}$
    (B) $\sqrt{64-36}$
    (C) $\sqrt{9-25}$
    (D) $\sqrt{25+9}$

9. What is the value of $\sqrt{\dfrac{1}{4}}$?

(A) $\dfrac{1}{16}$

(B) $\dfrac{1}{8}$

(C) $\dfrac{1}{2}$

(D) 2

10. What is the value of $\sqrt{\dfrac{9}{25}}$?

(A) $\dfrac{\sqrt{3}}{5}$

(B) $\dfrac{3}{\sqrt{5}}$

(C) $\dfrac{1}{8}$

(D) $\dfrac{3}{5}$

11. What is the value of $\sqrt{\dfrac{144}{81}}$?

(A) $\dfrac{\sqrt{12}}{9}$

(B) $\dfrac{\sqrt{16}}{9}$

(C) $\dfrac{4}{3}$

(D) 4

12. What is the value of $\sqrt{27}$?

(A) 3
(B) $3\sqrt{3}$
(C) $9\sqrt{3}$
(D) 13.5

13. What is the value of $\sqrt{48}$?

(A) $2\sqrt{6}$
(B) $4\sqrt{3}$
(C) 12
(D) 24

14. What is the value of $\sqrt{75}$?

(A) $3\sqrt{5}$
(B) $5\sqrt{3}$
(C) $25\sqrt{3}$
(D) 37.5

15. What is the value of $\sqrt{50}+\sqrt{18}$?

(A) $2\sqrt{8}$
(B) $8\sqrt{2}$
(C) $2\sqrt{17}$
(D) 34

16. What is the value of $\sqrt{108}-\sqrt{75}$?

(A) $\sqrt{3}$
(B) $3\sqrt{11}$
(C) $11\sqrt{3}$
(D) 11

17. What is the value of $\sqrt{32}+\sqrt{98}$?

(A) $2\sqrt{65}$
(B) $5\sqrt{16}$
(C) $11\sqrt{2}$
(D) $23\sqrt{2}$

18. What is the value of $\sqrt{80}+\sqrt{20}+\sqrt{45}$?

(A) $5\sqrt{9}$
(B) $9\sqrt{5}$
(C) $5\sqrt{29}$
(D) $29\sqrt{15}$

19. What is the value of $\sqrt{99} + \sqrt{44} + \sqrt{72}$?

   (A) $11\sqrt{5} + 2\sqrt{6}$
   (B) $+ 6\sqrt{2}$
   (C) $5\sqrt{11} + 2\sqrt{6}$
   (D) $5\sqrt{11} + 6\sqrt{2}$

20. What is the value of $\sqrt{250} - \sqrt{80} - \sqrt{90}$?

   (A) $2\sqrt{10} - 10$
   (B) $10\sqrt{2} - 10$
   (C) $2\sqrt{10} - 4\sqrt{5}$
   (D) $10\sqrt{2} - 4\sqrt{5}$

21. What is the value of $\sqrt{48} - \sqrt{8} + \sqrt{162}$?

   (A) $4\sqrt{3} + 7\sqrt{2}$
   (B) $4\sqrt{3} + 2\sqrt{7}$
   (C) $6 + 7\sqrt{2}$
   (D) $6 + 2\sqrt{7}$

22. What is the value of $\sqrt{8} \times \sqrt{2}$?

   (A)   4
   (B) $4\sqrt{2}$
   (C) $2\sqrt{8}$
   (D) $2\sqrt{2} + 2$

23. What is the value of $\sqrt{7} \times \sqrt{7}$?

   (A)   3.5
   (B)   7
   (C) $\sqrt{7}$
   (D) $\sqrt{14}$

24. What is the value of $\sqrt{20} \times \sqrt{5}$?

   (A)   10
   (B) $4\sqrt{5}$
   (C) $5\sqrt{2}$
   (D) $5\sqrt{10}$

25. What is the value of $\sqrt{15} \times \sqrt{5}$?

   (A) $3\sqrt{5}$
   (B) $5\sqrt{3}$
   (C) $25\sqrt{3}$
   (D)   37.5

26. What is the value of $\sqrt{20} \times \sqrt{80}$?

   (A) $5\sqrt{10}$
   (B)   16
   (C) $5\sqrt{16}$
   (D)   40

27. What is the value of $\sqrt{80} \div \sqrt{2}$?

   (A) $2\sqrt{10}$
   (B)   4
   (C) $10\sqrt{2}$
   (D)   40

28. What is the value of $\sqrt{27} \div (3\sqrt{3})$?

   (A)   1
   (B)   3
   (C)   9
   (D) $9\sqrt{3}$

Roots of Variables

Example: What is the value of $\sqrt{32x^{11}}$?

     (A) $16\sqrt{x^{11}}$
     (B) $16x^{10}\sqrt{x}$
     (C) $4x^{10}\sqrt{2x}$
     (D) $4x^5\sqrt{2x}$

Solution: (D). When finding the square root of a variable with a coefficient, find the root of each separately. Here, $\sqrt{32} = 4\sqrt{2}$. To find the square root of a variable, cut the variable in half. If the exponent is an odd number, factor out an x first. Here, $\sqrt{x^{11}}$ can first be rewritten as $\sqrt{x^{10}} \times \sqrt{x}$, which then simplifies to $x^5\sqrt{x}$. Lastly, combine all the factors back together. Here, the factors $4 \times \sqrt{2} \times x^5 \times \sqrt{x}$ can be rearranged as $4x^5\sqrt{2x}$.

1. If x is a positive integer, for which value of x could $\sqrt{x}$ be an integer?

    (A) 1
    (B) 2
    (C) 3
    (D) 6

2. If x is a positive integer, for which value of x could $\sqrt{\dfrac{x}{2}}$ be an integer?

    (A) 16
    (B) 18
    (C) 20
    (D) 22

3. If x is a positive integer, for which value of x could $\sqrt{\dfrac{3x}{2}}$ be an integer?

    (A) 12
    (B) 18
    (C) 24
    (D) 30

4. What is the value of $\sqrt{x^2}$?

    (A) x
    (B) $2x$
    (C) $x^{\frac{1}{2}}$
    (D) $\dfrac{x}{2}$

5. What is the value of $\sqrt{x^{16}}$?

    (A) x^2
    (B) x^4
    (C) x^8
    (D) $4x$

6. What is the value of $\sqrt{x^{100}}$?

    (A) x^{10}
    (B) x^{50}
    (C) $10x$
    (D) $50x$

7. What is the value of $\sqrt{9x^2}$?

    (A) $3x$
    (B) $3x^2$
    (C) $6x$
    (D) $9x$

8. What is the value of $\sqrt{36x^{18}}$?

   (A) $6x^3$
   (B) $6x^9$
   (C) $6x^{18}$
   (D) $18x^9$

9. What is the value of $\sqrt{25x^{50}}$?

   (A) $5x$
   (B) $5x^5$
   (C) $5x^{10}$
   (D) $5x^{25}$

10. What is the value of $\sqrt{64x^{128}}$?

   (A) $8x^{32}$
   (B) $8x^{64}$
   (C) $16x^{32}$
   (D) $16x^{64}$

11. What is the value of $\sqrt{16x^{16}}$?

   (A) $4x^4$
   (B) $4x^8$
   (C) $8x^4$
   (D) $8x^8$

12. What is the value of $\sqrt{x^3}$?

   (A) $x^2\sqrt{x}$
   (B) $x\sqrt{x}$
   (C) $3x$
   (D) $\dfrac{x}{3}$

13. What is the value of $\sqrt{x^7}$?

   (A) $x^6\sqrt{x}$
   (B) $x^3\sqrt{x}$
   (C) $7x$
   (D) $\dfrac{x}{7}$

14. What is the value of $\sqrt{x^{15}}$?

   (A) $15x$
   (B) $7x\sqrt{x}$
   (C) $x^7\sqrt{x}$
   (D) $x^{14}\sqrt{x}$

15. What is the value of $\sqrt{49x^9}$?

   (A) $14x^4\sqrt{x}$
   (B) $14x^8\sqrt{x}$
   (C) $7x^4\sqrt{x}$
   (D) $7x^8\sqrt{x}$

16. What is the value of $\sqrt{12x^{13}}$?

   (A) $2x^{12}\sqrt{3x}$
   (B) $2x^6\sqrt{3x}$
   (C) $6x^{12}\sqrt{x}$
   (D) $6x^6\sqrt{x}$

17. What is the value of $\sqrt{45x^3}$?

   (A) $3x\sqrt{5x}$
   (B) $9x\sqrt{5x}$
   (C) $3x^2\sqrt{5x}$
   (D) $9x^2\sqrt{5x}$

18. What is the value of $\sqrt{x^3y^4}$?

   (A) $xy^2\sqrt{x}$
   (B) $xy^3\sqrt{xy}$
   (C) $x^2y^2\sqrt{x}$
   (D) $x^2y^3\sqrt{xy}$

19. What is the value of $\sqrt{a^6b^5}$?

   (A) $a^5b^4\sqrt{ab}$
   (B) $a^5b^2\sqrt{ab}$
   (C) $a^3b^4\sqrt{b}$
   (D) $a^3b^2\sqrt{b}$

Imaginary Numbers

Example: What is the solution to $x^2 = -16$?

     (A) -4
     (B) 4
     (C) $4i$
     (D) $\pm 4i$

Solution: (D). To solve for x, find the square root of both sides of the equation, which will leave you with $x = \sqrt{-16}$. The square root of a negative number is impossible, so we factor the negative part out to $\sqrt{-1} \times \sqrt{16}$. $\sqrt{-1}$ is called an imaginary number, or i. And don't forget that the answer to a square root should include a $\pm$ sign (unless a problem specifically asks for only the positive square root).

1. What is the value of $\sqrt{-25}$?

     (A) -5
     (B) ± 5
     (C) $-5i$
     (D) $5i$

2. What is the value of $\sqrt{-196}$?

     (A) -14
     (B) ± 14
     (C) $-14i$
     (D) $14i$

3. If $i = \sqrt{-1}$, what is the value of i^2?

     (A) 1
     (B) -1
     (C) $\sqrt{-1}$
     (D) $-\sqrt{-1}$

4. If $i = \sqrt{-1}$, what is the value of i^3?

     (A) 1
     (B) -1
     (C) $\sqrt{-1}$
     (D) $-\sqrt{-1}$

5. What is the solution set for $x^2 = -100$?

     (A) 10
     (B) $10i$
     (C) ± 10
     (D) $\pm 10i$

6. What is the solution set for $x^2 + 144 = 0$?

     (A) 12
     (B) $12i$
     (C) ± 12
     (D) $\pm 12i$

7. What is the value of $\sqrt{-9} \times \sqrt{-4}$?

     (A) $-6i$
     (B) -6
     (C) 6
     (D) $6i$

8. What is the value of $\sqrt{50} \times \sqrt{-2}$?

     (A) 10
     (B) $10i$
     (C) ± 10
     (D) $\pm 10i$

Percents

> **Example:** A shirt was originally priced at $100. On Monday, it went on sale for 10% off. On Tuesday, it was marked back up 10% from its sale price. What is the price now?
>
> (A) $99
> (B) $100
> (C) $101
> (D) $102
>
> **Solution:** (A). On Monday, the price dropped 10% from $100, so you should subtract $10 to get $90. On Tuesday, the price went up 10% <u>from $90</u>, not $100, so you should add $9, not $10.

1. A rectangle is 20 meters long and 20 meters wide. If the length is increased by 10% and the width is decreased by 10%, what is the new area?

   (A) 320
   (B) 396
   (C) 400
   (D) 484

2. A rectangle is 50 feet long and 40 feet wide. The length is decreased by 20% and the width is increased by 20%. What is the percent decrease in the area?

   (A) 0%
   (B) 1%
   (C) 4%
   (D) 10%

3. The retail price for a book was $30. It was marked down 20% on Black Friday. The next day, it was marked back up 30%. What was the percent increase on the original price?

   (A) 0%
   (B) 4%
   (C) 6%
   (D) 10%

4. A number is decreased by 20%, and then the new number is decreased by another 20%. What is the percent decrease from the original number? *(Note: Always use 100% for the original number!)*

   (A) 36%
   (B) 40%
   (C) 60%
   (D) 64%

5. A number is increased by 30%, and then the new number is increased by another 30%. What is the percent increase from the original number?

   (A) 60%
   (B) 69%
   (C) 160%
   (D) 169%

6. On Thursday night, Juan slept 6 hours. On Friday night, he slept 50% more. How many hours did he sleep Friday night?

   (A) 3
   (B) 6
   (C) 9
   (D) 15

7. John ran 8 miles on Tuesday. On Wednesday, he ran 150% the distance he ran on Tuesday. How far did he run on Wednesday?

(A) $5\frac{1}{3}$

(B) 12

(C) 16

(D) 20

8. Kevin watched 2 hours of TV on Saturday. On Sunday, he watched 100% as many hours of TV as he did on Saturday. How much TV did he watch on Sunday?

(A) 2

(B) 3

(C) 4

(D) 6

Quantitative Comparison Practice – Answer Choices:

(A) The amount in column A is greater.

(B) The amount in column B is greater.

(C) The two amounts are equal.

(D) The relationship cannot be determined from the information provided.

The original price of a shirt goes up 20% in September, then drops 20% in October.

	Column A	Column B
9.	The percent decrease in October from the original price	0%

The length of a rectangle is increased by 30% and the width is decreased by 20%.

	Column A	Column B
10.	The percent increase in the area of the rectangle	10%

A store was selling a book for $25. They dropped the price 20% on Monday, then raised the price back up 20% on Tuesday.

	Column A	Column B
11.	The price of the book on Tuesday	$25

A student purchases a graphic novel for $100. It increases in value by 20% each year she owns it.

	Column A	Column B
12.	The amount of profit she would earn by selling the novel after 2 years	$40

Percent Change

Example: A shirt that originally cost $80 is on sale for $60. What is the percent decrease in the price?

(A) 20%
(B) 25%
(C) 33%
(D) 60%

Solution: (B). To find percent increase or decrease, create a fraction. Use the difference of the numbers as the numerator and the original number as the denominator. Here, the difference of $80 and $60 is $20 and the original price was $80, so the fraction should be $\frac{20}{80}$, which is equivalent to 25%.

1. On Friday, a pizzeria sold 90 pizza pies. On Saturday, it sold 180 pizza pies. What was the percent increase in the number of pizza pies sold?

(A) 50%
(B) 90%
(C) 100%
(D) 200%

2. On Saturday, a pizzeria sold 180 pizza pies. On Sunday, it sold 90 pizza pies. What was the percent decrease in the number of pizza pies sold?

(A) 25%
(B) 50%
(C) 100%
(D) 200%

3. Last week Flynn did 4 hours of community service. This week, he did 6 hours. What is the percent increase in the number of hours of community service Flynn did?

(A) 20%
(B) 25%
(C) 33%
(D) 50%

4. Last week Ella did 6 hours of community service. This week, she did 4 hours. What is the approximate percent decrease in the number of hours of community service Ella did?

(A) 20%
(B) 25%
(C) 33%
(D) 50%

5. An art dealer bought a painting for $600 and then sold it for $750. What is the percent increase in the price of the painting?

(A) 15%
(B) 20%
(C) 25%
(D) 33%

For questions 6-8, use the following information:

Mr. Jones bought a house in 2006 for $600,000.

6. In 2010, Mr. Jones' house was worth only $420,000. What is the percent decrease in the value of the house?

(A) 18%
(B) 28%
(C) 30%
(D) 43%

7. Mr. Jones' house was worth $630,000 in 2015. What was the percent increase in the value of the house since 2010?

    (A) 21%
    (B) 30%
    (C) 33%
    (D) 50%

8. What was the percent increase in the value of Mr. Jones' house from 2006 to 2015?

    (A) 5%
    (B) 15%
    (C) 20%
    (D) 30%

Quantitative Comparison Practice

Answer Choices:

(A) The amount in column A is greater.
(B) The amount in column B is greater.
(C) The two amounts are equal.
(D) The relationship cannot be determined from the information provided.

A supermarket sells boxes of granola for $2.40. Due to demand, they increase the prince to $6.00.

	Column A	Column B
9.	The percent increase in the price	250%

A supermarket sells boxes of granola for $6.00. This week, it is on sale for $2.40.

	Column A	Column B
10.	The percent decrease in the price	60%

Mary's electrical bill dropped from $40 in May to $30 in June.

	Column A	Column B
11.	The percent decrease in the cost of the bill	33%

Juanita's office rent increased from $7,000 to $9,200 last year.

	Column A	Column B
12.	The percent increase in her rent	30%

Scientific Notation

Example: What is the value of the numerical expression $(5 \times 10^3)(3 \times 10^5)$ in scientific notation?

    (A) 15×10^{15}
    (B) 1.5×10^{15}
    (C) 1.5×10^9
    (D) 15×10^8

Solution: (C). One way to solve arithmetic with scientific notation is to rewrite the numbers in standard form. $5 \times 10^3 = 5,000$ and $3 \times 10^5 = 300,000$, so their product is 1,500,000,000, which is equivalent to 1.5×10^9. If the problem involves multiplying or dividing of scientific notation, as this example does, another way is to use the factors to help you. Here, $5 \times 3 = 15$ and $10^3 \times 10^5 = 10^8$, which gives you 15×10^8. However, the first factor of any number in scientific notation must be at least 1 but less than 10, so 15×10^8 becomes 1.5×10^9.

1. Write 5×10^4 in standard form.

    (A)   50
    (B)   500
    (C)   5,000
    (D)   50,000

2. Write 8.52×10^6 in standard form.

    (A)   8,520,000
    (B)   85,200,000
    (C)   800,000,052
    (D)   852,000,000

3. Write 5×10^{-3} in standard form.

    (A)   0.000005
    (B)   0.00005
    (C)   0.0005
    (D)   0.005

4. Write 3.695×10^{-7} in standard form.

    (A)   0.00000003695
    (B)   0.0000003695
    (C)   0.000003695
    (D)   0.00003695

5. What is the value of 90,000 in scientific notation?

    (A) $9 \times 10,000$
    (B) 9×100^2
    (C) 9×10^5
    (D) 9×10^4

6. What is the value of 5,280,000 in scientific notation?

    (A) 5.28×10^6
    (B) 5.28×10^4
    (C) 528×10^6
    (D) 528×10^4

7. What is the value of 0.0002088 in scientific notation?

    (A) 2.088×10^{-4}
    (B) 2.088×10^{-3}
    (C) 2.88×10^{-4}
    (D) 2.88×10^{-3}

8. What is the value of the numerical expression $5 \times 10^4 + 6 \times 10^3$ in scientific notation?

    (A) 3.0×10^7
    (B) 1.1×10^7
    (C) 5.6×10^4
    (D) 30×10^4

9. What is the value of the numerical expression $7.41 \times 10^7 + 1.47 \times 10^4$ in scientific notation?

    (A) 7.41147×10^7
    (B) 7.4247×10^7
    (C) 8.88×10^{11}
    (D) 8.88×10^7

10. What is the value of the numerical expression $(3 \times 10^3)(2 \times 10^2)$ in scientific notation?

    (A) 6.0×10^5
    (B) 6.0×10^6
    (C) 5.0×10^5
    (D) 5.0×10^6

11. What is the value of the numerical expression $(5 \times 10^4)(6 \times 10^4)$ in scientific notation?

    (A) 3.0×10^9
    (B) 3.0×10^8
    (C) 30×10^9
    (D) 30×10^8

12. What is the value of the numerical expression $(5 \times 10^{-5})(5 \times 10^{-5})$ in scientific notation?

    (A) 2.5×10^{-10}
    (B) 25×10^{-10}
    (C) 2.5×10^{-9}
    (D) 25×10^{-9}

13. What is the value of the numerical expression $(2.5 \times 10^2)(2.4 \times 10^3)$ in scientific notation?

    (A) 60×10^6
    (B) 60×10^5
    (C) 6.0×10^6
    (D) 6.0×10^5

14. Which expression is equivalent to 5×10^{-6}?

    (A) $\dfrac{5}{6}$

    (B) $\dfrac{5}{10}$

    (C) $\dfrac{5}{10^6}$

    (D) $\dfrac{5}{10^{-6}}$

15. What is the value of the numerical expression $\dfrac{9 \times 10^6}{3 \times 10^4}$ in scientific notation?

    (A) 3.0×10^2
    (B) 3.0×10^1
    (C) 0.3×10^2
    (D) 0.3×10^1

16. What is the value of the numerical expression $\dfrac{4.8 \times 10^6}{1.2 \times 10^4}$ in scientific notation?

    (A) 4.0×10^1
    (B) 4.0×10^2
    (C) 4.0×10^3
    (D) 4.0×10^4

17. What is the value of the numerical expression $\dfrac{3.6 \times 10^8}{6.0 \times 10^4}$ in scientific notation?

    (A) 6.0×10^1
    (B) 6.0×10^2
    (C) 6.0×10^3
    (D) 6.0×10^4

Vocabulary

> Example: The number 0 falls under all of the following types of numbers EXCEPT:
>
> (A) counting numbers
> (B) rational numbers
> (C) real numbers
> (D) whole numbers
>
> Solution: (A). Whole numbers are all integers starting with 0. Counting numbers are all integers starting with 1, so they exclude 0. To solve the following questions, be sure to learn the definitions of the terms you don't know.

1. What type of number is $\sqrt{9}$?

   (A) complex number
   (B) imaginary number
   (C) irrational number
   (D) rational number

2. What type of number is $\sqrt{19}$?

   (A) complex number
   (B) imaginary number
   (C) irrational number
   (D) rational number

3. What type of number is $\sqrt{-1}$?

   (A) complex number
   (B) imaginary number
   (C) irrational number
   (D) rational number

4. What type of number is $5 + 3i$?

   (A) complex number
   (B) imaginary number
   (C) irrational number
   (D) rational number

5. What type of number MUST be the result from subtracting two positive integers?

   (A) complex number
   (B) imaginary number
   (C) rational number
   (D) whole number

6. What type of number is $\dfrac{2}{3}$ considered to be?

   (A) complex number
   (B) integer
   (C) irrational number
   (D) rational number

7. Mary says that 6^0 results in a whole number. Peter says it results in a counting number. Who is right?

   (A) Mary
   (B) Paul
   (C) both
   (D) neither

8. What type of number results from i^2?

   (A) complex number
   (B) irrational number
   (C) rational number
   (D) whole number

9. What is the product of $(x + 4)$ and its conjugate?

(A) $2x + 8$
(B) $x^2 - 16$
(C) $x^2 + 16$
(D) $x^2 + 8x + 16$

10. Thomas read pages 10 to 20 in his book, inclusive. How many pages did he read?

(A) 9
(B) 10
(C) 11
(D) 12

11. Daphne read pages 751 to 952 in her book, inclusive. How many pages did she read?

(A) 200
(B) 201
(C) 202
(D) 203

12. Evan added up all the integers from 1 to 5, inclusive, and got a sum of z. Which expression represents the sum of all integers from 3 to 5, inclusive?

(A) $z - 2$
(B) $z - 3$
(C) $z + 2$
(D) $z + 3$

13. Polly added up all the integers from 1 to 20, inclusive, and got a sum of x. Which expression represents the sum of all integers from 1 to 18, inclusive?

(A) $x - 19$
(B) $x - 20$
(C) $x - 39$
(D) $x + 39$

14. If the sum of all integers from 1 to 500, inclusive, is a, which expression represents the sum of all integers from 1 to 499, inclusive?

(A) $a - 1$
(B) $a - 500$
(C) $a + 1$
(D) $a + 500$

15. The sum of all the integers from 1,000 to 10,000, inclusive, is y. Which expression represents the sum of all integers from 1,003 to 10,000, inclusive?

(A) $y - 3$
(B) $y - 3,000$
(C) $y - 3,003$
(D) $y - 3,006$

16. The sum of all integers from 1 to 100, inclusive, is b. Which expression represents the sum of all integers from 1 to 104, inclusive?

(A) $b + 4$
(B) $b + 104$
(C) $b + 404$
(D) $b + 410$

17. What type of number does NOT result from the product of $\sqrt{8}$ and $\sqrt{18}$?

(A) real
(B) integer
(C) whole
(D) irrational

18. What type of number is i^4?

(A) imaginary
(B) whole
(C) irrational
(D) complex

Consecutive Integers

Example: The sum of two consecutive integers is 31. Which equation could be used to find the integers?

(A) $2x = 31$
(B) $x^2 - 1 = 31$
(C) $2x + 1 = 31$
(D) $2x - 1 = 31$

Solution: (C). When dealing with unknown numbers, use variables. The lowest number will be x. For consecutive integers, the next number will be $x + 1$. Then create an algebraic equation. Here, the sum of x and $x + 1$ is 31, so the equation should be $x + x + 1 = 31$.

1. Which of the following could represent three consecutive integers?

(A) $x, x + 1, x + 3$
(B) $x, x + 1, x + 2$
(C) $y, y + 2, y + 4$
(D) $z + 0.5, z + 1, z + 1.5$

2. Which of the following could represent three consecutive EVEN integers?

(A) $2z, 4z, 8z$
(B) $y + 3, y + 4, y + 5$
(C) $x, 2x + 1, 3x + 1$
(D) $y, y + 2, y + 4$

3. Which of the following could represent three consecutive ODD integers?

(A) $x, x + 1, x + 2$
(B) $x, x + 1, x + 3$
(C) $z, z + 2, z + 4$
(D) $z, 3, z + 2$

4. The sum of three consecutive even integers is 54. Which equation could be used to find the integers?

(A) $3x + 6 = 54$
(B) $x^3 + 6 = 54$
(C) $x(x + 2)(x + 4) = 54$
(D) $3x + 3 = 54$

5. The sum of four consecutive odd integers is 64. What is the smallest of the integers?

(A) 13
(B) 15
(C) 31
(D) 63

6. The product of two consecutive integers is 30. Which equation could be used to find the integers?

(A) $x^2 = 30$
(B) $2(x + 1) = 30$
(C) $2x + 1 = 30$
(D) $x(x + 1) = 30$

7. The product of two consecutive positive integers is 72. Which is the larger of the integers?

(A) 8
(B) 9
(C) 35
(D) 37

8. The product of three consecutive odd integers is 105. Which is the middle integer?

(A) 5
(B) 7
(C) 15
(D) 35

9. The product of three consecutive even integers is 480. What is the sum of the integers?

(A) 10
(B) 24
(C) 32
(D) 480

10. The sum of four consecutive odd integers is 16. What is the product of the integers?

(A) 0
(B) 16
(C) 64
(D) 105

11. The average of three consecutive integers is 8. What are the integers?

(A) 6, 8, 10
(B) 7, 8, 9
(C) 6, 7, 8
(D) 2, 3, 4

Quantitative Comparison Practice

Answer Choices:

(A) The amount in column A is greater.
(B) The amount in column B is greater.
(C) The two amounts are equal.
(D) The relationship cannot be determined from the information provided.

The sum of four consecutive integers is 54.

	Column A	Column B
12.	The largest of the four integers	12

The product of three consecutive integers is 120.

	Column A	Column B
13.	The largest of the three integers	12

The sum of four consecutive odd integers is 72.

	Column A	Column B
14.	The smallest of the four integers	16

The average of 7 consecutive integers is 23.

	Column A	Column B
15.	The smallest of the seven integers	20

The Tutorverse
www.thetutorverse.com

Matrices

Example: What is the result of the expression $\begin{bmatrix} 5 & 1 \\ 3 & 7 \end{bmatrix} + \begin{bmatrix} 2 & 9 \\ 4 & 6 \end{bmatrix}$?

(A) $\begin{bmatrix} 7 & 14 \\ 7 & 13 \end{bmatrix}$

(B) $\begin{bmatrix} 7 & 10 \\ 9 & 7 \end{bmatrix}$

(C) $\begin{bmatrix} 7 & 8 \\ 7 & 7 \end{bmatrix}$

(D) $\begin{bmatrix} 7 & 10 \\ 7 & 13 \end{bmatrix}$

Solution: (D). To add or subtract matrices, simply add or subtract the corresponding terms. In this case, 5+2=7, 1+9=10, 3+4=7, and 7+6=13. If there is a number in front of the matrix, it acts as a coefficient, so multiply every term in the matrix by that number.

1. What is the result of the expression $\begin{bmatrix} 13 & 2 \\ -3 & 17 \end{bmatrix} + \begin{bmatrix} 2 & -19 \\ 41 & 67 \end{bmatrix}$?

(A) $\begin{bmatrix} 11 & -17 \\ 38 & 84 \end{bmatrix}$

(B) $\begin{bmatrix} 15 & -17 \\ 38 & 84 \end{bmatrix}$

(C) $\begin{bmatrix} 15 & -17 \\ 44 & 84 \end{bmatrix}$

(D) $\begin{bmatrix} 4 & -17 \\ 38 & 84 \end{bmatrix}$

2. What is the result of the expression $\begin{bmatrix} 1 & 5 & 9 \\ -4 & 3 & -2 \end{bmatrix} - \begin{bmatrix} 9 & -5 & 1 \\ -2 & 3 & -4 \end{bmatrix}$?

(A) $\begin{bmatrix} 8 & 0 & 8 \\ 2 & 0 & 2 \end{bmatrix}$

(B) $\begin{bmatrix} -8 & 10 & 8 \\ -6 & 0 & -6 \end{bmatrix}$

(C) $\begin{bmatrix} -8 & 10 & 8 \\ -6 & 0 & -2 \end{bmatrix}$

(D) $\begin{bmatrix} -8 & 10 & 8 \\ -2 & 0 & 2 \end{bmatrix}$

3. What is the result of the expression
$$\begin{bmatrix} 4 & 2 \\ -8 & 9 \\ 3 & -5 \end{bmatrix} + \begin{bmatrix} 4 & 2 \\ -8 & 9 \\ 3 & -5 \end{bmatrix}?$$

(A) $\begin{bmatrix} 16 & 4 \\ -16 & 18 \\ 6 & -10 \end{bmatrix}$

(B) $\begin{bmatrix} 8 & 4 \\ -16 & 18 \\ 9 & -10 \end{bmatrix}$

(C) $\begin{bmatrix} 8 & 4 \\ -16 & 18 \\ 6 & -10 \end{bmatrix}$

(D) $\begin{bmatrix} 8 & 2 \\ 0 & 18 \\ 6 & 0 \end{bmatrix}$

4. What is the result of the expression
$$3\begin{bmatrix} -6 & 0 & 2 \\ 1 & -9 & 8 \\ 7 & 0 & -6 \end{bmatrix}?$$

(A) $\begin{bmatrix} -18 & 0 & 6 \\ 3 & -27 & 24 \\ 21 & 0 & -18 \end{bmatrix}$

(B) $\begin{bmatrix} -18 & 0 & 6 \\ 4 & -6 & 11 \\ 10 & 3 & -3 \end{bmatrix}$

(C) $\begin{bmatrix} -3 & 0 & 6 \\ 3 & 27 & 24 \\ 21 & 0 & 18 \end{bmatrix}$

(D) $\begin{bmatrix} -12 & 0 & 6 \\ 3 & -27 & 24 \\ 21 & 0 & -12 \end{bmatrix}$

5. What is the result of the expression
$$4\begin{bmatrix} 5 & 1 \\ 3 & 7 \end{bmatrix} + 2\begin{bmatrix} 2 & 9 \\ 4 & 6 \end{bmatrix}?$$

(A) $\begin{bmatrix} 24 & 22 \\ 20 & 40 \end{bmatrix}$

(B) $\begin{bmatrix} 24 & 22 \\ 7 & 13 \end{bmatrix}$

(C) $\begin{bmatrix} 24 & 22 \\ 12 & 42 \end{bmatrix}$

(D) $\begin{bmatrix} 10 & 22 \\ 12 & 42 \end{bmatrix}$

6. What is the result of the expression
$$\begin{bmatrix} 10a & a^2 \\ c^3 & -b \end{bmatrix} - \begin{bmatrix} 6a & 5a^2 \\ c^3 & 7b \end{bmatrix}?$$

(A) $\begin{bmatrix} 4a & -4a \\ c & 6b \end{bmatrix}$

(B) $\begin{bmatrix} 4a & -4a^2 \\ c^3 & -8b \end{bmatrix}$

(C) $\begin{bmatrix} 4a & -4a^2 \\ 0 & -8b \end{bmatrix}$

(D) $\begin{bmatrix} 16a & -4a^2 \\ 0 & -6b^2 \end{bmatrix}$

7. What is the result of the expression

$$-3\begin{bmatrix} 6 & 9x \\ 2y & -5 \\ -7x^2 & 0 \end{bmatrix}?$$

(A) $\begin{bmatrix} -18 & -27x \\ -6y & 15 \\ 21x^2 & 0 \end{bmatrix}$

(B) $\begin{bmatrix} 18 & 27x \\ 6y & -15 \\ -21x^2 & 0 \end{bmatrix}$

(C) $\begin{bmatrix} -18 & -27x \\ -6y & 15 \\ -21x^2 & -3 \end{bmatrix}$

(D) $\begin{bmatrix} -18 & 27x \\ -6y & 15 \\ -21x^2 & -3 \end{bmatrix}$

8. What is the result of the expression

$$5x\begin{bmatrix} 2 & 2x & -7 \\ 1 & -9y & 8x^2 \end{bmatrix}?$$

(A) $\begin{bmatrix} 10x & 10x^2 & -35x \\ 5x & -45xy & 40x^3 \end{bmatrix}$

(B) $\begin{bmatrix} 10x & 10x & -35x \\ 5x & -45x & 40x^2 \end{bmatrix}$

(C) $\begin{bmatrix} 10x & 10x^2 & -35x \\ 5x & 45xy & 40x^3 \end{bmatrix}$

(D) $\begin{bmatrix} 10x & 10x^2 & -35x \\ 5x & -45y & 40x^3 \end{bmatrix}$

9. What is the result of the expression

$$6\begin{bmatrix} 5x & -x \\ 3x & 7x \end{bmatrix} + x\begin{bmatrix} -2 & 9 \\ -3 & 6 \end{bmatrix}?$$

(A) $\begin{bmatrix} 28 & 3 \\ 15 & 48 \end{bmatrix}$

(B) $\begin{bmatrix} 28x & 3x \\ 15x & 48x \end{bmatrix}$

(C) $\begin{bmatrix} 28x & 3x \\ 21x & 48x \end{bmatrix}$

(D) $\begin{bmatrix} 28x & 3x \\ 15x & 48 \end{bmatrix}$

Algebraic Concepts

Algebraic Relationships

Example: If $x - 10 = 5 - 10$, what is the value of x?

    (A) -5
    (B) 5
    (C) 10
    (D) 15

Solution: (B). To solve these types of questions, remember that x represents a real number. Here, you do not need to solve anything. Simply substitute 5 for x to make the identity true.

1. If $3x = ax$, what is the value of a?

    (A) -3
    (B) 1
    (C) 3
    (D) 30

2. If $10c + 10 = bc + b$, what is the value of b?

    (A) 1
    (B) 5
    (C) 10
    (D) 100

3. If $15x = x$, what is the value of x?

    (A) 0
    (B) 1
    (C) 15
    (D) -14

4. If $m + n = 8$, then which expression is equal to n?

    (A) 4
    (B) $8 - m$
    (C) $8 + m$
    (D) 8

5. If $5x - 3 = 4$, then what must $15x - 9$ equal?

    (A) 6
    (B) 12
    (C) 15
    (D) 45

6. If $x = 5(y + 5)$, what is the value of $x - 1$?

    (A) $y + 4$
    (B) $y + 24$
    (C) $5y + 4$
    (D) $5y + 24$

7. If $m(a + b) = 80$ and $am = 20$, what is the value of bm?

    (A) 4
    (B) 20
    (C) 40
    (D) 60

8. Which has the greatest value?

    (A) $10 - 5$
    (B) $5 - 10$
    (C) $10 + 5$
    (D) $5^2 + 10^2$

9. If x and y are positive integers and x is greater than y, which has the greatest value?

    (A) $x - y$
    (B) $y - x$
    (C) $x + y$
    (D) $y^2 + x^2$

10. If x and y are positive integers and x is greater than y, which has the smallest value?

    (A) $x - y$
    (B) $y - x$
    (C) $x + y$
    (D) xy

11. If x and y are positive integers and x is greater than y, which has the greatest value?

    (A) $x - y$
    (B) $x^2 - y^2$
    (C) $x^2 + xy - y^2$
    (D) $x^2 - xy - y^2$

12. If $(x + y)^2 = 100$ and $x^2 + y^2 = 50$, what is the value of xy?

    (A) 2
    (B) 25
    (C) 50
    (D) 100

13. If $x + y = 10$ and $x - y = 3$, what is the value of $x^2 - y^2$?

    (A) 7
    (B) 13
    (C) 30
    (D) 49

14. If $\dfrac{x}{x+1} \cdot \dfrac{x}{x-1} = \dfrac{10}{x^2 - 1}$, then what is the value of $x^2 - 1$?

    (A) 9
    (B) 11
    (C) 99
    (D) 101

15. A right triangle is shown.

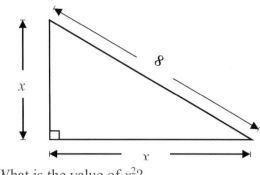

What is the value of x^2?

    (A) 8
    (B) 16
    (C) 32
    (D) 64

16. A right triangle is shown.

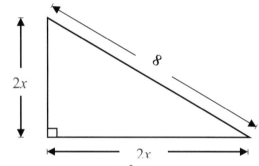

What is the value of x^2?

    (A) 8
    (B) 16
    (C) 32
    (D) 64

Quantitative Comparison Practice

Answer Choices:

(A) The amount in column A is greater.
(B) The amount in column B is greater.
(C) The two amounts are equal.
(D) The relationship cannot be determined from the information provided.

$x + y = 7$
x is an integer less than 4

	Column A	Column B
17.	$|x|$	y

$y = 3x + 4$

	Column A	Column B
18.	The value of y when $x = 5$	The value of x when $y = 19$

$x < y$

	Column A	Column B
19.	$x + 2$	$y + 1$

$x > y$

	Column A	Column B
20.	x^2	y^2

$4{,}200 = 10(4x + 20)$

	Column A	Column B
21.	x	10

$x > 0$ and $y < 0$

	Column A	Column B
22.	x^2	y^3

$y = -2x + 5$

	Column A	Column B
23.	The value of y when $x = -0.5$	The value of x when $y = 5$

$10(36 + 2x) = 720$

	Column A	Column B
24.	x	36

Simplifying Expressions

Example: Which expression is equivalent to the expression $2x + 5x^2 - (3x^2 + 4x)$?

(A) $2x^2 - 2x$
(B) $2x^2 + 6x$
(C) $8x^2 - 2x$
(D) $8x^2 - 6x$

Solution: (A). To combine like terms, you first want to get rid of any parentheses by distributing the factor or operation directly in front of the parentheses. Here, you can distribute the "–" sign to get $2x + 5x^2 - 3x^2 - 4x$. Then, combine terms that have the exact same variable and exponent. Here, $2x$ and $-4x$ combine to make $-2x$, and $5x^2$ and $-3x^2$ combine to make $2x^2$.

1. Which expression is equivalent to the expression $x + x$?

(A) 0
(B) x
(C) $2x$
(D) x^2

2. Which expression is equivalent to the expression $5y + 4y - 3y$?

(A) $3y$
(B) $6y$
(C) $6y^3$
(D) $12y$

3. Which expression is equivalent to the expression $x^2 + 4x + 2x^2 + 3x$?

(A) $10x^2$
(B) $10x$
(C) $3x^2 + 5x$
(D) $3x^2 + 7x$

4. Which expression is equivalent to the expression $4a + 2a^2 + 9a^3 + 8a - 7a^2$

(A) $4a^2 + 12a$
(B) $9a^3 - 5a^2 + 12a$
(C) $9a^3 - 14a^2 + 32a$
(D) $17a^3 - a^2$

5. Which expression is equivalent to the expression $7a + 4b + a - 2b$?

(A) $7a - 8b$
(B) $8a - 2b$
(C) $8a + 2b$
(D) $8a + 6b$

6. Which expression is equivalent to the expression $3m + 6n - 5m - 3n$?

(A) $-2m - 3n$
(B) $-2m + 3n$
(C) $2m - 3n$
(D) $2m + 3n$

7. Which expression is equivalent to the expression $3mn + 5mn + 8mn$?

(A) $16mn$
(B) $16(m+n)$
(C) $16m^3n^3$
(D) $120mn$

8. Which expression is equivalent to the expression $xy + xz + yz + xz + xy$?

(A) $5xyz$
(B) $2xy + 2xz + yz$
(C) $2xy + 2xz + 2yz$
(D) $(x + y + z)(x + y + z)$

9. Which expression is equivalent to the expression
$3ab + 5bc - 7ac + 9ab - 2ac + 4ab - 6bc$?

(A) $16ab - 9ac - bc$
(B) $16ab + 11ac + 9bc$
(C) $16ab - 5ac - bc$
(D) $16ab - 9ac + 11bc$

10. Which expression is equivalent to the expression $6x^2y + 3x^2y - 4xy^2 - 3xy^2$?

(A) $9x^2y - 7xy^2$
(B) $9x^2y + 7xy^2$
(C) $9x^2y - xy^2$
(D) $9x^2y + xy^2$

11. Which expression is equivalent to the expression
$9x^2y + 5xy^2 - 2x^2y + 6xy + 5x^2y^2 - xy^2$?

(A) $14x^2y^2 + 7x^2y + 4xy^2 + 6xy$
(B) $14x^2y^2 + 3x^2y + 4xy^2 + 5xy$
(C) $5x^2y^2 + 7x^2y + 4xy^2 + 6xy$
(D) $5x^2y^2 + 6x^2y + 2xy^2 + 5xy$

12. Which expression is equivalent to the expression $3x - (x + 2)$?

(A) $2x - 2$
(B) $2x + 2$
(C) $4x - 2$
(D) $4x + 2$

13. Which expression is equivalent to the expression $9x^2 - (5x^2 + 5x)$?

(A) $4x^2 - 5x$
(B) $4x^2 + 5x$
(C) $14x^2 - 5x$
(D) $14x^2 + 5x$

14. Which expression is equivalent to the expression $3x + 4y - (5x + 6y)$?

(A) $-2x - 2y$
(B) $-2x + 10y$
(C) $-8x - 2y$
(D) $8x + 10y$

15. Which expression is equivalent to
$5x^3 - x(2x + 4x^2) + 3x^2$?

(A) $10x^3$
(B) $x^3 + x^2$
(C) $8x^3 + 2x^2$
(D) $9x^3 + x^2$

16. Which expression is equivalent to the expression $9pq^3 - 8p^3q + (7pq^3 - 6pq)$?

(A) $-8p^3q + 16pq^3 - 6pq$
(B) $-8p^3q + 16pq^3 + 6pq$
(C) $16pq^3 - 14p^3q$
(D) $16pq^3 - 2p^3q$

17. Which expression is equivalent to
$xy(3xy^2 + 4x^2y) + x^2y(3y^2 + 4xy)$?

(A) $3xy^2 + 4x^2y$
(B) $6x^2y^3 + 8x^3y^2$
(C) $7x^3y^2 + 7x^2y^3$
(D) $6x^3y^2 + 8x^2y^3$

18. Which expression is equivalent to
$xy(3xy^2 - 4x^2y) - x^2y(3y^2 - 4xy)$?

(A) 0
(B) 1
(C) x^2y^3
(D) x^3y^2

Distributing

Example: Which expression is equivalent to the expression $(x + 5)(x - 6)$?

     (A) $x^2 + 5x - 6$
     (B) $x^2 - 30x - 1$
     (C) $x^2 - x - 30$
     (D) $x^2 - 6x + 5$

Solution: (C). To multiply polynomials, each term in the first set of parentheses must be distributed to each term in the second set of parentheses. Here, you must do $x \cdot x$, $x(-6)$, $5x$, and $5(-6)$. Then, you combine like terms. In this example, $-6x$ and $5x$ combine to make $-x$.

1. Which expression is equivalent to the expression $6(x + 4)$?

     (A) $6x + 6$
     (B) $6x + 24$
     (C) $x + 24$
     (D) $6x + 4$

2. Which expression is equivalent to the expression $12(y - 12)$?

     (A) $12y - 144$
     (B) $12y - 12$
     (C) $y - 144$
     (D) 0

3. Which expression is equivalent to the expression $9(n - 2)$?

     (A) $n - 18$
     (B) $2n - 18$
     (C) $9n - 2$
     (D) $9n - 18$

4. Which expression is equivalent to the expression $x + 9(x + 4)$?

     (A) $x^2 + 13x + 36$
     (B) $18x + 36$
     (C) $10x + 36$
     (D) $10x + 4$

5. Which expression is equivalent to the expression $(c + 6) - (c + 7)$?

     (A) -1
     (B) 13
     (C) $2c - 1$
     (D) $2c + 13$

6. Which expression is equivalent to the expression $(2h + 2) - 2(h + 2)$?

     (A) -2
     (B) 0
     (C) 2
     (D) $h + 2$

7. Which expression is equivalent to the expression $(a + 9)(a + 4)$?

     (A) $26a$
     (B) $2a + 13$
     (C) $a^2 + 36a + 13$
     (D) $a^2 + 13a + 36$

8. Which expression is equivalent to the expression $(m - 2)(m - 18)$?

     (A) $2m - 20$
     (B) $m^2 + 20m + 36$
     (C) $m^2 - 20m - 36$
     (D) $m^2 - 20m + 36$

9. Which expression is equivalent to the expression $(p + 1)(p - 36)$?

(A) $-35p$
(B) $p^2 - 36$
(C) $p^2 - 35p - 36$
(D) $p^2 - 35p + 36$

10. Which expression is equivalent to the expression $(c - 6)^2$?

(A) $c^2 + 36$
(B) $c^2 - 36$
(C) $c^2 - 12c + 36$
(D) $c^2 + 12c + 36$

11. Which expression is equivalent to the expression $(x + 3)(x - 12)$?

(A) $x^2 + 9x - 36$
(B) $x^2 + 9x + 36$
(C) $x^2 - 9x - 36$
(D) $x^2 - 9x + 36$

12. Which expression is equivalent to the expression $(x + c)(x + c)$?

(A) $x^2 + c^2$
(B) $x^2 + cx + c^2$
(C) $x^2 - 2cx + c^2$
(D) $x^2 + 2cx + c^2$

13. Which expression is equivalent to the expression $(x + z)(x - z)$?

(A) $x^2 + 2xz + z^2$
(B) $x^2 - 2xz + z^2$
(C) $x^2 - z^2$
(D) $x^2 + z^2$

14. Which expression is equivalent to the expression $(x + 5)(x - 5)$?

(A) $x^2 + 25$
(B) $x^2 - 25$
(C) $x^2 + 10x + 25$
(D) $x^2 - 10x$

15. Which expression is equivalent to the expression $(x - 9)(x + 9)$?

(A) $x^2 + 18x + 81$
(B) $x^2 + 81$
(C) $x^2 - 18x$
(D) $x^2 - 81$

16. If $(x + 2)^2 = x^2 + ax + 4$, what is the value of a?

(A) 2
(B) 4
(C) 8
(D) 16

17. If $(x - 5)^2 = x^2 + bx + 25$, what is the value of b?

(A) 10
(B) 5
(C) -5
(D) -10

18. If $(x + 8)^2 = x^2 + c + 64$, what is the value of c?

(A) 16
(B) $16x$
(C) 32
(D) $32x$

19. If $(x + 4)(x - 4) = 10$, what is the value of x^2?

(A) 4
(B) 10
(C) 16
(D) 26

20. If $(2x + 3)(2x - 3) = 7$, what is the value of $4x^2$?

   (A) 4
   (B) 7
   (C) 9
   (D) 16

21. If $(3x + 4)(3x - 4) = 16$, what is the value of $9x^2$?

   (A) −16
   (B) 0
   (C) 16
   (D) 32

22. Which expression is equivalent to the expression $(x + y)(x^2 - xy + y^2)$?

   (A) $x^3 + 2x^2y + 2xy^2 + y^3$
   (B) $x^3 + x^2y^2 + y^3$
   (C) $x^3 + y^3$
   (D) $x^3 - y^3$

23. Which expression is equivalent to the expression $(x + 2)(x - 2)(x^2 + 4)$?

   (A) $x^4 - 8x^2 + 16$
   (B) $x^4 + 8x^2 + 16$
   (C) $x^4 + 16$
   (D) $x^4 - 16$

Quantitative Comparison Practice

Answer Choices:

   (A)   The amount in column A is greater.
   (B)   The amount in column B is greater.
   (C)   The two amounts are equal.
   (D)   The relationship cannot be determined from the information provided.

	Column A	Column B
24.	$x + 7(x + 6)$	$8x + 6$

	Column A	Column B
25.	$(x + 9)^2$	$x^2 + 81$

x is a positive integer.

	Column A	Column B
26.	$(x - 10)^2$	$x^2 - 100$

	Column A	Column B
27.	$(x^2+1)(x-1)(x+1)$	$x^4 + 1$

	Column A	Column B
28.	$x - 1(x + 5)$	-5

Factoring

Example: Which expression is equivalent to the expression $x^2 + 5x + 6$?

    (A) $(x + 5)(x + 6)$
    (B) $(x + 5)(x + 1)$
    (C) $(x + 2)(x + 3)$
    (D) $(x + 6)(x - 1)$

Solution: (C). Here, the answer is $(x + 2)(x + 3)$ because 2 and 3 multiply to make 6 and add to make 5. To factor a quadratic expression, you want to find the factor pair of the last term that also adds to make the middle term.

1. Which expression is equivalent to $10x + 5$?

    (A) $2(5x + 1)$
    (B) $5(2x + 1)$
    (C) $5(2x + 5)$
    (D) $5x(2 + x)$

2. Which expression is equivalent to $8x^2 + 6x$?

    (A) $2(4x + 3x)$
    (B) $2x(4x + 3)$
    (C) $2x(4x + 3x)$
    (D) $4x(2x + 3)$

3. Which expression is equivalent to $12x^3 + 6x^2 + 18x$?

    (A) $6x(2x^2 + 1 + 3x)$
    (B) $6x^2(2x + x + 3)$
    (C) $6(2x^2 + x + 3x)$
    (D) $6x(2x^2 + x + 3)$

4. Which expression is equivalent to the expression $x^2 + 10x + 24$?

    (A) $(x + 6)(x + 4)$
    (B) $(x + 12)(x - 2)$
    (C) $(x + 6)(x - 4)$
    (D) $(x + 12)(x + 2)$

5. Which expression is equivalent to the expression $x^2 + 10x - 24$?

    (A) $(x + 6)(x + 4)$
    (B) $(x + 12)(x - 2)$
    (C) $(x + 6)(x - 4)$
    (D) $(x + 12)(x + 2)$

6. Which expression is equivalent to the expression $x^2 + 2x - 24$?

    (A) $(x + 6)(x + 4)$
    (B) $(x + 12)(x - 2)$
    (C) $(x + 6)(x - 4)$
    (D) $(x + 12)(x + 2)$

7. Which expression is equivalent to the expression $x^2 + 14x + 24$?

    (A) $(x + 6)(x + 4)$
    (B) $(x + 12)(x - 2)$
    (C) $(x + 6)(x - 4)$
    (D) $(x + 12)(x + 2)$

8. Which expression is equivalent to the expression $x^2 - 7x - 18$?

    (A) $(x - 2)(x - 9)$
    (B) $(x + 2)(x - 9)$
    (C) $(x - 9)^2$
    (D) $(x - 7)(x - 11)$

9. Which expression is equivalent to the expression $x^2 + 5x - 24$?

    (A) $(x + 12)(x - 2)$
    (B) $(x - 12)(x + 2)$
    (C) $(x + 6)(x - 1)$
    (D) $(x + 8)(x - 3)$

The Tutorverse
www.thetutorverse.com

10. Which expression is equivalent to the expression $x^2 - 49x + 48$?

    (A) $(x - 24)^2$
    (B) $(x - 48)(x - 1)$
    (C) $x(x - 49)$
    (D) $(x - 48)(x + 1)$

11. Which expression is equivalent to the expression $x^2 + x - 6$?

    (A) $(x + 3)(x - 2)$
    (B) $(x + 1)(x - 6)$
    (C) $(x + 1)(x + 6)$
    (D) $(x - 3)(x + 2)$

12. Which expression is equivalent to the expression $x^2 + 12x + 36$?

    (A) $(x + 6)^2$
    (B) $(x - 6)^2$
    (C) $(x + 9)(x + 4)$
    (D) $(x + 8)(x + 4)$

13. Which expression is equivalent to the expression $x^2 - 8x + 16$?

    (A) $(x - 4)^2$
    (B) $(x + 4)^2$
    (C) $(x + 4)(x - 4)$
    (D) $(x - 8)(x - 2)$

14. Which expression is equivalent to the expression $x^2 - 49$?

    (A) $x(x - 49)$
    (B) $7(x - 7)$
    (C) $(x + 7)(x - 7)$
    (D) $(x - 7)^2$

15. Which expression is equivalent to the expression $x^2 - 144$?

    (A) $(x - 12)^2$
    (B) $(x + 12)^2$
    (C) $(x - 12)(x + 12)$
    (D) $x(x - 144)$

16. If $x^2 + ax + 8 = (x + 2)(x + 4)$, which of the following is equivalent to a?

    (A) 1
    (B) 2
    (C) 6
    (D) 8

17. If $x^2 + ax + b = (x + 3)(x + 5)$, which of the following is equivalent to $a + b$?

    (A) 2
    (B) 8
    (C) 15
    (D) 23

18. If $x^2 + ax + b = (x + 4)(x - 3)$, which of the following is equivalent to $a - b$?

    (A) -13
    (B) -11
    (C) 11
    (D) 13

19. Which expression is equivalent to the expression $x^4 - 16$?

    (A) $(x - 2)^2(x + 2)^2$
    (B) $(x - 4)^2(x + 4)^2$
    (C) $(x - 2)(x + 2)(x^2 + 4)$
    (D) $(x^2 + 4)^2$

20. Which expression is equivalent to the expression $x^4 - 1$?

    (A) $(x + 1)(x - 1)(x^2 + 1)$
    (B) $(x - 1)^2(x + 1)^2$
    (C) $(x - 1)^2(x^2 + 1)$
    (D) $(x^2 + 1)^2$

21. If $x^2 - 6x - b = (x - 3)(x - 3)$, which of the following is equivalent to b?

    (A) -9
    (B) -6
    (C) 6
    (D) 9

Creating Expressions & Equations

Example: Brent has 3 more quarters than dimes. The total value of all his quarters and dimes is $2.50.
Which equation represents the amount of money, in dollars, that Brent has?

(A) $x + (x + 3) = 2.50$
(B) $10x + 25(x + 3) = 2.50$
(C) $0.10x + 0.25x = 2.50$
(D) $0.10x + 0.25(x + 3) = 2.50$

Solution: (D). In a problem where you don't know any quantity, use a variable. Here, the number of
dimes can be x, and the number of quarters can be $x + 3$. However, that merely represents the
number of coins Brent has. To find the value of his coins, you must multiply the number of
dimes by 0.10 and the number of quarters by 0.25. We know the sum of the two values must
equal 2.50 because that is how much money Brent has in total, so $0.10x + 0.25(x + 3) = 2.50$.

1. Simon has x books. Julie has twice as many
books as Simon. In terms of x, how many
books does Julie have?

(A) 2
(B) $2x$
(C) $x + 2$
(D) $\dfrac{2}{x}$

2. Jack has y books. Percy has 5 more than
twice as many books as Jack. In terms of y,
how many books does Percy have?

(A) $2y + 5$
(B) $5y + 2$
(C) $(5 + 2)y$
(D) $7y$

3. Bob baked 3 times as many cookies as Lucy.
If they baked 36 cookies altogether, which
equation can be used to find out how many
cookies Bob baked?

(A) $4x = 36$
(B) $3x = 36$
(C) $3x + 1 = 36$
(D) $2x + x = 36$

4. Brent mowed m lawns. Jane mowed 6 more
lawns than Brent. If they mowed 30 lawns
altogether, which equation can be used to
find out how many lawns Jane mowed?

(A) $m + 6 = 30$
(B) $2m + 6 = 30$
(C) $6m - 6 = 30$
(D) $7m = 30$

5. A machine can weld 10 times as many car
bumpers as a human in any given amount of
time. In one day, a machine and a human
can weld a combined 550 car bumpers.
How many did the machine weld?

(A) 450
(B) 495
(C) 500
(D) 540

6. Al biked 3 times the number of miles Bob
did yesterday. They biked 72 miles
altogether. How many miles did Al bike?

(A) 18
(B) 24
(C) 48
(D) 54

7. Sue read 12 more than twice as many pages as Tom did last week. If Sue read 90 pages, how many pages did Tom read?

(A) 33
(B) 39
(C) 168
(D) 192

8. In right triangle ABC, angle C is a right angle, and angle B is 18 less than twice angle A. How many degrees is angle B?

(A) 27
(B) 36
(C) 54
(D) 63

9. If the degree measures of the angles of a triangle are in the ratio 1:2:3, what is the degree measure of the largest angle?

(A) 30
(B) 45
(C) 60
(D) 90

10. If the degree measures of the angles of a triangle are in the ratio 3:4:5, what is the degree measure of the smallest angle?

(A) 30
(B) 45
(C) 60
(D) 75

11. If a certain number is doubled and the result is increased by 12, the resulting number is 34. What is the original number?

(A) 5
(B) $7\frac{1}{3}$
(C) 11
(D) 23

12. If 5 more than twice a number is 23, what is 4 times the number?

(A) 14
(B) 18
(C) 36
(D) 56

13. Peter has 10 quarters and 5 nickels. Which expression represents the amount of money, in dollars, that Peter has?

(A) $25 + 5 \times 10 + 5$
(B) $10 \times 25 + 5 \times 5$
(C) $10 \times 0.25 + 5 \times 0.5$
(D) $10 \times 0.25 + 5 \times 0.05$

14. Wendy has 3 more pennies than nickels. Which expression represents the amount of money, in dollars, that Wendy has?

(A) $8x$
(B) $(x + 3) + 5x$
(C) $0.05x + 0.01(x + 3)$
(D) $0.05(x + 3) + 0.01x$

15. Carl has 9 fewer pennies than dimes. Which expression represents the amount of money, in dollars, that Carl has?

(A) $10(x - 9) + x$
(B) $10x + 1(x - 9)$
(C) $0.10x + 0.01(x - 9)$
(D) $0.10(x - 9) + 0.01x$

16. Thomas has 6 more nickels than dimes. The total amount of his nickels and dimes is $1.05. Which equation represents the amount of money, in dollars, that Thomas has?

   (A) $0.10x + 0.05(x + 6) = 1.05$
   (B) $0.05x + 0.10(x + 6) = 1.05$
   (C) $10x + 5(x + 6) = 1.05$
   (D) $5x + 10(x + 6) = 1.05$

17. James has 5 more nickels than quarters. The total value of all his coins is $1.75. How many nickels does he have?

   (A) 10
   (B) 17
   (C) 30
   (D) 85

18. Julie has twice as many dimes as nickels. The total value of all her coins is $3.00. How many nickels does she have?

   (A) 10
   (B) 12
   (C) 18
   (D) 20

19. A phone company charges 2 dollars for the first minute of international calling, plus an additional 30 cents for each minute after the first. Which expression represents the cost, in dollars, of an international phone call that lasts x minutes?

   (A) $2x + 30$
   (B) $2 + .3x$
   (C) $2 + 30(x - 1)$
   (D) $2 + .3(x - 1)$

Quantitative Comparison Practice

Answer Choices:

   (A) The amount in column A is greater.
   (B) The amount in column B is greater.
   (C) The two amounts are equal.
   (D) The relationship cannot be determined from the information provided.

Harry has $2.40 in nickels and quarters. He has three times as many nickels as quarters.

Column A	Column B
20. The total value of the nickels	$1.80

A motorized lawn mower can mow lawns five times faster than a man-powered lawn mower. Jim pushes a man-powered lawn mower while his brother uses a motorized lawn mower. Together, they mow 300 square meters of lawn.

Column A	Column B
21. The number of square meters of lawn the motorized lawn mower mowed	240

Function Notation

Example: If $f(x) = 4x - 6$, what is the value of $f(3)$?

    (A) 3   (B) 6   (C) 9   (D) 12

Solution: (B). A function takes an input and produces an output. In this case, the function is f (x), which is equal to $4x - 6$. The input in this function is x, which is a variable that represents some number. We're told to find the value of $f(3)$, which means we must substitute in 3 for every instance of x in the function. This gives us $4(3) - 6$, which simplifies to $12 - 6 = 6$.

1. If $g(x) = -2x + 3x$, what is the value of $g(5)$?

   (A) −10
   (B) −5
   (C) 5
   (D) 15

2. If $f(x) = -|x| + x^2$, what is the value of $f(-3)$?

   (A) −12
   (B) −3
   (C) 6
   (D) 9

3. If $f(x) = 2x$ and $g(x) = 0.5x$, what is the value of $f(g(4))$?

   (A) 2
   (B) 4
   (C) 6
   (D) 8

4. If $f(x) = 3x + 5$ and $g(x) = (x - 1)^2$, what is the value of $g(f(2))$?

   (A) 2
   (B) 11
   (C) 100
   (D) 121

5. $n(p) = p - 1$
   $m(q) = q + 1$

   If $n(m(q)) = 1$, what is the value of q?

   (A) −2
   (B) −1
   (C) 1
   (D) 2

6. $g(t) = t^2$
   $h(u) = \sqrt{u}$

   If $h(g(t)) = 2$, what is the value of t if $t > 0$?

   (A) 2
   (B) 4
   (C) 8
   (D) 64

7. If $f(x) = x^2$, and $x \neq 0$, which of the following statements must be true?

   I. $f(x)$ must be positive
   II. $f(x)$ must be even

   (A) Statement I only
   (B) Statement II only
   (C) Both Statement I & II
   (D) Neither Statement I nor Statement II

8. If $f(x) = x^3$, which of the following inequalities must be true?

   (A) $f(2) > f(\frac{1}{2})$

   (B) $f(2) < f(\frac{1}{2})$

   (C) $f(2) = f(\frac{1}{2})$

   (D) $f(0) > f(\frac{1}{2})$

For questions 9-11, use the following operation:

$$\square b = 6b - 12$$

9. What is the value of $\square 4$?

(A) −48
(B) 0
(C) 12
(D) 24

10. What is the value of $\square 7 - \square 3$?

(A) 4
(B) 12
(C) 24
(D) 30

11. What is the value of b if $\square b = 42$?

(A) 7
(B) 9
(C) 180
(D) 240

For questions 12–14, use the following operation:

$$\wedge x \wedge = x^2 + 6x + 9$$

12. What is the value of $\wedge 2 \wedge$?

(A) −3
(B) 1
(C) 13
(D) 25

13. What is the value of $\wedge(-3)\wedge$?

(A) −18
(B) 0
(C) 18
(D) 36

14. What is the value of $\sqrt{\wedge x \wedge}$?

(A) $x + 3$
(B) $(x + 3)^2$
(C) $x + \sqrt{6x} + 3$
(D) $x^2 + 3x + 4.5$

For questions 15–17, use the following operation:

$$x@y = 2x - 3y$$

15. What is the value of $5@3$?

(A) −8
(B) 1
(C) 9
(D) 21

16. What is the value of $7@y$?

(A) $2y - 21$
(B) $14 - 3y$
(C) $14 - y$
(D) $21 - 3y$

17. What is the value of $x@7$?

(A) $21 - 3x$
(B) $14 - 3x$
(C) $2x - 21$
(D) $2x - 14$

For questions 18–20, use the following operation:

$$c\#d = c^2 + cd + 16$$

18. What is the value of 2#3?

(A) 10
(B) 17
(C) 26
(D) 31

19. What is the value of 10#4 − 4#10?

(A) −84
(B) 0
(C) 84
(D) 116

20. What is the value of 4#d?

(A) 4d
(B) 4d + 32
(C) d^2 + 16
(D) d^2 + 4d + 16

For questions 21–23, use the following operation:

$$p\sim = \frac{1}{p} + p^2$$

21. What is the value of (−5)~?

(A) $-25\frac{1}{5}$
(B) $-24\frac{4}{5}$
(C) $24\frac{4}{5}$
(D) $25\frac{1}{5}$

22. Which value of p would NOT result in an integer?

(A) −1
(B) 0
(C) 1
(D) All real number values of p will result in an integer.

23. What is the value of p if $p\sim = 0$?

(A) −1
(B) 0
(C) $\frac{1}{2}$
(D) 1

For questions 24–26, use the following operation:

$$\left(x\right) = \frac{x}{4} + x^2$$

24. What is the value of $\left(1\right)$?

(A) $\frac{1}{4}$
(B) $\frac{1}{2}$
(C) $\frac{5}{4}$
(D) $\frac{25}{16}$

25. What is the value of x if $\left(x\right) = 17$?

(A) −6
(B) −4
(C) 4
(D) 6

26. What is the value of $\left(-2\right)$?

(A) −4.5
(B) −3.5
(C) 3.5
(D) 4.5

Quantitative Comparison Practice

Answer Choices:

(A) The amount in column A is greater.
(B) The amount in column B is greater.
(C) The two amounts are equal.
(D) The relationship cannot be determined from the information provided.

⇨$x = \dfrac{1}{x} + 1$

Column A	Column B

27. ⇨$\dfrac{1}{2}$ 2

$\sim y = y^2 + y$

Column A	Column B

28. ~ 3 9

$<<<z = 5z - 4$

Column A	Column B

29. $<<<10$ 54

$/a/ = 3a + 4$

Column A	Column B

30. The value of a $/10/$
when $/a/ = 10$

Solving for Zero

Example: For what value of x is the equation $\dfrac{x-2}{2-x} = 0$ true?

(A) 0
(B) 2
(C) all real numbers
(D) There are no values for x that would make the equation true.

Solution: (D). For a fraction to be equal to zero, the numerator must be zero. However, the denominator can never be zero, because then the fraction does not exist. Here, if $x = 2$, then the numerator equals zero, but so does the denominator, so there is no value of x that will work to make the whole fraction equal to zero.

1. If $x + 5 = 0$, then what does x equal?

(A) −5
(B) 0
(C) 1
(D) 5

2. If $5y = 0$, then what does y equal?

(A) $-\dfrac{1}{5}$
(B) 0
(C) 1
(D) $\dfrac{1}{5}$

The Tutorverse
www.thetutorverse.com

3. If $ab = 0$, then which **must** be true?

    I. $a = 0$
    II. $b = 0$
    III. either $a = 0$ or $b = 0$

(A) I only
(B) II only
(C) III only
(D) I, II, and III

4. If $a + b = 0$, then which **must** be true?

    I. $a = 0$
    II. $b = 0$
    III. either $a = 0$ or $b = 0$

(A) I and II
(B) II and III
(C) I, II, and III
(D) neither I, II, nor III

5. If $x = 5$, then what does $(x + 5)(x - 5)$ equal?

(A) 0
(B) 5
(C) 10
(D) 25

6. If $(x + 5)(x + 3) = 0$, then what could x equal?

(A) 3
(B) 5
(C) 3 or 5
(D) −3 or −5

7. Which fraction is <u>not</u> a real number?

    I. $\dfrac{0}{5}$

    II. $\dfrac{5}{0}$

(A) I only
(B) II only
(C) both I and II
(D) neither I nor II

8. For what value(s) of x is the expression $5x$ a real number?

(A) all real numbers
(B) any real or imaginary number
(C) only 0
(D) any real number except 0

9. For which value of x <u>could</u> the equation $(x + 9)(x - 9) = 0$ be true?

(A) 0
(B) −9
(C) all real numbers
(D) There are no values for x that would make the equation true.

10. For which value of x could the equation $x^2 + 7x + 10 = 0$ be true?

(A) 2
(B) 0
(C) $-\dfrac{10}{7}$
(D) −5

11. For what value of x is the equation
$x^2 + 8x - 20 = 0$ true?

(A) -10
(B) -2
(C) $\dfrac{5}{4}$
(D) $\sqrt{20}$

12. For what value of x is the equation
$x^2 - 5x - 36 = 0$ true?

(A) 4
(B) 5
(C) 6
(D) 9

13. For what value of x is the equation
$x^2 - 12x + 11 = 0$ true?

(A) -11
(B) -10
(C) 10
(D) 11

14. For what value of x is the equation
$x^2 - 100 = 0$ true?

(A) 10 only
(B) -10 only
(C) 10 or -10
(D) There are no values for x that would make the equation true

15. For what value of x is the equation $\dfrac{x+8}{8+x} = 0$

true?

(A) -8
(B) 0
(C) all real numbers
(D) There are no values for x that would make the equation true

16. For what value of x is the equation
$\dfrac{x^2 - 16}{(x+6)(x-8)} = 0$ true?

(A) 8 only
(B) -6 only
(C) 4 or -4
(D) 4, -6, or 8

17. For what value of x is the equation
$(x^3 + 8) \div 2x = 0$ true?

(A) 0, 2, or -2
(B) 0 or -2
(C) -2
(D) 2

18. If $(2x - 6) \times 4x = 0$, then what could x equal?

(A) $\dfrac{1}{4}$ or 3
(B) 1 or 0
(C) 3 or 0
(D) 4 or 0

The Tutorverse
www.thetutorverse.com

Inequalities

Example: Which graph represents the solution set for $2 \leq x + 1 \leq 10$?

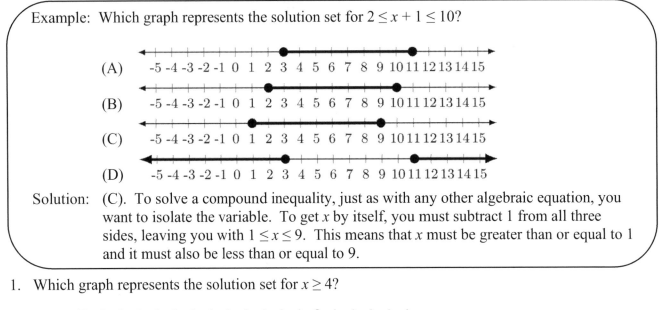

Solution: (C). To solve a compound inequality, just as with any other algebraic equation, you want to isolate the variable. To get x by itself, you must subtract 1 from all three sides, leaving you with $1 \leq x \leq 9$. This means that x must be greater than or equal to 1 and it must also be less than or equal to 9.

1. Which graph represents the solution set for $x \geq 4$?

(A) -9 -8 -7 -6 -5 -4 -3 -2 -1 0 1 2 3 4 5 6 7 8 9

(B) -9 -8 -7 -6 -5 -4 -3 -2 -1 0 1 2 3 4 5 6 7 8 9

(C) -9 -8 -7 -6 -5 -4 -3 -2 -1 0 1 2 3 4 5 6 7 8 9

(D) -9 -8 -7 -6 -5 -4 -3 -2 -1 0 1 2 3 4 5 6 7 8 9

2. Which graph represents the solution set for $a < -6$?

(A) -9 -8 -7 -6 -5 -4 -3 -2 -1 0 1 2 3 4 5 6 7 8 9

(B) -9 -8 -7 -6 -5 -4 -3 -2 -1 0 1 2 3 4 5 6 7 8 9

(C) -9 -8 -7 -6 -5 -4 -3 -2 -1 0 1 2 3 4 5 6 7 8 9

(D) -9 -8 -7 -6 -5 -4 -3 -2 -1 0 1 2 3 4 5 6 7 8 9

3. Which graph represents the solution set for $-3 \leq m \leq 9$?

(A) -16 -14 -12 -10 -8 -6 -4 -2 0 2 4 6 8 10 12 14 16

(B) -16 -14 -12 -10 -8 -6 -4 -2 0 2 4 6 8 10 12 14 16

(C) -16 -14 -12 -10 -8 -6 -4 -2 0 2 4 6 8 10 12 14 16

(D) -16 -14 -12 -10 -8 -6 -4 -2 0 2 4 6 8 10 12 14 16

4. What is the solution set for $3x + 3 \geq 6$?

(A) ![number line with filled dot at 1, shaded left] -9 -8 -7 -6 -5 -4 -3 -2 -1 0 1 2 3 4 5 6 7 8 9

(B) ![number line with filled dot at 1, shaded right] -9 -8 -7 -6 -5 -4 -3 -2 -1 0 1 2 3 4 5 6 7 8 9

(C) ![number line with filled dot at 2, shaded left] -9 -8 -7 -6 -5 -4 -3 -2 -1 0 1 2 3 4 5 6 7 8 9

(D) ![number line with filled dot at 2, shaded right] -9 -8 -7 -6 -5 -4 -3 -2 -1 0 1 2 3 4 5 6 7 8 9

5. What is the solution set for $-5c + 10 > 15$? *(Reminder: when you multiply or divide by a negative number, the inequalities all switch direction!)*

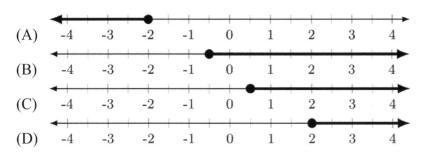

(A) -6 -5 -4 -3 -2 -1 0 1 2 3 4 5 6

(B) -6 -5 -4 -3 -2 -1 0 1 2 3 4 5 6

(C) -6 -5 -4 -3 -2 -1 0 1 2 3 4 5 6

(D) -6 -5 -4 -3 -2 -1 0 1 2 3 4 5 6

6. What is the solution set for $-4y - 2 \leq 0$?

(A) ![number line filled dot at -2, shaded left] -4 -3 -2 -1 0 1 2 3 4

(B) ![number line filled dot at -1, shaded right] -4 -3 -2 -1 0 1 2 3 4

(C) ![number line filled dot at 1, shaded right] -4 -3 -2 -1 0 1 2 3 4

(D) ![number line filled dot at 2, shaded right] -4 -3 -2 -1 0 1 2 3 4

7. What is the solution set for $-3a + 5 \geq -7$?

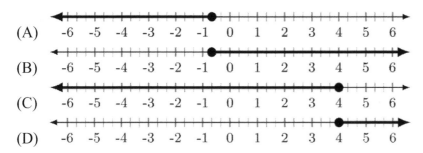

(A) -6 -5 -4 -3 -2 -1 0 1 2 3 4 5 6

(B) -6 -5 -4 -3 -2 -1 0 1 2 3 4 5 6

(C) -6 -5 -4 -3 -2 -1 0 1 2 3 4 5 6

(D) -6 -5 -4 -3 -2 -1 0 1 2 3 4 5 6

8. What is the solution set for $-9 \leq 3h + 3 \leq 6$?

(A)

(B)

(C)

(D)

9. What is the solution set for $-1 \leq -2f + 1 \leq 9$?

(A)

(B)

(C)

(D)

10. Which graph represents the solution set for $6 \geq -p + 3 \geq -1$?

(A)

(B)

(C)

(D)

11. Which graph represents the solution set for $-5 < -3w + 3 < -1$?

(A)

(B)

(C)

(D)

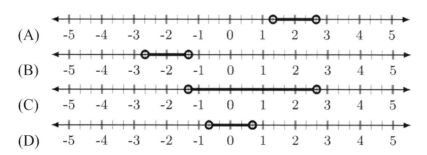

Absolute Value Inequalities

Example: Which graph represents the solution set of the absolute value inequality $|x + 3| < 5$?

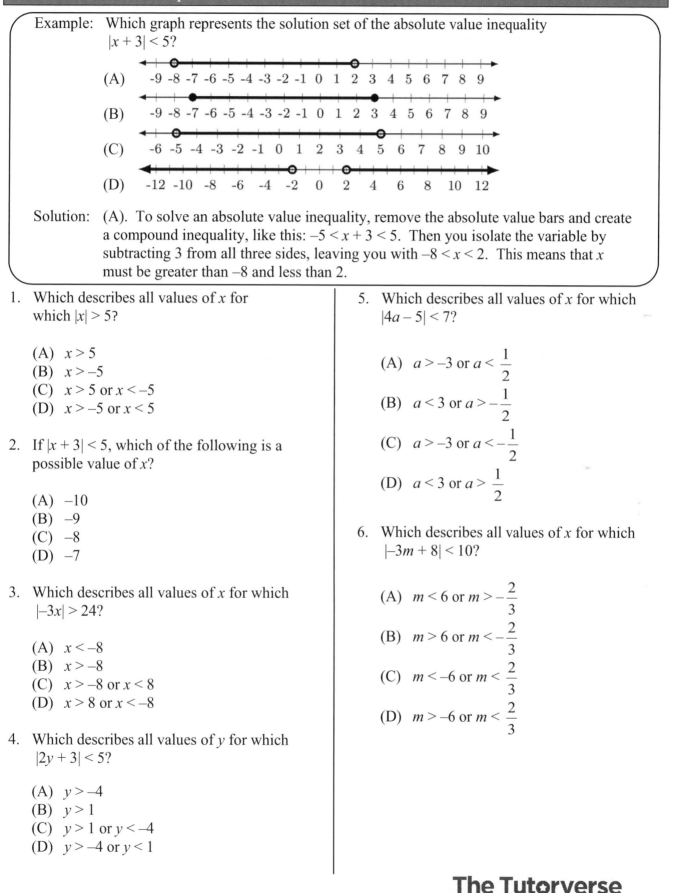

Solution: (A). To solve an absolute value inequality, remove the absolute value bars and create a compound inequality, like this: $-5 < x + 3 < 5$. Then you isolate the variable by subtracting 3 from all three sides, leaving you with $-8 < x < 2$. This means that x must be greater than -8 and less than 2.

1. Which describes all values of x for which $|x| > 5$?

   (A) $x > 5$
   (B) $x > -5$
   (C) $x > 5$ or $x < -5$
   (D) $x > -5$ or $x < 5$

2. If $|x + 3| < 5$, which of the following is a possible value of x?

   (A) -10
   (B) -9
   (C) -8
   (D) -7

3. Which describes all values of x for which $|-3x| > 24$?

   (A) $x < -8$
   (B) $x > -8$
   (C) $x > -8$ or $x < 8$
   (D) $x > 8$ or $x < -8$

4. Which describes all values of y for which $|2y + 3| < 5$?

   (A) $y > -4$
   (B) $y > 1$
   (C) $y > 1$ or $y < -4$
   (D) $y > -4$ or $y < 1$

5. Which describes all values of x for which $|4a - 5| < 7$?

   (A) $a > -3$ or $a < \dfrac{1}{2}$

   (B) $a < 3$ or $a > -\dfrac{1}{2}$

   (C) $a > -3$ or $a < -\dfrac{1}{2}$

   (D) $a < 3$ or $a > \dfrac{1}{2}$

6. Which describes all values of x for which $|-3m + 8| < 10$?

   (A) $m < 6$ or $m > -\dfrac{2}{3}$

   (B) $m > 6$ or $m < -\dfrac{2}{3}$

   (C) $m < -6$ or $m < \dfrac{2}{3}$

   (D) $m > -6$ or $m < \dfrac{2}{3}$

7. Which of the following is the graph of the solution to $|x| < 3$?

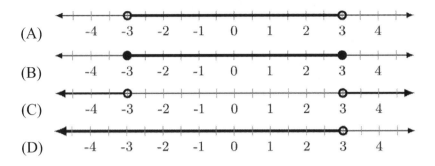

(A)

(B)

(C)

(D)

8. Which of the following is the graph of the solution to $|5x| > 30$?

(A)

(B)

(C)

(D)

9. Which of the following is the graph of the solution to $|y + 3| > 5$?

(A)

(B)

(C)

(D)

10. Which of the following is the graph of the solution to $|x + 5| - 5 < 2$?

(A)

(B)

(C)

(D)

11. Which of the following is the graph of the solution to $|x-8|+2<6$?

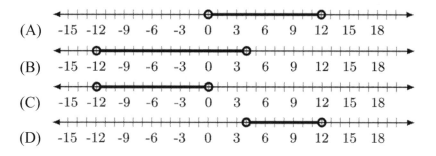

(A) -15 -12 -9 -6 -3 0 3 6 9 12 15 18

(B) -15 -12 -9 -6 -3 0 3 6 9 12 15 18

(C) -15 -12 -9 -6 -3 0 3 6 9 12 15 18

(D) -15 -12 -9 -6 -3 0 3 6 9 12 15 18

12. Which of the following is the graph of the solution to $3|x-1|<7$?

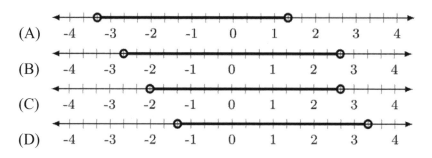

(A) -4 -3 -2 -1 0 1 2 3 4

(B) -4 -3 -2 -1 0 1 2 3 4

(C) -4 -3 -2 -1 0 1 2 3 4

(D) -4 -3 -2 -1 0 1 2 3 4

13. Which of the following is the graph of the solution to $\frac{1}{4}|x-1|<5$?

(A) -25 -20 -15 -10 -5 0 5 10 15 20 25

(B) -25 -20 -15 -10 -5 0 5 10 15 20 25

(C) -25 -20 -15 -10 -5 0 5 10 15 20 25

(D) -25 -20 -15 -10 -5 0 5 10 15 20 25

14. Which of the following is the graph of the solution to $\frac{1}{2}|x+3|-3<1$?

(A) -11-10-9 -8 -7 -6 -5 -4 -3 -2 -1 0 1 2 3 4 5 6 7 8 9 10 11

(B) -11-10-9 -8 -7 -6 -5 -4 -3 -2 -1 0 1 2 3 4 5 6 7 8 9 10 11

(C) -11-10-9 -8 -7 -6 -5 -4 -3 -2 -1 0 1 2 3 4 5 6 7 8 9 10 11

(D) -11-10-9 -8 -7 -6 -5 -4 -3 -2 -1 0 1 2 3 4 5 6 7 8 9 10 11

15. A solution set is graphed on the number line shown.

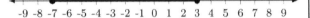

The solution set of which inequality is shown?

(A) $|x| < 2$
(B) $|x| > 2$
(C) $|x + 1| < 3$
(D) $|x - 1| < 1$

16. A solution set is graphed on the number line shown.

The solution set of which inequality is shown?

(A) $|x + 2| \leq 5$
(B) $|x - 2| \leq 5$
(C) $|x + 5| \leq 2$
(D) $|x - 5| \leq 2$

17. A solution set is graphed on the number line shown.

The solution set of which inequality is shown?

(A) $|x - 2| \leq 1$
(B) $|x + 2| \leq 1$
(C) $|x - 1| \leq 2$
(D) $|x + 1| \leq 2$

18. A solution set is graphed on the number line shown.

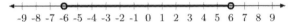

The solution set of which inequality is shown?

(A) $|5x| < 1$
(B) $|-2x| < 10$
(C) $|x + 5| < 0$
(D) $|x - 5| < 0$

19. A solution set is graphed on the number line shown.

The solution set of which inequality is shown?

(A) $|\frac{1}{2}x| < 3$
(B) $|x - 3| < 3$
(C) $|2x| < 3$
(D) $|-2x| < 3$

20. Which describes all values of x for which $|2m - 7| < 7$?

(A) $m > 0$ or $m < 7$
(B) $m < 0$ or $m > 7$
(C) $m > -7$ or $m < 0$
(D) $m < -7$ or $m > 0$

Slope

Example: Find the slope of the line that passes through points (–8,4) and (4,10).

    (A) –2

    (B) $-\dfrac{1}{2}$

    (C) $\dfrac{1}{2}$

    (D) 2

Solution: (C). To find slope from two coordinate points, use $\dfrac{\Delta y}{\Delta x}$, meaning subtract the first y value from the second y value and the first x value from the second x value. Here, that means $\dfrac{10-4}{4--8} = \dfrac{6}{12} = \dfrac{1}{2}$.

1. The graph of a line is shown.

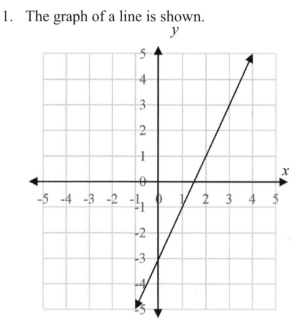

What is the slope of the line?

    (A) –3
    (B) –2
    (C) 2
    (D) 3

2. The graph of a line is shown.

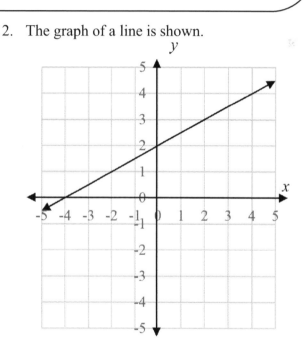

What is the slope of the line?

    (A) –2

    (B) $-\dfrac{1}{2}$

    (C) $\dfrac{1}{2}$

    (D) 2

3. The graph of a line is shown.

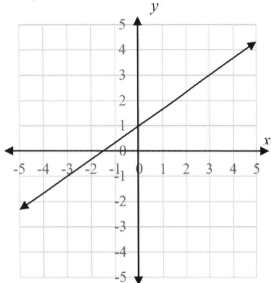

What is the slope of the line?

(A) $\dfrac{3}{2}$

(B) $\dfrac{2}{3}$

(C) $-\dfrac{2}{3}$

(D) $-\dfrac{3}{2}$

4. What is the slope of the line represented by $y = 5x - 7$?

(A) −2
(B) 5
(C) 7
(D) 12

5. The graph of a line is shown.

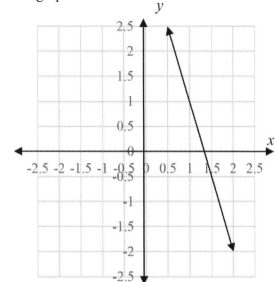

What is the slope of the line?

(A) −3

(B) $-\dfrac{1}{3}$

(C) $\dfrac{1}{3}$

(D) 3

6. The graph of a line is shown.

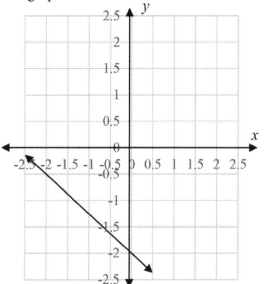

What is the slope of the line?

(A) $-\dfrac{4}{3}$

(B) $-\dfrac{3}{4}$

(C) $\dfrac{3}{4}$

(D) $\dfrac{4}{3}$

7. What is the slope of the line parallel to the line $y = -\dfrac{2}{3}x + 7$?

(A) $-\dfrac{3}{2}$

(B) $-\dfrac{2}{3}$

(C) $\dfrac{2}{3}$

(D) $\dfrac{3}{2}$

8. A function is shown.

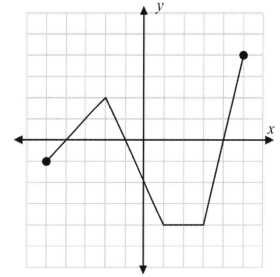

What are the values of x for which the slope of the function is negative?

(A) $-5 < x < -2$

(B) $-2 < x < 1$

(C) $1 < x < 3$

(D) $3 < x < 5$

9. Find the slope of the line that passes through points (0,3) and (2,–5).

(A) –4

(B) –1

(C) $-\dfrac{1}{4}$

(D) 1

10. Find the slope of the line that passes through points (2,6) and (3,11).

(A) –5

(B) $-\dfrac{1}{5}$

(C) $\dfrac{1}{5}$

(D) 5

11. Find the slope of the line that passes through points (−3,1) and (3,5).

    (A) $\dfrac{3}{2}$

    (B) $\dfrac{2}{3}$

    (C) $-\dfrac{2}{3}$

    (D) $-\dfrac{3}{2}$

12. Find the slope of the line that passes through points (−2, −7) and (−10, −9).

    (A)   −4

    (B) $-\dfrac{1}{4}$

    (C) $\dfrac{1}{4}$

    (D)   4

13. A line that passes through points (x,1) and (3,5) has a slope of 2. What is the value of x?

    (A)   0
    (B)   1
    (C)   2
    (D)   3

14. A line that passes through points (−5,4) and (x,7) has a slope of $\dfrac{1}{2}$. What is the value of x?

    (A)   −2
    (B)   −1
    (C)   0
    (D)   1

15. A line that passes through points (−8, −4) and (8,y) has a slope of $\dfrac{3}{4}$. What is the value of y?

    (A)   5
    (B)   6
    (C)   7
    (D)   8

16. What is the slope of a line perpendicular to $y = 2x + 3$? *(Reminder: the slopes of perpendicular lines are negative reciprocals.)*

    (A)   −2

    (B) $-\dfrac{1}{2}$

    (C) $\dfrac{1}{2}$

    (D)   2

17. Line a is represented by $y = 4x − 6$ and line b is perpendicular to line a. What is the product of the slopes of lines a and b?

    (A)   −1

    (B) $-\dfrac{1}{4}$

    (C) $\dfrac{1}{4}$

    (D)   1

18. Line m has a slope of 2. Line n is perpendicular to line m. What is the product of their slopes?

    (A)   −1

    (B) $-\dfrac{1}{2}$

    (C) $\dfrac{1}{2}$

    (D)   1

19. Line *a* passes through both the origin and point (5,5).

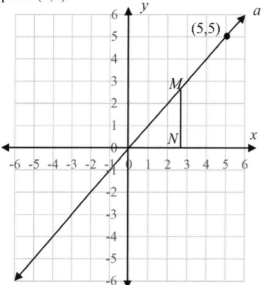

Line *b* (not shown) also passes through the origin, and intersects $\overline{MN}$ between *M* and *N*. Which of the following could be the slope of line *b*?

(A) 5
(B) 2.5
(C) 0.5
(D) –5

20. What is the slope of the line perpendicular to $y = mx + b$?

(A) $-m$

(B) $-\dfrac{1}{m}$

(C) $\dfrac{1}{m}$

(D) m

21. Line *a* passes through both the origin and point (3,–6).

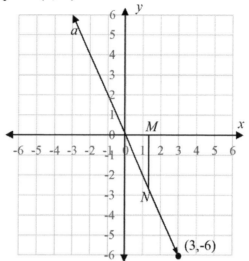

Line *b* (not shown) also passes through the origin, and intersects $\overline{MN}$ between *M* and *N*. Which of the following could be the slope of line *b*?

(A) –3
(B) –0.5
(C) 0.5
(D) 3

22. The line shown represents $y = mx + b$.

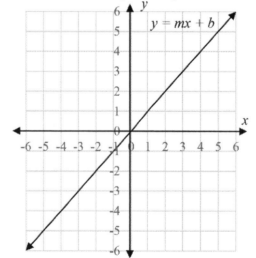

What is the slope of $y = 2mx + b$?

(A) 0.5
(B) 1
(C) 2
(D) 4

Quantitative Comparison Practice

Answer Choices:

    (A)   The amount in column A is greater.
    (B)   The amount in column B is greater.
    (C)   The two amounts are equal.
    (D)   The relationship cannot be determined from the information provided.

	Column A	Column B
23.	The slope of the line $y = 2x + 4$	The slope of the line $4x + 2y = 8$

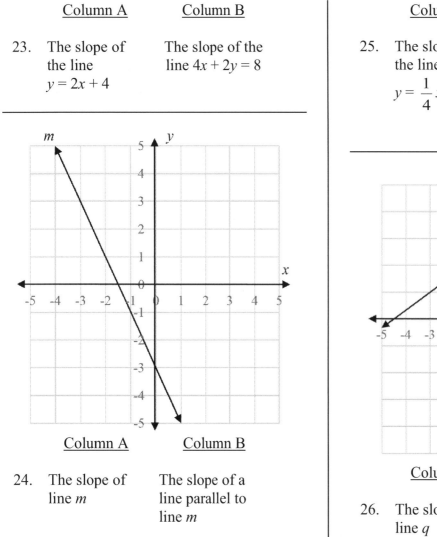

	Column A	Column B
24.	The slope of line m	The slope of a line parallel to line m

	Column A	Column B
25.	The slope of the line $y = \dfrac{1}{4}x - 6$	The slope of the line perpendicular to $y = \dfrac{1}{4}x - 6$ at $(4,-5)$

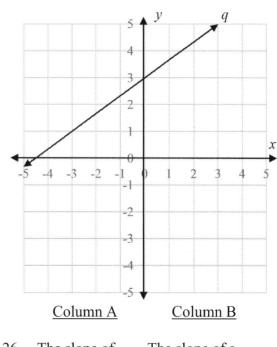

	Column A	Column B
26.	The slope of line q	The slope of a line perpendicular to line q

Equation of a Line

Example: Find the equation of the line that passes through points (–2,–3) and (4,9).

$\quad$ (A) $\quad y = \dfrac{1}{2}x + 1$

$\quad$ (B) $\quad y = \dfrac{1}{2}x - 3$

$\quad$ (C) $\quad y = 2x + 1$

$\quad$ (D) $\quad y = 2x - 3$

Solution: (C). To find the equation of a line, find the slope first using $\dfrac{\Delta y}{\Delta x}$. Here, that means the

slope is $\dfrac{9--3}{4--2} = \dfrac{12}{6} = 2$. Plug in the slope for m in the formula for a line,

$y = mx + b$. Here, that gives you $y = 2x + b$. Then, choose any given point and plug the x and y coordinates in for x and y in the equation. Here, you can do $9 = 2(4) + b$, which gives you $b = 1$.

1. Find the equation of the line that passes through points (3,3) and (9,5).

$\quad$ (A) $\quad y = 3x - 6$

$\quad$ (B) $\quad y = \dfrac{1}{3}x + 2$

$\quad$ (C) $\quad y = -3x + 12$

$\quad$ (D) $\quad y = -\dfrac{1}{3}x + 4$

2. Find the equation of the line that passes through points (0,–6) and (3,0).

$\quad$ (A) $\quad y = 2x - 3$

$\quad$ (B) $\quad y = 2x - 6$

$\quad$ (C) $\quad y = -2x - 3$

$\quad$ (D) $\quad y = -2x - 6$

3. Find the equation of the line that passes through points (–4,4) and (8,–5).

$\quad$ (A) $\quad y = -\dfrac{3}{4}x + 1$

$\quad$ (B) $\quad y = -\dfrac{3}{4}x - 2$

$\quad$ (C) $\quad y = -\dfrac{4}{3}x + 1$

$\quad$ (D) $\quad y = -\dfrac{4}{3}x - 2$

4. Find the equation of the line that is parallel to $y = 3x + 2$ and passes through point (5,5). *(Note: Remember that parallel lines have the same slope.)*

$\quad$ (A) $\quad y = -3x - 5$

$\quad$ (B) $\quad y = -3x - 10$

$\quad$ (C) $\quad y = 3x - 5$

$\quad$ (D) $\quad y = 3x - 10$

5. Find the equation of the line that is parallel to $y = -2x + 5$ and passes through point (–3,6).

$\quad$ (A) $\quad y = -2x$

$\quad$ (B) $\quad y = -2x - 5$

$\quad$ (C) $\quad y = 2x$

$\quad$ (D) $\quad y = 2x - 5$

6. Find the equation of the line that is parallel to $y = \dfrac{1}{2}x - 4$ and passes through point (8, –1).

$\quad$ (A) $\quad y = \dfrac{1}{2}x - 5$

$\quad$ (B) $\quad y = \dfrac{1}{2}x - 19$

$\quad$ (C) $\quad y = 2x - 5$

$\quad$ (D) $\quad y = 2x - 19$

7. Find the equation of the line that is perpendicular to $y = 3x + 10$ and passes through point $(6,-7)$.

   (Note: Remember that perpendicular lines have slopes that are negative reciprocals of each other.)

   (A) $y = \dfrac{1}{3}x - 5$

   (B) $y = \dfrac{1}{3}x - 26$

   (C) $y = -\dfrac{1}{3}x - 5$

   (D) $y = -\dfrac{1}{3}x - 26$

8. Find the equation of the line that is perpendicular to $y = -2x + 5$ and passes through point $(0,0)$.

   (A) $y = -\dfrac{1}{2}x$

   (B) $y = -\dfrac{1}{2}x - 5$

   (C) $y = \dfrac{1}{2}x$

   (D) $y = \dfrac{1}{2}x - 5$

9. Line m is represented by the equation $y = \dfrac{1}{2}x - 4$. Line n is perpendicular to line m. The two lines intersect at $(8,0)$. What is the equation of line n?

   (A) $y = -2x + 8$
   (B) $y = -2x + 16$
   (C) $y = 2x + 8$
   (D) $y = 2x + 16$

10. The graph of a line is shown.

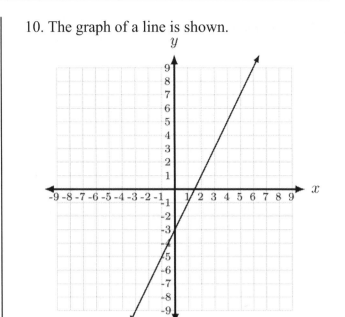

   What is the equation of the line?

   (A) $y = 2x + 1.5$
   (B) $y = 2x - 3$
   (C) $y = 3x + 1.5$
   (D) $y = 3x - 3$

11. The graph of a line is shown.

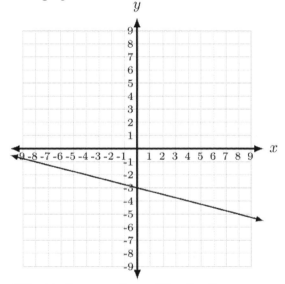

   What is the equation of the line?

   (A) $y = -4x - 3$

   (B) $y = -4x - 10$

   (C) $y = -\dfrac{1}{4}x - 3$

   (D) $y = -\dfrac{1}{4}x - 10$

12. The graph of a line is shown.

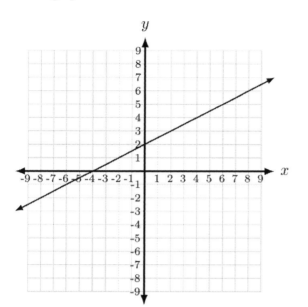

What is the equation of the line?

(A) $y = \dfrac{1}{2}x - 4$

(B) $y = \dfrac{1}{2}x + 2$

(C) $y = 2x - 4$

(D) $y = 2x + 2$

13. The graph of line q is shown.

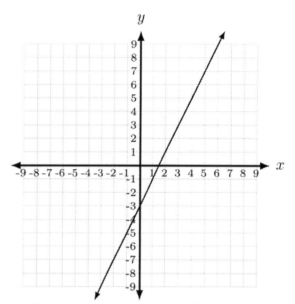

What is the equation of the line perpendicular to line q at $(4,5)$?

(A) $y = -\dfrac{1}{2}x + 7$

(B) $y = -\dfrac{1}{2}x - 3$

(C) $y = 2x + 7$

(D) $y = 2x - 3$

14. Line k is represented by the equation $y = -\dfrac{1}{3}x + 7$. Line l is perpendicular to line k. The two lines intersect at $(3, 6)$. What is the equation of line l?

(A) $y = -\dfrac{1}{3}x - 3$

(B) $y = 3x - 3$

(C) $y = 3x + 7$

(D) $y = \dfrac{1}{3}x + 7$

Sequences

Example: The first five terms of a geometric sequence of numbers are shown.

6, 12, 24, 48, 96

Which expression represents the nth term of this sequence?

(A) $n + 6$
(B) $6n + 6$
(C) $6(2)^{n-1}$
(D) $2(6)^{n-1}$

Solution: (C). If you are comfortable with sequences, you can recognize that each proceeding term is being multiplied by 2. The fact that each proceeding term is being multiplied instead of added makes it a geometric sequence instead of an arithmetic sequence. Since the first term is 6, that means the expression should be $6(2)^{n-1}$.

If you are not comfortable with sequences, you can still figure the problem out using a simple plugging-in strategy. If you are given a list of five terms, just pick any number 1 to 5 (try the highest number first, not 1 or 2), plug it in for the n in each answer choice, and see which one gives you the corresponding term. Here, if you pick 5 and plug it into each answer choice, only answer choice (C) will give you 96, which is the 5th term.

1. The first five terms of an arithmetic sequence of numbers are shown.

1, 3, 5, 7, 9

Which expression represents the nth term of this sequence?

(A) $n + 2$
(B) $2n$
(C) $2n + 2$
(D) $2n - 1$

2. The first four terms of an arithmetic sequence of numbers are shown.

−1, 3, 7, 11

Which expression represents the nth term of this sequence?

(A) $n - 1$
(B) $n + 4$
(C) $4n - 5$
(D) $4n - 1$

3. The first six terms of an arithmetic sequence of numbers are shown.

15, 10, 5, 0, −5, −10

Which expression represents the nth term of this sequence?

(A) $-n$
(B) $-5n + 10$
(C) $-5n + 20$
(D) $n - 14$

4. The first five terms of an arithmetic sequence of numbers are shown.

$$\frac{1}{2}, \frac{3}{2}, \frac{5}{2}, \frac{7}{2}, \frac{9}{2}$$

Which expression represents the nth term of this sequence?

(A) $n - \dfrac{1}{2}$

(B) $n + 1$

(C) $\dfrac{1}{2}n + 1$

(D) $\dfrac{1}{2}n + 2$

5. The first five terms of an arithmetic sequence of numbers are shown.

1, 3, 5, 7, 9

What is the 10th term of this sequence?

(A) 15
(B) 17
(C) 19
(D) 21

6. The first four terms of an arithmetic sequence of numbers are shown.

2, 7, 12, 17

What is the 50th term of this sequence? *(Note: the numbers in the sequence are skip-counting by 5. Look back at the first four questions. How can taking note of the skip-counting help you find the right answer?)*

(A) 247
(B) 252
(C) 257
(D) 262

7. The first six terms of an arithmetic sequence of numbers are shown.

−4, −1, 2, 5, 8, 11

What is the 100th term of this sequence?

(A) 292
(B) 293
(C) 294
(D) 295

8. The first five terms of a geometric sequence of numbers are shown.

2, 6, 18, 54, 162

Which expression represents the nth term of this sequence?

(A) 3^{n-1}
(B) $4^{n-1} + 2$
(C) $2(3)^{n-1}$
(D) $2(3)^{n}$

9. The first four terms of a geometric sequence of numbers are shown.

$-5, -15, -45, -135$

Which expression represents the nth term of this sequence?

(A) $-3(5)^{n-1}$
(B) $(-5)^{n-1}$
(C) $-5(3)^{n-1}$
(D) $-5(-3)^{n-1}$

10. The first five terms of a geometric sequence of numbers are shown.

$12, 6, 3, \dfrac{3}{2}, \dfrac{3}{4}$

Which expression represents the nth term of this sequence?

(A) $12\left(\dfrac{1}{2}\right)^{n-1}$

(B) $12(2)^{n-1}$

(C) $12\left(\dfrac{1}{2}\right)^{n}$

(D) $12(2)^{n}$

11. The first four terms of a geometric sequence of numbers are shown.

$\dfrac{2}{3}, \dfrac{2}{9}, \dfrac{2}{27}, \dfrac{2}{81}$

Which expression represents the nth term of this sequence?

(A) $\dfrac{2}{3}\left(\dfrac{1}{3}\right)^{n-1}$

(B) $\dfrac{1}{3}\left(\dfrac{2}{3}\right)^{n-1}$

(C) $2(3)^{n-1}$

(D) $\dfrac{2}{3n}$

12. The first four terms of a geometric sequence of numbers are shown.

$4, 8, 16, 32$

What is the 6th term of this sequence?

(A) 64
(B) 96
(C) 128
(D) 256

13. The first five terms of a geometric sequence of numbers are shown.

$20, 10, 5, \dfrac{5}{2}, \dfrac{5}{4}$

What is the 8th term of this sequence?

(A) $\dfrac{5}{32}$

(B) $\dfrac{5}{64}$

(C) $\dfrac{5}{128}$

(D) $\dfrac{5}{256}$

Permutations & Combinations

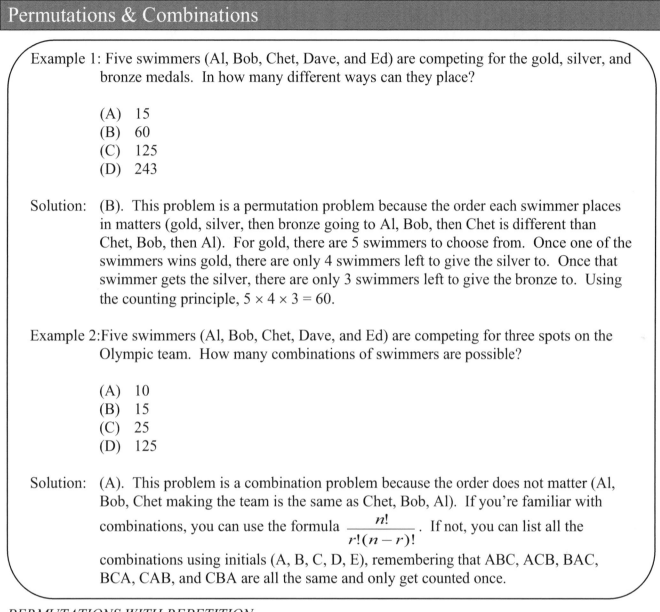

Example 1: Five swimmers (Al, Bob, Chet, Dave, and Ed) are competing for the gold, silver, and bronze medals. In how many different ways can they place?

(A) 15
(B) 60
(C) 125
(D) 243

Solution: (B). This problem is a permutation problem because the order each swimmer places in matters (gold, silver, then bronze going to Al, Bob, then Chet is different than Chet, Bob, then Al). For gold, there are 5 swimmers to choose from. Once one of the swimmers wins gold, there are only 4 swimmers left to give the silver to. Once that swimmer gets the silver, there are only 3 swimmers left to give the bronze to. Using the counting principle, $5 \times 4 \times 3 = 60$.

Example 2: Five swimmers (Al, Bob, Chet, Dave, and Ed) are competing for three spots on the Olympic team. How many combinations of swimmers are possible?

(A) 10
(B) 15
(C) 25
(D) 125

Solution: (A). This problem is a combination problem because the order does not matter (Al, Bob, Chet making the team is the same as Chet, Bob, Al). If you're familiar with combinations, you can use the formula $\dfrac{n!}{r!(n-r)!}$. If not, you can list all the combinations using initials (A, B, C, D, E), remembering that ABC, ACB, BAC, BCA, CAB, and CBA are all the same and only get counted once.

PERMUTATIONS WITH REPETITION

1. Billy has 10 different shirts and 4 different pairs of pants. How many different outfits can he make from one shirt and one pair of pants?

(A) 6
(B) 14
(C) 20
(D) 40

2. Brad must create a code for his locker. It must be 3 characters long. For each character, he may choose from all ten digits (0-9), and he may repeat digits. How many different codes can he create?

(A) 30
(B) 100
(C) 720
(D) 1,000

3. Mason is choosing a password for his phone using any letters from the alphabet, A-Z. It must be four letters long, and he can repeat letters. How many different passwords can he create?

   (A) 4^{26}
   (B) 26^4
   (C) 26×4
   (D) $26 \times 25 \times 24 \times 23$

4. A multiple choice quiz has only 3 questions, each one with answer choices A, B, C, and D. Assuming a student answers every question, in how many ways could he fill in the answers?

   (A) 9
   (B) 12
   (C) 64
   (D) 81

5. A deli offers 3 kinds of bread, 4 kinds of deli meat, and 3 types of cheese. How many different sandwiches can be made from 1 type of bread, 1 type of meat, and 1 type of cheese?

   (A) 3
   (B) 10
   (C) 12
   (D) 36

6. Alex is ordering a custom license plate. It must be 6 characters long. For each of the first three characters he may choose any letter A through Z and for each of the last three characters he may choose any digit 0 through 9. How many different license plates can Alex choose from?

   (A) $3(26 \times 10)$
   (B) $26^3 \times 10^3$
   (C) $26 \times 3 \times 10 \times 3$
   (D) $26^3 \times 26^3 \times 26^3 \times 10^3 \times 10^3 \times 10^3$

PERMUTATIONS WITHOUT REPETITION

7. Brad must create a code for his locker. It must be 3 digits. For each digit, he may choose from all ten digits (0-9), and he may NOT repeat digits. How many different codes can he create?

   (A) 30
   (B) 100
   (C) 720
   (D) 1,000

8. Mason is choosing a password for his phone using any letters from the alphabet, A-Z. It must be four letters long, and he cannot repeat letters. How many different passwords can he create?

   (A) 4^{26}
   (B) 26^4
   (C) 26×4
   (D) $26 \times 25 \times 24 \times 23$

9. In how many different ways can the letters MATH be arranged?

   (A) 12
   (B) 16
   (C) 24
   (D) 64

10. Polly has 7 different books. She is going to arrange three of them on the shelf above her desk. In how many different ways can she arrange three books?

   (A) 21
   (B) 81
   (C) 210
   (D) 343

11. Brittany is ordering a custom license plate. It must be 6 characters long. For each of the first three characters she may choose any letter A through Z and for each of the last three characters she may choose any digit 0 through 9, but no letter or digit can be repeated. How many different license plates can Brittany choose from?

(A) $26^3 \times 10^3$
(B) $26 \times 3 \times 10 \times 3$
(C) $26 \times 25 \times 24 \times 10 \times 9 \times 8$
(D) $26^3 \times 25^3 \times 24^3 \times 10^3 \times 9^3 \times 8^3$

12. Walt, Xander, Yoko, and Zack run a race. In how many different ways can they finish?

(A) 4
(B) 16
(C) 24
(D) 64

COMBINATIONS

13. There are four pieces of fruit lying on a counter – an apple, a banana, an orange, and a peach. Dorothy wants to eat two pieces of fruit with her lunch. How many combinations of 2 pieces of fruit are possible from the four pieces of fruit?

(A) 6
(B) 8
(C) 12
(D) 16

14. Logan's swim team has 5 members. It plans to send 2 of its members to represent them at a swim meet. How many combinations of 2 members are possible from the 5-member team?

(A) 5
(B) 10
(C) 15
(D) 20

15. Mrs. Thompson has 7 children. She wants to choose two to go clean the garage. How many different pairs can go?

(A) 14
(B) 21
(C) 49
(D) 128

16. Tina's little sister has 5 dolls, but she can only take 4 on vacation with them. How many combinations of 4 dolls can Tina's sister make?

(A) 5
(B) 10
(C) 15
(D) 20

17. 6 players entered a chess tournament. Matches are played one pair at a time, with the players picked randomly. How many different combinations of 2 players can be made for the first match?

(A) 12
(B) 15
(C) 24
(D) 36

18. Abby has 6 board games, and can take 3 of them to camp with her. How many combinations of 3 games can she take?

(A) 3
(B) 12
(C) 18
(D) 20

(E)

Proportions

Example: Rectangle *ABCD* is similar to rectangle *WXYZ*.

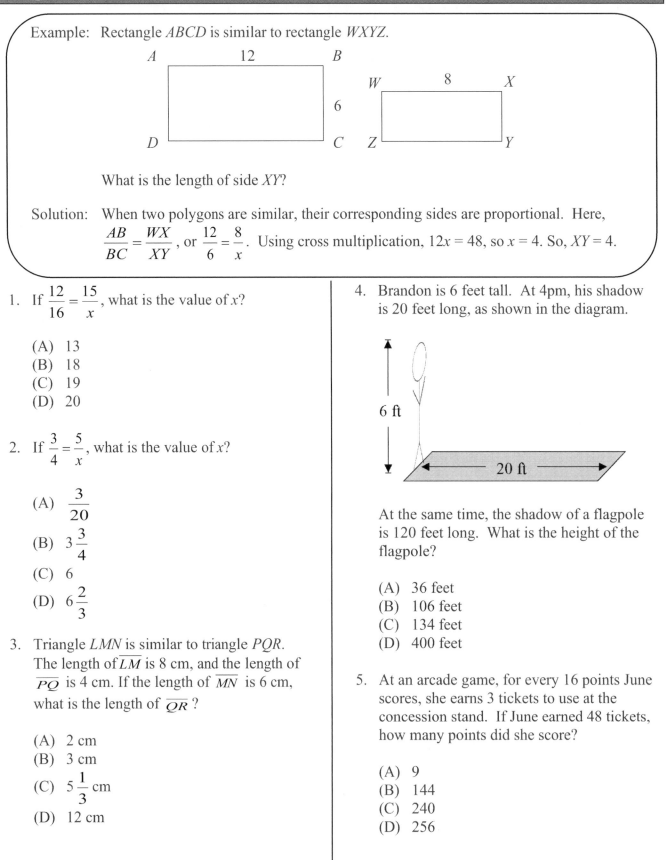

What is the length of side *XY*?

Solution: When two polygons are similar, their corresponding sides are proportional. Here,
$\frac{AB}{BC} = \frac{WX}{XY}$, or $\frac{12}{6} = \frac{8}{x}$. Using cross multiplication, $12x = 48$, so $x = 4$. So, $XY = 4$.

1. If $\frac{12}{16} = \frac{15}{x}$, what is the value of x?

   (A)   13
   (B)   18
   (C)   19
   (D)   20

2. If $\frac{3}{4} = \frac{5}{x}$, what is the value of x?

   (A) $\frac{3}{20}$
   (B) $3\frac{3}{4}$
   (C)   6
   (D) $6\frac{2}{3}$

3. Triangle *LMN* is similar to triangle *PQR*.
    The length of $\overline{LM}$ is 8 cm, and the length of
    $\overline{PQ}$ is 4 cm. If the length of $\overline{MN}$ is 6 cm,
    what is the length of $\overline{QR}$?

   (A)   2 cm
   (B)   3 cm
   (C) $5\frac{1}{3}$ cm
   (D)   12 cm

4. Brandon is 6 feet tall. At 4pm, his shadow
    is 20 feet long, as shown in the diagram.

    6 ft

    20 ft

    At the same time, the shadow of a flagpole
    is 120 feet long. What is the height of the
    flagpole?

   (A)   36 feet
   (B)   106 feet
   (C)   134 feet
   (D)   400 feet

5. At an arcade game, for every 16 points June
    scores, she earns 3 tickets to use at the
    concession stand. If June earned 48 tickets,
    how many points did she score?

   (A)   9
   (B)   144
   (C)   240
   (D)   256

The Tutorverse

6. Ingrid usually runs 12 miles in 2 hours. If she only has 40 minutes to run today, how many miles can she run?

   (A) 2.4
   (B) 3
   (C) 4
   (D) 5

7. Triangle *ABC* is similar to Triangle *DEF*.

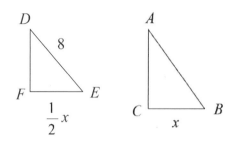

   What is the length of side *AB*?

   (A) 4
   (B) 8
   (C) 12
   (D) 16

8. Triangle *GHI* is similar to Triangle *JKL*.

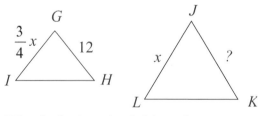

   What is the length of side *JK*?

   (A) 8
   (B) 9
   (C) 15
   (D) 16

9. A model of a real ship is built at a scale of 1 inch represents 6 yards. If the model is 2.5 feet long, how long is the real ship? *(Note: 1 yard = 3 feet)*

   (A) 60 feet
   (B) 180 feet
   (C) 360 feet
   (D) 540 feet

10. A farmer has 4 cows that can eat all the grass in a field in 10 days. If the farmer buys 1 more cow, how many days will it take the cows to eat all the grass?

   (A) 8
   (B) 10
   (C) 12
   (D) 12.5

11. Two hoses can fill a bucket in 5 hours. How long will it take 5 hoses to fill the bucket?

   (A) 2 hours
   (B) 5 hours
   (C) 10 hours
   (D) 12.5 hours

Quantitative Comparison Practice

Answer Choices:

   (A)   The amount in column A is greater.
   (B)   The amount in column B is greater.
   (C)   The two amounts are equal.
   (D)   The relationship cannot be determined from the information provided.

$$\frac{6}{15} = \frac{15}{x}$$

	Column A	Column B
12.	x	6

Triangle *ABC* is similar to Triangle *DEF*

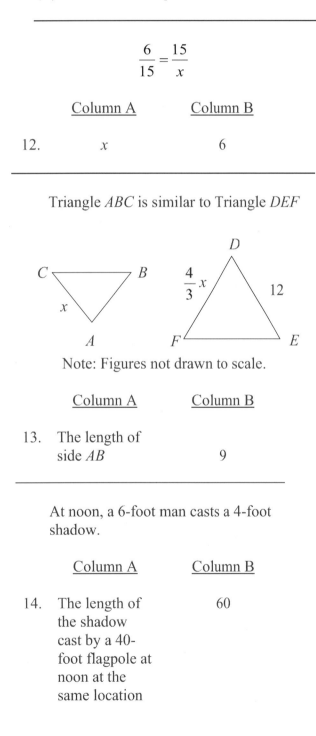

Note: Figures not drawn to scale.

	Column A	Column B
13.	The length of side *AB*	9

At noon, a 6-foot man casts a 4-foot shadow.

	Column A	Column B
14.	The length of the shadow cast by a 40-foot flagpole at noon at the same location	60

Jennifer buys 3 textbooks for $51.

	Column A	Column B
15.	The number of textbooks she can buy at the same rate if she has $130	8

Cho has to read 78 pages of a book for school and reads 6 pages every hour.

	Column A	Column B
16.	The number of minutes it takes him to read all 78 pages at the same rate.	800 minutes

Geometry

Geometry with Variables

Example: A rectangle has a length of $x + 7$ and a width of $x - 3$. What is the area of the rectangle?

(A)   21
(B) $2x + 4$
(C) $x^2 - 21$
(D) $x^2 + 4x - 21$

Solution: (D). To find area of a rectangle, you multiply the length by the width. The same holds true when the length and width are algebraic expressions. Here, the area is $(x + 7)(x - 3)$. To multiply binomials, use the distributive property.

1. What is the area of the square?

2. What is the perimeter of the square?

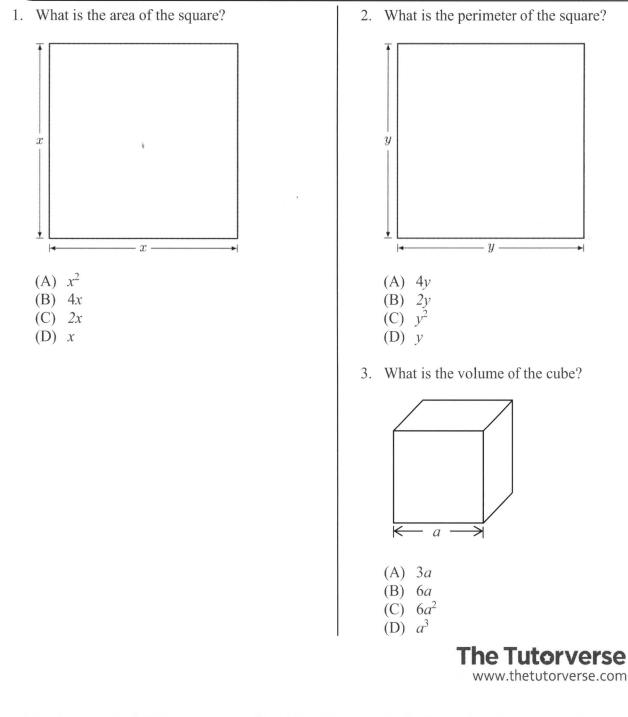

(A) x^2
(B) $4x$
(C) $2x$
(D) x

(A) $4y$
(B) $2y$
(C) y^2
(D) y

3. What is the volume of the cube?

(A) $3a$
(B) $6a$
(C) $6a^2$
(D) a^3

The Tutorverse
www.thetutorverse.com

4. What is the area of the rectangle?

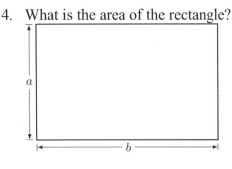

(A) $a + b$
(B) $2a + 2b$
(C) ab
(D) $\dfrac{ab}{2}$

5. What is the perimeter of the rectangle?

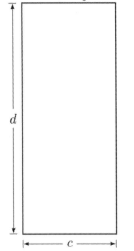

(A) cd
(B) $c + d$
(C) $2c + 2d$
(D) $4c + 4d$

6. What is the perimeter of the rectangle?

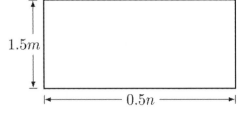

(A) $m + n$
(B) $3m + n$
(C) $2m + 2n$
(D) $1.5m + 0.5n$

7. What is the area of the rectangle?

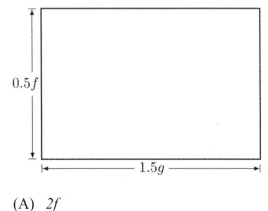

(A) $2f$
(B) $2g$
(C) $0.75fg$
(D) $2.25fg$

8. A cube has a length of a, a width of b, and a depth of c. What is the volume?

(A) b^3
(B) $3abc$
(C) $a^3b^3c^3$
(D) $a + b + c$

9. A rectangular prism sits atop a larger rectangular prism, as shown.

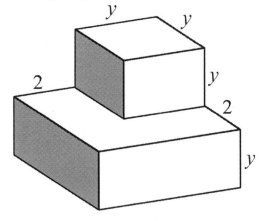

Which expression represents the total volume of both rectangular prisms?

(A) $4y^4$
(B) $y^3 + 4y$
(C) $y^3 + 4y^3$
(D) $y^3 + y(y + 2)(y + 2)$

10. The formula for the area of a circle is $A = \pi r^2$, where r is the radius. If the radius of a circle is doubled, what happens to the area of the circle?

   (A)   The area is multiplied by 2.
   (B)   The area is multiplied by 4.
   (C)   The area is multiplied by 6.28.
   (D)   The area does not change.

11. Ben draws a large red circle and a small blue circle. The red circle has an area exactly 9 times that of the blue circle. Which statement is true?

   (A)   The diameter of the red circle is 9 times as long as the diameter of the blue circle.
   (B)   The diameter of the blue circle is $\dfrac{1}{9}$ the length of the diameter of the red circle.
   (C)   The circumference of the blue circle is $\dfrac{1}{3}$ the circumference of the red circle.
   (D)   The length of radius of the blue circle is 3 times the length of the radius of the red circle.

12. The formula used to find the volume of a sphere is $V = \dfrac{4}{3}\pi r^3$, where r is the radius. The radius of Sphere A is 3 times the length of the radius of Sphere B. Which statement is true?

   (A)   The volume of Sphere A is 3 times the volume of Sphere B.
   (B)   The volume of Sphere A is 6 times the volume of Sphere B.
   (C)   The volume of Sphere A is 9 times the volume of Sphere B.
   (D)   The volume of Sphere A is 27 times the volume of Sphere B.

13. Cube Q has a side length of 2 inches. Cube R has a side length of 4 inches. Which statement is true?

   (A)   The volume of Cube R is 2 times the volume of Cube Q.
   (B)   The volume of Cube R is 4 times the volume of Cube Q.
   (C)   The volume of Cube R is 8 times the volume of Cube Q.
   (D)   The volume of Cube R is 16 times the volume of Cube Q.

14. Cube V has a side length of $3x$ inches. Cube W has a side length of x inches. Which statement is true?

   (A)   The volume of Cube V is 3 times the volume of Cube W.
   (B)   The volume of Cube V is 9 times the volume of Cube W.
   (C)   The volume of Cube V is 27 times the volume of Cube W.
   (D)   The volume of Cube V is 81 times the volume of Cube W.

15. Two circles are shown.

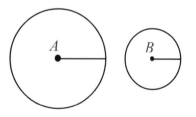

The area of circle A is 4 times the area of circle B. If the radius of circle A is 12, what is the radius of circle B?

   (A)   1.5
   (B)   3
   (C)   6
   (D)   8

Quantitative Comparison Practice

Answer Choices:

(A)   The amount in column A is greater.
(B)   The amount in column B is greater.
(C)   The two amounts are equal.
(D)   The relationship cannot be determined from the information provided.

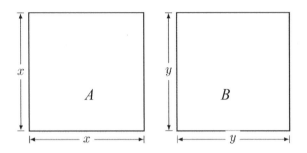

Note: Figures not drawn to scale.

	Column A	Column B
16.	The area of Square A	The area of Square B

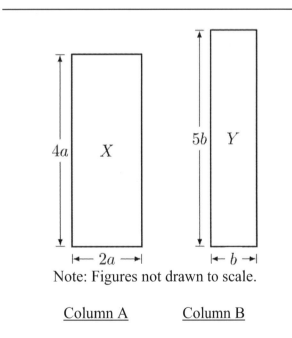

Note: Figures not drawn to scale.

	Column A	Column B
17.	The perimeter of Rectangle X	The perimeter of Rectangle Y

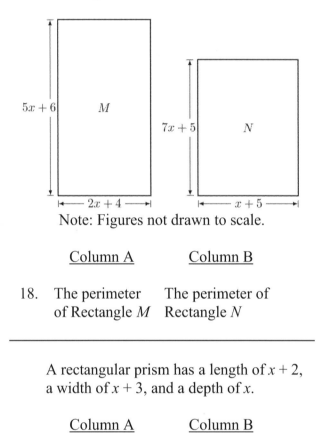

Note: Figures not drawn to scale.

	Column A	Column B
18.	The perimeter of Rectangle M	The perimeter of Rectangle N

A rectangular prism has a length of $x + 2$, a width of $x + 3$, and a depth of x.

	Column A	Column B
19.	The volume of the rectangular prism	$x^2 + 5x + 6$

A square and a triangle have equal perimeters. The square has a side length of 6.

	Column A	Column B
20.	The length of the base side of the triangle	8

Angle Sums

Example: An isosceles trapezoid has a base angle of 70°, as shown in the diagram.

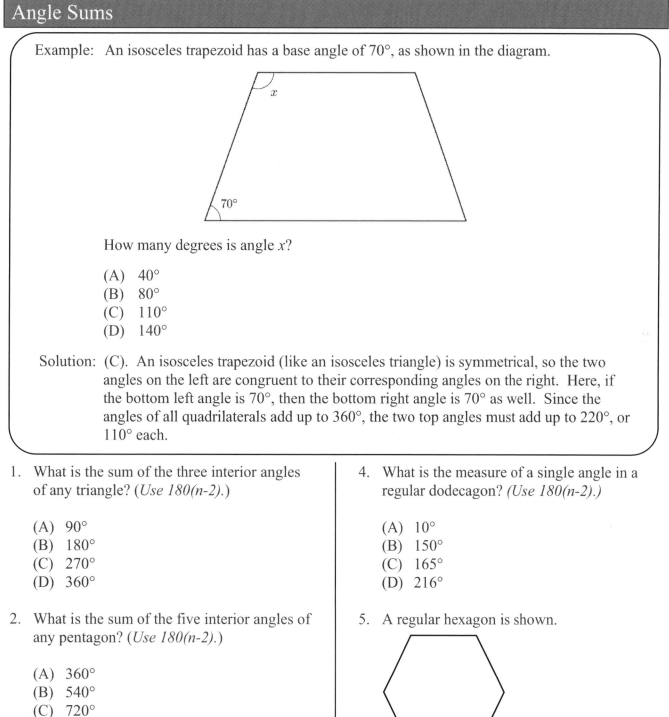

How many degrees is angle *x*?

(A) 40°
(B) 80°
(C) 110°
(D) 140°

Solution: (C). An isosceles trapezoid (like an isosceles triangle) is symmetrical, so the two angles on the left are congruent to their corresponding angles on the right. Here, if the bottom left angle is 70°, then the bottom right angle is 70° as well. Since the angles of all quadrilaterals add up to 360°, the two top angles must add up to 220°, or 110° each.

1. What is the sum of the three interior angles of any triangle? (*Use 180(n-2).*)

   (A) 90°
   (B) 180°
   (C) 270°
   (D) 360°

2. What is the sum of the five interior angles of any pentagon? (*Use 180(n-2).*)

   (A) 360°
   (B) 540°
   (C) 720°
   (D) 900°

3. What is the sum of the eight interior angles of any octagon? (*Use 180(n-2).*)

   (A) 720°
   (B) 900°
   (C) 1080°
   (D) 1260°

4. What is the measure of a single angle in a regular dodecagon? (*Use 180(n-2).*)

   (A) 10°
   (B) 150°
   (C) 165°
   (D) 216°

5. A regular hexagon is shown.

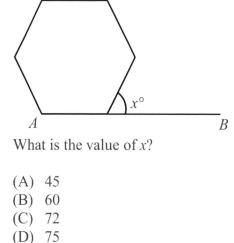

   What is the value of *x*?

   (A) 45
   (B) 60
   (C) 72
   (D) 75

The Tutorverse
www.thetutorverse.com

6. The measures of two angles of a triangle are 45° and 54°. What is the measure of the third angle?

    (A) 81°
    (B) 91°
    (C) 99°
    (D) 261°

7. A right triangle is shown.

    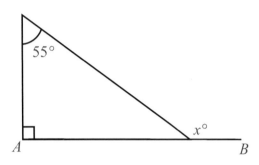

    What is the value of *x*?

    (A) 125
    (B) 135
    (C) 145
    (D) 155

8. The two base angles of an isosceles trapezoid are each 65°. What is the measure of each of the two top angles?

    (A) 25°
    (B) 50°
    (C) 90°
    (D) 115°

9. In parallelogram *ABCD* (not shown), angle *A* has a measure of 32°. What is the measure of its adjacent angle, angle *B*?

    (A) 32°
    (B) 58°
    (C) 90°
    (D) 148°

10. The measures of four of the angles of a pentagon are shown in the diagram.

    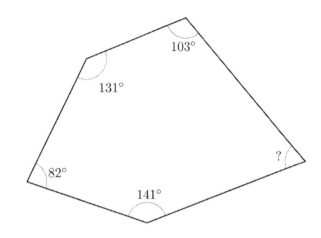

    What is the measure of the fifth angle?

    (A) 67°
    (B) 82°
    (C) 83°
    (D) 173°

11. The measures of seven of the angles of an octagon are shown in the diagram.

    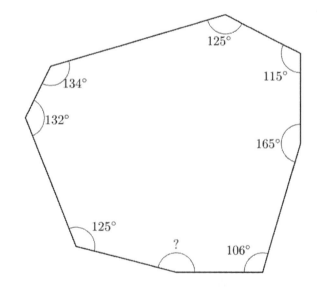

    What is the measure of the eighth angle?

    (A) 89°
    (B) 139°
    (C) 165°
    (D) 178°

Polygons on a Coordinate Grid

Example: The grid shows two vertices of a right triangle.

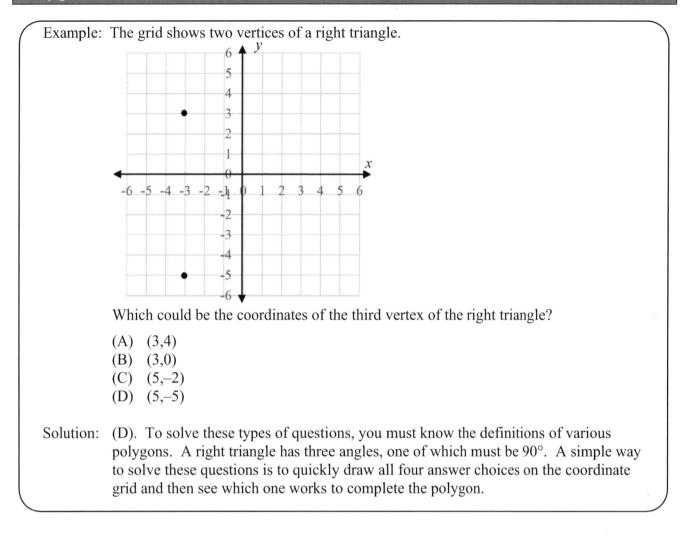

Which could be the coordinates of the third vertex of the right triangle?

(A) (3,4)
(B) (3,0)
(C) (5,–2)
(D) (5,–5)

Solution: (D). To solve these types of questions, you must know the definitions of various polygons. A right triangle has three angles, one of which must be 90°. A simple way to solve these questions is to quickly draw all four answer choices on the coordinate grid and then see which one works to complete the polygon.

1. Three vertices of a rectangle are (–5,6), (–2,6) and (–2,–2). Which could be the coordinates of the fourth vertex of the rectangle?

(A) (1,6)
(B) (–2,3)
(C) (–6,0)
(D) (–5,–2)

2. Three vertices of a square are (1,3), (6,3) and (1,–2). Which could be the coordinates of the fourth vertex of the square?

(A) (6,–2)
(B) (3,–2)
(C) (6,1)
(D) (–2,3)

3. The grid shows three vertices of a rhombus.

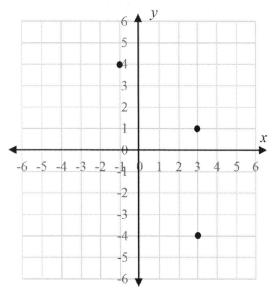

Which could be the coordinates of the fourth vertex of the rhombus?

(A) (0,–3)
(B) (–1,–1)
(C) (–2,–2)
(D) (0,0)

4. The grid shows two vertices of a right triangle.

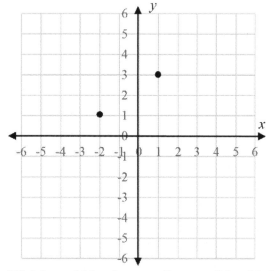

Which could be the coordinates of the third vertex of the right triangle?

(A) (4,–1)
(B) (2,–5)
(C) (–2,4)
(D) (1,–4)

5. The grid shows three vertices of an isosceles trapezoid.

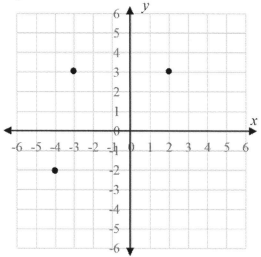

Which could be the coordinates of the fourth vertex of the regular trapezoid?

(A) (3, –2)
(B) (4, –3)
(C) (1, –1)
(D) (–5,0)

6. The grid shows two vertices of an obtuse triangle.

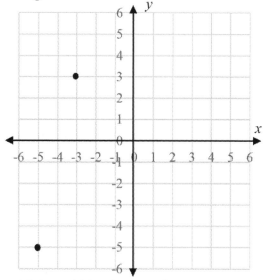

Which could be the coordinates of the third vertex of the obtuse triangle?

(A) (5,1)
(B) (3,–1)
(C) (0,0)
(D) (–4,3)

The Tutorverse
www.thetutorverse.com

Distance on a Coordinate Grid

Example: In right triangle *ABC*, right angle *B* is at (10,10) and hypotenuse $\overline{AC}$ has endpoints (2,10) and (10,4). What is the length of hypotenuse $\overline{AC}$?

(A) 6
(B) 8
(C) 10
(D) 14

Solution: (C). To find the length of a diagonal line on a coordinate grid, always think of it as the hypotenuse of a right triangle and use the Pythagorean Theorem. It can also help to draw a rough sketch of the figure. Here, the right triangle has base lengths of 6 and 8. Using $a^2 + b^2 = c^2$, the hypotenuse is proven to be 10.

1. What is the length of the line connecting coordinate points (2,3) and (6,3), in coordinate units?

   (A) 1
   (B) 3
   (C) 4
   (D) 6

2. How far apart are the coordinate points (4,5) and (4,–2)?

   (A) 1 coordinate unit
   (B) 3 coordinate units
   (C) 6 coordinate units
   (D) 7 coordinate units

3. How many coordinate units apart are the coordinate points (3,3) and (7,6)?

   (A) 3
   (B) 4
   (C) 5
   (D) 6

4. What is the distance, in coordinate units, between coordinate points (–4,3) and (4,–3)?

   (A) 6
   (B) 8
   (C) 10
   (D) 14

5. Line segment $\overline{AB}$ has endpoints at (–5,3) and (4,–9). How long is line segment $\overline{AB}$?

   (A) 15 coordinate units
   (B) 18 coordinate units
   (C) 21 coordinate units
   (D) 24 coordinate units

6. Right triangle *XYZ* has vertices at *X*(–1,–1), *Y*(–7,–1), and *Z*(–1,–9). What is the length of hypotenuse $\overline{YZ}$, in coordinate units?

   (A) 6
   (B) 8
   (C) 10
   (D) 12

7. Circle *O* lies on a coordinate grid. Coordinate points (2,–3) and (–10,13) are the endpoints of the diameter of Circle *O*. What is the length of the diameter of Circle *O*?

   (A) 14 coordinate units
   (B) 20 coordinate units
   (C) 24 coordinate units
   (D) 28 coordinate units

The Tutorverse
www.thetutorverse.com

8. The hypotenuse of right triangle *GHI* has a length of 20 coordinate units and a right angle at *H*(5,18). If *G*(5,6) is another vertex, which could be the coordinates of vertex *I*?

   (A) (21,18)
   (B) (18,–11)
   (C) (5, –11)
   (D) (18,21)

9. Point *C* (not shown) is the midpoint of $\overline{AB}$ and has coordinates (*m*,*n*).

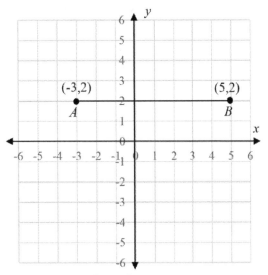

   What is the value of *m*?

   (A) –2
   (B) 1
   (C) 2
   (D) 4

10. Points A, B, C, and D are shown on a coordinate grid.

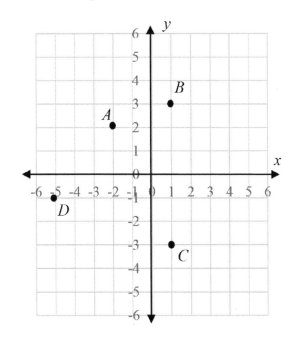

    For which point does the (*x*,*y*) coordinate pair satisfy the equation $|x| - |y| = 4$?

    (A) *A*
    (B) *B*
    (C) *C*
    (D) *D*

11. What is the distance, in coordinate units, between coordinate points (–5, 3) and (7, –2)?

    (A) 5
    (B) 12
    (C) 13
    (D) 17

Nets

Example: A cube is shown.

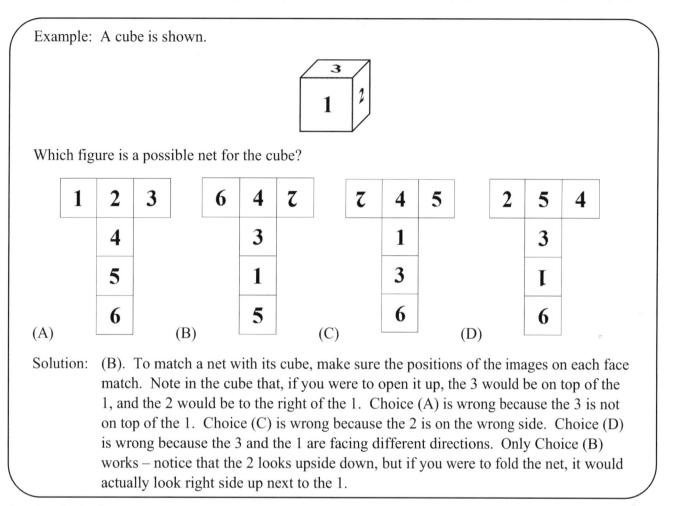

Which figure is a possible net for the cube?

Solution: (B). To match a net with its cube, make sure the positions of the images on each face match. Note in the cube that, if you were to open it up, the 3 would be on top of the 1, and the 2 would be to the right of the 1. Choice (A) is wrong because the 3 is not on top of the 1. Choice (C) is wrong because the 2 is on the wrong side. Choice (D) is wrong because the 3 and the 1 are facing different directions. Only Choice (B) works – notice that the 2 looks upside down, but if you were to fold the net, it would actually look right side up next to the 1.

1. A cube is shown.

Which figure is a possible net for the cube?

(A)   (B)   (C)   (D)

2. A cube is shown.

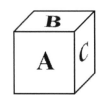

Which figure is a possible net for the cube?

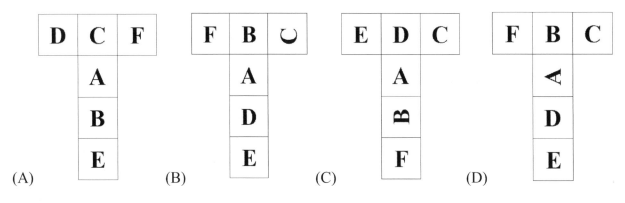

(A)   (B)   (C)   (D)

3. A cube is shown.

Which figure is a possible net for the cube?

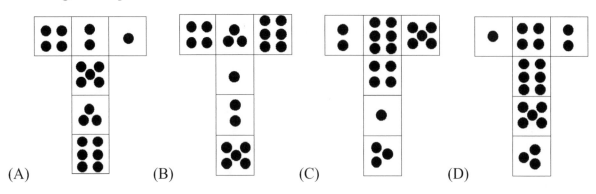

(A)   (B)   (C)   (D)

4. A cube is shown.

Which figure is a possible net for the cube?

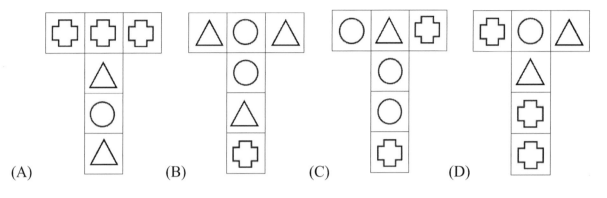

(A) (B) (C) (D)

---

5. A net is shown.

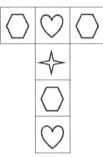

Which of the following is a possible cube for the net shown?

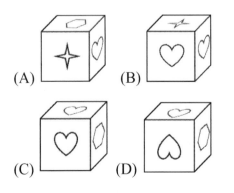

(A) (B)

(C) (D)

6. A net is shown.

Which of the following is a possible cube for the net shown?

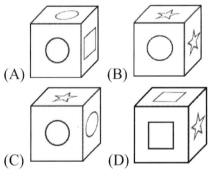

(A) (B)

(C) (D)

7. A net is shown.

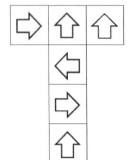

Which of the following is a possible cube for the net shown?

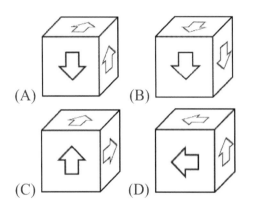

(A)　　　　(B)

(C)　　　　(D)

8. The pattern shown below can be folded into a polyhedron.

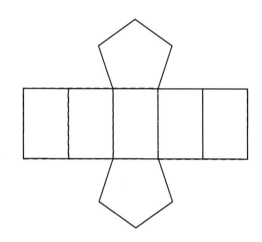

Which of the following would result from folding the above pattern?

(A)　　　　　　　(B)

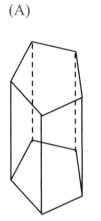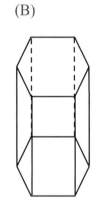

(C)　　　　　　　(D)

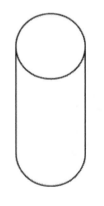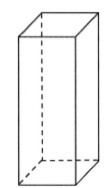

Trigonometry

Example: Triangle *ABC* is shown. The length of $\overline{AB}$ is 6 in. The measure of angle *C* is 35°.

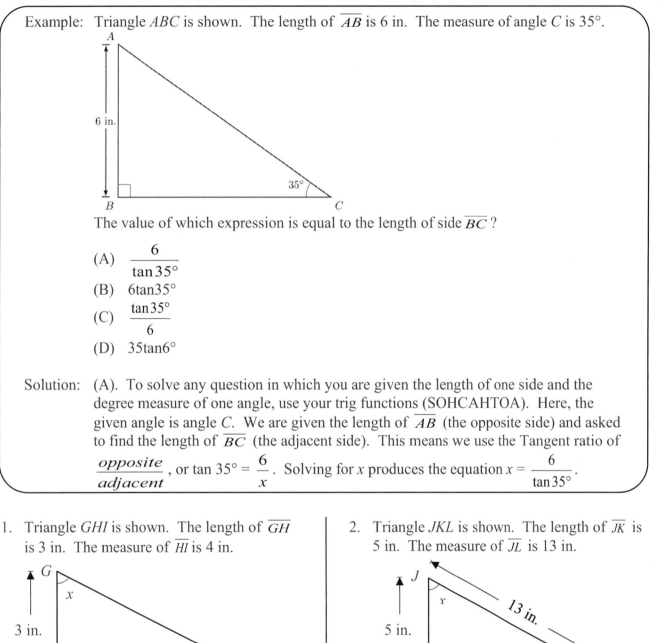

The value of which expression is equal to the length of side $\overline{BC}$?

(A) $\dfrac{6}{\tan 35°}$

(B) $6\tan 35°$

(C) $\dfrac{\tan 35°}{6}$

(D) $35\tan 6°$

Solution: (A). To solve any question in which you are given the length of one side and the degree measure of one angle, use your trig functions (SOHCAHTOA). Here, the given angle is angle *C*. We are given the length of $\overline{AB}$ (the opposite side) and asked to find the length of $\overline{BC}$ (the adjacent side). This means we use the Tangent ratio of $\dfrac{opposite}{adjacent}$, or $\tan 35° = \dfrac{6}{x}$. Solving for *x* produces the equation $x = \dfrac{6}{\tan 35°}$.

1. Triangle *GHI* is shown. The length of $\overline{GH}$ is 3 in. The measure of $\overline{HI}$ is 4 in.

The value of which expression is equal to $\dfrac{4}{3}$?

(A) $\cos x$
(B) $\csc x$
(C) $\sin x$
(D) $\tan x$

2. Triangle *JKL* is shown. The length of $\overline{JK}$ is 5 in. The measure of $\overline{JL}$ is 13 in.

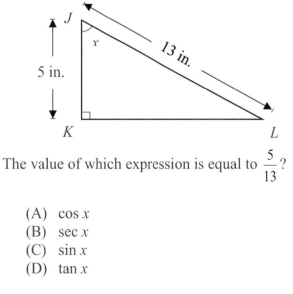

The value of which expression is equal to $\dfrac{5}{13}$?

(A) $\cos x$
(B) $\sec x$
(C) $\sin x$
(D) $\tan x$

The Tutorverse
www.thetutorverse.com

3. Triangle *MNO* is shown. The length of $\overline{MO}$ is 25 in. The measure of $\overline{NO}$ is 24 in.

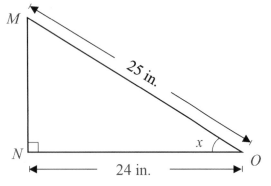

The value of which expression is equal to $\dfrac{24}{25}$?

  (A) cos *x*
  (B) cot *x*
  (C) sin *x*
  (D) tan *x*

4. Triangle *PQR* is shown. The length of $\overline{PR}$ is 15 in. The measure of $\overline{PQ}$ is 9 in.

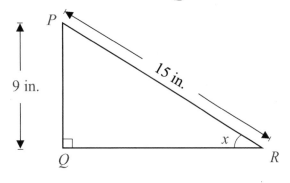

The value of which expression is equal to $\dfrac{9}{15}$?

  (A) cos *x*
  (B) csc *x*
  (C) sin *x*
  (D) tan *x*

5. Triangle *DEF* is shown. The length of $\overline{DE}$ is 4 in. The measure of angle *D* is 64°.

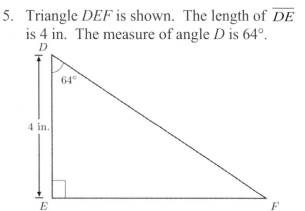

The value of which expression is equal to the length of side $\overline{DF}$?

  (A) $\dfrac{\sin 64°}{4}$

  (B) $\dfrac{4}{\sin 64°}$

  (C) $\dfrac{\cos 64°}{4}$

  (D) $\dfrac{4}{\cos 64°}$

6. Triangle *GHI* is shown. The length of $\overline{GH}$ is 2 in. The measure of angle *I* is 34°.

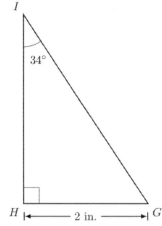

The value of which expression is equal to the length of side $\overline{HI}$?

  (A) 2tan34°

  (B) $\dfrac{2}{\tan 34°}$

  (C) $\dfrac{\tan 34°}{2}$

  (D) 34 tan 2°

7. Triangle *JKL* is shown. The length of $\overline{JL}$ is 4 in. The measure of angle *J* is 22°.

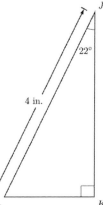

The value of which expression is equal to the length of side $\overline{KL}$?

(A) 4sin22°

(B) $\dfrac{4}{\sin 22°}$

(C) $\dfrac{\cos 22°}{4}$

(D) 4cos22°

8. Triangle *JNO* is shown. The length of $\overline{NO}$ is 11 in. The measure of angle *O* is 42°.

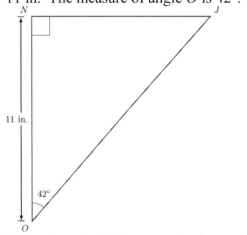

The value of which expression is equal to the length of side $\overline{NJ}$?

(A) 11cos42°

(B) $\dfrac{\cos 42°}{11}$

(C) 11tan42°

(D) $\dfrac{\tan 42°}{11}$

9. Triangle *PQR* is shown. The length of $\overline{QR}$ is 9 in. The measure of angle *P* is 46°.

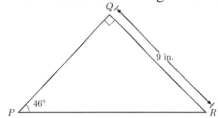
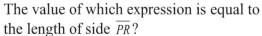

The value of which expression is equal to the length of side $\overline{PR}$?

(A) $\dfrac{\sin 46°}{9}$

(B) $\dfrac{9}{\sin 46°}$

(C) $\dfrac{\tan 46°}{9}$

(D) $\dfrac{9}{\tan 46°}$

10. Triangle *STU* is shown. The length of $\overline{TU}$ is 8 in. The measure of angle *U* is 10°.

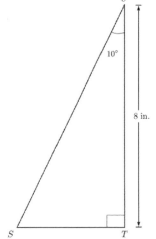

The value of which expression is equal to the length of side $\overline{SU}$?

(A) 8cos10°

(B) $\dfrac{8}{\cos 10°}$

(C) 8tan10°

(D) $\dfrac{8}{\tan 10°}$

Measurements

Appropriate Units

Example: Which is the most reasonable unit to use to measure the height of an adult human?

(A) centimeters
(B) grams
(C) kilometers
(D) milligrams

Solution: (A). Grams and milligrams both measure weight, not height/length. Kilometers measure length, but they are far too large to use to measure the length/height of a person (1 kilometer is a little more than half a mile). When using the metric system to measure the height of people, we typically use centimeters (a 6-foot man is approximately 182 centimeters).

1. Which is the most reasonable unit to use when measuring the volume of water in a bathtub?

   (A) centimeters
   (B) grams
   (C) kilograms
   (D) liters

2. Which is the most reasonable unit to use when measuring the length of an ant?

   (A) feet
   (B) milligrams
   (C) milliliters
   (D) millimeters

3. Which is the most reasonable unit to use when measuring the weight of a car?

   (A) cubic feet
   (B) grams
   (C) square feet
   (D) tons

4. Which is the most reasonable unit to use when measuring the height of a skyscraper?

   (A) kiloliters
   (B) meters
   (C) square feet
   (D) tons

5. Which is the most reasonable unit to use when measuring the distance between two cities?

   (A) centimeters
   (B) feet
   (C) kilometers
   (D) tons

6. Which is the most reasonable unit to use when measuring the capacity of an eyedropper?

   (A) centimeters
   (B) gallons
   (C) milliliters
   (D) pounds

7. Which is the most reasonable unit to use when measuring the length of a city block?

   (A) acres
   (B) grams
   (C) tons
   (D) yards

Area & Perimeter

Example: A sheet of gray paper that is 11 inches long and 8 inches wide has a hole cut out of the center in the shape of a square with side length of 4 inches, as shown in the accompanying diagram.

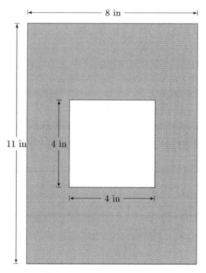

What is the area of the remaining paper?

(A) 28 square inches
(B) 66 square inches
(C) 72 square inches
(D) 104 square inches

Solution: (C). To solve most "shaded area" questions, subtract the area of the inner shape from the area of the outer shape. Here, the area of the sheet of paper is 88 square inches and the area of the hole is 16 square inches. The remaining paper is 88 − 16 = 72.

1. A square has an area of 36 square centimeters. What is its perimeter, in centimeters?

(A) 18
(B) 24
(C) 36
(D) 81

2. A square has a perimeter of 36 centimeters. What is its area, in square centimeters?

(A) 18
(B) 24
(C) 36
(D) 81

3. A large square has had a smaller square cut from its top left corner, as shown.

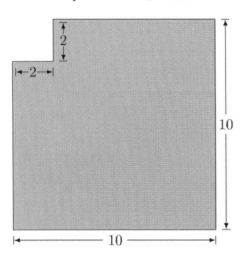

Which expression represents the area of the shaded region?

(A) 8×8
(B) $10 \times 10 - 8$
(C) $10^2 + 2^2$
(D) $10^2 - 2^2$

4. A large square has had a smaller square cut from its top left corner, as shown.

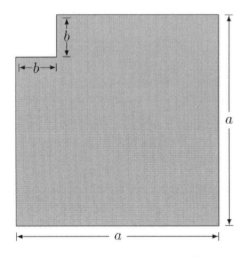

Which expression represents the area of the shaded region?

(A) $(a - b)^2$
(B) $a^2 - b$
(C) $a^2 - b^2$
(D) $a^2 + b^2$

5. A circle lies inside a square, as shown.

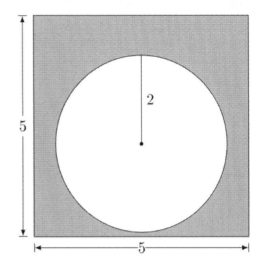

Which expression represents the area of the shaded region?

(A) $20 - 2\pi$
(B) $20 - 4\pi$
(C) $25 - 2\pi$
(D) $25 - 4\pi$

6. A rectangle has had its corners rounded, as shown.

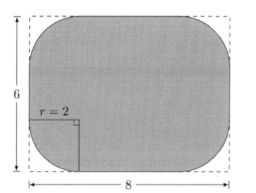

Which expression represents the area of the shaded region? *(Note: draw lines to split the figure into more familiar shapes, like rectangles and circle sections.)*

(A) $2\pi + 24$
(B) $2\pi + 32$
(C) $4\pi + 24$
(D) $4\pi + 32$

7. A circle is inscribed in a square, as shown.

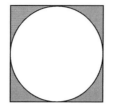

If the side length of the square is 10 inches, what is the area of the shaded region, in square inches?

(A) $40 - 10\pi$
(B) $40 - 25\pi$
(C) $100 - 10\pi$
(D) $100 - 25\pi$

8. A trapezoid is shown.

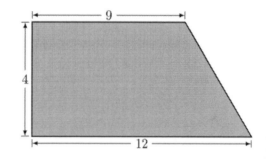

What is the area of the figure?

(A) 29 units
(B) 36 units
(C) 42 units
(D) 48 units

9. The figure shows a square with a square portion missing.

If the large gray square has a side length of 6 inches, what is the area of the shaded region?

(A) 3 square inches
(B) 9 square inches
(C) 18 square inches
(D) 24 square inches

10. Each square in the grid shown has an area of 16 in^2.

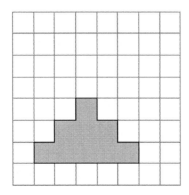

What is the perimeter of the shaded region, in inches?

(A) 16
(B) 48
(C) 64
(D) 256

11. The shaded figure has a total area of 99 ft^2.

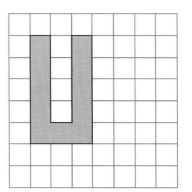

What is the length of each grid square?

(A) 3 ft
(B) 5 ft
(C) 7 ft
(D) 9 ft

12. Each square in the grid shown has a length of $\frac{1}{2}$ in.

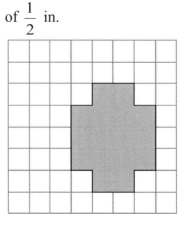

What is the area of the shaded region?

(A) 4 in^2
(B) 8 in^2
(C) 9.5 in^2
(D) 16 in^2

Quantitative Comparison Practice

Answer Choices:

(A) The amount in column A is greater.
(B) The amount in column B is greater.
(C) The two amounts are equal.
(D) The relationship cannot be determined from the information provided.

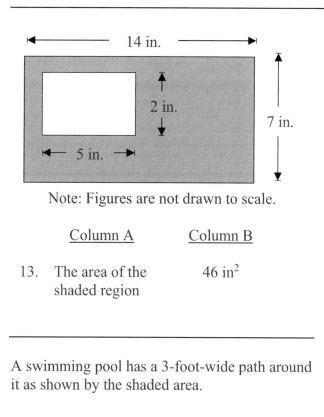

Note: Figures are not drawn to scale.

Column A	Column B
13. The area of the shaded region	46 in²

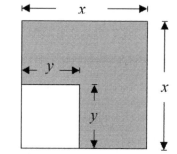

Note: Figures are not drawn to scale.

Column A	Column B
15. The area of the shaded region	$(x - y)^2$

A swimming pool has a 3-foot-wide path around it as shown by the shaded area.

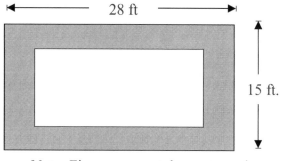

Note: Figures are not drawn to scale.

Column A	Column B
14. The area of the pool	300

A garden is 16 feet long and 12 feet wide, and has a 4-foot-wide concrete path around it as shown by the shaded area.

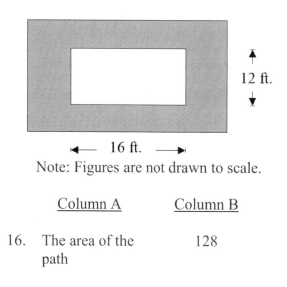

Note: Figures are not drawn to scale.

Column A	Column B
16. The area of the path	128

The Tutorverse
www.thetutorverse.com

Speed

Example: Zoe and Yanni were both driving their cars from Appleville to Brownville. Yanni drove at an average speed of 40 miles per hour and reached Brownville in three hours. Which one piece of additional information could be used to determine how long it took Zoe to reach Brownville?

(A) Appleville is exactly 80 miles from Brownville.
(B) Zoe caught up to Yanni while he was stopped to get gas exactly 40 miles from Appleville.
(C) Zoe caught up with Yanni at the exact moment they both reached Brownville.
(D) Zoe's average speed was 20 miles per hour faster than Yanni's.

Solution: (D). For a problem involving missing information, try each answer choice and see if you can then solve the problem. Here, we know that if Yanni made the trip in three hours going 40 miles per hour, then the two towns must be 120 miles apart. If we know that Zoe was going 60 miles per hour, then it must have taken her exactly 2 hours to reach Brownville.

1. Train A traveled 40 miles in 2 hours and Train B traveled twice as far in half the time. What was Train B's average speed, in miles per hour?

(A) 20
(B) 40
(C) 80
(D) 160

2. Alice is jogging at a constant speed of 6 miles per hour. Bob is jogging at a constant speed of 5 miles per hour. How much longer will it take Bob to jog 15 miles?

(A) 15 minutes
(B) 30 minutes
(C) 45 minutes
(D) 60 minutes

3. Mike is roller-skating at a constant speed of 8 kilometers per hour. Nancy is skating at a constant speed of 12 kilometers per hour. How much longer will it take Mike to skate 36 kilometers?

(A) 45 minutes
(B) 1 hour
(C) 90 minutes
(D) 9 hours

4. Owen is swimming at a constant speed of 50 meters per minute. Penny is swimming at a constant speed of 40 meters per minute. How much longer will it take Penny to swim 200 meters?

(A) 1 minute
(B) 4 minutes
(C) 5 minutes
(D) 20 minutes

5. Caitlin is driving a car at a constant speed of 50 kilometers per hour. David is driving another car at a constant speed of 70 kilometers per hour. How much farther will David drive in 6 hours?

(A) 20 kilometers
(B) 120 kilometers
(C) 300 kilometers
(D) 420 kilometers

6. Elon and Frances start riding their bikes on the same path at the same moment. Elon rides his bike at a constant speed of 10 miles per hour. Frances rides her bike a constant speed of 12 miles per hour. Frances stops riding after two and a half hours. How long will she have to wait for Elon to catch up to her?

(A) 2 minutes
(B) 5 minutes
(C) 30 minutes
(D) 60 minutes

7. Katherine started rollerblading down a path at a constant rate of 2 miles per hour. One hour later, Leon started rollerblading down the same path at a constant rate. If Leon skates 4 miles per hour faster than Katherine, how long does it take Leon to catch up to Katherine?

(A) 2.0 hours
(B) 1.5 hours
(C) 1.0 hour
(D) 0.5 hour

8. George and Helen were both canoeing down the same river, each at a constant speed, and George at a faster speed than Helen. George canoed 3 miles in 30 minutes. It took Helen 40 minutes to canoe the same distance. How fast was Helen going?

(A) 2 miles per hour
(B) 4 miles per hour
(C) 4.5 miles per hour
(D) 6 miles per hour

9. Quentin and Randy had an ice skating race across a huge frozen lake. Quentin skated at a constant speed of 10 miles per hour. Randy finished the race in 10 minutes. Which additional piece of information would be needed to determine who won?

(A) The winner won by 2 minutes.
(B) The distance they raced was 1 mile.
(C) When the winner finished, the loser was halfway done.
(D) The area of the lake was 200 sq. feet.

10. Ursula and Victor were riding go-carts down a hill, each at a constant speed, and Ursula at a faster speed than Victor. When Ursula started riding, Victor had already traveled 1 mile. Which piece of additional information could be used to determine how long Ursula had been riding when she caught up with Victor?

(A) Ursula was riding at a speed of 12 miles per hour.
(B) Victor was riding at a speed of 9 miles per hour.
(C) The sum of Ursula and Victor's speeds was 5 miles per hour.
(D) Ursula was riding 2 miles per hour faster than Victor.

11. Sue and Thomas were skiing down a mountain, each at a constant speed. Sue skied faster than Thomas, but when Sue started skiing, Thomas had already skied 1 mile. Which additional piece of information would be needed to determine how long it took Sue to catch up to Thomas?

(A) Sue reached the bottom in 12 minutes.
(B) Thomas reached the bottom 2 minutes after Sue.
(C) Sue's speed was 4 miles per hour faster than Thomas' speed.
(D) The ski path was 4 miles long.

Converting Units

Example: There are 5,280 feet in 1 mile. A car is driving at a speed of 30 miles per hour. Which expression has a value equal to the car's speed, in feet per minute?

(A) $\dfrac{30 \times 5{,}280}{60}$

(B) $\dfrac{60 \times 5{,}280}{30}$

(C) $\dfrac{30 \times 60}{5{,}280}$

(D) $\dfrac{60}{30 \times 5{,}280}$

Solution: (A). To convert units, start by writing the given rate as a ratio. Here, it would be $\dfrac{30 \text{ miles}}{1 \text{ hour}}$. Then, multiply by equivalent ratios that will cancel out unwanted units and leave you with your desired units. Here, our desired unit ratio is feet per minute, or $\dfrac{\text{feet}}{\text{minute}}$. That means multiplying $\dfrac{30 \text{ miles}}{1 \text{ hour}} \times \dfrac{5{,}280 \text{ feet}}{1 \text{ mile}} \times \dfrac{1 \text{ hour}}{60 \text{ minutes}}$. The miles cancel each other out and the hours cancel each other out, leaving you with feet per minute.

1. There are 3 feet in one yard. A man is walking at a speed of 90 yards per minute. Which expression has a value equal to the man's speed, in feet per second?

(A) $\dfrac{90}{60 \times 3}$

(B) $\dfrac{90 \times 3}{60}$

(C) $\dfrac{60 \times 3}{90}$

(D) $\dfrac{60}{90 \times 3}$

2. There are 0.305 meters in one foot. A woman is jogging at a rate of 2 meters per second. Which expression has a value equal to the woman's speed, in feet per minute?

(A) $\dfrac{2 \times 60}{0.305}$

(B) $\dfrac{2}{0.305 \times 60}$

(C) $\dfrac{0.305 \times 60}{2}$

(D) $\dfrac{0.305}{2 \times 60}$

3. There are 1,760 yards in a mile. A cheetah can run at a speed of up to 70 miles per hour. Which expression has a value equal to a cheetah's maximum speed, in yards per minute?

(A) $\dfrac{70 \times 1,760}{60}$

(B) $\dfrac{60 \times 1,760}{70}$

(C) $\dfrac{70}{60 \times 1,760}$

(D) $\dfrac{60}{70 \times 1,760}$

4. There are 5,280 feet in 1 mile. If Brenda runs at a rate of 6 miles per hour, the value of which numerical expression is her speed in feet per second?

(A) $\dfrac{6 \times 60}{5280}$

(B) $\dfrac{6 \times 5,280}{60}$

(C) $\dfrac{6 \times 60 \times 60}{5280}$

(D) $\dfrac{6 \times 5,280}{60 \times 60}$

5. There are 12 inches in a foot. A snail is crawling at a speed of 2 inches per minute. What is the snail's speed, in feet per hour?

(A) 1
(B) 2.5
(C) 4
(D) 10

6. There are 12 inches in one foot. There are 3 feet in one yard. A cyclist is biking at a rate of 5 yards per second. Which expression has a value equal to the cyclist's speed, in inches per hour?

(A) $5 \times 3 \times 12 \times 60 \times 60$

(B) $\dfrac{5 \times 3 \times 12}{60 \times 60}$

(C) $\dfrac{5 \times 60 \times 60}{3 \times 12}$

(D) $\dfrac{60 \times 60}{5 \times 3 \times 12}$

7. There are 5,280 feet in a mile. There are 12 inches a foot. If an airplane was flying at a rate of 614 miles per hour, the value of which numerical expression is its speed in inches per second?

(A) $\dfrac{12 \times 60 \times 60}{614 \times 5,280}$

(B) $\dfrac{614 \times 60 \times 60}{5,280 \times 12}$

(C) $\dfrac{5,280 \times 60 \times 60}{614 \times 12}$

(D) $\dfrac{614 \times 12 \times 5,280}{60 \times 60}$

Formulas

Example: The formula for the volume of a cone is $V = \dfrac{1}{3} Bh$, where B is the area of the base and h is the length of the height. A cone has a volume of 30π in^3, and a height of 10 in. What is the area of the base, B?

(A) 3π
(B) 9π
(C) 20π
(D) 60π

Solution: (B). Formula questions on this test have nothing to do with being familiar with obscure formulas. Instead, these questions are about solving for a variable algebraically. Take the formula $V = \dfrac{1}{3} Bh$ and plug in 30π for V and 10 for h, then solve for B.

1. The formula for the area of a triangle is $A = \dfrac{1}{2} bh$, where b is the base length and h is the length of the height. A triangle has an area of 100 in^2 and a height of 2 in. What is its base length?

(A) 25 in.
(B) 50 in.
(C) 100 in.
(D) 200 in.

2. The formula used to find the area of a circle is $A = \pi r^2$, where r is the radius. If the diameter of a circle is 18 cm, what is its area, in cm^2?

(A) 18π
(B) 36π
(C) 81π
(D) 324π

3. The formula for the area of a trapezoid is $A = \dfrac{1}{2} (b_1 + b_2)h$, where h is the length of the altitude, and b_1 and b_2 are the lengths of the bases. If the bases of a trapezoid are 10 inches and 12 inches, and its height is 4 inches, what is its area, in inches^2?

(A) 22
(B) 44
(C) 80
(D) 88

4. The formula for the volume of a rectangular pyramid is $V = \dfrac{lwh}{3}$, where l is the base length, w is the base width, and h is the height. If the area of the base of a pyramid is 24 square feet, and the height is 6 feet, what is the volume of the pyramid?

(A) 24 feet^3
(B) 48 feet^3
(C) 72 feet^3
(D) 144 feet^3

5. The formula used to find the surface area of a rectangular prism is $SA = 2lw + 2lh + 2hw$, where l is length, w is width, and h is height. If a rectangular prism has a length of 6 meters, a width of 8 meters, and a height of 10 meters, what is its surface area, in meters^2?

(A) 188
(B) 240
(C) 376
(D) 480

6. The formula for the surface area of a cylinder is $SA = 2B + Ch$, where B is the area of each base, C is the circumference, and h is the vertical height. A cylinder has a surface area of 24π meters^2, a base area of 4π meters^2, and a circumference of 4π meters. What is the vertical height?

(A) 2 in.
(B) 4 in.
(C) 6 in.
(D) 12 in.

7. The formula for converting degrees in Celsius to Fahrenheit is $F = \dfrac{9}{5}C + 32$. If the temperature is 25 degrees Celsius, what is the temperature, in degrees Fahrenheit?

(A) –13
(B) –7
(C) 45
(D) 77

8. The formula used to find the surface area of a cone is $SA = B + \dfrac{1}{2}Cl$, where B is the area of the base, C is the circumference, and l is the slant height. A cone has a surface area of 70π in^2, a base area of 10π in^2, and a circumference of 12π in. What is the slant height?

(A) 7 in.
(B) 10 in.
(C) 14 in.
(D) 7π in.

9. The formula for converting degrees in Fahrenheit to Celsius is $C = \dfrac{5}{9}(F - 32)$. If the temperature is 100 degrees Celsius, what is the temperature in Fahrenheit?

(A) 37°
(B) 68°
(C) 180°
(D) 212°

10. The formula for the volume of a cone is $V = \dfrac{1}{3}\pi r^2 h$, where r is the radius of the base and h is the height. If a cone has a volume of 16π cm^3 and a height of 3 cm, what is the radius, in cm?

(A) 2
(B) 3
(C) 4
(D) 5

11. The formula used to find the area of a circle is $A = \pi r^2$, where r is the radius and A is the area. If the area of a circle is 36π cm^2, what is its diameter, in cm?

(A) 3
(B) 6
(C) 12
(D) 18

Data & Probability

Probability

> **Example:** Tom is playing a game in which he must roll a six-sided die and spin a spinner with four equal spaces labelled A, B, C, and D. What is the probability that he will roll a prime number on the die and spin a C?
>
> (A) $\dfrac{1}{24}$
>
> (B) $\dfrac{1}{9}$
>
> (C) $\dfrac{1}{8}$
>
> (D) $\dfrac{1}{6}$
>
> **Solution:** (C). To find the probability of two or more events happening, find each probability separately, then multiply the fractions. Here, the probability of rolling a prime number on a die (2, 3, or 5) is 1 out of 2. The probability of spinning a C is 1 out of 4. The probability of both events happening is 1 out of 8.

1. A bowl contains 3 red marbles, 4 white marbles, and 5 blue marbles. If one marble is chosen at random, what is the probability that it will be white?

   (A) $\dfrac{1}{12}$

   (B) $\dfrac{1}{4}$

   (C) $\dfrac{1}{3}$

   (D) $\dfrac{4}{9}$

2. The probability of picking a piece of chocolate out of a bowl of candy is $\dfrac{5}{6}$.
   Which of the following could NOT be the number of pieces of candy in the bowl?

   (A) 6
   (B) 15
   (C) 30
   (D) 60

3. A coin is tossed twice. What is the probability that it will land on heads both times?

   (A) $\dfrac{1}{8}$

   (B) $\dfrac{1}{4}$

   (C) $\dfrac{1}{2}$

   (D) $\dfrac{2}{3}$

4. If every student in a class puts his or her name in a hat, the probability of picking a boy's name is $\dfrac{2}{5}$. If there are 35 students in the class, how many boys are in the class?

   (A) 10
   (B) 14
   (C) 15
   (D) 21

5. If a coin is flipped 4 times, what is the probability of its landing on heads 4 times in a row?

    (A) $\dfrac{1}{16}$

    (B) $\dfrac{1}{8}$

    (C) $\dfrac{1}{4}$

    (D) $\dfrac{1}{2}$

6. Dustin is playing a board game in which everyone takes turns rolling two six-sided dice. Dustin wins the game if he rolls a 12 on his next turn. What is the probability that he will roll a 12?

    (A) $\dfrac{1}{16}$

    (B) $\dfrac{1}{12}$

    (C) $\dfrac{1}{36}$

    (D) $\dfrac{1}{144}$

7. In a deck of 52 playing cards, there are 4 queens. If one card is chosen at random, and then returned to the deck, and a second card is chosen at random, what is the probability that both cards will be queens?

    (A) $\dfrac{2}{52}$

    (B) $\dfrac{1}{13} \times \dfrac{1}{13}$

    (C) $\dfrac{2}{52} \times \dfrac{1}{52}$

    (D) $\dfrac{4}{52} \times \dfrac{3}{52}$

8. In a deck of 52 playing cards, there are 4 aces. If one card is chosen at random, NOT returned to the deck, and then a second card is chosen at random, what is the probability that both cards will be aces?

    (A) $\dfrac{1}{13} \times \dfrac{1}{12}$

    (B) $\dfrac{1}{13} \times \dfrac{1}{13}$

    (C) $\dfrac{1}{13} \times \dfrac{1}{17}$

    (D) $\dfrac{4}{13} \times \dfrac{3}{52}$

9. A bowl has only red, green, and purple grapes. The probability of picking a red grape out of the bowl, eating it, and then picking a green grape out of the bowl is $\dfrac{1}{8}$. The probability of picking just a red grape is $\dfrac{1}{4}$. What is the probability of picking a green grape?

    (A) $\dfrac{1}{2}$

    (B) $\dfrac{1}{8}$

    (C) $\dfrac{1}{12}$

    (D) $\dfrac{1}{32}$

10. The children at a party are bobbing for apples from a bucket containing a total of 10 red and green apples. The probability of a child getting two red apples in a row, without replacement, is $\dfrac{12}{90}$. How many red apples are in the bucket?

    (A) 2
    (B) 3
    (C) 4
    (D) 6

11. A group of friends is playing a game of darts on a dartboard of various colors. The probability of throwing a dart onto the green section of the dartboard twice in a row is $\frac{9}{100}$. What is the probability of throwing a dart onto the green section of the dartboard once?

(A) $\frac{3}{50}$

(B) $\frac{3}{10}$

(C) $\frac{9}{50}$

(D) $\frac{9}{10}$

12. A six-sided die is tossed 30 times. What is the expected number of 3's?

(A) 5
(B) 6
(C) 10
(D) 15

13. A coin is flipped ten times. What is the expected number of tails?

(A) 2
(B) 3
(C) 5
(D) 8

14. A six-sided die is tossed 15 times. What is the expected number of 5's?

(A) 2.5
(B) 3
(C) 4
(D) 6

15. A coin is flipped seven times. What is the expected number of heads?

(A) 3
(B) 3.5
(C) 4
(D) 4.5

16. A coin is flipped five times. The table shows the possible outcomes and the probability of each outcome.

Number of Heads	Probability
0	$\frac{1}{32}$
1	$\frac{5}{32}$
2	$\frac{10}{32}$
3	$\frac{10}{32}$
4	$\frac{5}{32}$
5	$\frac{1}{32}$

What is the expected number of tails?

(A) 1
(B) 2.5
(C) 10
(D) 16

Quantitative Comparison Practice

Answer Choices:

(A)   The amount in column A is greater.
(B)   The amount in column B is greater.
(C)   The two amounts are equal.
(D)   The relationship cannot be determined from the information provided.

Sandra's closet has 6 orange shirts, 7 green shirts, and 8 purple shirts.

	Column A	Column B
17.	The probability of picking out an orange shirt	$\dfrac{2}{5}$

A class of students all put pieces of paper with their names on them into a hat. The probability of picking out a name that starts with the letter A is $\dfrac{2}{15}$.

The probability of picking out a name that starts with A, replacing it into the hat, and then picking out a name that starts with M is $\dfrac{1}{45}$.

	Column A	Column B
18.	The probability of picking out a name that starts with M.	$\dfrac{1}{6}$

A coin is flipped 25 times.

	Column A	Column B
19.	The expected number of tails	5

Frank has a bucket full of equally-sized red, yellow, and green apples. The probability of picking out a red apple is $\dfrac{1}{4}$. There are twice as many yellow apples as red apples.

	Column A	Column B
20.	The probability of picking out a green apple	$\dfrac{1}{8}$

Sam is on a game show. He is blindfolded and standing in front of a bowl with 10 equally sized plastic balls, each a different color. In order to win a new car, he has to pick out a ball, place it back into the bowl, and then pick out the same ball a second time.

	Column A	Column B
21.	The probability that Sam wins the car	$\dfrac{1}{100}$

A six-sided die is rolled 85 times.

	Column A	Column B
22.	The expected number of 5's	17

Probability – Conditional

Example: If Sue flips a fair coin ten times and it lands on heads all ten times in a row, what is the probability that it will land on heads the eleventh time?

(A) $\dfrac{1}{2,048}$

(B) $\dfrac{1}{22}$

(C) $\dfrac{1}{11}$

(D) $\dfrac{1}{2}$

Solution: (D). With probability questions, be careful that you understand what you are being asked to find the probability of. If the problem had asked "What is the probability that a coin will land on heads 11 times in a row?" the answer would be 1 out of 2,048. Here, the fact that the coin landed on heads 10 times is irrelevant. All the question is asking is for the probability that the coin will land on heads again, which is 1 out of 2.

1. If Jack rolls a fair six-sided number cube 100 times and he rolls a 6 every single time, what is the probability that his next roll will be a 6?

(A) $\dfrac{1}{600}$

(B) $\dfrac{1}{101}$

(C) $\dfrac{1}{100}$

(D) $\dfrac{1}{6}$

2. Tom has a standard deck of 52 playing cards, which has four of each number (four A's, four 2's, four 3's, etc.). If he draws (picks out) three 10's in a row, keeping the card every time, what is the probability that the next card he picks out will be a 10?

(A) $\dfrac{1}{208}$

(B) $\dfrac{1}{52}$

(C) $\dfrac{1}{49}$

(D) $\dfrac{1}{13}$

3. A bowl contains 5 red candies and 5 white candies. Catherine picks out a candy at random, places it back in the bowl, then picks out a second candy at random. What is the probability that the first candy was red and the second candy was white?

(A) $\dfrac{1}{25}$

(B) $\dfrac{2}{10}$

(C) $\dfrac{1}{4}$

(D) $\dfrac{5}{18}$

4. A bowl contains 5 red candies and 5 white candies. Catherine picks out a candy, then places it back into the bowl and picks out another candy. If the first candy Catherine picks out is red, what is the probability that the second candy Catherine picks out will be white?

(A) $\dfrac{1}{5}$

(B) $\dfrac{1}{4}$

(C) $\dfrac{1}{2}$

(D) $\dfrac{2}{3}$

5. A bag contains 5 red marbles, 6 yellow marbles, and 7 blue marbles. Paul picks out three marbles from the bag. What is the probability that Paul picks out 3 blue marbles in a row?

(A) $\dfrac{5}{16}$

(B) $\dfrac{7}{18}$

(C) $\dfrac{7^3}{18^3}$

(D) $\dfrac{7 \times 6 \times 5}{18 \times 17 \times 16}$

6. A bag contains 5 red marble, 6 yellow marbles, and 7 blue marbles. Paul picks out three marbles from the bag. If the first two marbles are blue, what is the probability that the third marble he picks out will also be blue?

(A) $\dfrac{5}{16}$

(B) $\dfrac{7}{18}$

(C) $\dfrac{7^3}{18^3}$

(D) $\dfrac{7 \times 6 \times 5}{18 \times 17 \times 16}$

7. A bag contains 2 green lollipops, 4 yellow lollipops and 6 purple lollipops. If Jackie picks out a green lollipop and does not place it back into the bag, what is the probability that the next lollipop she picks out will be purple?

(A) $\dfrac{1}{12}$

(B) $\dfrac{1}{11}$

(C) $\dfrac{6}{11}$

(D) $\dfrac{1}{2}$

8. A bag contains 2 green lollipops, 4 yellow lollipops and 6 purple lollipops. If Jackie picks two lollipops without replacement, what is the probability that Jackie will pick out a green lollipop and then pick out a purple lollipop?

(A) $\dfrac{1}{12}$

(B) $\dfrac{1}{11}$

(C) $\dfrac{6}{11}$

(D) $\dfrac{1}{2}$

9. Kevin rolls a six-sided number cube twice. If the first number he rolls is a 1, what is the probability that the next number he rolls is a 2?

(A) $\dfrac{1}{36}$

(B) $\dfrac{1}{12}$

(C) $\dfrac{1}{6}$

(D) $\dfrac{1}{3}$

10. A bucket contains 10 yellow pencils, 4 white pencils, 6 green pencils, and 10 black pencils. Damon picks out a pencil and does not place it back into the bucket, then picks out another pencil. What is the probability that the first pencil Damon picked out was yellow, and the second pencil he picked out was black?

(A) $\dfrac{1}{9}$

(B) $\dfrac{10}{87}$

(C) $\dfrac{1}{3}$

(D) $\dfrac{10}{29}$

Quantitative Comparison Practice

Answer Choices:

  (A) The amount in column A is greater.
  (B) The amount in column B is greater.
  (C) The two amounts are equal.
  (D) The relationship cannot be determined from the information provided.

A 6-sided number cube is rolled twice.

	Column A	Column B
11.	If the first roll results in a number less than 5, the probability of the second roll resulting in an even number	If the first roll results in a number less than 3, the probability of the second roll resulting in a prime number

A coin is flipped and a 6-sided number cube is rolled.

	Column A	Column B
12.	The probability of the coin landing on heads and the die resulting in an even number.	If the coin lands on tails, the probability of the die landing on a 4.

Averages

Example: A set of five numbers has an average of 12. If one more number is added to the set, the new average will be 16. What is that number?

(A) 4
(B) 20
(C) 24
(D) 36

Solution: (D). Remember that to find an average you take the sum of a set of numbers and divide it by the quantity of numbers in the set. If you are given the average and the quantity of numbers but don't know what the sum is, you do the opposite of divide, which is multiply. Here, 12×5 tells you that the sum of the set of numbers is 60. The new average is 16, and now has six numbers in the set, so 16×6 gives you a new sum of 96. The missing number is $96 - 60 = 36$.

1. James took four quizzes. His quiz average was 84. What was the total of all four quiz scores?

    (A) 21
    (B) 84
    (C) 168
    (D) 336

2. Over the course of three basketball games, Bonnie scored a total of 36 points. What was her point average per game?

    (A) 12
    (B) 18
    (C) 72
    (D) 108

3. Daphne played four soccer games and scored an average of 12 points per game. How many points did she score in all?

    (A) 3
    (B) 12
    (C) 24
    (D) 48

4. The average height of 6 students is x inches. In terms of x, what is the total height of all the students, in inches?

    (A) $6 + x$
    (B) $x - 6$
    (C) $\dfrac{x}{6}$
    (D) $6x$

5. Ellen will take 5 tests this semester. If she wants to end her semester with a 95 test average, what must the sum of all her tests be?

    (A) 380
    (B) 455
    (C) 475
    (D) 625

6. Susie was trying to calculate the mean of her five test scores. She forgot what she had scored on each of the first 4 tests but knew that the sum of those four scores was 374. If Susie scored a 96 on her fifth test, then what was the mean of all 5 scores?

    (A) 94
    (B) 94.75
    (C) 235
    (D) 470

7. Paul took three tests. His grades were 92, 85, and 87. He will take one more test before the end of the semester. If he wants a test average of 90, what must he score on his fourth test?

(A) 90
(B) 92
(C) 96
(D) 99

8. A set of 6 numbers has a mean of 12. What additional number must be included in this set to create a new set with a mean that is 3 more than the mean of the original set?

(A) 15
(B) 33
(C) 45
(D) 48

9. A set of 9 numbers has a mean of 20. What additional number must be included in this set to create a new set with a mean that is 4 less than the mean of the original set?

(A) −40
(B) −20
(C) 0
(D) 20
(E)

10. After three tests, Brandon had a test average of 90. After his fourth test, his average dropped to an 85. What did he score on his fourth test?

(A) 70
(B) 75
(C) 80
(D) 82

11. Daniel scored at least one point during each of 5 games. If the average number of points he scored is 10, what is the greatest possible number of points he could have scored in one game?

(A) 50
(B) 49
(C) 46
(D) 45

12. If the mean of x, $2x$, and $3x$ is 30, what is the value of x?

(A) 2
(B) 5
(C) 10
(D) 15

Quantitative Comparison Practice

Answer Choices:

(A)   The amount in column A is greater.
(B)   The amount in column B is greater.
(C)   The two amounts are equal.
(D)   The relationship cannot be determined from the information provided.

Sam took 5 tests. The mean of his tests was 90.

	Column A	Column B
13.	Sam's median test score	90

A class of 24 students read an average of 12 books each over the summer

	Column A	Column B
14.	The total number of books read by the whole class	252

Julie scored an average of 12 points over 3 soccer games

	Column A	Column B
15.	Julie's new point average over all 4 games, if she scores 15 points in her fourth game	15

After Donny's fourth test, his test average went up 5 points, to a 93.

	Column A	Column B
16.	The sum of Donny's first three test scores	274

The average of x and $5x$ is 18.

	Column A	Column B
17.	x	3

Dot, Bill, and Rosie baked a total of 159 cookies. Dot baked 95 of them.

	Column A	Column B
18.	The average number of cookies baked by Bill and Rosie	22

Interpreting Graphs

Example: The graph shows the distance Charlie was from home as a function of time one morning before school.

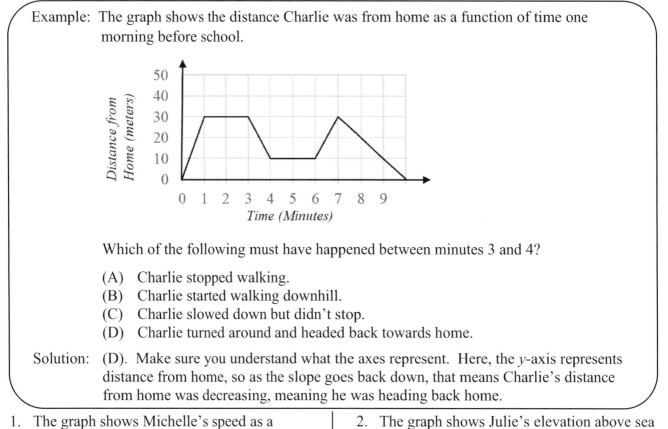

Which of the following must have happened between minutes 3 and 4?

(A)   Charlie stopped walking.
(B)   Charlie started walking downhill.
(C)   Charlie slowed down but didn't stop.
(D)   Charlie turned around and headed back towards home.

Solution: (D). Make sure you understand what the axes represent. Here, the *y*-axis represents distance from home, so as the slope goes back down, that means Charlie's distance from home was decreasing, meaning he was heading back home.

1.   The graph shows Michelle's speed as a function of time one day while driving to work.

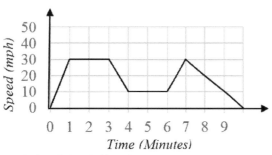

Which of the following must have happened between minutes 3 and 6?

(A)   Michelle slowed her car to a stop.
(B)   Michelle started driving downhill.
(C)   Michelle slowed down but didn't stop.
(D)   Michelle turned around and headed back towards home.

2.   The graph shows Julie's elevation above sea level while she was hiking up a mountain from a beach at sea level one weekend morning.

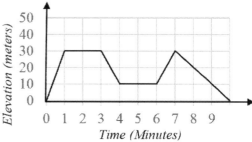

Which of the following most likely happened between minutes 3 and 7?

(A)   Julie slowed down but didn't stop hiking.
(B)   Julie slowed to a stop, and then started hiking again.
(C)   Julie hiked back down to the beach, then back up the mountain.
(D)   Julie hiked downhill, paused for two minutes, then hiked back up the same mountain.

Frequency Charts & Graphs

Example: The frequency chart shows how many movies each kid in a class of 21 students saw in a movie theater last month.

Number of Movies	Number of Kids Who Saw That Many Movies
0	1
1	4
2	8
3	5
4	3

What is the range of the data?

(A) 8
(B) 7
(C) 4
(D) 3

Solution: (C). Frequency charts and graphs condense long lists of numbers. Here, we are tracking how many movies were seen. The column on the left shows us that the only responses by the students were 0, 1, 2, 3, and 4 (no one saw more than 4 movies). The column on the right tells us how many of each data point there are. Specifically, going down the list, there is one 0, four 1's, eight 2's, five 3's, and three 4's, giving us 21 data points. We could list all 21 data points out on paper, but we don't need to. The range is simply the difference of the largest and smallest numbers in a set of data. Here, the most movies seen was 4 and the fewest was 0, so the range is $4 - 0 = 4$.

(practice begins on the next page)

1. The frequency chart shows the number of books read by each student in a class last week.

Number of Books	Number of Students Who Read That Many Books
1	10
2	9
3	7
4	4
5	1

What is the median of the data?

(A) 2
(B) 3
(C) 7
(D) 9

2. The frequency chart shows the number of birds witnessed by bird watchers over several days.

Number of Birds	Number of Days During Which That Number of Birds Was Spotted
1	6
2	6
3	1
4	6
5	6

What is the mean of the data?

(A) 3
(B) 3.7
(C) 4.4
(D) 6

3. The frequency chart shows the number of slices of pizza eaten by the staff of an office one Friday.

Number of Slices of Pizza	Number of Workers Who Ate That Many Slices
0	4
1	9
2	8
3	4
4	2

What is the mode of the data?

(A) 1
(B) 2
(C) 4
(D) 9

4. The graph shows the number of hours spent trick-or-treating by each kid in a class last Halloween. The numbers on the horizontal axis represent the number of hours spent trick-or-treating; the numbers on the vertical axis represent the number of kids who trick-or-treated for this number of hours.

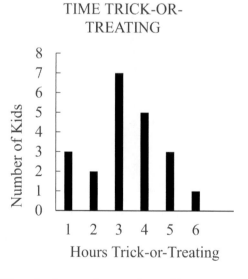

TIME TRICK-OR-TREATING

What is the mode number of hours spent trick-or-treating?

(A) 3
(B) 5
(C) 6
(D) 7

5. The graph shows the amount of money donated by certain families during a fundraiser.

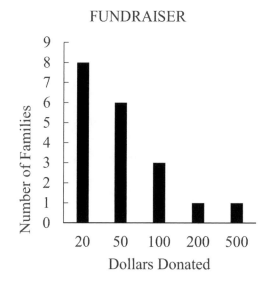

FUNDRAISER

What is the range of the number of dollars donated during the fundraiser?

(A) 8
(B) 9
(C) 480
(D) 500

6. The graph shows the number of peas Jodie pushed off her dinner plate each day her family had peas with dinner.

DISCARDED PEAS

What is the mean number of peas discarded?

(A) 2
(B) 3
(C) 4
(D) 5

7. The graph shows the number of miles Jason biked on certain days last spring.

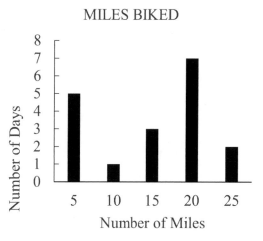

MILES BIKED

What is the median number of miles Jason biked?

(A) 12.5
(B) 15
(C) 17.5
(D) 20

8. The graph shows the number of apples picked each day by a farmer last fall, but the graph is incomplete, as one of the bars is missing.

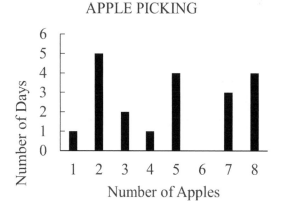

APPLE PICKING

If the farmer picked a total of 100 apples last fall, on how many days did he pick 6 apples?

(A) 0
(B) 1
(C) 2
(D) 3

Circle Graphs

Example: A class of 30 students took a survey in which each student chose his or her favorite pizza topping. 10 students chose pepperoni. A circle graph was made using the data. What was the central angle of the portion of the graph representing pepperoni?

   (A)   10°
   (B)   30°
   (C)   120°
   (D)   135°

Solution: (C). A circle has 360°. Since 10 out of 30 is equal to $\frac{1}{3}$, the portion of the circle representing pepperoni would be $\frac{1}{3}$ of the circle, or 120°.

1. Brent kept track of his monthly expenses. He found out he spent 30% of his income on rent, 20% on food, 15% on utilities, and 35% on clothes. Which of the following circle graphs represents Brent's expenses?

(A)

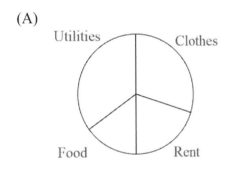

(C)

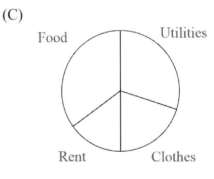

(B)

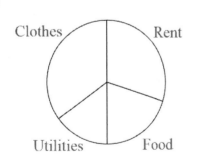

(D)

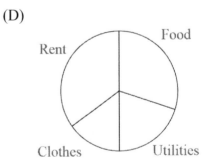

2. The circle graph shows the favorite fruit of 240 shoppers at a farmer's market.

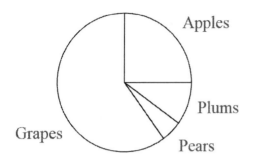

The portion labelled Apples has a central angle of 90°. How many of the 240 shoppers chose apples as their favorite fruit?

(A) 24
(B) 60
(C) 80
(D) 90

3. The table shows the favorite color of 90 students.

FAVORITE COLOR

Color	Number of Students
Red	23
Yellow	12
Blue	15
Orange	10
Purple	30

Which portion of a circle graph will have a central angle of 60°?

(A) blue
(B) red
(C) purple
(D) yellow

4. The circle graph shows the number of animals on a farm.

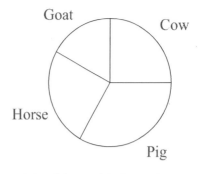

Which table could show the same data?

(A)

ANIMALS ON A FARM

Animal	Quantity
Cow	30
Goat	30
Horse	50
Pig	85

(B)

ANIMALS ON A FARM

Animal	Quantity
Cow	25
Goat	15
Horse	15
Pig	50

(C)

ANIMALS ON A FARM

Animal	Quantity
Cow	35
Goat	15
Horse	12
Pig	25

(D)

ANIMALS ON A FARM

Animal	Quantity
Cow	35
Goat	23
Horse	35
Pig	47

5. Hunter tracked how many miles he ran each month for one year, and then made a circle graph from the data. He ran exactly 24 miles each month. What was the central angle of the portion of the graph representing December?

(A) 12°
(B) 24°
(C) 30°
(D) 36°

6. A circle graph (not shown) displays the results of a poll asking people what their favorite color is. 50 people chose orange. If the central angle of the portion of the graph representing orange is 40°, how many people took the poll?

(A) 75
(B) 225
(C) 400
(D) 450

7. The circle graph shows a group of students' favorite day of the week.

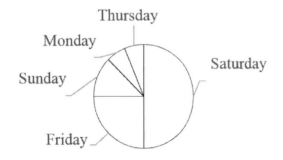

If 48 people chose Saturday, approximately how many people chose Sunday?

(A) 3
(B) 6
(C) 12
(D) 24

8. The circle graph shows the distribution of grades for a state-wide math test.

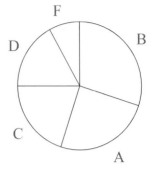

If 3,000 students earned a D, how many students took the test in all?

(A) 12,000
(B) 18,000
(C) 24,000
(D) 27,000

9. The table shows the favorite fruit of all the students in a school's 8th grade class. The data for orange is missing.

FAVORITE FRUIT

Fruit	Number of Students
Apple	30
Banana	20
Orange	
Peach	40
Mango	10

A circle graph is made from the data. If the central angle of the portion of the graph representing peach is 120°, how many people chose orange?

(A) 10
(B) 20
(C) 30
(D) 40

10. Philip is making a circle graph to represent his expenses. Rent takes up $\frac{1}{2}$ of the circle and food takes up $\frac{1}{3}$ of the circle. How many more degrees is the central angle of the portion representing rent than the central angle of the portion representing food?

(A) 45
(B) 60
(C) 75
(D) 90

11. Cindy is making a circle graph to represent her expenses. Transportation takes up $\frac{1}{6}$ of the circle and utilities takes up $\frac{1}{8}$ of the circle. How many more degrees is the central angle of the portion representing transportation than the central angle of the portion representing utilities?

(A) 15
(B) 20
(C) 30
(D) 45

12. A circle graph has three sections. If the degree measure of the central angles of the three sections are in the ratio 2:3:4, what is the degree measure of the largest angle?

(A) 40
(B) 80
(C) 120
(D) 160

13. A pizza was cut into 8 equal slices. Nigel ate 3 slices. What is the total degree measure of the central angle representing the slices Nigel ate?

(A) 67.5°
(B) 90°
(C) 135°
(D) 225°

Box-and-Whisker Plots

Example: The box-and-whisker plot shows the scores every student in a class earned on an English exam.

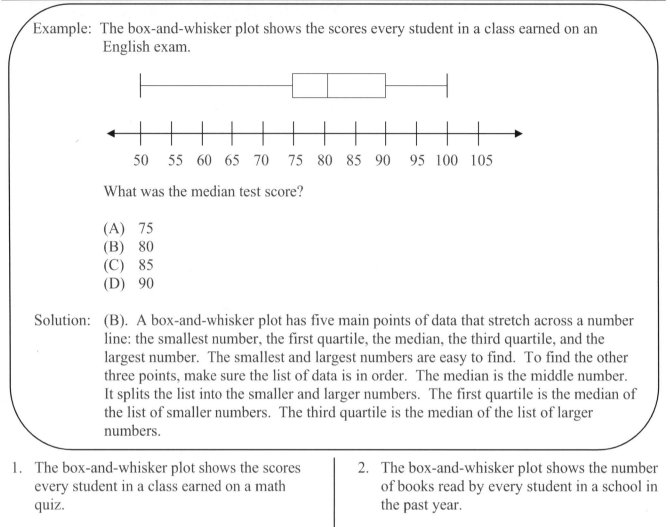

What was the median test score?

(A) 75
(B) 80
(C) 85
(D) 90

Solution: (B). A box-and-whisker plot has five main points of data that stretch across a number line: the smallest number, the first quartile, the median, the third quartile, and the largest number. The smallest and largest numbers are easy to find. To find the other three points, make sure the list of data is in order. The median is the middle number. It splits the list into the smaller and larger numbers. The first quartile is the median of the list of smaller numbers. The third quartile is the median of the list of larger numbers.

1. The box-and-whisker plot shows the scores every student in a class earned on a math quiz.

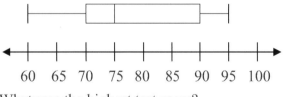

What was the highest test score?

(A) 75
(B) 90
(C) 95
(D) 100

2. The box-and-whisker plot shows the number of books read by every student in a school in the past year.

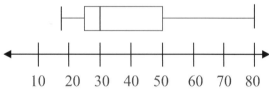

What was the least number of books read?

(A) 10
(B) 18
(C) 24
(D) 30

3. The box-and-whisker plot shows the number of times a group of people brushed their teeth during one month.

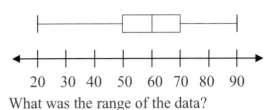

What was the range of the data?

(A) 90
(B) 70
(C) 60
(D) 20

4. The following data shows how many movies each person in a movie club watched last month.

3, 4, 5, 5, 6, 7, 8, 8, 9, 10, 11

Which of the following box-and-whisker plots correctly represents the data?

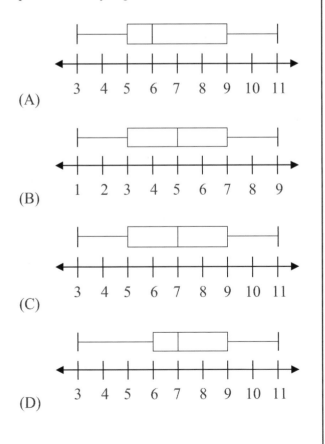

5. The following data shows how many students in a class earned an A on each of the last 12 math tests.

12, 8, 9, 12, 7, 6, 8, 4, 1, 3, 9, 5

Which of the following box-and-whisker plots correctly represents the data?

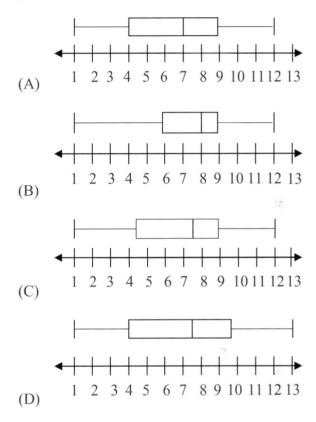

6. The following data shows the number of hours each member of a gym spent exercising in the gym last year.

52, 85, 65, 58, 45, 41, 65, 68, 40, 45, 65, 85, 35, 44, 75

Which of the following box-and-whisker plots correctly represents the data?

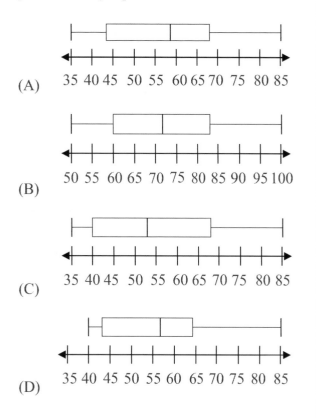

(A)

(B)

(C)

(D)

Stem-and-Leaf Plots

Example: The stem-and-leaf plot below shows the grade each student in a class earned on a science test.

Stem	Leaf
7	2 6 8 9
8	1 3 4 6 7 7 8 9
9	2 3 7 8 9

What is the range of the test grades?

(A) 7
(B) 8
(C) 13
(D) 27

Solution: (D). Stem-and-leaf plots separate numbers into their tens and ones. 7 | 2 6 8 9 represents the numbers 72, 76, 78, and 79. Here, the largest number is 99 and the smallest number is 72, so the range is 99 − 72 = 27.

1. The stem-and-leaf plot below shows the number of hours each student in a class spent reading last month.

Stem	Leaf
0	0 0 1 1 1 1 2 5 7 8
1	0 0 0 3 3 4 8
2	0 0 1

What is the mode of the data?

(A) 0
(B) 1
(C) 10
(D) 21

2. The stem-and-leaf plot below shows the number of minutes Keith spent exercising each day last month.

Stem	Leaf
3	1 2 5 5 6
4	1 2 3 5 6 7 8
5	1 2 3 3 5 7 7 7
6	1 2 2 3 6 6 7 7
7	4 7 8

What is the median of the data?

(A) 48
(B) 53
(C) 57
(D) 61

3. The stem-and-leaf plot below shows the number of points Josie scored during all 10 of her basketball games last season.

Stem	Leaf
0	3 5 5 6
1	0 0 1 2
2	0 1

What is the mean of Josie's points scored?

(A) 2.3
(B) 3
(C) 8
(D) 10.3

4. The stem-and-leaf plot below shows the ages of every person who went to the park yesterday.

Stem	Leaf
0	1
1	0 3 3 3 6
2	1 1 2
3	5 9
4	0
5	1 7
6	3

What is the mode of the ages?

(A) 1
(B) 3
(C) 13
(D) 21

5. The stem-and-leaf plot below shows the number of pencils owned by every student in a class.

Stem	Leaf
0	1 1 2 2 2 3 5
1	0 2
2	0

What is the mean of the pencils?

(A) 2.5
(B) 5.8
(C) 8
(D) 10

6. The stem-and-leaf plot below shows the ages of every person who went to the town library yesterday. One piece of data is missing, as shown by the box.

Stem	Leaf
0	☐ 2 2 5 5 5 7
1	0 1 2
5	1 5 9 9
6	1 3 3 4 5 8 9

If the range of the data is 67, what is the mode of the data?

(A) 2
(B) 5
(C) 2 and 5
(D) 2, 5, and 9

Histograms

Example: The histogram shows the ages of everyone who attended a health fair.

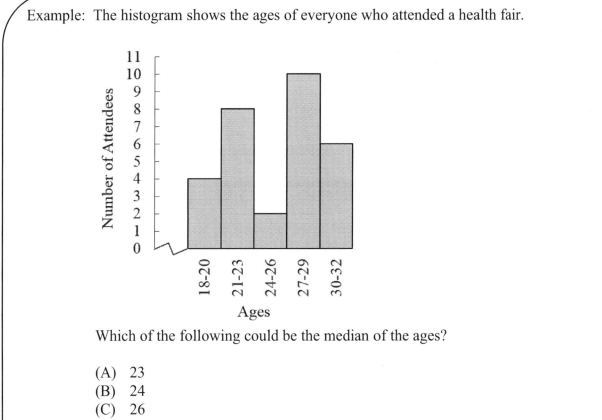

Which of the following could be the median of the ages?

(A) 23
(B) 24
(C) 26
(D) 29

Solution: (D). Like a frequency chart, the height of each bar shows how many data points you have. Here, the number of attendees is exactly 30, which means that if you put all the numbers in order, the median must be the average of the 15th and 16th numbers. We don't know exactly what the numbers are, but we know that both the 15th and 16th numbers lie within the "27-29" range. Just because the bar is labelled "27-29" doesn't mean that all three numbers must be included. It's possible that they could be all 29's, hence the use of the word "could" in the question.

(practice begins on the next page)

1. The histogram shows the weights of everyone who signed up at a gym last week.

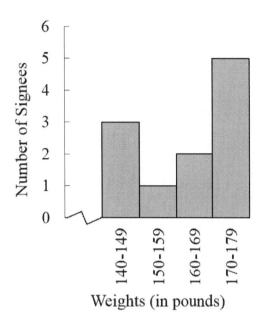

How many people weighed less than 160 pounds?

(A) 1
(B) 3
(C) 4
(D) 5

2. The histogram shows the test grades of everyone who took a math test.

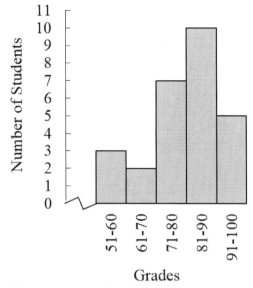

Which of the following could be the range of all the test grades?

(A) 30
(B) 40
(C) 50
(D) 60

Quantitative Comparison Practice

Answer Choices:

(A) The amount in column A is greater.
(B) The amount in column B is greater.
(C) The two amounts are equal.
(D) The relationship cannot be determined from the information provided.

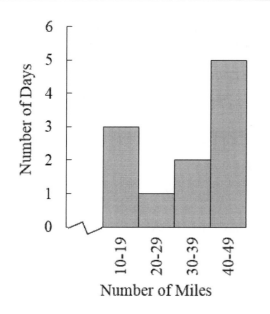

The histogram shows the number of miles travelled by a bus over several days.

Column A	Column B
3. The number of days it travelled fewer than 30 miles	The number of days it travelled more than 30 miles

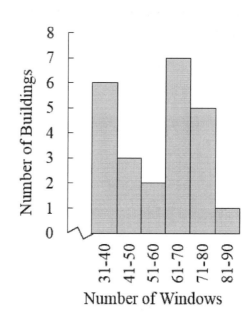

The histogram shows the number of windows counted in several buildings.

Column A	Column B
5. The median	61

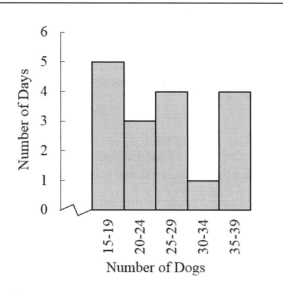

The histogram shows the number of dogs counted in a park over the course of a month.

Column A	Column B
4. The mode	15

Survey Samples

Example: John wants to conduct a survey to try to determine what percent of his school takes the school bus to school each morning. Which sample of students will give him the most reliable information about the students in his school?

(A)   the students in his class
(B)   all of the people walking by a supermarket one morning
(C)   all of the students getting off the school bus one morning
(D)   all of the students coming into the school building one morning

Solution: (D). Surveys should always be given to the broadest, most random and unbiased sample available, but only of the relevant demographic. Here, since John is only interested in students in his school, the closer he can get to his entire school, the more representative the data will be.

1. Four students – April, Ben, Cindy, and Daniel – each have to conduct a survey to find out how many hours the students of their school spend reading each week. Who obtained the most reliable results?

(A)   April, who surveyed 30 students as they walked out of the library
(B)   Ben, who surveyed 30 people as they walked by the school's front entrance
(C)   Cindy, who surveyed 30 students as they walked into the cafeteria during lunch
(D)   Daniel, who surveyed 30 people in the teachers' lounge

2. A politician's campaign team wants to know what percent of voters will vote for him in a certain city. Which is the best sample for them to ask?

(A)   5,000 randomly selected people across the entire country
(B)   1,000 people randomly chosen in the city phone book
(C)   2,000 people who attended his opponent's campaign party
(D)   1,000 students in the city's largest middle school

3. An 8th grade class is conducting a survey to determine the most popular animals among the students in all three 8th grade classes in their school. Which sample will give the most reliable information?

(A)   only their class
(B)   all the parents of 8th graders who attend parent-teacher conferences
(C)   a random selection of students from the entire middle school
(D)   every person who attends the school play

4. Water runs from a mountaintop, through a forest river, and into a city reservoir where it waits to be pumped into the city's plumbing system. A scientist wants to test the cleanliness of the city's drinking water. Which sample will give the most accurate information regarding the city's drinking water?

(A)   the water at the top of the mountain
(B)   the water halfway down the river
(C)   the water in the reservoir
(D)   the water coming out of his faucet.

The Essay

Overview

The essay is the only section of the test that is not multiple-choice. It is also the only section that is not scored by the ERB. Instead, copies of your essay will be sent to every school to which you apply. The admissions departments will read your essay, and they will use it as part of your application. This means that even though it is not scored, the essay is still a very important part of the test.

You will have 30 minutes to complete your essay. Consider mapping out your time as follows:

3 minutes – PLAN. Brainstorm ideas and jot down notes. Organize your essay into five paragraphs (a brief introduction, three body paragraphs, and a brief conclusion).

25 minutes – WRITE. If you've planned well, the actual writing of the essay should not be difficult.

2 minutes – PROOFREAD. This is very important! You want to catch and fix all errors in punctuation, spelling and grammar. Never let anyone else read what you have written before you have read it to yourself carefully.

You might see some of the following three types of personal essays on the ISEE – what we will call Personal Statements, Real-Life Experiences, and Hypothetical Scenarios. They may seem different, but they all ask you to do the same thing – talk about yourself in some way.

Below are 15 essay prompts (five for each of the three types of personal essay):

Personal Statements

In a Personal Statement essay, you will be asked to describe your character, opinions, or interests. Here are five examples of Personal Statement essays:

1. Tell us about a person you admire.
2. Write about a character in fiction, a historical figure, or a creative work (as in art, music, science, etc.) that has had an influence on you, and explain that influence.
3. Describe an attribute, a quality, or a skill that distinguishes you from everyone else.
4. What do you think makes a person a good teacher? What kind of qualities do you look for in a teacher? Describe the best teacher you ever had and what made him/her so special.
5. What is your favorite book, and why?

Real-Life Experiences

In a Real-Life Experience essay, you will be asked to discuss an event that actually happened to you. Here are five examples of Real-Life Experience essays:

1. Describe a time when you experienced failure. How did it affect you, and what did you learn from the experience?
2. Write about a time you struggled and succeeded.
3. Describe a time you changed your mind about a certain belief or idea. What prompted the change? How did it affect you going forward?
4. Write about your most embarrassing moment.
5. Describe the best gift you ever gave to someone.

Hypothetical Scenarios

Hypothetical Scenario essays ask a form of "What if?" They are asking what you would do in a certain situation. Here are five examples of Hypothetical Scenario essays:

1. Choose a prominent person (living or deceased) that you would like to interview and explain why.
2. If you could travel to either the past or the future, to what year would you travel, and why?
3. What would you do with one million dollars?
4. If you could have any superpower, what superpower would you choose to have, and what would you do with it?
5. If you were going to be stranded on a deserted island and could take three items with you, what three items would you take and why?

How to Use This Section

Choose one of the above 15 topics. Set a timer for 30 minutes, then make your notes and write your essay on a separate sheet of lined paper. Copy the prompt into the box at the top of the essay page and begin writing. You are limited to two pages for the essay, so plan accordingly. Remember to proofread!

Tutorverse Tips!

Remember that the essay has two purposes. Schools want to see how well you can write and also want to learn something about you as a person. Think of the essay as a written interview. If you are asked to describe the best birthday party you have ever attended, consider focusing on the experience itself and how it made you feel. Why was the birthday party special to you? How did the party make you feel? Instead of focusing only on describing the events that happened, ask yourself "So what?" – why were the events special?

Remember to plan thoroughly before you start writing and to proofread carefully when you are done. The planning is important because admissions directors can identify well organized essays versus those essays that lack structure. Proofreading is important because you want to remove careless mistakes – such as simple punctuation or spelling errors – that will reflect poorly on your writing skills.

Final Practice Test (Form B)

Overview

The practice test is designed to assess your understanding of key skills and concepts. It is important to take the final practice test after completing the diagnostic test and after you have spent time studying and practicing.

This practice test assesses your mastery of certain skills and concepts that you may see on the actual exam. The main difference between the practice test and the actual test is that the practice test is scored differently from how the actual exam is scored. On the actual exam, certain questions will not count towards your actual score, and your score will be determined how you did compared with other students in your grade. On this practice test, however, we will score every question in order to gauge your mastery over skills and concepts.

This practice test should *not* be used as a gauge of how you will score on the test.

Format

The format of the practice test is similar to that of the actual test. The number of questions included in each section mirror those of the actual test, *even though the actual test includes questions that will not be scored*. This is done by design, in order to help familiarize you with the actual length of the test.

Practice Test Section	Questions	Time Limit
Verbal Reasoning	40	20 minutes
Quantitative Reasoning	37	35 minutes
Break #1	N/A	5 minutes
Reading Comprehension	36	35 minutes
Mathematics Achievement	47	40 minutes
Break #2	N/A	5 minutes
Essay Prompt	1	30 minutes
Total	**161**	**170 minutes**

Answering

Use the answer sheet provided on the next several pages to record your answers. You may wish to tear these pages out of the workbook.

Practice Test Answer Sheet

Section 1: Verbal Reasoning

1. Ⓐ Ⓑ Ⓒ Ⓓ   8. Ⓐ Ⓑ Ⓒ Ⓓ   15. Ⓐ Ⓑ Ⓒ Ⓓ   22. Ⓐ Ⓑ Ⓒ Ⓓ   29. Ⓐ Ⓑ Ⓒ Ⓓ   36. Ⓐ Ⓑ Ⓒ Ⓓ
2. Ⓐ Ⓑ Ⓒ Ⓓ   9. Ⓐ Ⓑ Ⓒ Ⓓ   16. Ⓐ Ⓑ Ⓒ Ⓓ   23. Ⓐ Ⓑ Ⓒ Ⓓ   30. Ⓐ Ⓑ Ⓒ Ⓓ   37. Ⓐ Ⓑ Ⓒ Ⓓ
3. Ⓐ Ⓑ Ⓒ Ⓓ   10. Ⓐ Ⓑ Ⓒ Ⓓ   17. Ⓐ Ⓑ Ⓒ Ⓓ   24. Ⓐ Ⓑ Ⓒ Ⓓ   31. Ⓐ Ⓑ Ⓒ Ⓓ   38. Ⓐ Ⓑ Ⓒ Ⓓ
4. Ⓐ Ⓑ Ⓒ Ⓓ   11. Ⓐ Ⓑ Ⓒ Ⓓ   18. Ⓐ Ⓑ Ⓒ Ⓓ   25. Ⓐ Ⓑ Ⓒ Ⓓ   32. Ⓐ Ⓑ Ⓒ Ⓓ   39. Ⓐ Ⓑ Ⓒ Ⓓ
5. Ⓐ Ⓑ Ⓒ Ⓓ   12. Ⓐ Ⓑ Ⓒ Ⓓ   19. Ⓐ Ⓑ Ⓒ Ⓓ   26. Ⓐ Ⓑ Ⓒ Ⓓ   33. Ⓐ Ⓑ Ⓒ Ⓓ   40. Ⓐ Ⓑ Ⓒ Ⓓ
6. Ⓐ Ⓑ Ⓒ Ⓓ   13. Ⓐ Ⓑ Ⓒ Ⓓ   20. Ⓐ Ⓑ Ⓒ Ⓓ   27. Ⓐ Ⓑ Ⓒ Ⓓ   34. Ⓐ Ⓑ Ⓒ Ⓓ
7. Ⓐ Ⓑ Ⓒ Ⓓ   14. Ⓐ Ⓑ Ⓒ Ⓓ   21. Ⓐ Ⓑ Ⓒ Ⓓ   28. Ⓐ Ⓑ Ⓒ Ⓓ   35. Ⓐ Ⓑ Ⓒ Ⓓ

Section 2: Quantitative Reasoning

1. Ⓐ Ⓑ Ⓒ Ⓓ   8. Ⓐ Ⓑ Ⓒ Ⓓ   15. Ⓐ Ⓑ Ⓒ Ⓓ   22. Ⓐ Ⓑ Ⓒ Ⓓ   29. Ⓐ Ⓑ Ⓒ Ⓓ   36. Ⓐ Ⓑ Ⓒ Ⓓ
2. Ⓐ Ⓑ Ⓒ Ⓓ   9. Ⓐ Ⓑ Ⓒ Ⓓ   16. Ⓐ Ⓑ Ⓒ Ⓓ   23. Ⓐ Ⓑ Ⓒ Ⓓ   30. Ⓐ Ⓑ Ⓒ Ⓓ   37. Ⓐ Ⓑ Ⓒ Ⓓ
3. Ⓐ Ⓑ Ⓒ Ⓓ   10. Ⓐ Ⓑ Ⓒ Ⓓ   17. Ⓐ Ⓑ Ⓒ Ⓓ   24. Ⓐ Ⓑ Ⓒ Ⓓ   31. Ⓐ Ⓑ Ⓒ Ⓓ
4. Ⓐ Ⓑ Ⓒ Ⓓ   11. Ⓐ Ⓑ Ⓒ Ⓓ   18. Ⓐ Ⓑ Ⓒ Ⓓ   25. Ⓐ Ⓑ Ⓒ Ⓓ   32. Ⓐ Ⓑ Ⓒ Ⓓ
5. Ⓐ Ⓑ Ⓒ Ⓓ   12. Ⓐ Ⓑ Ⓒ Ⓓ   19. Ⓐ Ⓑ Ⓒ Ⓓ   26. Ⓐ Ⓑ Ⓒ Ⓓ   33. Ⓐ Ⓑ Ⓒ Ⓓ
6. Ⓐ Ⓑ Ⓒ Ⓓ   13. Ⓐ Ⓑ Ⓒ Ⓓ   20. Ⓐ Ⓑ Ⓒ Ⓓ   27. Ⓐ Ⓑ Ⓒ Ⓓ   34. Ⓐ Ⓑ Ⓒ Ⓓ
7. Ⓐ Ⓑ Ⓒ Ⓓ   14. Ⓐ Ⓑ Ⓒ Ⓓ   21. Ⓐ Ⓑ Ⓒ Ⓓ   28. Ⓐ Ⓑ Ⓒ Ⓓ   35. Ⓐ Ⓑ Ⓒ Ⓓ

Section 3: Reading Comprehension

1. Ⓐ Ⓑ Ⓒ Ⓓ   7. Ⓐ Ⓑ Ⓒ Ⓓ   13. Ⓐ Ⓑ Ⓒ Ⓓ   19. Ⓐ Ⓑ Ⓒ Ⓓ   25. Ⓐ Ⓑ Ⓒ Ⓓ   31. Ⓐ Ⓑ Ⓒ Ⓓ
2. Ⓐ Ⓑ Ⓒ Ⓓ   8. Ⓐ Ⓑ Ⓒ Ⓓ   14. Ⓐ Ⓑ Ⓒ Ⓓ   20. Ⓐ Ⓑ Ⓒ Ⓓ   26. Ⓐ Ⓑ Ⓒ Ⓓ   32. Ⓐ Ⓑ Ⓒ Ⓓ
3. Ⓐ Ⓑ Ⓒ Ⓓ   9. Ⓐ Ⓑ Ⓒ Ⓓ   15. Ⓐ Ⓑ Ⓒ Ⓓ   21. Ⓐ Ⓑ Ⓒ Ⓓ   27. Ⓐ Ⓑ Ⓒ Ⓓ   33. Ⓐ Ⓑ Ⓒ Ⓓ
4. Ⓐ Ⓑ Ⓒ Ⓓ   10. Ⓐ Ⓑ Ⓒ Ⓓ   16. Ⓐ Ⓑ Ⓒ Ⓓ   22. Ⓐ Ⓑ Ⓒ Ⓓ   28. Ⓐ Ⓑ Ⓒ Ⓓ   34. Ⓐ Ⓑ Ⓒ Ⓓ
5. Ⓐ Ⓑ Ⓒ Ⓓ   11. Ⓐ Ⓑ Ⓒ Ⓓ   17. Ⓐ Ⓑ Ⓒ Ⓓ   23. Ⓐ Ⓑ Ⓒ Ⓓ   29. Ⓐ Ⓑ Ⓒ Ⓓ   35. Ⓐ Ⓑ Ⓒ Ⓓ
6. Ⓐ Ⓑ Ⓒ Ⓓ   12. Ⓐ Ⓑ Ⓒ Ⓓ   18. Ⓐ Ⓑ Ⓒ Ⓓ   24. Ⓐ Ⓑ Ⓒ Ⓓ   30. Ⓐ Ⓑ Ⓒ Ⓓ   36. Ⓐ Ⓑ Ⓒ Ⓓ

Section 4: Mathematics Achievement

1. Ⓐ Ⓑ Ⓒ Ⓓ   9. Ⓐ Ⓑ Ⓒ Ⓓ   17. Ⓐ Ⓑ Ⓒ Ⓓ   25. Ⓐ Ⓑ Ⓒ Ⓓ   33. Ⓐ Ⓑ Ⓒ Ⓓ   41. Ⓐ Ⓑ Ⓒ Ⓓ
2. Ⓐ Ⓑ Ⓒ Ⓓ   10. Ⓐ Ⓑ Ⓒ Ⓓ   18. Ⓐ Ⓑ Ⓒ Ⓓ   26. Ⓐ Ⓑ Ⓒ Ⓓ   34. Ⓐ Ⓑ Ⓒ Ⓓ   42. Ⓐ Ⓑ Ⓒ Ⓓ
3. Ⓐ Ⓑ Ⓒ Ⓓ   11. Ⓐ Ⓑ Ⓒ Ⓓ   19. Ⓐ Ⓑ Ⓒ Ⓓ   27. Ⓐ Ⓑ Ⓒ Ⓓ   35. Ⓐ Ⓑ Ⓒ Ⓓ   43. Ⓐ Ⓑ Ⓒ Ⓓ
4. Ⓐ Ⓑ Ⓒ Ⓓ   12. Ⓐ Ⓑ Ⓒ Ⓓ   20. Ⓐ Ⓑ Ⓒ Ⓓ   28. Ⓐ Ⓑ Ⓒ Ⓓ   36. Ⓐ Ⓑ Ⓒ Ⓓ   44. Ⓐ Ⓑ Ⓒ Ⓓ
5. Ⓐ Ⓑ Ⓒ Ⓓ   13. Ⓐ Ⓑ Ⓒ Ⓓ   21. Ⓐ Ⓑ Ⓒ Ⓓ   29. Ⓐ Ⓑ Ⓒ Ⓓ   37. Ⓐ Ⓑ Ⓒ Ⓓ   45. Ⓐ Ⓑ Ⓒ Ⓓ
6. Ⓐ Ⓑ Ⓒ Ⓓ   14. Ⓐ Ⓑ Ⓒ Ⓓ   22. Ⓐ Ⓑ Ⓒ Ⓓ   30. Ⓐ Ⓑ Ⓒ Ⓓ   38. Ⓐ Ⓑ Ⓒ Ⓓ   46. Ⓐ Ⓑ Ⓒ Ⓓ
7. Ⓐ Ⓑ Ⓒ Ⓓ   15. Ⓐ Ⓑ Ⓒ Ⓓ   23. Ⓐ Ⓑ Ⓒ Ⓓ   31. Ⓐ Ⓑ Ⓒ Ⓓ   39. Ⓐ Ⓑ Ⓒ Ⓓ   47. Ⓐ Ⓑ Ⓒ Ⓓ
8. Ⓐ Ⓑ Ⓒ Ⓓ   16. Ⓐ Ⓑ Ⓒ Ⓓ   24. Ⓐ Ⓑ Ⓒ Ⓓ   32. Ⓐ Ⓑ Ⓒ Ⓓ   40. Ⓐ Ⓑ Ⓒ Ⓓ

Section 5: Essay

Final Practice Test (Form B)

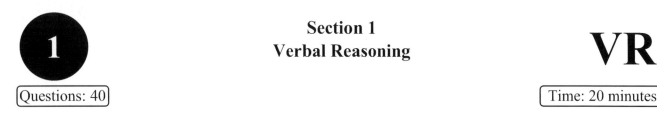

Section 1
Verbal Reasoning

VR

Questions: 40

Time: 20 minutes

There are two different types of questions in this section. Each question has four answer choices. Record your answer choice on your answer sheet. Once you have finished work on Part One, you may continue to work on Part Two. Writing or taking notes in your test booklet is permitted.

Part One – Synonyms

In Part One, four possible answers follow a word written in capital letters. Choose one of the four possible answers that is most nearly the same meaning as the word in capital letters.

Sample Question:

BOON:

(A) benefit
(B) trouble
(C) vibration
(D) virtue

Sample Answer:

Ⓐ B C D

Part Two – Sentence Completion

In Part Two, four possible answers follow a sentence with one or two missing words. One missing word will be denoted by one blank. Two missing words will be denoted by two blanks. The correct answer is the single word or pair of words that contextually completes the sentence.

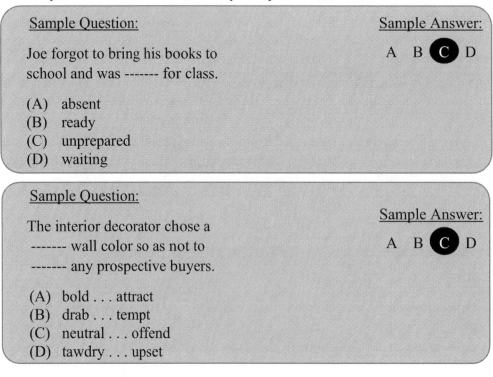

Sample Question:

Joe forgot to bring his books to school and was ------- for class.

(A) absent
(B) ready
(C) unprepared
(D) waiting

Sample Answer:

A B Ⓒ D

Sample Question:

The interior decorator chose a ------- wall color so as not to ------- any prospective buyers.

(A) bold . . . attract
(B) drab . . . tempt
(C) neutral . . . offend
(D) tawdry . . . upset

Sample Answer:

A B Ⓒ D

VR

Part One – Synonyms

Directions: Select the word that is most nearly the same in meaning as the word in capital letters.

1. MOCK:

   (A) flock
   (B) genuine
   (C) original
   (D) tease

2. PREVENT:

   (A) deter
   (B) encourage
   (C) fortify
   (D) permit

3. INSTILL:

   (A) concentrate
   (B) condense
   (C) postpone
   (D) teach

4. CUNNING:

   (A) absurdity
   (B) resourceful
   (C) swift
   (D) victorious

5. WAVER:

   (A) hesitate
   (B) roll
   (C) surrender
   (D) swell

6. HAVOC:

   (A) callousness
   (B) certainty
   (C) chaos
   (D) privilege

7. RIVAL:

   (A) adversary
   (B) friend
   (C) restoration
   (D) revival

8. IMPERIOUS:

   (A) arrogant
   (B) majestic
   (C) meek
   (D) royal

9. CONSPICUOUS:

   (A) discreet
   (B) guilty
   (C) obvious
   (D) suspicious

10. GRUELING:

   (A) brilliant
   (B) commanding
   (C) demanding
   (D) simple

11. AMELIORATE:

   (A) cancel
   (B) curate
   (C) enhance
   (D) organize

12. EGREGIOUS:

   (A) aggressive
   (B) awful
   (C) fluent
   (D) joyous

Go on to the next page. ➡

The Tutorverse

1

VR

13. APLOMB:

   (A) composure
   (B) explosion
   (C) fanfare
   (D) talent

14. TEMPESTUOUS:

   (A) angry
   (B) fickle
   (C) predictable
   (D) reckless

15. CONCURRENT:

   (A) advantageous
   (B) separate
   (C) simultaneous
   (D) temporal

16. MALLEABLE:

   (A) impressionable
   (B) malicious
   (C) resistant
   (D) wicked

17. ACUMEN:

   (A) anxiety
   (B) precision
   (C) seriousness
   (D) wisdom

18. FACETIOUS:

   (A) beautiful
   (B) inscribed
   (C) serious
   (D) silly

19. SUCCUMB:

   (A) combine
   (B) succeed
   (C) tousle
   (D) yield

Go on to the next page. ➡

VR

Part Two – Sentence Completion

Directions: Select the word or pair of words that best completes the meaning of the sentence.

20. In order to fit in with his friends, Carl pretended to be ------- about his schoolwork; in reality, he cared deeply about his grades.

    (A) apathetic
    (B) blissful
    (C) concerned
    (D) enthusiastic

21. Before a tsunami strikes, the water along the coast often ------- into the ocean, withdrawing many yards from shore.

    (A) bubbles
    (B) evaporates
    (C) rains
    (D) recedes

22. The pirates had nothing but ------- for authority, choosing always to raid and pillage despite the law.

    (A) ambivalence
    (B) contempt
    (C) deference
    (D) respect

23. Before the printing press, which automated and simplified the process of copying texts, making copies of books manually must have been -------.

    (A) effortless
    (B) gratifying
    (C) impossible
    (D) tedious

24. Some parts of the action movie were -------, not serving to advance the plot or develop the characters.

    (A) frivolous
    (B) important
    (C) integral
    (D) thrilling

25. The rain showed no signs of -------, for the wet season had arrived and it would continue raining for many months.

    (A) abating
    (B) improving
    (C) melting
    (D) starting

26. The accountant was well compensated, for he was ------- in carrying out his duties; the executive was pleased to have such a thorough and precise professional on his team.

    (A) careless
    (B) impatient
    (C) meticulous
    (D) regular

Go on to the next page. ➡

The Tutorverse
www.thetutorverse.com

1

VR

27. During the 1960s and 1970s, the government sought to ------- an otherwise stagnant national sense of purpose by investing in space exploration.

    (A) destroy
    (B) engender
    (C) replicate
    (D) standardize

28. Compared with the sailor's tiny ship, the whale he spotted was a -------.

    (A) behemoth
    (B) disaster
    (C) monstrosity
    (D) toy

29. Directly overhead, the moon had reached its -------.

    (A) base
    (B) nadir
    (C) potential
    (D) zenith

30. After many years of prosperity, the crash of the stock market marked a ------- of fortune.

    (A) bias
    (B) catalyst
    (C) paragon
    (D) vicissitude

31. References to well-known scientific studies and journals helped lend some ------- to the otherwise far-fetched science-fiction novel.

    (A) credence
    (B) deposition
    (C) incredulity
    (D) susceptibility

32. Despite his mother's best efforts to ------- him, Jeremy remained ------- for many weeks after losing his favorite stuffed animal, blaming his mother for his loss.

    (A) comfort . . . pacified
    (B) console . . . indignant
    (C) distress . . . resentful
    (D) sadden . . . content

33. The politician was very successful in his presidential bid because he was a(n) ------- speaker and had a(n) ------- personality; people were captivated by his speeches and found him to be charming.

    (A) avid . . . alluring
    (B) dull . . . dry
    (C) eloquent . . . charismatic
    (D) powerful . . . tiring

Go on to the next page. ➡

VR

1

34. The writer used humor at just the right times in his otherwise ------- play; by only telling a joke at the most ------- moment, he succeeded in lifting the mood of the entire play.

    (A) depressing . . . unsuitable
    (B) mediocre . . . fleeting
    (C) melancholy . . . opportune
    (D) uplifting . . . appropriate

35. Known for her -------, the counselor always had a schedule full of people who valued her sensitivity and -------.

    (A) callousness . . . sympathy
    (B) impudence . . . refinement
    (C) subtlety . . . garrulousness
    (D) tact . . . discretion

36. The people demanded that the ------- give up his power and ------- his throne; they would no longer tolerate or obey his harsh rule.

    (A) judge . . . abandon
    (B) king . . . seize
    (C) lord . . . regain
    (D) tyrant . . . abdicate

37. In order to ------- their numbers, the rebels sought to ------- support by handing out pamphlets along with free food and water.

    (A) augment . . . garner
    (B) diminish . . . gather
    (C) increase . . . bequeath
    (D) multiply . . . dampen

38. Zoe was puzzled by the ------- instructions on the box; what should have been clear directions were instead -------, open to multiple interpretations.

    (A) confusing . . . obvious
    (B) cryptic . . . ambiguous
    (C) explicit . . . concise
    (D) simple . . . complicated

39. The judge was a ------- and ------- woman, which made it difficult for the gangsters to influence her decision regarding the case.

    (A) decadent . . . amoral
    (B) righteous . . . venal
    (C) scrupulous . . . incorruptible
    (D) sedate . . . incorrigible

40. The chatter was both ------- and -------; it seemed that the foolish, pointless conversation would never end.

    (A) engaging . . . constant
    (B) inane . . . incessant
    (C) stimulating . . . persistent
    (D) vapid . . . sporadic

STOP. Do not go on until instructed to do so.

STOP

The Tutorverse

2

Section 2
Quantitative Reasoning

QR

Questions: 37   Time: 35 minutes

This section contains two parts. As soon as you finish Part One, continue on to Part Two. Remember to fill in the corresponding bubbles on your answer sheet. You may write in your test booklet.

Part One – Word Problems

Each question in this part is a word problem followed by four answer choices. Select the best answer from the four answer choices. You may write in your test booklet.

Example: A square has an area of 16 square inches. What is the perimeter, in inches?

(A) 4
(B) 8
(C) 16
(D) 64

The correct answer is 16, so circle C is darkened.

Example Answer

A   B   **C**   D

Part Two – Quantitative Comparison

Part Two is comprised of quantitative comparisons between amounts shown in Column A and Column B. Using the given information, compare the two amounts and choose one of the answer choices below:

(A) The amount in Column A is greater.
(B) The amount in Column B is greater.
(C) The two amounts are equal.
(D) The relationship cannot be determined from the information provided.

Example:

$x < 0$

Column A	Column B
x^2	x^3

Example Answer

A   B   C   D

Even though we don't know exactly what the value of x is, the given information states that x must be a negative number. Squaring a negative number results in a positive number. Raising a negative number to the third power results in a negative number, so the amount in Column A must be greater than the amount in Column B.

The Tutorverse
www.thetutorverse.com

QR

Part One – Word Problems

2

Directions – Choose the best of the four possible answers.

1. If $(x + a)(x + 2) = x^2 + mx + 10$, then what is the value of m?

   (A) 2
   (B) 5
   (C) 7
   (D) 10

2. Morty's piggy bank has $4.20 in quarters and dimes. There are 7 more quarters than dimes. Which equation represents the amount of money, in dollars, that Morty has?

   (A) $10x + 25(x + 7) = 4.2$
   (B) $25x + 10(x + 7) = 4.2$
   (C) $0.25x + 0.10(x + 7) = 4.2$
   (D) $0.10x + 0.25(x + 7) = 4.2$

3. A six-sided die is tossed 60 times. What is the expected number of 4's?

   (A) 10
   (B) 12
   (C) 15
   (D) 30

4. If $f(x) = x^3$ and $g(x) = \sqrt{x}$, which of the following inequalities must be true?

   (A) $f(-1) < g(0.1) < f(1)$
   (B) $g(0.1) < f(-1) < f(1)$
   (C) $f(1) < f(-1) < g(0.1)$
   (D) $f(1) < g(.01) < f(-1)$

5. If $\dfrac{x}{x-7} = \dfrac{50}{43}$, what is the value of x?

   (A) 57
   (B) 50
   (C) 43
   (D) 36

6. Two cruise ships, the Opulence and the Astound, set sail at the same time from New York to another port 1,000 miles away. The Opulence sailed at an average speed of 25 miles per hour. Which one piece of additional information could be used to determine the Astound's average speed?

   (A) The Opulence made the return trip in 35 hours.
   (B) The Opulence reached its destination in 40 hours.
   (C) The Opulence reached its destination 10 hours before the Astound.
   (D) The Opulence made the trip back to New York in 5 hours' less time than the Astound.

7. Rick has taken three tests so far in his math class. His scores on these tests are 89, 95, and 80. The score on his final exam will be counted twice in his mean. What is the lowest score he can get on his final exam and have a mean score of no less than 90?

   (A) 88
   (B) 92
   (C) 93
   (D) 95

8. The original retail price for a phone case was marked down 30% on Black Friday. The next day, it was marked back up 20% from the Black Friday sale price. What was the percent decrease from the original price?

   (A) 6%
   (B) 10%
   (C) 15%
   (D) 16%

Go on to the next page.

www.thetutorverse.com

2

QR

9. What is the value of the expression
$$\frac{4^3(2^2+2^3)}{4^2(2^3+2^4)}?$$

  (A) $\dfrac{1}{4}$

  (B) $\dfrac{1}{2}$

  (C) 1

  (D) 2

10. Which of the following represents 7^8 in terms of 49?

  (A) 49^2

  (B) 49^4

  (C) 49^8

  (D) 49^{16}

11. A scale model is built of a ship at a scale of 1 inch represents 4 yards. If the model is 3.5 feet long, how long will the real ship be?
(Note: 1 yard = 3 feet)

  (A) 14 feet

  (B) 42 feet

  (C) 168 feet

  (D) 504 feet

12. If $n*m = 3m + \dfrac{n}{m}$, what is the value of 10*5?

  (A) 15.5

  (B) 17

  (C) 30.5

  (D) 32

13. A roller coaster has a minimum height requirement of 54 inches. The histogram shows the heights of everyone who lined up to ride the roller coaster.

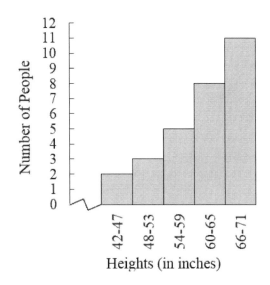

How many people were allowed to ride the roller coaster?

  (A) 5

  (B) 6

  (C) 24

  (D) 27

14. The product of three consecutive even integers is 960. What is the sum of the integers?

  (A) 20

  (B) 24

  (C) 30

  (D) 32

Go on to the next page. ➡

QR

15. What is the value of $\left(\dfrac{1}{25}\right)^{-\frac{1}{2}}$?

   (A) -5

   (B) $-\dfrac{1}{5}$

   (C) $\dfrac{1}{5}$

   (D) 5

16. The line shown represents $y = mx + b$ and has a slope of -4.

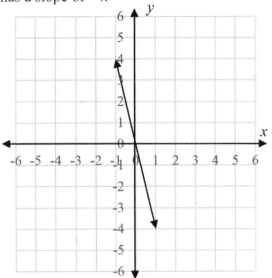

What could be the slope of $y = 2mx + b$?

   (A) -1.5
   (B) -2
   (C) -6
   (D) -8

17. If $i = \sqrt{-1}$, what is the value of i^5?

   (A) 1
   (B) -1
   (C) $\sqrt{-1}$
   (D) $-\sqrt{-1}$

18. A drawer contains 15 blue pens, 4 black pens, and 6 red pens. If Alyssa picks out a blue pen and does not place it back into the bag, what is the probability that the next pen she picks out will be black?

   (A) $\dfrac{1}{6}$

   (B) $\dfrac{4}{25}$

   (C) $\dfrac{1}{5} \times \dfrac{1}{6}$

   (D) $\dfrac{1}{5} \times \dfrac{4}{25}$

19. A net is shown.

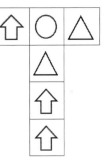

Which is a possible cube for the net?

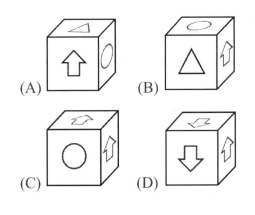

   (A)   (B)

   (C)   (D)

Go on to the next page. ➡

2

QR

20. If $\sqrt{5} = x + 1$, what is the value of $(x + 1)^2$?

(A) $\sqrt{5}$
(B) 5
(C) 25
(D) 36

21. Which is the most reasonable unit to use when measuring the volume of gasoline in a car's gas tank?

(A) feet
(B) gallons
(C) inches
(D) milliliters

Part Two – Quantitative Comparisons

Directions – Compare the amount in Column A to the amount in Column B using the information provided in each question. All questions in this part have the following answer choices:

(A) The amount in column A is greater.
(B) The amount in column B is greater.
(C) The two amounts are equal.
(D) The relationship cannot be determined from the information provided.

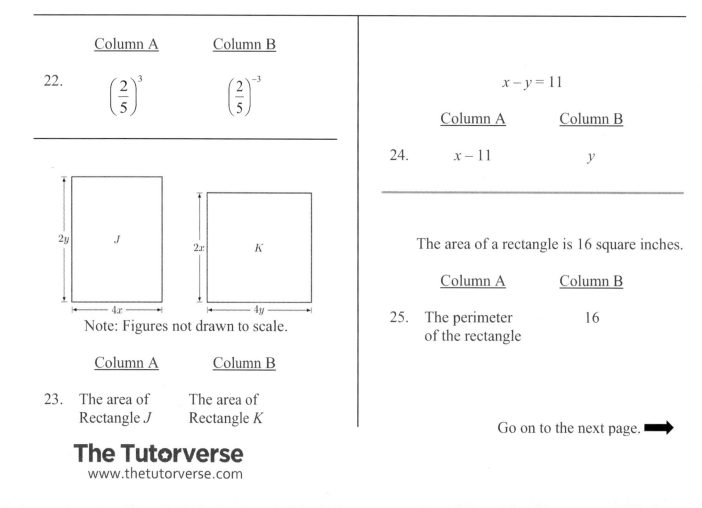

	Column A	Column B
22.	$\left(\dfrac{2}{5}\right)^3$	$\left(\dfrac{2}{5}\right)^{-3}$

	Column A	Column B
23.	The area of Rectangle J	The area of Rectangle K

Note: Figures not drawn to scale.

$x - y = 11$

	Column A	Column B
24.	$x - 11$	y

The area of a rectangle is 16 square inches.

	Column A	Column B
25.	The perimeter of the rectangle	16

Go on to the next page. ➡

QR

2

All questions in this part have the following answer choices:
(A)   The amount in column A is greater.
(B)   The amount in column B is greater.
(C)   The two amounts are equal.
(D)   The relationship cannot be determined from the information provided.

On Monday, one share of Company A stock was selling for $500. On Tuesday, the stock was worth 10% less than it was on Monday. On Wednesday, the stock was worth 10% less than it was on Tuesday.

Column A	Column B
26. The price of one share of Company A stock on Wednesday	$400

The sum of all integers from 50 to 200, inclusive, is a.

Column A	Column B
27. The sum of all integers from 50 to 199, inclusive	$a - 1$

A 6-sided cube, numbered 1 to 6, and a 4-sided die, numbered 1 to 4, are both rolled.

Column A	Column B
28. The probability of rolling a 2 or a 4 on the 4-sided die	The probability of rolling a 2 or a 4 on the 6-sided cube

The formula used to find the area of a circle is $A = \pi r^2$, where r is the radius. The area of Circle G is π.

Column A	Column B
29. The value of r	$\dfrac{1}{2}$

Column A	Column B
30. $30 - 5 \times 2^2 + 5$	15

Bea scored a total of 114 points this season. The graph shows the number of points Bea scored during each game this season, but the graph is incomplete, as one of the bars is missing.

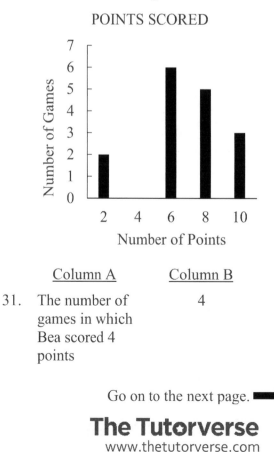

POINTS SCORED

Column A	Column B
31. The number of games in which Bea scored 4 points	4

Go on to the next page. ➡

The Tutorverse
www.thetutorverse.com

2 QR

All questions in this part have the following answer choices:
(A) The amount in column A is greater.
(B) The amount in column B is greater.
(C) The two amounts are equal.
(D) The relationship cannot be determined from the information provided.

$3x + 2y = x$

	Column A	Column B
32.	$12x + 12y$	24

Before Mrs. Schroeder decided to add 3 points to the quiz grades of everyone in her class, 5 of the students had scored an 85.

	Column A	Column B
33.	The mode after the points were added	88

The graph shows the speed at which Jon was driving as a function of time during his 10-minute car ride home from school.

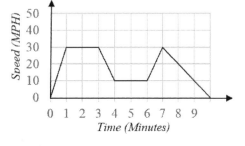

	Column A	Column B
34.	The number of minutes Jon's car was stopped from the time he left school to the time he got home	4

The formula used to find the volume of a cone is $\frac{1}{3}\pi r^2 h$, with radius r and height h.

Cone A is 4 times the volume of Cone B.

	Column A	Column B
35.	The radius of Cone A	4 times the radius of Cone B

The following spinner is spun twice.

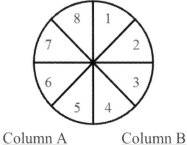

	Column A	Column B
36.	The probability the spinner will land on an odd number followed by an even number	If the first number is even, the probability of the second number being odd

---

A state map has a scale of 3 cm = 500 km.

	Column A	Column B
37.	The actual distance between two towns that are 1 meter apart on the map	1500 km

STOP. Do not go on until instructed to do so.

STOP

RC

Section 3

Reading Comprehension

3

Questions: 36

Time: 35 minutes

There are six passages in this section. There are six questions associated with each passage, for a total of 36 questions. The correct answer for each question will be based on what is either stated or implied in the related passage. You may take notes in your test pamphlet.

RC

Questions 1-6

1   The transformation of water into
2 different physical states is described as the
3 water cycle. Like all matter, water can take
4 on various forms, including liquid, gaseous,
5 and solid states. The transformation of water
6 into these different states involves different
7 chemical and physical reactions and
8 processes. Each form and each process has
9 different effects on the environment.
10   On Earth, the sun powers the water cycle.
11 The heat from the sun causes liquid water
12 found in oceans, lakes, and rivers – even in
13 plants and soil – to evaporate. Evaporation
14 transforms liquid water into water vapor,
15 which rises high into the air as a result of its
16 buoyancy and molecular mass. Some
17 estimates suggest that almost 90% of global
18 evaporation takes place over the oceans.
19   The higher the water vapor rises, the less
20 atmospheric pressure there is, and the colder
21 it becomes. As a result of the lower
22 temperature, water vapor begins to condense
23 into water droplets, much like it does on the
24 outside of a glass of ice-water on a hot day.
25 As it condenses, during a phenomenon
26 known as precipitation, the droplets start to
27 fall out of the sky in the form of liquid water.
28 Many scientists estimate that 80% of global
29 precipitation takes place over the ocean. The
30 form of the precipitation itself – rain, snow,
31 hail, etc. – depends on local climate
32 conditions.
33   Though much of the precipitation falls
34 back into bodies of water or onto land, where
35 it helps to perpetuate the water cycle, some
36 precipitation falls as frozen water and can
37 stay frozen for years. Snow and ice can stay
38 frozen for hundreds and even thousands of
39 years, effectively removing that water from
40 the water cycle until it melts again. Ice in
41 Antarctica and Greenland, for example, have

42 been dated to be approximately 800,000
43 years old.
44   Though it may seem as if frozen water
45 can do little once removed from the water
46 cycle, in reality the power of snow and ice
47 has shaped much of present-day Earth. As
48 global temperatures change, mountains of ice
49 known as glaciers advance and retreat,
50 grinding valleys into the earth and defining
51 mountains in their wake. While this process
52 can take thousands of years, the frequency
53 and intensity of liquid rain precipitation can
54 be so intense that it can lead to soil erosion
55 and even violent landslides in a matter of
56 minutes. Rain slowly chisels away at stones
57 and other hard matter, helping to pulverize
58 even the mightiest mountain or boulder; over
59 time, rain even helps to gouge rivers and
60 canyons into the land.
61   Water also plays a large role in shaping
62 environmental temperatures as it evaporates
63 and subsequently condenses. The process of
64 evaporation uses up energy from the
65 surrounding environment, thus generating a
66 cooling effect. The process of condensation
67 gives off energy into the surrounding
68 environment, thus generating a warming
69 effect.
70   The water cycle is an integral part of the
71 global environment, influencing everything
72 from entire climates and ecosystems to the
73 geological features of the earth itself.

Go on to the next page. ➡

RC

1. The primary purpose of the passage is to

   (A) discuss the benefits of water.
   (B) describe how water is precious to life.
   (C) document in detail the steps and reasons for certain natural processes.
   (D) explain the significance of certain natural processes to the environment.

2. Based on lines 10-18, it can be inferred that the water cycle would cease to exist if

   (A) global temperatures increased.
   (B) the sun disappeared or burned out.
   (C) all water was trapped in a frozen state.
   (D) people used up all of the water in the world.

3. Which best describes the organization of lines 10-32?

   (A) The author makes recommendations.
   (B) The author presents a number of arguments.
   (C) The author describes a process in chronological order.
   (D) The author compares the water cycle with other phenomenon.

4. According to lines 44-60, though water is frozen for long periods of time, it continues to have an impact on the environment by

   (A) creating various geological features.
   (B) contributing to landslides and soil erosion.
   (C) causing earthquakes that result in tsunamis.
   (D) grinding boulders into smaller stones and eventually into sand.

5. In line 59, "gouge" most nearly means

   (A) consume.
   (B) devour.
   (C) dig.
   (D) poke.

6. The tone of the passage can best be described as

   (A) derogatory.
   (B) objective.
   (C) pleading.
   (D) uncertain.

Go on to the next page. ➡

3

Questions 7 – 12

1　　The Works Progress Administration
2　(WPA) was a brilliant solution to the
3　difficult problem of the Great Depression.
4　While the WPA did not single-handedly lift
5　the United States out of its depression, it
6　played a major role in doing so while at the
7　same time investing in the country's future.
8　　　One of the many effects of the Great
9　Depression was the loss of millions of jobs.
10　Some estimates suggest that at its peak, one-
11　in-four able-bodied workers were
12　unemployed, impacting millions upon
13　millions of families.
14　　　For an economy, large-scale and
15　entrenched unemployment is devastating.
16　Because the unemployed have little or no
17　money to spend on goods and services,
18　businesses suffer. During the Great
19　Depression, many businesses either closed
20　entirely or fired many of their workers. This
21　exacerbated already high levels of
22　unemployment and put more pressure on
23　businesses that had remained open.
24　　　Unemployment in the Great Depression
25　resulted in mass poverty and homelessness,
26　as the unemployed were unable to pay for
27　even basic necessities such as food and
28　shelter. In 1932, according to *Fortune*
29　magazine, 34 million people had no income.
30　　　President Roosevelt's decision to invest
31　in employment was an inspired way to break
32　the self-perpetuating cycle of economic
33　depression. By providing Americans with
34　jobs, the President and his administration
35　hoped that they could revitalize the economy
36　by infusing it with consumer money to spend
37　on goods and services. As a result of
38　increased demand for their goods and
39　services, the administration hoped that
40　businesses would hire workers again.
41　　　The WPA was the largest of the New
42　Deal programs, employing approximately

43　three million Americans simultaneously at
44　its zenith. The WPA, whose goal was to
45　provide a paid job to the most needy,
46　provided nearly a million new jobs each year
47　between 1935 and 1943. These jobs were
48　primarily related to the construction of
49　public infrastructure. In all, the WPA built
50　some 40,000 new buildings and renovated
51　nearly 90,000 more. Americans continue to
52　use and rely on much of the infrastructure
53　that was built by the hands of the WPA.
54　　　The WPA also invested in the nation's
55　culture. Federal Project Number One was
56　the umbrella project under which the Federal
57　Art, Music, Theatre, and Writers Projects
58　operated. These projects employed over
59　40,000 artists, some of whom today are
60　highly regarded and well-known – Jackson
61　Pollock and Mark Rothko among them.
62　　　President Roosevelt himself highlighted
63　the impact of the WPA:
64　　"By building airports, schools, highways,
65　　and parks . . . by almost immeasurable
66　　kinds and quantities of service the Work
67　　Projects Administration has reached a
68　　creative hand into every county in this
69　　Nation . . . By employing eight millions of
70　　Americans, with thirty millions of
71　　dependents, it has brought to these people
72　　renewed hope and courage. It has
73　　maintained and increased their working
74　　skills; and it has enabled them once more
75　　to take their rightful places in public or in
76　　private employment."

Go on to the next page. ➡

RC

3

7. Which of the following best describes the main idea of the passage?

 (A) Unemployment has many negative consequences.
 (B) The Great Depression resulted in mass poverty and homelessness.
 (C) Government intervention mitigated the effects of a national plight.
 (D) Federal Project Number One was integral to the cultural development of the country.

8. In lines 30-40, the author suggests that the WPA was created in order to

 (A) arrest the downward spiral of the economy and help it recover.
 (B) help combat the negative emotional consequences of unemployment.
 (C) support American businesses that were struggling to find workers.
 (D) artificially make the number of unemployed appear lower than it was.

9. In lines 41-61, the author does all of the following EXCEPT

 (A) describe the scale and scope of WPA projects.
 (B) describe the reason for the creation of the WPA.
 (C) describe the impact of the WPA on infrastructure.
 (D) describe the number of people employed by the WPA.

10. In line 21, "exacerbated" most nearly means

 (A) improved.
 (B) neutralized.
 (C) nullified.
 (D) worsened.

11. In the final paragraph (lines 64-76), the author quotes President Roosevelt in order to

 (A) highlight the misery caused by the Great Depression.
 (B) describe in detail all of the contributions of the WPA.
 (C) illustrate how President Roosevelt was proud of the WPA.
 (D) reiterate the impact of the WPA on the people and on the country.

12. The author of the passage appears to care most deeply about the fact that the WPA

 (A) helped foster the next generation of American artists.
 (B) was created in response to an article by *Fortune* magazine.
 (C) is unfairly credited with helping to end the Great Depression.
 (D) was a good program, having both short-term and long-term benefits.

Go on to the next page. ➡

The Tutorverse
www.thetutorverse.com

3

RC

Questions 13 – 18

1　　As soon as I stepped outside and without
2　looking at the weather forecast, I knew that
3　we were due for a thunderstorm.
4　　The clouds – once white and fluffy –
5　were angry and dark as coal. Everything
6　seemed to be tinged a sickly greenish-
7　yellow. A barely-audible buzzing – an
8　electrical humming, almost – played in the
9　periphery of my hearing. The little hairs on
10　the back of my neck and on my arms stood
11　on end.
12　　Yes, I knew that we were due for a
13　thunderstorm. I had witnessed this same
14　scene unfold before me time and time again
15　right before a big storm.
16　　There were a number of things I needed
17　to do, and I ran through the checklist in my
18　mind: close the windows; close the storm
19　shutter; get flashlights and candles ready;
20　double check my battery supply. As I went
21　around the house on autopilot, checking
22　batteries and closing windows, a deep
23　rumbling rolled over my house. The storm
24　was coming, and thunder was its herald.

25　　A few drops of rain quickly gave way to
26　a deafening deluge, a million nails being
27　hammered into my roof. The wind began a
28　relentless campaign to break into my house,
29　shaking my storm shutters violently and
30　searching for gaps in my windows. The
31　thunder, once a dulcet bass in the distance,
32　split the air like a giant's war drums, shaking
33　the contents of my house.
34　　Through the slats of my shutters came a
35　blinding flash, casting a striped shadow
36　against the walls and floors of my living
37　room. The lightning was followed by a
38　violent peal of thunder, sending one of my
39　picture frames crashing to the
40　floor. Somewhere out there, the branches of
41　a tree – a victim of the wind or lightning –
42　fell to the earth, taking with it the electrical
43　lines that powered my home
44　　But for the lightning and the weak glow
45　from my candle and flashlight, I sat in near
46　darkness and waited for the storm to pass.

Go on to the next page. ➡

RC

13. The passage's primary purpose is to

    (A) explain the cause of a thunderstorm.
    (B) highlight the features of a thunderstorm.
    (C) describe the author's personal experience.
    (D) list the steps to take to prepare for a thunderstorm.

14. According to the passage, the author indicates that he knew a thunderstorm was coming because

    (A) he has very sensitive hearing.
    (B) his eyesight is extremely acute.
    (C) the hairs on his neck and arms are a type of sixth sense.
    (D) he had seen similar phenomena presage thunderstorms in the past.

15. It can be inferred that the author "went around the house on autopilot" (lines 20-21) because

    (A) he had performed his checklist many times before.
    (B) he was uninterested in performing his checklist.
    (C) he needed to think carefully about his checklist.
    (D) the author relies on outside help to manage his checklist.

16. In line 26, "deluge" most nearly means

    (A) blaze.
    (B) collision.
    (C) inferno.
    (D) torrent.

17. The phrase "split the air like a giant's war drums" (line 32) refers to

    (A) the volume of the rain.
    (B) the loudness of the thunder
    (C) the harshness of the rain.
    (D) the brightness of the lightning.

18. The final sentence of the passage (lines 44-46) is included in order to

    (A) communicate the author's helplessness.
    (B) emphasize the impact that rain has in a thunderstorm.
    (C) persuade the reader to invest in flashlights and candles.
    (D) explain how the author's preparedness helped save him from total darkness.

Go on to the next page. ➡

3

RC

Questions 19 – 24

1　　I looked forward to my biology class
2　every day. In fact, you could say that I
3　loved my biology class. The different
4　topics fascinated me, and I would sit in
5　class furiously taking notes about
6　everything from cell division to the Krebs
7　Cycle.
8　　At the beginning of the school year, my
9　teacher, Mr. Smith, grouped everyone in the
10　class into pairs. Each pair consisted of two
11　lab partners, who would work on projects
12　together throughout the year and be graded
13　on those projects together.
14　　I liked and generally got along with my
15　lab partner, Charlie. For the most part, we
16　worked well together, sharing
17　responsibilities equally. We'd meet up after
18　school to work on our projects, compare
19　notes, or study for the next test. Still, we'd
20　sometimes argue about whose turn it was to
21　check the petri dish or who was supposed to
22　note our observations about Spot, the class
23　plant. We weren't exactly friends, but we
24　didn't dislike each other, either; we had a
25　simple working relationship with one
26　another, and that was that.
27　　Things went along as they always did
28　until the day that Mr. Smith announced that
29　our next project would be to dissect a frog.
30　My heart skipped a beat – I had been
31　looking forward to this project since I first
32　read about it on our class syllabus!

33　　Charlie, however, did not share my
34　zeal.
35　　As we stared down at the pale frog
36　lying on the shiny metal dissection tray,
37　Charlie leaned over, grabbed my arm, and
38　whispered, "I don't think I can do this. I
39　think I'm going to be sick."
40　　Charlie's face was shrouded in panic
41　and fear. I could tell by the pleading,
42　searching look in Charlie's eyes that this
43　was a pure and powerful anxiety.
44　　"Don't worry about it," I said. "I'll
45　handle this one. You can help with the next
46　project that we have."
47　　Charlie nodded and seemed relieved, if
48　not a little bit surprised at my generosity.
49　　For my part, I put on my gloves and
50　started to go to work.
51　　At first, Charlie was fine. We
52　examined the exterior of the frog (which we
53　determined to be male), and identified a few
54　interesting features as we listened to Mr.
55　Smith's instructions. I picked up my
56　scalpel and made the first incision.
57　　Almost immediately, Charlie's face
58　turned a shade curiously akin to the frog
59　that we were dissecting.
60　　As I lengthened the incision, exposing
61　the most intimate parts of the frog, Charlie
62　bolted out of the classroom, knocking over
63　lab stools and papers on the way out.

Go on to the next page. ➡

RC

19. Which of the following best describes the main idea of the passage?

   (A) Working with other people can lead to unexpected outcomes.
   (B) Dissecting animals in school is inhumane and should not be permitted.
   (C) Students should be friends if they are to partner together on projects.
   (D) Teachers must be aware of their students' sensitivities prior to assigning projects.

20. In line 34, "zeal" most nearly means

   (A) enthusiasm.
   (B) furor.
   (C) reticence.
   (D) satisfaction.

21. According to the passage, the author first knew that Charlie's feelings about dissecting the frog were genuine because

   (A) Charlie ran out of the room.
   (B) she could see the distress in Charlie's eyes.
   (C) Charlie's grip on her arm was strong and painful.
   (D) she knew Charlie very well, as they were good friends.

22. It can be inferred that Charlie was surprised at the author's generosity (lines 47-48) because

   (A) the author was doing Charlie a favor.
   (B) Charlie knows that the author is generally mean-spirited and spiteful.
   (C) the author has in the past allowed Charlie to avoid project responsibilities.
   (D) the two students previously did not have a particularly friendly relationship.

23. In lines 57-59, the author compares Charlie's face with the appearance of the frog in order to

   (A) highlight differences between she and Charlie.
   (B) compare and contrast different shades of green.
   (C) note the irony and help the reader visualize the situation.
   (D) disparage Charlie's appearance and mock Charlie's predicament.

24. The author of the passage does all of the following EXCEPT

   (A) illustrate her relationship with Charlie.
   (B) relate Charlie's reaction to dissecting a frog.
   (C) explain why Charlie disliked dissecting a frog.
   (D) describe the first few steps in dissecting a frog.

Go on to the next page. ➡

3

RC

Questions 25-30

1   Indoor and outdoor plumbing has
2 improved hygiene, extended the human
3 lifespan, and facilitated the growth of cities
4 and other areas of high population density.
5 Modern plumbing traces its roots back to
6 ancient civilizations.
7   As populations grew and more people
8 started to live in smaller and smaller areas,
9 the need to provide potable water, as well as
10 the need to remove wastewater, grew
11 increasingly important. In ancient times,
12 diseases were poorly understood, and
13 mortality rates due to dirty water and
14 unsanitary conditions were extremely high.
15 Early waste disposal consisted of merely
16 gathering waste and throwing it onto the
17 ground or into a nearby river or lake – often
18 the same body of water from which drinking
19 water was drawn. Open sewage ditches and
20 cesspools were eventually eliminated in
21 favor of underground sewage and water
22 systems.
23   One of the most well-known examples
24 of plumbing in the ancient world was the
25 system used by the Romans. In this highly

26 advanced plumbing system, huge aqueducts
27 brought fresh water into the Roman
28 metropolis, and pipes carried the water into
29 people's homes and businesses. As a result,
30 public baths were erected, and wastewater
31 was efficiently removed. Due in part to this
32 innovation, Rome flourished.
33   While the Romans were clearly
34 advanced in their administration of the
35 public water supply, other civilizations were
36 just as savvy, if not more so, with their
37 plumbing techniques. Historians believe
38 that the city of Lothal in the Indus Valley,
39 for example, was a place where every
40 private home had a toilet that was connected
41 to a subterranean sewer network. The
42 network collected waste and centralized it
43 into a regularly cleaned cesspit. In ancient
44 Greece, the Minoan civilization on the
45 island of Crete was one of the first to use
46 underground water supply networks to
47 provide clean drinking water and to remove
48 waste water. It even allowed for the
49 collection and removal of overflow in the
50 event of heavy rainfall.

Go on to the next page. ➡

RC

3

25. The passage is primarily concerned with

   (A) comparing different ancient plumbing systems.
   (B) comparing ancient plumbing with modern plumbing.
   (C) diminishing the accomplishments of ancient plumbers.
   (D) explaining how ancient plumbing evolved into modern plumbing.

26. The "smaller and smaller areas" referred to in line 8 are most likely

   (A) coastal areas.
   (B) cities and towns.
   (C) dormitory-style apartments.
   (D) rural farms and communities.

27. The author uses the word "merely" in line 15 in order to convey a sense of

   (A) foreboding and dread for the future.
   (B) confusion and uncertainty about the past.
   (C) the lack of sophistication of early waste disposal.
   (D) surprise and admiration for ancient people's simplicity.

28. In line 36, "savvy" most nearly means

   (A) advanced.
   (B) frugal.
   (C) obtrusive.
   (D) plain.

29. The author suggests that Rome flourished in part because

   (A) every home had a toilet.
   (B) the Roman sewer network was subterranean.
   (C) the Roman plumbing system improved hygiene.
   (D) public baths led to an advanced plumbing system.

30. In the final paragraph (lines 33-50), the author cites Lothal and Crete as examples in order to

   (A) undermine the sophistication of their plumbing systems.
   (B) illustrate other examples of ancient plumbing ingenuity.
   (C) provide a scientific analysis of their plumbing and sewer systems.
   (D) describe the circumstances by which certain archaeological discoveries were made.

Go on to the next page. ➡

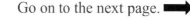

3

RC

Questions 31 – 36

1 Since ancient times, people around the
2 world have prized diamonds for their beauty
3 and desired them for their rarity. One of the
4 most coveted and valuable minerals on
5 Earth, diamonds come in many different
6 sizes, colors, and qualities. Though all
7 diamonds are precious, certain diamonds
8 exhibit unique qualities which make them
9 exceptionally valuable – for example, some
10 diamonds are unusually large, while others
11 are unusually colored. Such diamonds
12 become more than just gemstones – they
13 become famous, even legendary.
14   Widely regarded as one of the largest
15 gem-quality diamonds ever found, the
16 *Cullinan* diamond was found in a South
17 African mine, weighing over 3,106 carats.
18 The original diamond was then split into
19 over 100 separate stones. The two largest
20 stones, the *Cullinan I & II*, were set into the
21 Crown Jewels of the United Kingdom, with
22 the former and larger set into the scepter and
23 the latter and smaller set into the crown.
24 Though the *Cullinan I* weighed only 17% of
25 the original, its still-prodigious size earned it
26 the nickname *Great Star of Africa*.
27   Diamonds are not only prized for their
28 size, but are also valued for their color – or
29 lack thereof – and clarity. Discovered in
30 Zaire, the *Millennium Star* is far from the
31 largest diamond in the world. However, the
32 *Millennium Star* is actually the second-
33 largest colorless, flawless diamond in the
34 world. The diamond possesses no internal or
35 external imperfections nor does it contain
36 any chemical discolorations.
37   Many diamonds become famous because
38 of their physical attributes. The *Amarillo*
39 *Starlight*, *Eye of Brahma*, *Heart of Eternity*,
40 and *Mountain of Light* are just a few of the
41 many diamonds that have come to exemplify
42 perfection in either size, color, or quality.
43 Some diamonds, however, transcend mere
44 fame and become truly legendary despite
45 their physical attributes.

46   The *Tavernier Blue*, a 115-carat rare
47 diamond, surfaced some time during the 17th
48 century. A French merchant-traveler by the
49 name of Jean-Baptiste Tavernier sold the
50 diamond to King Louis XIV of France.
51 Louis XIV had the stone recut, after which it
52 became known as the *French Blue*. *French*
53 *Blue* became part of the French Crown
54 Jewels and eventually became the property
55 of King Louis XVI and his queen, Marie
56 Antoinette. During the French Revolution,
57 which resulted in the execution of Louis XVI
58 and Marie Antoinette, *French Blue* was
59 stolen and never recovered.
60   Decades after the theft of *French Blue*, a
61 similar but smaller diamond emerged in the
62 United Kingdom. While history is unclear as
63 to how, this diamond became the property of
64 Thomas Hope and was henceforth known as
65 the *Hope Diamond*. The diamond would go
66 on to change hands many times, becoming
67 the property of jewelers, heiresses, dukes,
68 lords, and possibly even a sultan.
69   Though the *Hope Diamond* is beautiful
70 by many physical standards, it is the
71 diamond's long, rich, and sometimes
72 mysterious history that truly sets it apart
73 from other famous diamonds. The diamond
74 is surrounded by intrigue and enigma, which
75 over time has turned speculation into fact
76 and fact into legend. Many believe the
77 diamond to be cursed, citing the unfavorable
78 fates of many of the diamond's owners as
79 proof. The diamond became so well-known
80 that newspapers around the world published
81 stories about how the diamond had brought
82 misfortune to its owners.
83   Though *Cullinan I* and the *Millennium*
84 *Star* are estimated to be more valuable than
85 the *Hope Diamond*, it's possible that many
86 more people have heard of the latter than the
87 former. And while color, size, and quality
88 matter when judging diamonds, the *Hope*
89 *Diamond* suggests that they aren't
90 everything.

Go on to the next page. ➡

RC

31. The passage is primarily concerned with

    (A) listing every famous diamond in the world.
    (B) explaining how objects can be valuable for different reasons.
    (C) documenting the criteria for evaluating the value of diamonds.
    (D) describing the experience of looking and handling a perfect diamond.

32. In lines 14-36, the author cites the *Great Star of Africa* and the *Millennium Star* as prime examples of diamonds

    (A) that are part of royal crown jewels.
    (B) that are surrounded by myth and legend.
    (C) exhibiting superior craftsmanship and cut.
    (D) possessing extraordinary physical properties.

33. In line 43, "transcend" most nearly means

    (A) become.
    (B) change.
    (C) exceed.
    (D) ruin.

34. Which best describes the organization of lines 46-68?

    (A) A gemstone is described in detail.
    (B) A chronological list of events is presented.
    (C) The qualities important in gemstones is emphasized.
    (D) The legend and lore surrounding a gemstone is explained.

35. According to lines 69-82, the author suggests that the *Hope Diamond*

    (A) is actually just a legend and does not exist.
    (B) is responsible for the execution of Louis XVI and Marie Antoinette.
    (C) is evidence that physical properties alone don't determine a diamond's worth.
    (D) is more valuable than the *Great Star of Africa* and the *Mountain of Light* combined.

36. Throughout the passage, the author uses the proper names of diamonds in order to

    (A) describe each diamond's appearance.
    (B) emphasize the importance and fame of these diamonds.
    (C) explain how the diamond's appearance affects its name.
    (D) illustrate the clarity, color, and size of each diamond.

STOP. Do not go on until instructed to do so.

The Tutorverse

Section 4
Mathematics Achievement

MA

Questions: 47

Time: 40 minutes

Each question in this section is followed by four answer choices. Select the best answer from the four answer choices. You may write in your test booklet. Remember to fill in the corresponding bubbles on your answer sheet.

Example: Ann has twice as many books as Bob. Bob has twice as many books as Cindy. If Cindy has 20 books, how many books does Ann have?

Example Answer

A   B   C   **D**

(A) 5
(B) 10
(C) 40
(D) 80

The correct answer is 80, so circle D is darkened.

MA

1. The first five terms of an arithmetic sequence of numbers are shown.

$$-10, -4, 2, 8, 14$$

What is the 50th term of this sequence?

(A) 284
(B) 286
(C) 288
(D) 290

2. Which expression is equivalent to the expression $x^2 - 100$?

(A) $(x - 10)^2$
(B) $(x + 10)^2$
(C) $(x - 10)(x + 10)$
(D) $x(x - 100)$

3. The box-and-whisker plot shows the number of burgers sold by a restaurant each day during the month of July.

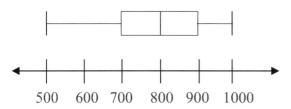

Which value represents the third quartile of the data?

(A) 600
(B) 700
(C) 800
(D) 900

4. The stem-and-leaf plot below shows the number of guests a hotel had each night last month.

Stem	Leaf
11	1 3 3 5 7 7
12	3 6 7 7 9
13	0 1 5 6 7 9 9
14	0 0 1 2 4
15	5 6 9 9
16	7 7 9

What is the range of the number of guests?

(A) 8
(B) 15
(C) 30
(D) 58

5. A rectangular prism has a length of x, a width of $2x$, and a depth of y. What is the volume of the prism?

(A) xy^3
(B) $2xy$
(C) $2x^2y$
(D) $2x^3y$

6. If $9x - 15 = 30$, what is the value of $27x - 40$?

(A) 80
(B) 85
(C) 90
(D) 95

Go on to the next page. ➡

www.thetutorverse.com

MA

7. Nathan's robot can fold towels four times as fast as Nathan. In one minute Nathan and his robot can fold a total of 40 towels. How many towels can Nathan's robot fold in one minute?

(A) 30
(B) 32
(C) 35
(D) 36

8. A circle graph (not shown) displays the results of a poll asking people what their favorite animal is. 40 people chose giraffe. If the central angle of the portion of the graph representing giraffe is 30°, how many people chose an animal other than giraffe?

(A) 180
(B) 240
(C) 440
(D) 480

9. The formula used to find the volume of a sphere is $V = \frac{4}{3}\pi r^3$, where r is the radius. A sphere has a volume of 36π yards^3. What is the radius of this sphere?

(A) 3
(B) 9
(C) 13.5
(D) 16

10. Find the slope of the line that passes through points (1,10) and (10,–5).

(A) $-\frac{5}{3}$

(B) $-\frac{3}{5}$

(C) $\frac{3}{5}$

(D) $\frac{5}{3}$

11. A standard deck of 52 playing cards includes 4 jacks and 4 kings. If one card is chosen at random, and then returned to the deck, and a second card is chosen at random, what is the probability that the first card chosen will be a jack and the second card chosen will be a king?

(A) $\frac{8}{52}$

(B) $\frac{1}{13} \times \frac{1}{13}$

(C) $\frac{1}{26} \times \frac{1}{52}$

(D) $\frac{4}{52} \times \frac{3}{52}$

12. A set of 5 numbers has a mean of 10. What additional number must be included in this set to create a new set with a mean that is 15?

(A) 15
(B) 20
(C) 40
(D) 60

Go on to the next page. ➡

MA

4

13. Carrie is 5 feet tall. At 7pm, her shadow is 9 feet long, as shown in the diagram.

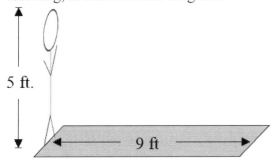

5 ft.

9 ft

At the same time, the shadow of a flagpole is 45 feet long. What is the height of the flagpole?

(A) 14 feet
(B) 25 feet
(C) 27 feet
(D) 41 feet

14. Which expression is equivalent to the expression $(x + a)(x - b)$?

(A) $x^2 - bx + ax - ab$
(B) $x^2 + bx - ax - ab$
(C) $x^2 - bx + ax + ab$
(D) $x^2 - bx - ax + ab$

15. What is the result of the expression
$$\begin{bmatrix} x & 1 \\ 3 & 2y \end{bmatrix} + \begin{bmatrix} x & -5 \\ 9 & 3y \end{bmatrix}?$$

(A) $\begin{bmatrix} x^2 & -5 \\ 12 & 6y^2 \end{bmatrix}$

(B) $\begin{bmatrix} 2x & -5 \\ 27 & 5y^2 \end{bmatrix}$

(C) $\begin{bmatrix} 2x & -4 \\ 27 & 6y \end{bmatrix}$

(D) $\begin{bmatrix} 2x & -4 \\ 12 & 5y \end{bmatrix}$

16. Line segment $\overline{AB}$ has endpoints at $(-7,1)$ and $(1,-5)$. How long is line segment $\overline{AB}$?

(A) 6 coordinate units
(B) 8 coordinate units
(C) 10 coordinate units
(D) 14 coordinate units

17. Which of the following is the graph of the solution to $|-5q - 5| > 5$?

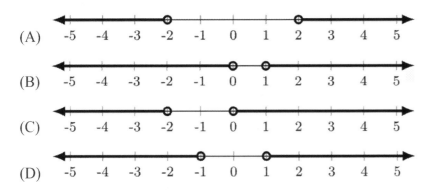

Go on to the next page. ➡

The Tutorverse
www.thetutorverse.com

4

MA

18. The measures of five of the angles of a hexagon are shown in the diagram.

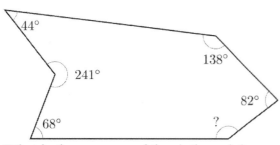

What is the measure of the sixth angle?

(A) 57°
(B) 135°
(C) 138°
(D) 147°

19. Triangle ABC is shown. The length of $\overline{BC}$ is 8 in. The measure of angle A is 27°.

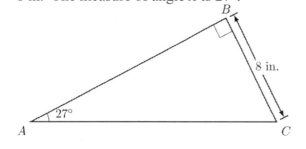

The value of which expression is equal to the length of side $\overline{AB}$?

(A) $\dfrac{8}{\sin 27°}$

(B) $\dfrac{\sin 27°}{8}$

(C) $\dfrac{8}{\tan 27°}$

(D) $\dfrac{\tan 27°}{8}$

20. The grid shows three vertices of a square.

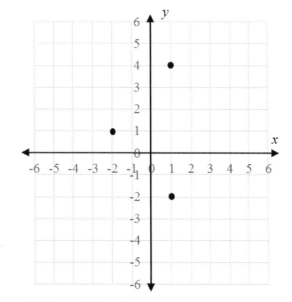

Which could be the coordinates of the fourth vertex of the square?

(A) (1,4)
(B) (3,3)
(C) (4,1)
(D) (4,2)

21. Which expression is equivalent to the expression $3c^2d^3 - 8c^2d^3 - (2c^3d^2 - 5c^3d^2)$?

(A) $5c^3d^2 - 3c^2d^3$
(B) $3c^3d^2 - 5c^2d^3$
(C) $c^3d^2 - 3c^2d^3$
(D) $-8c^3d^2 + 5c^2d^3$

22. A club of 6 members must elect four officers: President, Vice President, Secretary, and Treasurer. In how many different ways can they fill these positions?

(A) 24
(B) 256
(C) 360
(D) 1,296

Go on to the next page. ➡

The Tutorverse
www.thetutorverse.com

MA

23. The graph of a line is shown.

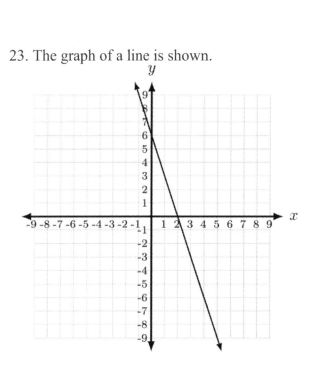

What is the equation of the line?

(A) $y = -4x + 2$
(B) $y = -4x + 6$
(C) $y = -3x + 2$
(D) $y = -3x + 6$

24. For what value(s) of x is the equation
$\dfrac{(x+4)(x-2)}{x^2-1} = 0$ true?

(A) 4 and –2
(B) 2 and –4
(C) 1 and –1
(D) 1, –1, 2, and 4

25. An entomologist believes that a certain type of mosquito found across the northeastern United States is causing disease in humans. She wants to test a sample of mosquitoes to find out. From which sample can she obtain the most reliable results?

(A) 5,000 mosquitoes found in sub-Saharan Africa
(B) 2,000 mosquitoes found in northern California
(C) 1,000 mosquitoes found across New York and Maine
(D) 500 mosquitoes found in central Vermont

26. The frequency chart shows the number of goldfish owned by each student in a class.

Number of Goldfish	Number of Students Owning That Number of Goldfish
0	9
1	5
2	3
3	2
4	1

What is the range of the data?

(A) 4
(B) 5
(C) 8
(D) 9

27. What is the value of $\sqrt{16x^{144}}$?

(A) $4x^{12}$
(B) $4x^{72}$
(C) $8x^{12}$
(D) $8x^{72}$

Go on to the next page. ➡

The Tutorverse
www.thetutorverse.com

4

MA

28. Which graph represents the solution set for $-4 \leq -2j + 3 < 11$?

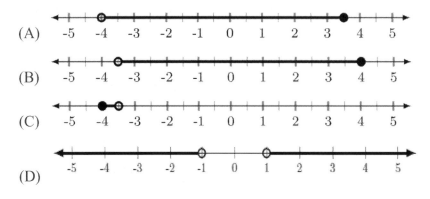

(A)

(B)

(C)

(D)

---

29. Which is the most reasonable unit to use when measuring the weight of a cruise ship?

(A) kilograms
(B) liters
(C) grams
(D) kilometers

30. What is the solution set for $x^2 = -400$?

(A) 20
(B) $20i$
(C) ± 20
(D) $\pm 20i$

31. If a and b are prime numbers, what is the least common multiple of $2a$, $4ab$, and $6b^2$?

(A) $12ab^2$
(B) $12ab$
(C) $2ab^2$
(D) $2ab$

32. What is the value of the expression $\sqrt{100 - 64}$?

(A) 2
(B) 6
(C) 8
(D) 18

33. What is the value of the numerical expression $\dfrac{7.2 \times 10^{10}}{8.0 \times 10^{-5}}$ in scientific notation?

(A) 9.0×10^{16}
(B) 9.0×10^{15}
(C) 9.0×10^{14}
(D) 9.0×10^{5}

34. A circle with radius 4 inches is missing a portion, as shown.

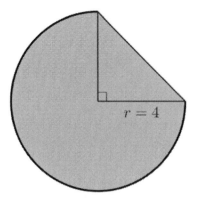

Which expression represents the area of the shaded region?

(A) $12\pi + 8$
(B) $12\pi + 16$
(C) $16\pi + 8$
(D) $16\pi + 16$

Go on to the next page. ➡

The Tutorverse
www.thetutorverse.com

MA

35. There are 0.305 meters in one foot. There are 3 feet in 1 yard. A woman is jogging at a rate of 80 meters per minute. Which expression has a value equal to the woman's speed, in yards per hour?

(A) $\dfrac{80 \times 60}{0.305 \times 3}$

(B) $\dfrac{80 \times 3}{0.305 \times 60}$

(C) $\dfrac{0.305 \times 60}{80 \times 3}$

(D) $\dfrac{0.305 \times 3}{80 \times 60}$

36. Adam has a standard deck of 52 playing cards, which includes 4 queens. If he picks out a queen and puts it in his pocket, what is the probability that the second card he picks out will also be a queen?

(A) $\dfrac{3}{52}$

(B) $\dfrac{3}{51}$

(C) $\dfrac{4}{52} \times \dfrac{3}{52}$

(D) $\dfrac{4}{52} \times \dfrac{3}{51}$

37. The shaded figure has an area of 64 m².

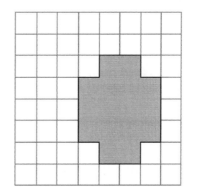

What is the perimeter of the shaded figure, in meters?

(A) 14
(B) 18
(C) 28
(D) 36

38. $\sqrt{5}$ can be described as which of the following?

(A) real number
(B) natural number
(C) rational number
(D) complex number

Go on to the next page. ➡

The Tutorverse
www.thetutorverse.com

4

MA

39. The diameter of the cone shown is half its height. The formula used to find the volume of the cone is $V = \frac{1}{3}r^2h\pi$, where r is the radius of the cone and h is the height of the cone.

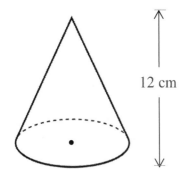

12 cm

If the height of the cone is 12 cm., what is its volume, in cm³?

(A) 36π
(B) 108π
(C) 144π
(D) 432π

40. If $\frac{x}{25+9} = x$, then what is the value of x?

(A) 34
(B) 1
(C) $\frac{1}{34}$
(D) 0

41. Alice, Bob, and Carol picked an average of 85 peaches. If Alice picked 105 peaches, what is the average of the number of peaches Bob and Carol picked?

(A) 20
(B) 40
(C) 50
(D) 75

42. Last night, Michael had 4 hours of homework. Today, the teacher gave 100% more homework. How many hours of homework does Michael have tonight?

(A) 4
(B) 6
(C) 8
(D) 12

43. Each square in the grid shown has an area of 4 in².

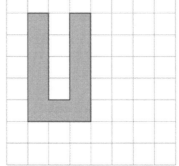

What is the area of the shaded region?

(A) 40 in²
(B) 44 in²
(C) 48 in²
(D) 52 in²

Go on to the next page. ➡

MA

4

44. A quadrilateral is shown.

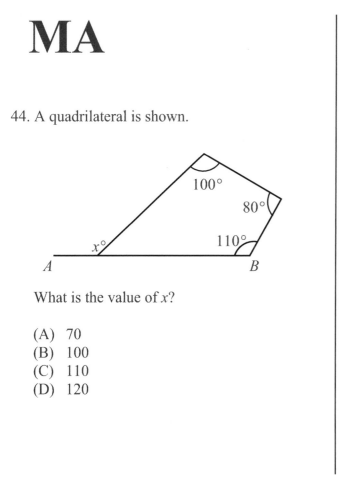

What is the value of *x*?

(A) 70
(B) 100
(C) 110
(D) 120

45. An art dealer bought a painting for $750 and then sold it for $600. What is the percent decrease in the price of the painting?

(A) 15%
(B) 20%
(C) 25%
(D) 30%

46. Lori has taken four tests so far in her math class. Her scores on these tests are 94, 100, 88, and 80. The score on her final exam will be counted twice in her mean. What is the lowest score she can get on her final exam and have a mean score of no less than 92?

(A) 200
(B) 190
(C) 100
(D) 95

47. A solution set is graphed on the number line shown.

$$-15 \quad -12 \quad -9 \quad -6 \quad -3 \quad 0 \quad 3 \quad 6 \quad 9 \quad 12 \quad 15$$

The solution set of which inequality is shown?

(A) $|x + 7| < 5$
(B) $|x - 7| < 5$
(C) $|x + 5| < 7$
(D) $|x - 5| < 7$

STOP. Do not go on until instructed to do so.

STOP

The Tutorverse
www.thetutorverse.com

Essay Topic Sheet

Use the pre-lined pages in the answer sheet of this practice test to answer the essay topic.

You have 30 minutes to complete the essay. This includes planning and writing time. You are **only** to write on the topic written on the other side of this page. You **may not** write on another topic. No other topic will be acceptable.

This essay is an opportunity for you to show how you write. You should try to express your thoughts clearly enough for a reader to understand what you mean. However, how well you write is more important than how much you write.

You may want to write more than a brief paragraph. A copy of this essay will be sent to each school that is receiving your test results. You may only write on the pre-lined pages in the answer sheet. Print or write in cursive legibly, so that someone who has not seen your handwriting before can read your writing.

You may plan and take notes on the other side of this page. However, only the writing on the pre-lined pages of your answer sheet will be accepted.

You may write only in black or blue ink.

There are additional directions on the other side of this page.

The Tutorverse
www.thetutorverse.com

Essay Topic

Describe the best day you've ever had in your life.

You may only write on this essay question.

Write down the topic below on the first few lines of your answer sheet.

Only the pre-lined pages of the answer sheet will be sent to schools.

Only write in black or blue ink.

Notes

_____

_____

_____

_____

_____

_____

_____

_____

_____

_____

_____

_____

_____

Scoring the Final Practice Test (Form B)

Using your answer sheet and referring to the answer key at the back of the book, calculate the percentage of questions you answered correctly in each section by taking the number of questions you answered correctly in that section and dividing it by the number of questions in that section. Multiply this number by 100 to determine your percentage score. The higher the percentage, the stronger your performance in that section. Note that the actual test will not evaluate your score based on percentage correct or incorrect. Instead, it will evaluate your performance relative to all other students in your grade who took the test.

Section	Questions Correct	Total Questions	Percent Questions Correct
Verbal Reasoning		40	%
Quantitative Reasoning		37	%
Reading Comprehension		36	%
Mathematics Achievement		47	%

Carefully consider the results from your practice test. If you're not happy with any of the results, take another look through the related section's practice questions to see if there is any more studying and preparing you can do. If necessary, revise your study plan based on these results.

Remember, the Upper Level ISEE is given to students from grades 8 through 12. When you take the actual test, your scores will only be compared with other scores of students in your grade. Unless you've finished high school, chances are that there is material on this test that you have not yet been taught. If this is the case, and you would like to improve your score beyond what is expected of your grade, consider outside help – such as a tutor or teacher – who can help you learn more about the topics that are new to you.

Answer Key

The answer key to this practice test can be found at the back of the book in the Answer Key section. The keys are organized by section, and each question has an answer associated with it. Visit www.thetutorverse.com for detailed answer explanations.

Note that there are no answers provided to the essay sections. Instead, consider having a tutor, teacher, or other educator review your writing and give you constructive feedback.

Get a Scaled Score Report @ thetutorverse.com/digital

Looking for an estimated Scaled Score Report? First, save your printed bubble sheet!

Then, navigate to thetutorverse.com/digital. Scroll to the "Get a Score Report" feature and follow the on-screen instructions. You'll be prompted to create or log in to your account on thetutorverse.com.

More Practice Tests Available Online

Need to take more practice tests? Want to work through more practice sections? Check out our computer-based practice on thetutorverse.com/digital. Take a fully-timed, automated practice test. Or, work through thousands of additional practice questions. Get this workbook for FREE using the code at the front of this workbook.

Answer Keys

This section provides the answer solutions to the practice questions in each section of the workbook except for the diagnostic test, practice test, and essay sections. The answers to the diagnostic and practice tests immediately follow their respective tests. There are no answers provided to the essay sections. Instead, consider having a tutor, teacher, or other educator review your writing and give you constructive feedback. Remember: there are detailed answer explanations available online at www.thetutorverse.com. Be sure to obtain permission before going online.

Diagnostic Practice Test (Form A)

Verbal Reasoning

1. B	6. C	11. D	16. A	21. C	26. B	31. D	36. C
2. D	7. D	12. A	17. C	22. D	27. B	32. C	37. D
3. B	8. A	13. B	18. D	23. D	28. B	33. C	38. D
4. A	9. D	14. C	19. C	24. D	29. D	34. D	39. C
5. A	10. B	15. C	20. A	25. B	30. D	35. D	40. D

Quantitative Reasoning

1. C	6. A	11. B	16. A	21. B	26. B	31. B	36. A
2. B	7. D	12. A	17. C	22. B	27. B	32. C	37. C
3. D	8. A	13. C	18. C	23. C	28. B	33. B	
4. C	9. D	14. C	19. A	24. A	29. A	34. C	
5. B	10. A	15. A	20. B	25. B	30. B	35. A	

Reading Comprehension

1. C	6. D	11. C	16. A	21. B	26. C	31. B	36. D
2. B	7. A	12. A	17. A	22. C	27. A	32. D	
3. A	8. C	13. B	18. B	23. B	28. A	33. C	
4. A	9. B	14. B	19. B	24. C	29. D	34. A	
5. B	10. A	15. D	20. D	25. D	30. A	35. D	

Mathematics Achievement

1. C	7. D	13. D	19. C	25. B	31. B	37. A	43. C
2. A	8. B	14. C	20. B	26. A	32. A	38. D	44. D
3. B	9. A	15. A	21. C	27. D	33. D	39. B	45. B
4. D	10. D	16. A	22. B	28. A	34. C	40. B	46. B
5. C	11. D	17. B	23. D	29. B	35. B	41. D	47. D
6. A	12. B	18. A	24. A	30. B	36. C	42. C	

Verbal Reasoning – Synonyms

Connotations

1. D	9. B	17. A	25. A	33. A	41. A	49. D	57. C
2. A	10. C	18. B	26. C	34. C	42. B	50. C	58. D
3. D	11. D	19. C	27. D	35. D	43. B	51. A	59. A
4. B	12. D	20. B	28. C	36. D	44. A	52. A	60. C
5. A	13. B	21. A	29. A	37. A	45. D	53. D	61. A
6. B	14. C	22. B	30. A	38. A	46. D	54. B	
7. B	15. D	23. D	31. C	39. D	47. A	55. A	
8. A	16. B	24. D	32. D	40. B	48. D	56. C	

Root Words

1.	D	9.	C	17.	C	25.	B	33.	D	41.	A	49.	D	57.	D
2.	D	10.	C	18.	C	26.	A	34.	B	42.	D	50.	C	58.	A
3.	C	11.	D	19.	B	27.	D	35.	C	43.	C	51.	D	59.	C
4.	C	12.	C	20.	D	28.	A	36.	A	44.	B	52.	C	60.	D
5.	C	13.	A	21.	C	29.	C	37.	A	45.	D	53.	D	61.	B
6.	C	14.	A	22.	B	30.	C	38.	D	46.	B	54.	B		
7.	A	15.	A	23.	A	31.	B	39.	B	47.	D	55.	D		
8.	D	16.	B	24.	A	32.	D	40.	D	48.	A	56.	C		

Vocabulary

1.	D	9.	D	17.	A	25.	A	33.	C	41.	C	49.	B	57.	C
2.	C	10.	A	18.	B	26.	D	34.	D	42.	D	50.	B	58.	A
3.	D	11.	D	19.	C	27.	D	35.	D	43.	C	51.	D	59.	B
4.	B	12.	B	20.	B	28.	B	36.	A	44.	B	52.	C	60.	A
5.	A	13.	A	21.	D	29.	D	37.	B	45.	B	53.	C	61.	D
6.	C	14.	B	22.	B	30.	C	38.	A	46.	D	54.	B		
7.	D	15.	D	23.	B	31.	C	39.	C	47.	A	55.	C		
8.	C	16.	A	24.	C	32.	B	40.	D	48.	D	56.	A		

Association

1.	D	9.	A	17.	C	25.	A	33.	C	41.	B	49.	C	57.	C
2.	B	10.	B	18.	B	26.	B	34.	B	42.	A	50.	B	58.	B
3.	D	11.	A	19.	C	27.	D	35.	A	43.	C	51.	C	59.	A
4.	D	12.	B	20.	B	28.	B	36.	B	44.	A	52.	B	60.	B
5.	B	13.	B	21.	D	29.	B	37.	C	45.	D	53.	B		
6.	B	14.	D	22.	A	30.	D	38.	D	46.	C	54.	A		
7.	B	15.	B	23.	B	31.	B	39.	D	47.	B	55.	A		
8.	B	16.	B	24.	D	32.	A	40.	B	48.	C	56.	A		

Verbal Reasoning – Sentence Completion

Single Blank

1.	C	11.	C	21.	B	31.	C	41.	A	51.	A	61.	C	71.	D
2.	A	12.	C	22.	A	32.	C	42.	A	52.	D	62.	D	72.	C
3.	A	13.	A	23.	D	33.	B	43.	A	53.	C	63.	A	73.	A
4.	D	14.	C	24.	A	34.	C	44.	A	54.	A	64.	A	74.	B
5.	A	15.	B	25.	B	35.	B	45.	B	55.	B	65.	C	75.	D
6.	C	16.	C	26.	D	36.	B	46.	A	56.	B	66.	A	76.	B
7.	B	17.	A	27.	B	37.	D	47.	C	57.	A	67.	C	77.	A
8.	C	18.	D	28.	C	38.	C	48.	A	58.	D	68.	B		
9.	A	19.	D	29.	B	39.	A	49.	B	59.	A	69.	D		
10.	A	20.	A	30.	A	40.	C	50.	A	60.	C	70.	A		

Double Blank

1.	A	6.	A	11.	D	16.	C	21.	C	26.	A	31.	B	36.	B
2.	C	7.	B	12.	A	17.	C	22.	C	27.	C	32.	B	37.	A
3.	A	8.	A	13.	C	18.	A	23.	C	28.	D	33.	D	38.	A
4.	D	9.	B	14.	B	19.	A	24.	B	29.	D	34.	C		
5.	A	10.	A	15.	D	20.	B	25.	B	30.	B	35.	D		

Reading Comprehension

Narrative

Passage 1	Passage 3	Passage 5	Passage 7	Passage 9
1. D	1. A	1. D	1. D	1. D
2. D	2. A	2. D	2. B	2. B
3. A	3. D	3. B	3. A	3. A
4. C	4. D	4. B	4. A	4. B
5. A	5. A	5. B	5. A	5. A
6. B	6. B	6. A	6. C	6. D

Passage 2	Passage 4	Passage 6	Passage 8
1. D	1. C	1. C	1. B
2. A	2. B	2. C	2. A
3. A	3. A	3. D	3. D
4. C	4. C	4. D	4. A
5. D	5. C	5. D	5. D
6. A	6. A	6. C	6. B

Persuasive

Passage 1	Passage 2	Passage 3	Passage 4	Passage 5	Passage 6	Passage 7	Passage 8
1. D	1. D	1. C	1. D	1. D	1. D	1. D	1. D
2. C	2. C	2. C	2. B	2. B	2. A	2. D	2. C
3. A	3. B	3. B	3. D	3. C	3. D	3. C	3. C
4. A	4. D	4. B	4. C	4. D	4. D	4. D	4. B
5. C	5. B	5. C	5. D	5. C	5. C	5. C	5. D
6. C	6. D	6. D	6. A	6. D	6. D	6. B	6. C

Descriptive

Passage 1	Passage 2	Passage 3	Passage 4	Passage 5	Passage 6	Passage 7	Passage 8
1. D	1. A	1. A	1. D	1. A	1. D	1. D	1. C
2. D	2. D	2. B	2. A	2. A	2. A	2. B	2. A
3. A	3. C	3. A	3. C	3. D	3. C	3. A	3. D
4. A	4. A	4. A	4. C	4. C	4. C	4. B	4. C
5. B	5. D	5. C	5. B	5. D	5. D	5. C	5. B
6. B	6. B	6. B	6. A	6. B	6. C	6. B	6. B

Expository

Passage 1	Passage 2	Passage 3	Passage 4	Passage 5	Passage 6	Passage 7	Passage 8
1. A	1. D	1. C	1. C	1. C	1. D	1. A	1. B
2. D	2. D	2. B	2. A	2. D	2. C	2. D	2. D
3. A	3. C	3. D	3. B	3. D	3. D	3. D	3. A
4. C	4. D	4. C	4. B	4. C	4. A	4. B	4. C
5. D	5. B	5. A	5. A	5. A	5. D	5. C	5. C
6. C	6. A	6. C	6. C	6. C	6. B	6. D	6. B

The Tutorverse
www.thetutorverse.com

Passage 9   Passage 10

1.	D	1.	C
2.	C	2.	D
3.	C	3.	C
4.	A	4.	B
5.	A	5.	D
6.	D	6.	A

Quantitative Reasoning & Mathematics Achievement

Arithmetic

1.	B	3.	A	5.	C	7.	A	9.	A	11.	B	13.	B	15.	B
2.	B	4.	B	6.	D	8.	B	10.	C	12.	B	14.	C		

Factors

1.	D	3.	A	5.	A	7.	D	9.	D	11.	C	13.	A	15.	D
2.	A	4.	B	6.	A	8.	A	10.	A	12.	D	14.	D	16.	C

Multiples

1.	D	2.	D	3.	A	4.	A	5.	A	6.	B	7.	A	8.	B

Exponents

1.	D	3.	C	5.	B	7.	C	9.	C	11.	A	13.	A	15.	B
2.	C	4.	B	6.	C	8.	B	10.	D	12.	C	14.	C		

Negative Exponents

1.	B	5.	D	9.	B	13.	C	17.	A	21.	B	25.	D
2.	D	6.	D	10.	C	14.	B	18.	B	22.	D	26.	C
3.	C	7.	D	11.	D	15.	A	19.	C	23.	A	27.	A
4.	D	8.	B	12.	D	16.	B	20.	C	24.	B	28.	D

Fractional Exponents

1.	B	4.	B	7.	B	10.	A	13.	B	16.	A	19.	A
2.	C	5.	B	8.	C	11.	A	14.	B	17.	D	20.	B
3.	D	6.	A	9.	B	12.	A	15.	A	18.	D		

Roots of Numbers

1.	B	5.	B	9.	C	13.	B	17.	C	21.	A	25.	B
2.	A	6.	A	10.	D	14.	B	18.	B	22.	A	26.	D
3.	B	7.	A	11.	C	15.	B	19.	D	23.	B	27.	A
4.	B	8.	A	12.	B	16.	A	20.	C	24.	A	28.	A

Roots of Variables

1.	A	4.	A	7.	A	10.	B	13.	B	16.	B	19.	D
2.	B	5.	C	8.	B	11.	B	14.	C	17.	A		
3.	C	6.	B	9.	D	12.	B	15.	C	18.	A		

Imaginary Numbers

1.	D	2.	D	3.	B	4.	D	5.	D	6.	D	7.	B	8.	B

Percents

1.	B	3.	B	5.	B	7.	B	9.	A	11.	B
2.	C	4.	A	6.	C	8.	A	10.	B	12.	A

Percent Change

1.	C	3.	D	5.	C	7.	D	9.	B	11.	B
2.	B	4.	C	6.	C	8.	A	10.	C	12.	A

Scientific Notation

1. D	4. B	7. A	10. A	13. D	16. B
2. A	5. D	8. C	11. A	14. C	17. C
3. D	6. A	9. A	12. C	15. A	

Vocabulary

1. D	4. A	7. C	10. C	13. C	16. D
2. C	5. C	8. C	11. C	14. B	17. D
3. B	6. D	9. B	12. B	15. C	18. B

Consecutive Integers

1. B	3. C	5. A	7. B	9. B	11. B	13. B	15. C
2. D	4. A	6. D	8. A	10. D	12. A	14. B	

Matrices

1. B	3. C	5. A	7. A	9. B
2. D	4. A	6. C	8. A	

Algebraic Relationships

1. C	4. B	7. D	10. B	13. C	16. A	19. D	22. A
2. C	5. B	8. D	11. C	14. A	17. B	20. D	23. A
3. A	6. D	9. D	12. B	15. C	18. A	21. A	24. B

Simplifying Expressions

1. C	4. B	7. A	10. A	13. A	16. A
2. B	5. C	8. B	11. C	14. A	17. B
3. D	6. B	9. A	12. A	15. B	18. A

Distributing

1. B	5. A	9. C	13. C	17. D	21. D	25. D
2. A	6. A	10. C	14. B	18. B	22. C	26. D
3. D	7. D	11. C	15. D	19. D	23. D	27. B
4. C	8. D	12. D	16. B	20. D	24. A	28. C

Factoring

1. B	4. A	7. D	10. B	13. A	16. C	19. C
2. B	5. B	8. B	11. A	14. C	17. D	20. A
3. D	6. C	9. D	12. A	15. C	18. D	21. A

Creating Expressions & Equations

1. B	4. B	7. B	10. B	13. D	16. A	19. D
2. A	5. C	8. C	11. C	14. C	17. A	20. B
3. A	6. D	9. D	12. C	15. C	18. B	21. A

Function Notation

1. C	5. C	9. C	13. B	17. C	21. C	25. C	29. B
2. C	6. A	10. C	14. A	18. C	22. B	26. C	30. B
3. B	7. A	11. B	15. B	19. C	23. A	27. A	
4. C	8. A	12. D	16. B	20. B	24. C	28. A	

Solving for Zero

1. A	4. D	7. B	10. D	13. D	16. C
2. B	5. A	8. A	11. A	14. C	17. C
3. C	6. D	9. B	12. D	15. D	18. C

Inequalities

1. D	3. B	5. C	7. C	9. A	11. A
2. A	4. B	6. B	8. A	10. A	

Absolute Value Inequalities

1. C	4. D	7. A	10. A	13. C	16. A	19. A
2. D	5. B	8. C	11. D	14. B	17. D	20. A
3. D	6. A	9. C	12. D	15. A	18. B	

Slope

1. C	5. A	9. A	13. B	17. A	21. B	25. A
2. C	6. B	10. D	14. D	18. A	22. C	26. A
3. B	7. B	11. B	15. D	19. C	23. A	
4. B	8. B	12. C	16. B	20. B	24. C	

Equation of a Line

1. B	3. A	5. A	7. C	9. B	11. C	13. A
2. B	4. D	6. A	8. C	10. B	12. B	14. B

Sequences

1. D	3. C	5. C	7. B	9. C	11. A	13. A
2. C	4. A	6. A	8. C	10. A	12. C	

Permutations & Combinations

1. D	4. C	7. C	10. C	13. A	16. A
2. D	5. D	8. D	11. C	14. B	17. B
3. B	6. B	9. C	12. C	15. B	18. D

Proportions

1. D	3. B	5. D	7. D	9. D	11. A	13. C	15. B
2. D	4. A	6. C	8. D	10. A	12. A	14. B	16. B

Geometry with Variables

1. A	4. C	7. C	10. B	13. C	16. D	19. D
2. A	5. C	8. A	11. C	14. C	17. D	20. D
3. D	6. B	9. D	12. D	15. C	18. D	

Angle Sums

1. B	3. C	5. B	7. C	9. D	11. D
2. B	4. B	6. A	8. D	10. C	

Polygons on a Coordinate Grid

1. D	2. A	3. B	4. B	5. A	6. D

Distance on a Coordinate Grid

1. C	3. C	5. A	7. B	9. B	11.C
2. D	4. C	6. C	8. A	10. D	

Nets

1. D	2. B	3. D	4. A	5. C	6. A	7. A	8. A

Trigonometry

1. D	3. A	5. D	7. A	9. B
2. A	4. C	6. B	8. C	10. B

Appropriate Units

1. D	2. D	3. D	4. B	5. C	6. C	7. D

Area & Perimeter

1. B	3. D	5. D	7. D	9. C	11. A	13. A	15. A
2. D	4. C	6. D	8. C	10. C	12. A	14. B	16. A

Speed

| 1. C | 3. C | 5. B | 7. D | 9. B | 11. C |
| 2. B | 4. A | 6. C | 8. C | 10. D | |

Converting Units

| 1. B | 2. A | 3. A | 4. D | 5. D | 6. A | 7. D |

Formulas

| 1. C | 3. B | 5. C | 7. D | 9. D | 11. C |
| 2. C | 4. B | 6. B | 8. B | 10. C | |

Probability

1. C	4. B	7. B	10. C	13. C	16. B	19. A	22. B
2. B	5. A	8. C	11. B	14. A	17. B	20. A	
3. B	6. C	9. A	12. A	15. B	18. C	21. A	

Probability – Conditional

| 1. D | 3. C | 5. D | 7. C | 9. C | 11. C |
| 2. C | 4. C | 6. A | 8. B | 10. B | 12. A |

Averages

1. D	4. D	7. C	10. A	13. D	16. B
2. A	5. C	8. B	11. C	14. A	17. A
3. D	6. A	9. B	12. D	15. B	18. A

Interpreting Graphs

| 1. C | 2. D |

Frequency Charts & Graphs

| 1. A | 2. A | 3. A | 4. A | 5. C | 6. A | 7. C | 8. B |

Circle Graphs

| 1. B | 3. A | 5. C | 7. C | 9. B | 11. A | 13. C |
| 2. B | 4. D | 6. D | 8. B | 10. B | 12. D | |

Box-and-Whisker Plots

| 1. C | 2. B | 3. B | 4. C | 5. C | 6. A |

Stem-and-Leaf Plots

| 1. B | 2. B | 3. D | 4. C | 5. B | 6. C |

Histograms

| 1. C | 2. B | 3. B | 4. D | 5. D |

Survey Samples

| 1. C | 2. B | 3. A | 4. D |

Final Practice Test (Form B)

Verbal Reasoning

1. D	6. C	11. C	16. A	21. D	26. C	31. A	36. D
2. A	7. A	12. B	17. D	22. B	27. B	32. B	37. A
3. D	8. A	13. A	18. D	23. D	28. A	33. C	38. B
4. B	9. C	14. B	19. D	24. A	29. D	34. C	39. C
5. A	10. C	15. C	20. A	25. A	30. D	35. D	40. B

(continued on next page)

The Tutorverse

Quantitative Reasoning

1.	C	6.	C	11.	D	16.	D	21.	B	26.	A	31.	B	36.	B
2.	D	7.	C	12.	B	17.	C	22.	B	27.	B	32.	B	37.	A
3.	A	8.	D	13.	C	18.	A	23.	C	28.	A	33.	D		
4.	A	9.	D	14.	C	19.	D	24.	C	29.	A	34.	B		
5.	B	10.	B	15.	D	20.	B	25.	D	30.	C	35.	D		

Reading Comprehension

1.	D	6.	B	11.	D	16.	D	21.	B	26.	B	31.	B	36.	B
2.	B	7.	C	12.	D	17.	B	22.	D	27.	C	32.	D		
3.	C	8.	A	13.	C	18.	A	23.	C	28.	A	33.	C		
4.	A	9.	B	14.	D	19.	A	24.	C	29.	C	34.	B		
5.	C	10.	D	15.	A	20.	A	25.	A	30.	B	35.	C		

Mathematics Achievement

1.	A	7.	B	13.	B	19.	C	25.	C	31.	A	37.	D	43.	B
2.	C	8.	C	14.	A	20.	C	26.	A	32.	B	38.	A	44.	C
3.	D	9.	A	15.	D	21.	B	27.	B	33.	C	39.	A	45.	B
4.	D	10.	A	16.	C	22.	C	28.	A	34.	A	40.	D	46.	D
5.	C	11.	B	17.	C	23.	D	29.	A	35.	A	41.	D	47.	C
6.	D	12.	C	18.	D	24.	B	30.	D	36.	B	42.	C		

Made in the USA
Middletown, DE
20 February 2024

50056974R00190